450 Two-Story HOME PLANS

S0-AFY-422

COPYRIGHT © 1998
CREATIVE HOMEOWNER PRESS®
A Division of Federal Marketing Corp.
Upper Saddle River, NJ

Library of Congress
Catalog Card No.: 98-72200
ISBN:1-58011-020-7

CREATIVE HOMEOWNER PRESS
A Division of
Federal Marketing Corp.
24 Park Way,
Upper Saddle River, NJ 07458

Manufactured in the
United States of America
Printed at: Webcrafters, Inc.

Current Printing (last digit)
1 0 9 8 7 6 5 4 3 2

COVER PHOTOGRAPHY BY
James Rueter Jr.

TABLE OF CONTENTS

Wrap-Around Porch

plan no.

**2
4
2
4
5**

Photography by John Ehrenclou

plan info

First Floor	**1,113 sq. ft.**
Second Floor	**970 sq. ft.**
Basement	**1,113 sq. ft.**
Garage	**480 sq. ft.**
Bedrooms	**Three**
Baths	**2(full), 1(half)**
Foundation	**Basement**

Picture a porch swing, cozy rocking chairs and a pitcher of lemonade on this country porch. What an inviting picture. The homey feel continues throughout this house. The formal areas are located in the traditional places, flanking the entry hall. The living room includes a wonderful fireplace and the dining room has direct access to the kitchen. The U-shaped kitchen includes a breakfast bar, built-in pantry, planning desk and a double sink. A mudroom entry will help keep the dirt from muddy shoes away from the rest of the house. A convenient laundry area is close at hand in the half-bath off the mudroom. The sunny breakfast nook is a cheerful place to start your day, and the expansive family room has direct access to the rear wood deck. Sleeping quarters are located on the second floor. The master suite is highlighted by a walk-in closet and private master bath. The two additional bedrooms, one with a built-in desk, share a full hall bath with a double vanity. A window seat in the hallway provides a cozy place to curl up with a book. In fact, bookshelves have been built-in on either side of the seat. The photographed home may have been modified to suit individual tastes.

This U-shaped kitchen is user-friendly and convenient to both the dining and family rooms.

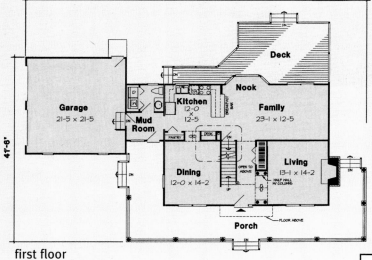

first floor

74'-0"

41'-6"

Garage
21-5 x 21-5

Mud Room

Kitchen
12-0 x 12-5

Nook

Deck

Family
23-1 x 12-5

Dining
12-0 x 14-2

Living
13-1 x 14-2

OPEN TO ABOVE

PANTRY

DESK

HALF HALL W/ COLUMNS

FLOOR ABOVE

Porch

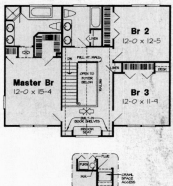

second floor

Master Br
12-0 x 15-4

Br 2
12-0 x 12-5

Br 3
12-0 x 11-9

FULL HT. HALL

OPEN TO FOYER BELOW

RAILING

LINEN

BUILT-IN BOOK SHELVES

WINDOW SEAT

DESK

Crawl Space/Slab Option

FURN

FLUE

CRAWL SPACE ACCESS

Cozy up in this bright nook with a spot of tea for some afternoon reading.

Loft, Windows, Decks

plan no.

10515

Photography by John Ehrenclou

Bring the outdoors in with plenty of windows, wrap-around porch and backyard greenhouse.

plan info

First Floor	**1,280 sq. ft.**
Second Floor	**735 sq. ft.**
Greenhouse	**80 sq. ft.**
Playhouse	**80 sq. ft.**
Bedrooms	**Three**
Baths	**2(full), 1(half)**
Foundation	**Crawl Space**

The first floor living space of this inviting home blends the family room and the dining room for comfortable family living. The large kitchen shares a preparation/eating bar with the dining room. The ample utility room is designed with a pantry, plus room for a freezer, a washer and a dryer. Also on the first floor is the master suite with its two closets and five piece bath which opens into a greenhouse. The second floor is highlighted by a loft which overlooks the first floor living area. The two upstairs bedrooms each have double closets and share a four-piece, compartmentalized bath. The photographed home may have been modified to suit individual tastes.

When the sun sets, retreat to a cozy family room with a stone fireplace.

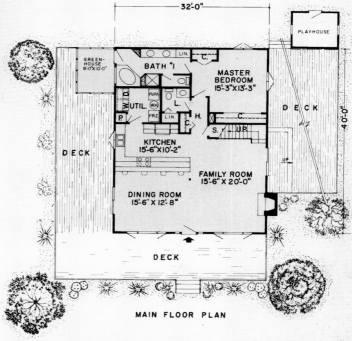

MAIN FLOOR PLAN

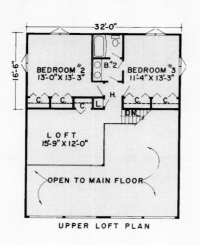

UPPER LOFT PLAN

This design boasts a bright, cheery place for family dining.

price code **D**

total living area: **2,464 sq. ft.**

Wrap-Around Porch

plan no.

9
3
2
0
9

Photography by John Ehrenclou

Enjoy warm evenings with the
family on this classic porch.

An
EXCLUSIVE DESIGN
By Jannis Vann & Associates, Inc.

plan info

First Floor	**1,250 sq. ft.**
Second Floor	**1,166 sq. ft.**
Basement	**448 sq. ft.**
Finished Stairs	**48 sq. ft.**
Garage	**706 sq. ft.**
Bedrooms	**Four**
Baths	**2(full), 1(half)**
Foundation	**Basement**

The wrap-around porch on this home adds to the classic
styling and gives curb appeal. Upon entering the home, the
formal living room and dining room are to your left and right,
respectively. Columns accentuate the Great room, while the
fireplace adds to the mood of the room. A well-appointed
kitchen is conveniently placed between the formal dining room
and the informal breakfast room. There is a screened porch
and a sun deck for outdoor living space. Four bedrooms
occupy the second floor. The master suite includes a private
master bath, walk-in closet and a private deck. The three
additional bedrooms share the full hall bath. The
photographed home may have been modified to suit individual
tastes.

This staircase lends elegance to the open foyer and makes this design a winner.

first floor

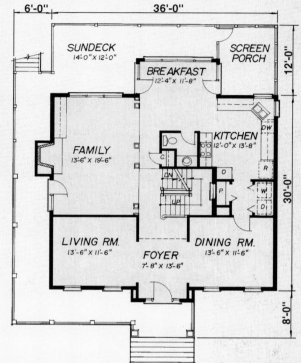

6'-0" 36'-0"

SUNDECK 14'-0" X 12'-0"

BREAKFAST 12'-4" X 11'-8"

SCREEN PORCH

12'-0"

FAMILY 13'-6" X 19'-6"

KITCHEN 12'-0" X 13'-8"

30'-0"

LIVING RM. 13'-6" X 11'-6"

FOYER 7'-8" X 13'-6"

DINING RM. 13'-6" X 11'-6"

8'-0"

second floor

DECK

MASTER BR. 12'-4" X 17'-6"

BEDROOM·4 13'-6" X 11'-6"

M. BATH

BATH·2

BEDROOM·3 13'-6" X 11'-6"

OPEN TO FOYER

BEDROOM·2 13'-6" X 11'-6"

The large master bedroom has a deck to the outdoors and private bath.

Home With Views

plan no.

2 4 3 1 9

Photography by John Ehrenclou

This home is perfect for enjoying the landscape with three floors of windows.

plan info

Main Floor	**728 sq. ft.**
Upper Floor	**573 sq. ft.**
Lower Floor	**409 sq. ft.**
Garage	**244 sq. ft.**
Bedrooms	**Three**
Baths	**2(full)**
Foundation	**Basement**

This home is a vacation haven with views from every room whether it is situated on a lake or a mountaintop. The main floor features a living room and dining room split by a fireplace. The kitchen flows into the dining room and is gracefully separated by a bar. There is a bedroom and a full bath on the main floor. The second floor has a bedroom or library loft, with clerestory windows, which opens above the living room. The master bedroom and bath are also on the top floor. The lower floor has a large recreation room with a whirlpool tub and a bar, a laundry room and a garage. This home has large decks and windows on one entire side. The photographed home may have been modified to suit individual tastes.

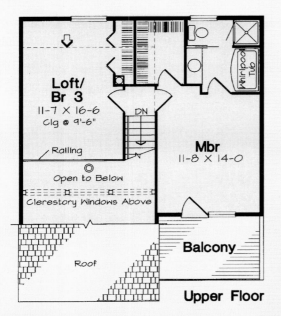

You won't miss out enjoying the fire while you're preparing meals in the kitchen. The split fireplace is shared by both the living and kitchen areas.

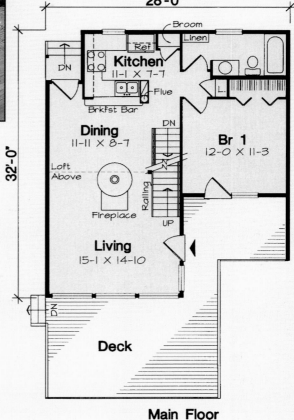

28'-0"

32'-0"

Kitchen
11-1 X 7-7

Ref

Broom

Linen

DN

Flue

Brkfst Bar

Dining
11-11 X 8-7

Loft Above

Fireplace

DN

Railing

UP

Br 1
12-0 X 11-3

Living
15-1 X 14-10

DN

Deck

Main Floor

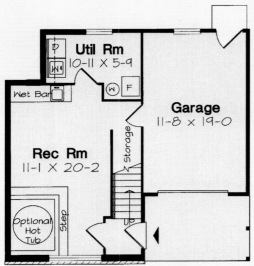

Util Rm
10-11 X 5-9

Wet Bar

W

F

Garage
11-8 X 19-0

Rec Rm
11-1 X 20-2

Storage

Step

UP

Optional Hot Tub

Lower Floor

An
EXCLUSIVE DESIGN
By Marshall Associates

Loft/ Br 3
11-7 X 16-6
Clg @ 9'-6"

DN

Whirlpool Tub

Mbr
11-8 X 14-0

Railing

Open to Below

Clerestory Windows Above

Roof

Balcony

Upper Floor

total living area: 1,328 sq. ft.

Rustic Exterior

plan no.

34600

Photography by Beth Steele

▲

Small, but with all the amenities, this design is a great get-away.

plan info

Main Floor	1,013 sq. ft.
Upper Floor	315 sq. ft.
Basement	1,013 sq. ft.
Bedrooms	Three
Baths	2(full)
Foundation	Basement/Slab Crawl Space

Although rustic in appearance, the interior of this cabin is quiet, modern and comfortable. Small in overall size, it still contains three bedrooms and two baths in addition to a large, two-story living room with exposed beams. As a hunting/ fishing lodge or mountain retreat, this compares well. The photographed home may have been modified to suit individual tastes.

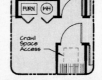

Crawl Space / Slab Plan

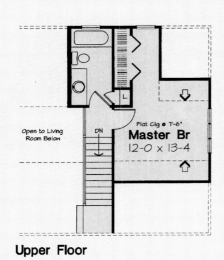

Open to Living
Room Below

DN

L.

Flat Clg @ 7'-6"

Master Br
12-0 x 13-4

Upper Floor

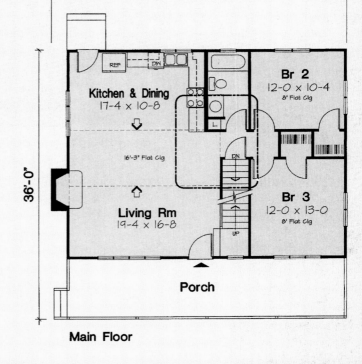

38'-0"

36'-0"

REF DW

Kitchen & Dining
17-4 x 10-8

16'-3" Flat Clg

Living Rm
19-4 x 16-8

L.

DN

UP

Br 2
12-0 x 10-4
8' Flat Clg

Br 3
12-0 x 13-0
8' Flat Clg

Porch

Main Floor

The owners of this plan
chose to modify this home
and include a spectacular
sunroom. ▶

Covered Porch

An EXCLUSIVE DESIGN
By Karl Kreeger

plan no.

3
4
9
0
1

Photography by John Ehrenclou

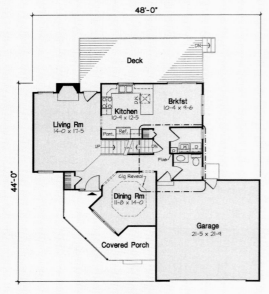

48'-0"

44'-0"

Deck

Kitchen
10-4 x 12-5

Brkfst
10-4 x 9-6

Living Rm
14-0 x 17-5

Pant. | Ref.

UP

Flue

Gig Reveal

Dining Rm
11-8 x 14-0

Garage
21-5 x 21-4

Covered Porch

First Floor

Line of Floor Below

Master Br
14-3 x 17-5

Br 3
12-2 x 10-1

DN

Railing

Flue

Second Floor

Br 2
13-11 x 11-9

Opt. Slab/ Crawl Space

Furn.

plan info

First Floor	909 sq. ft.
Second Floor	854 sq. ft.
Basement	899 sq. ft.
Garage	491 sq. ft.
Bedrooms	Three
Baths	2(full), 1(half)
Foundation	Basement/Slab Crawl Space

This pleasant Traditional design has a farmhouse flavor exterior that incorporates a covered porch and features a circle wood louver on its garage, giving this design a feeling of sturdiness. Inside, on the first level to the right of the foyer, is a formal dining room complete with a bay window and an elevated ceiling. To the left of the foyer is the living room with a wood-burning fireplace. The kitchen is connected to the breakfast room and there is also a room for the laundry facilities. A half-bath is also featured on the first floor. The master bedroom, on the second floor, has its own private bath and walk-in closet. The other two bedrooms share a full bath. A two-car garage is also added into this design. The photographed home may have been modified to suit individual tastes.

Extraordinary Home

plan no.

92642

Photography by Donna & Rob Kolb, Exposures Unlimited/Builder: Ralph Brothers

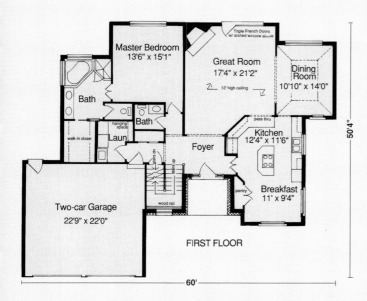

FIRST FLOOR

Master Bedroom
13'6" x 15'1"

Bath

hanging space

Bath

walk-in closet

Laun.

Two-car Garage
22'9" x 22'0"

Triple French Doors w/ arched window above

Great Room
17'4" x 21'2"

12' high ceiling

Dining Room
10'10" x 14'0"

pass thru

Foyer

Kitchen
12'4" x 11'6"

pantry

Breakfast
11' x 9'4"

wood rail

50'4"

60'

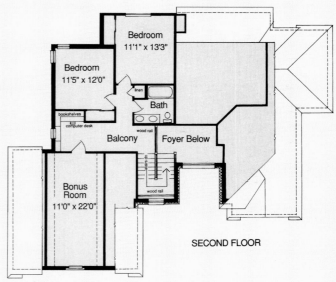

SECOND FLOOR

Bedroom
11'1" x 13'3"

Bedroom
11'5" x 12'0"

linen

Bath

bookshelves

computer desk

Balcony

Foyer Below

wood rail

Bonus Room
11'0" x 22'0"

wood rail

plan info

First Floor	1,524 sq. ft.
Second Floor	558 sq. ft.
Basement	1,460 sq. ft.
Bonus Room	267 sq. ft.
Bedrooms	Three
Baths	2(full), 1(half)
Foundation	Basement

Upon entering the foyer, your view will go directly to the cozy fireplace and stylish French doors of the Great room. A grand entry into the formal dining room, coupled with the volume ceiling, pulls these two rooms together for a spacious feeling. From the roomy, well-equipped kitchen, there is a pass-through to the Great room. Natural light will flood the breakfast area through large windows. Located between the first floor master bedroom suite and the garage is the laundry, adding convenience and protecting the living areas from noise and disorder. Split stairs, graced with wood railings, lead to the versatile second floor with two additional bedrooms. The photographed home may have been modified to suit individual tastes.

Pie-Shaped Lot Design

plan no.

93034

Photography Supplied by Build One Design

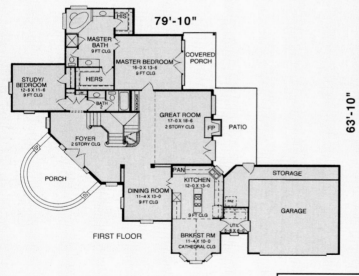

79'-10"

MASTER BATH
9 FT CLG

HIS

MASTER BEDROOM
16-0 X 13-6
9 FT CLG

COVERED PORCH

STUDY/ BEDROOM
12-6 X 11-6
9 FT CLG

HERS

BATH

FOYER
2 STORY CLG

GREAT ROOM
17-0 X 18-6
2 STORY CLG

FP

PATIO

PORCH

DINING ROOM
11-4 X 13-0
9 FT CLG

PAN

KITCHEN
12-0 X 13-0

FRZ

STORAGE

GARAGE

9 FT CLG

FIRST FLOOR

UTIL

BRKFST RM
11-4 X 10-0
CATHEDRAL CLG

63'-10"

SECOND FLOOR

BEDROOM 2
12-6 X 11-6

BATH 3

LIN

BEDROOM 3
12-6 X 12-6

BALCONY

OPEN TO FOYER BELOW

BALCONY

OPEN TO GREAT ROOM BELOW

BEDROOM 4
11-4 X 13-6

ATTIC

plan info

First Floor	1,966 sq. ft.
Second Floor	872 sq. ft.
Garage	569 sq. ft.
Bedrooms	Four
Baths	3(full)
Foundation	Crawl Space/Slab

Designed for the corner or pie shaped lot, this home features mirror elevations on right and left. Entering the foyer, a lovely split stair moves upward to the second floor. The dining room opens to the right and features an elegant entrance flanked with square columns. The kitchen with a cooktop work island features a pantry and angled window sink. A vaulted ceiling gives the breakfast room a distinctive look and adds character to the kitchen wing. A private study can double as bedroom five if needed. The rear master suite has access to an outdoor covered porch. The master bath provides a sumptuous retreat for the homeowner. Separate his-n-her vanities, a corner whirlpool tub and separate showers are standard. Upstairs, three bedrooms and a bath are included in the plan. No materials list available for this plan. The photographed home may have been modified to suit individual tastes.

total living area: 3,397 sq. ft.

F price code

ⴽ R

Old Fashioned Look

An EXCLUSIVE DESIGN
By Ahmann Design Inc.

plan no.

93118

Photography Supplied by Ahmann Design/Builder: Sattler Homes

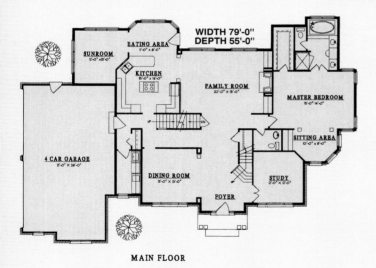

WIDTH 79'-0"
DEPTH 55'-0"

SUNROOM
EATING AREA
KITCHEN
FAMILY ROOM
20'-0" X 15'-0"
MASTER BEDROOM
15'-0" X 14'-0"
4 CAR GARAGE
25'-0" X 38'-0"
SITTING AREA
10'-0" X 8'-0"
DINING ROOM
15'-0" X 13'-0"
STUDY
12'-0" X 12'-0"
FOYER

MAIN FLOOR

OPEN TO
FAMILY RM.

BEDROOM #2
15'-0" X 15'-0"

BEDROOM #4
15'-0" X 15'-0"

OPEN TO
FOYER

BEDROOM #3
12'-0" X 12'-0"

SECOND FLOOR

*This plan is not to be built within a 75 mile radius of Cedar Rapids, IA.

plan info

First Floor	2,385 sq. ft.
Second Floor	1,012 sq. ft.
Basement	2,385 sq. ft.
Garage	846 sq. ft.
Bedrooms	Four
Baths	3(full), 1(half)
Foundation	Basement

This-two story brick home features the old fashioned look of turn-of-the-century homes mixed with a contemporary floor plan. The bright two story foyer is framed by an elegant dining room to the left and a study, for after hours work, on the right. The generous, island kitchen opens into a breakfast area surrounded by glass and perfect for reading the morning paper. The enticing master suite features a sitting area that makes the perfect get-away. Upstairs you'll enjoy a dramatic view of both the foyer and the family room below as you cross the bridge to any of the three additional bedrooms, all with walk-in closets and one with a private bath. No materials list is available for this plan. The photographed home may have been modified to suit individual tastes.

price code **E** total living area: 2,692 sq. ft.

Stately Elegance

plan no.

99853

Photography by Jon Riley, Riley & Riley Photographers

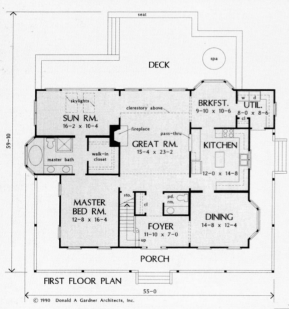

FIRST FLOOR PLAN

59-10

55-0

DECK · spa · seat

SUN RM. 16-2 x 10-4 · skylights · clerestory above · BRKFST. 9-10 x 10-6 · UTIL. 8-0 x 8-6 · w d · cl

fireplace · pass-thru

GREAT RM. 15-4 x 23-4 · KITCHEN

master bath · walk-in closet · 12-0 x 14-8

MASTER BED RM. 12-8 x 16-4 · sto. · cl · pd. rm. · DINING 14-8 x 12-4

FOYER 11-10 x 7-0 · up

PORCH

© 1990 Donald A Gardner Architects, Inc.

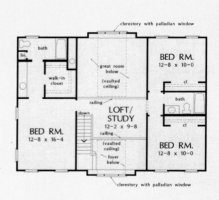

SECOND FLOOR PLAN

clerestory with palladian window

bath · lin.

walk-in closet · great room below (vaulted ceiling) · BED RM. 12-8 x 10-0 · cl

BED RM. 12-8 x 16-4 · down · LOFT/ STUDY 12-2 x 9-8 · railing · bath · cl

railing · (vaulted ceiling) · foyer below · BED RM. 12-8 x 10-0

clerestory with palladian window

plan info

First Floor	1,734 sq. ft.
Second Floor	958
Bedrooms	Four
Baths	3(full), 1(half)
Foundation	Crawl Space

A double gabled roof with front and rear palladian windows give this wrap-around porch plan a stately elegance. Vaulted ceilings in the two-story foyer and Great room reinforce the visual drama of the palladian windows while a loft/study overlooks both areas. The spacious first floor master suite accesses the large sun room from a luxurious master bath with garden tub, shower, and double vanity. The covered porch and outstanding deck with seating and optional spa expand living space outdoors. Upstairs, one of the three bedrooms could be a second master with private bath. The photographed home may have been modified to suit individual tastes.

total living area: 1,668 sq. ft.

Country Porch

B price code

Photography by by John Ehrenclou

plan no. 93219

As you enter the home through the country porch, the dining room is close at hand for an elegant dinner party. The U-shaped kitchen services both the formal dining room and informal breakfast area. The master suite includes a luxurious master bath with a double vanity, walk-in closet, tub, and shower. The second floor bedrooms are large and have ample closet space. The photographed home may have been modified to suit individual tastes

first floor

Deck

Brkfst. 9-0 x 8-0

Kit. 9-0 x 9-6

Dining 9-10 x 11-4

Lav.

W/D

M.Bath

Living 18-0 x 13-6

Mstr. Bdrm. 15-6 x 13-6

38'-0"

Porch

38'-0"

An EXCLUSIVE DESIGN *By Jannis Vann & Associates, Inc.*

second floor

Bath

Bdrm. 2 15-8 x 13-4

Bdrm. 3 15-6 x 11-0

plan info

First Flr.	1,057 sq. ft.
Second Flr.	611 sq. ft.
Basement	511 sq. ft.
Garage	546 sq. ft.
Bedrooms	Three
Baths	2(full), 1(half)
Foundation	Basement

---

total living area: 1,768 sq. ft.

A Little Drama

B price code

Photography by Donna & Rob Kolb, Exposures Unlimited/Builders: Stephen Due Builders

plan no. 92609

This home's dramatic exterior features a 12' high entry with transom and sidelights, multiple gables and a box window. The foyer and sunken Great room feel very open with 12' high ceilings. The Great room and the breakfast room access a rear porch. On the second floor is the master bedroom suite with a whirlpool tub and a walk-in closet. The photographed home may have been modified to suit individual tastes.

Bedroom 11-4 x 11-4

Bath

Hall

Master Bedroom 12 x 16

stairs dn

Great Room Below 12' ceiling

Foyer Below 12' ceiling

Bedroom 11-4 x 9-6

Bath

tray ceiling

walk in closet

second floor

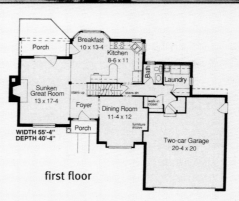

Porch

Breakfast 10 x 13-4

Kitchen 8-6 x 11

Sunken Great Room 13 x 17-4

stairs up

stairs dn

Laundry

Bath

walk-in closet

Foyer

Dining Room 11-4 x 12

Porch

WIDTH 55'-4" DEPTH 40'-4"

furniture alcove

Two-car Garage 20-4 x 20

first floor

plan info

First Flr.	960 sq. ft.
Second Flr.	808 sq. ft.
Bedrooms	Three
Baths	2(full), 1(half)
Foundation	Basement

Flexibility to Expand

plan no.

99859

Photography by Jon Riley, Riley &Riley Photographers

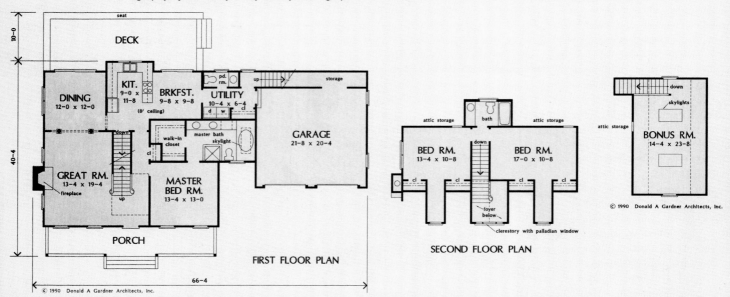

FIRST FLOOR PLAN

© 1990 Donald A Gardner Architects, Inc.

SECOND FLOOR PLAN

© 1990 Donald A Gardner Architects, Inc.

plan info

First Floor	1,289 sq. ft.
Second Floor	542 sq. ft.
Bonus Room	393 sq. ft.
Garage	521 sq. ft.
Bedrooms	Three
Baths	2(full), 1(half)
Foundation	Basement/Crawl Space

The growing family will appreciate the flexibility offered by an unfinished bonus room and an optional basement in this three bedroom country cottage that lives bigger than it looks. An elegant palladian window in a clerestory dormer washes the two-story foyer in natural light. Columns between Great room and dining room add drama and accent nine foot ceilings. A luxurious first level master suite makes a great parent get-away. The master bath features a cheery skylight above the whirlpool tub. This plan is available with a basement or crawl space foundation. Please specify when ordering. The photographed home may have been modified to suit individual tastes.

A price code 🏠

Neat and Tidy

plan no.

91033

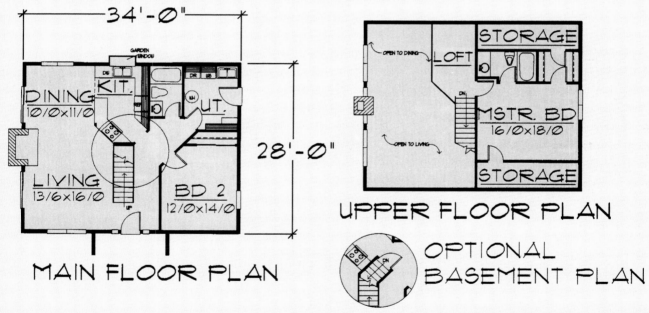

34'-0"

DINING
10/0x11/0

KIT.

GARDEN WINDOW

DR WB

U.T.

LIVING
13/6x16/0

BD 2
12/0x14/0

28'-0"

MAIN FLOOR PLAN

OPEN TO DINING

LOFT

STORAGE

DN

MSTR. BD
16/0x18/0

OPEN TO LIVING

STORAGE

UPPER FLOOR PLAN

DN

OPTIONAL BASEMENT PLAN

plan info

Main Floor	952 sq. ft.
Upper Floor	297 sq. ft.
Bedrooms	Two
Baths	2(full)
Foundation	Basement/Crawl Space

This compact house has plenty of closets and storage areas. The utility room is also larger than most, and opens directly outside, so there's no reason for anyone to track in snow or mud. Sliding glass doors lead from the two-story living room and dining room out to a paved patio. Tucked into a corner, the kitchen is both out of the way and convenient. A handsome stone fireplace adds a functional and a decorative element to both the interior and the exterior of the home. A downstairs bedroom will sleep either children or guests. Beyond the railed loft, a master suite with a full bath and a walk-in closet provides the owner of this home with every comfort. This plan is available with a basement or crawl space foundation. Please specify when ordering.

National Treasure

plan no.

24400

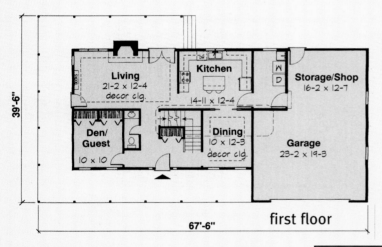

Living
21-2 x 12-4
decor clg.

Kitchen
14-11 x 12-4

Storage/Shop
16-2 x 12-7

Den/
Guest
10 x 10

Dining
10 x 12-3
decor clg.

Garage
23-2 x 19-3

39'-6"

67'-6"

first floor

An EXCLUSIVE DESIGN
By Upright Design

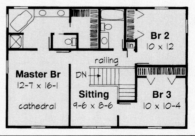

second floor

Master Br
12-7 x 16-1
cathedral

Br 2
10 x 12

railing

DN

Sitting
9-6 x 8-6

Br 3
10 x 10-4

plan info

First Floor	1,034 sq. ft.
Second Floor	944 sq. ft.
Basement	944 sq. ft.
Garage	675 sq. ft.
Bedrooms	Three
Baths	2(full), 1(half)
Foundation	Basement/Slab Crawl Space

This delightful home's wrap-around covered porch recalls the warmth and charm of days past. Inside, a spacious foyer provides easy access to the formal dining room, secluded den/guest room (which might serve as your home office), and the large living room. Ceilings downstairs are all 9' high, with decorative vaults in the living and dining rooms. The kitchen, with its island/breakfast bar, is large enough for two people to work in comfortably. The adjacent laundry room also serves as a mud room for boots and clothes, and leads directly to the garage, which features an ample storage/shop area at the rear. Upstairs, three bedrooms, each with cathedral ceilings, share a sitting area. For privacy, the master bedroom is separated from the other bedrooms, and boasts a palatial bathroom, complete with a whirlpool tub. If room to relax is what you're after, this home is loaded with irresistible features.

C price code

Traditional Two-Story

plan no.

92631

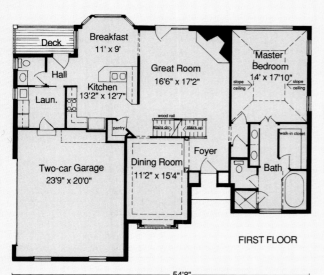

Deck

Breakfast 11' x 9'

Hall

Kitchen 13'2" x 12'7"

Great Room 16'6" x 17'2"

Master Bedroom 14' x 17'10"

slope ceiling | slope ceiling

Laun.

wood rail | stairs dn | stairs up

pantry

walk-in closet

Two-car Garage 23'9" x 20'0"

Dining Room 11'2" x 15'4"

Foyer

Bath

46'8"

FIRST FLOOR

54'8"

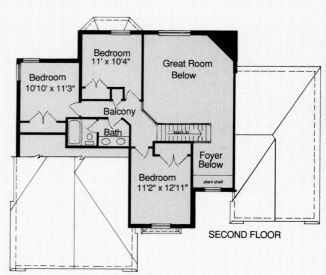

Bedroom 11' x 10'4"

Great Room Below

Bedroom 10'10' x 11'3"

Balcony

Bath

stairs dn

Bedroom 11'2" x 12'11"

Foyer Below

plant shelf

SECOND FLOOR

plan info

First Floor	1,511 sq. ft.
Second Floor	646 sq. ft.
Basement	1,479 sq. ft.
Garage	475 sq. ft.
Bedrooms	Four
Baths	2(full), 1(half)
Foundation	Basement

Interesting angles and varied ceiling treatments set the stage for pride of ownership, while an easy-flow traffic pattern, a kitchen pantry and large closet in the back hall, provides convenience. A high window above the door in the Great room, and the breakfast bay surrounded by windows, provide a bright place for the family to gather. Serving meals is a pleasure in the spacious kitchen with a peninsula. A tray ceiling in the dining room, columns at the corner and a box window will make you eager to entertain. Rounding out the first floor is the master bedroom suite with an ultra bath featuring a dual bowl vanity and whirlpool tub. An elegant staircase leads to the second floor, where an expansive balcony overlooks the Great room and foyer.

price code

D

total living area: 2,188 sq. ft.

Two-Story Great Room

plan no.

99801

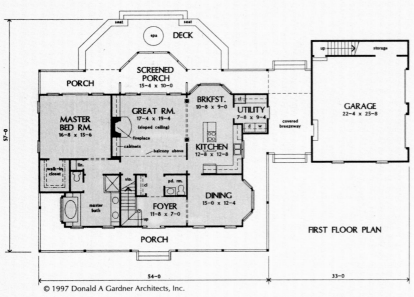

© 1997 Donald A Gardner Architects, Inc.

FIRST FLOOR PLAN

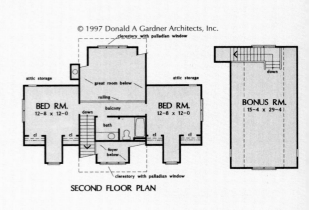

© 1997 Donald A Gardner Architects, Inc.

SECOND FLOOR PLAN

plan info

First Floor	1,618 sq. ft.
Second Floor	570 sq. ft.
Bonus Room	495 sq. ft.
Garage	649 sq. ft.
Bedrooms	Three
Baths	2(full), 1(half)
Foundation	Crawl Space

A two-story Great room and two-story foyer, both with dormer windows, welcome natural light into this graceful country classic with wrap-around porch. The large kitchen, featuring a center cooking island with counter and large breakfast area, opens to the Great room for easy entertaining. Columns punctuate the interior spaces and a separate dining room provides a formal touch to the plan. The master suite, privately situated on the first floor, has a double vanity, garden tub, and separate shower. The semi-detached garage features a large bonus room.

Grand Traditional

plan no.

94230

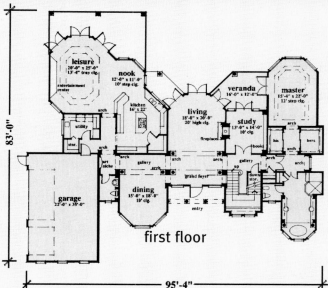

first floor

83'-0"

95'-4"

second floor

plan info

First Floor	3,546 sq. ft.
Second Floor	1,213 sq. ft.
Garage	822 sq. ft.
Bedrooms	Four
Baths	3(full), 1(half)
Foundation	Basement/Slab

Inside the foyer area, double arches lead into the formal living room and out to the rear through triple french doors. A two-sided fireplace is shared with the owners study. The expansive kitchen easily serves the dining room and informal nook area. The kitchen has plenty of work space, a walk-in pantry area, a cooktop island, an eating bar, and a pass-through that serves the veranda. The expansive kitchen easily serves the dining room and informal nook area. Double doors lead into the owners suite. Large his and her wardrobe closets framed with arches lead into the sleeping area. The bayed suite has doors to the veranda, a high stepped ceiling and a sitting area. The elegant bath is well appointed. Up the grand staircase are three secondary suites. No materials list is available for this plan.

price code

B

total living area: 1,560 sq. ft.

Cozy Country

plan no.

34602

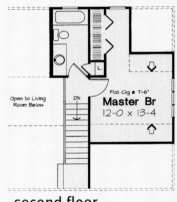

first floor

- 44'-0"
- 34'-0"
- Dining 9-3 x 12-7
- Kitchen 8-7 x 12-7
- Ref
- island
- breakfast bar
- line of floor above
- flat clg @ 17'
- DN
- UP
- storage
- Optional Deck w/ Hot Tub
- privacy fence
- Master Br 12-0 x 14-6
- Flat clg. @ 15'-7"
- Great Room 19-7 x 14-10
- Porch

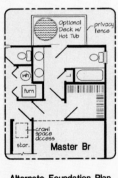

Alternate Foundation Plan

- Optional Deck w/ Hot Tub
- privacy fence
- wh
- furn
- crawl space access
- stor.
- Master Br

second floor

- Flat Clg @ 7'-6"
- Master Br 12-0 x 13-4
- Open to Living Room Below
- DN

plan info

First Floor	1,061 sq. ft.
Second Floor	499 sq. ft.
Basement	1,061 sq. ft.
Bedrooms	Three
Baths	2(full), 1(half)
Foundation	Basement/Slab Crawl Space

A wrap-around porch and dormer windows lend an old-fashioned country feeling to this home. Yet inside, a floor plan designed for today's lifestyle unfolds. A great room enhanced by a large hearth fireplace and a vaulted ceiling gives a cozy welcome to guests. It is separated by the breakfast bar from the kitchen/dining area. An island extends the work space in this efficiently laid out area. The dining area has direct access to the rear yard. The first floor master suite also includes a vaulted ceiling and is highlighted by a private, double vanity bath. Two additional bedrooms on the second floor share a full double vanity bath in the hall.

Happy Hill House

price code

91026

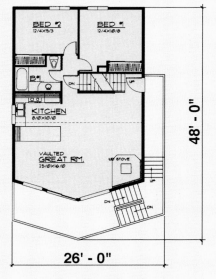

BED #2
12/4X9/3

BED #1
12/4X10/8

B #1

KITCHEN
8/0X10/2

VAULTED
GREAT RM.
25/0X16/0

48' - 0"

26' - 0"

MAIN FLOOR PLAN

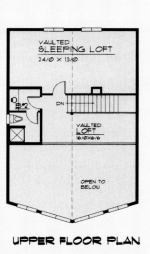

VAULTED
SLEEPING LOFT
24/0 X 13/0

B #2

VAULTED
LOFT
16/0X6/6

OPEN TO
BELOW

UPPER FLOOR PLAN

plan info

Main Floor	**988 sq. ft.**
Upper Level	**366 sq. ft.**
Basement	**988 sq. ft.**
Bedrooms	**Three**
Baths	**2(full)**
Foundation	**Basement**

Built into a hill, this vacation house takes advantage of your wonderful view. It features a Great room that opens out on a deck and brings earth and sky into the home through sweeping panels of glass. The open plan draws the kitchen into the celebration of the outdoors and shares the warmth of the sturdy wood stove. Two bedrooms on the main level share a bath. Two large, upstairs lofts, one overlooking the Great room, have a full bath all to themselves. This house feels as airy and delightful as a tree house.

C

Luxury Plan

plan no.

92610

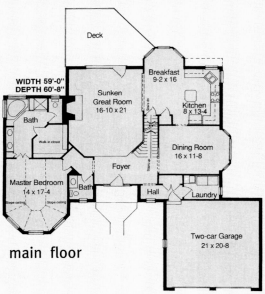

WIDTH 59'-0"
DEPTH 60'-8"

Deck

Breakfast
9-2 x 16

Sunken
Great Room
16-10 x 21

Kitchen
8 x 13-4

Bath

Walk-in closet

Dining Room
16 x 11-8

Foyer

Master Bedroom
14 x 17-4

Slope ceiling   Slope ceiling

Bath

Hall

Laundry

Two-car Garage
21 x 20-8

main floor

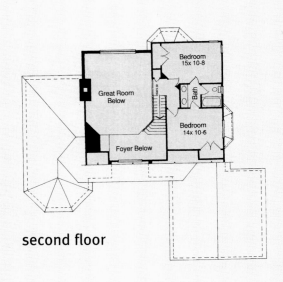

Bedroom
15x 10-8

Great Room
Below

Bath

Bedroom
14x 10-6

Foyer Below

second floor

plan info

First Floor	1,626 sq. ft.
Second Floor	475 sq. ft.
Bedrooms	Three
Baths	2(full), 1(half)
Foundation	Basement

An octagonal master bedroom with a vaulted ceiling, a sunken Great room with a balcony above, and an exterior with an exciting roof line provide this home with all the luxurious amenities in a moderate size. The first floor master bedroom targets this home to the empty-nester market. The elegant exterior has a rich solid look that is very important to the discriminating buyer. The kitchen features a center island and a breakfast nook. The sunken Great room has a cozy fire-place. Elegant and luxurious in a moderate size, this home has what your looking for.

total living area: 2,563 sq. ft.

E price code

The Great Outdoors

plan no.

9 9 8 4 3

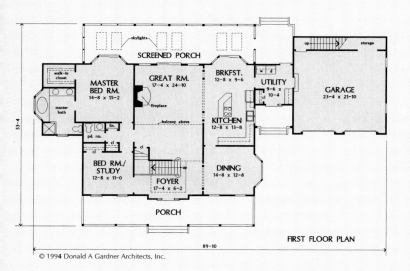

skylights
SCREENED PORCH

| walk-in closet | | | storage |
| MASTER BED RM. 14-8 x 15-2 | GREAT RM. 17-4 x 24-10 | BRKFST. 12-8 x 9-6 | UTILITY 9-6 x 10-4 | GARAGE 23-4 x 21-10 |

master bath
fireplace
balcony above
KITCHEN 12-8 x 13-8
pd. rm.
BED RM./STUDY 12-8 x 11-0
FOYER 17-4 x 6-2
DINING 14-8 x 12-8

53-4

PORCH

89-10

FIRST FLOOR PLAN

© 1994 Donald A Gardner Architects, Inc.

great room below
attic storage
attic storage
railing
BED RM. 12-8 x 14-0
BED RM. 12-8 x 14-0
down
bath
foyer below

© 1994 Donald A Gardner Architects, Inc.

SECOND FLOOR PLAN

down
BONUS RM. 16-10 X 25-4

plan info

First Floor	1,907 sq. ft.
Second Floor	656 sq. ft.
Bonus Room	467 sq. ft.
Garage	580 sq. ft.
Bedrooms	Four
Baths	2(full), 1(half)
Foundation	Crawl Space

Bay windows and a long, skylit rear screened porch make this four bedroom dormered country home a haven for outdoor enthusiasts. The designer has opened the foyer to take advantage of light from the central dormer with palladian window, then vaulted the great room for more vertical drama. A grand room emerges by opening the contemporary kitchen to the great room. The master suite is privately tucked away with a large, luxurious bath complete with a bay window, corner shower, and garden tub. Use the front bedroom as a study if you like, and finish out the bonus room at your leisure. The photographed home may have been modified to suit individual tastes.

Farmhouse Flavor

An
EXCLUSIVE DESIGN
By Karl Kreeger

plan no.

10785

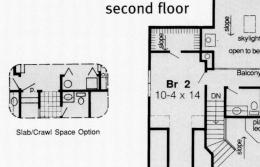

first floor

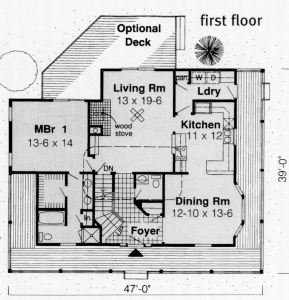

Optional Deck

Living Rm
13 x 19-6

Ldry

W D pan.

wood stove

MBr 1
13-6 x 14

Kitchen
11 x 12

DN

Dining Rm
12-10 x 13-6

Foyer

47'-0"

39'-0"

Slab/Crawl Space Option

second floor

slope

slope

skylight

open to below

slope

Balcony

Br 2
10-4 x 14

DN

Br 3
11 x 14

plant ledge

slope

plan info

First Floor	1,269 sq. ft.
Second Floor	638 sq. ft.
Basement	1,269 sq. ft.
Bedrooms	Three
Baths	2full), 1(half)
Foundation	Basement/Slab Crawl Space

The charm of an old fashioned farmhouse combines with sizzling contemporary excitement in this three-bedroom home. Classic touches abound, from the clapboard exterior with its inviting, wrap-around porch to the wood stove that warms the entire house. Inside, the two-story foyer, crowned by a plant ledge high overhead, affords a view of the soaring, skylit living room and rear deck beyond sliding glass doors. To the right, there's a formal dining room with bay window, just steps away from the kitchen. The well-appointed master suite completes the first floor. Upstairs, you'll find a full bath and two more bedrooms, each with a walk-in closet and cozy gable sitting nook.

total living area: 1,785 sq. ft.

B price code

Second Floor Balcony

An
EXCLUSIVE DESIGN
By Greg Stafford

plan no.

24610

46'-8"

Dining
12-1 x 11-4

Kitchen
13 x 11-4

W
D

pantry

DN

Great Rm
14 x 21-8

UP

open to above

Garage
22 x 23-4

35'-8"

First Floor

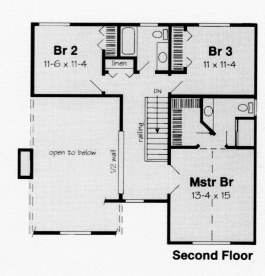

Br 2
11-6 x 11-4

linen

Br 3
11 x 11-4

DN

open to below

1/2 wall

railing

Mstr Br
13-4 x 15

Second Floor

plan info

First Floor	**891 sq. ft.**
Second Floor	**894 sq. ft.**
Basement	**891 sq. ft.**
Garage	**534 sq. ft.**
Bedrooms	**Three**
Baths	**2(full), 1(half)**
Foundation	**Basement/Slab Crawl Space**

The Great room of this home is made more elegant by the fireplace and the fact that it is two stories high. A beautiful multi-paned, arched window naturally illuminates the room and provides a view of the front yard. An efficient kitchen is located at the rear of the home. The conveniences included in the layout of the kitchen are many. A central island, a built-in pantry, double sinks, not to mention the ample storage and counter space, give the advantages today's family demands. The second floor overlooks the Great room. The master bedroom has a private bath and a walk-in closet. The two additional bedrooms share a full hall bath.

total living area: 4,106 sq. ft.

Traditional Stucco

plan no.

94239

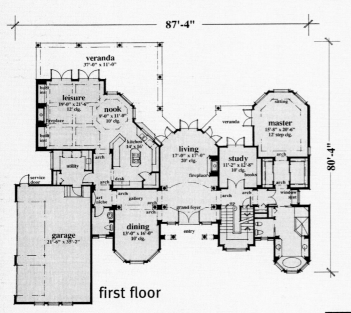

first floor

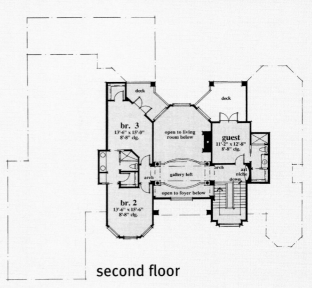

second floor

plan info

First Floor	3,027 sq. ft.
Second Floor	1,079 sq. ft.
Basement	3,027 sq. ft.
Garage	802 sq. ft.
Bedrooms	Four
Baths	3(full), 1(half)
Foundation	Basement/Slab

This traditional elevation features stucco and stone. Round columns grace the double door covered entryway. The living room features a fireplace, a two-story ceiling and bayed glass doors to the rear yard. The gallery leads past the dining room to the family areas. The kitchen serves the dining room and family nook. The leisure room has a fireplace, television niche, coffered ceiling and French doors leading to a covered veranda in the rear. The master wing is located apart from the family areas. The bath has a walk-in shower, a large tub, and his and her vanities. Upstairs, three bedrooms provide privacy from the ground floor. One bedroom is a full suite with a private bath and deck. A gallery catwalk overlooks the two-story living room and foyer. No materials list available for this plan.

total living area: 2,411 sq. ft.   Stylized Roof   D price code

plan no. 24262

Efficiently designed, the kitchen easily serves both the formal dining room and the nook. Upstairs, four bedrooms accommodate your sleeping hours. The master bedroom adds interest with a vaulted ceiling. The master bath has a large double vanity, linen closet, corner tub, separate shower, compartmented toilet, and huge walk-in closet. The three additional bedrooms, one with a walk-in closet, share the full hall bath.

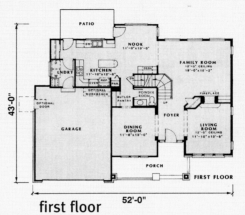

second floor

first floor

plan info

First Flr.	1,241 sq. ft.
Second Flr.	1,170 sq. ft.
Garage	500 sq. ft.
Bedrooms	Four
Baths	2(full), 1(half)
Foundation	Basement/Slab Crawl Space

---

total living area: 1,883 sq. ft.   Growing Families   C price code

plan no. 96479

We opened up the foyer with a dormer, and columns accent the adjacent dining room. The Great room boasts a cathedral ceiling, while living and entertaining space expands to the deck. A tray ceiling adds interest and volume to the master bedroom. The suite includes a walk-in closet and a skylit bath with a garden tub and double vanity. A flexible bedroom/ study shares a bath with another bedroom.

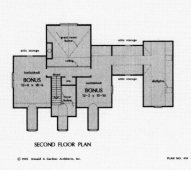

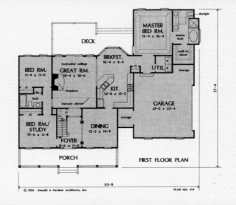

plan info

First Flr.	1,803 sq. ft.
Second Flr.	80 sq. ft.
Bonus Rm.	918 sq. ft.
Garage	569 sq. ft.
Bedrooms	Three
Baths	2(full)
Foundation	Crawl Space

total living area: 1,554 sq. ft.

Country Influence

plan no.

24654

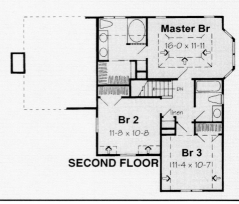

50'-0"

40'-0"

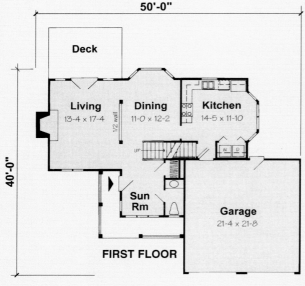

Deck

Living
13-4 x 17-4

1/2 wall

Dining
11-0 x 12-2

Kitchen
14-5 x 11-10

UP

W D

Sun Rm

Garage
21-4 x 21-8

FIRST FLOOR

Master Br
16-0 x 11-11

DN

linen

Br 2
11-8 x 10-8

Br 3
11-4 x 10-7

SECOND FLOOR

plan info

First Floor	**806 sq. ft.**
Second Floor	**748 sq. ft.**
Garage	**467 sq. ft.**
Bedrooms	**Three**
Baths	**2(full), 1(half)**
Foundation	**Basement/Slab Crawl Space**

A cozy porch sets the tone for this comfortable home. Enter into the sun room that includes a coat closet and convenient access to a half bath. A simple half wall separates the living room and the dining room. The efficient kitchen is equipped with a laundry center and a sunny bayed area. The bedrooms are on the second floor. A walk-in closet, private bath with an oval tub and a decorative ceiling and bay window highlight the master suite. The two additional bedrooms share a full bath.

An EXCLUSIVE DESIGN
By Plan One Homes, Inc.

No. 92618

■ **This plan features:**

— Four bedrooms

— Two full and one half baths

■ The spacious Living Room flows easily into the Dining Room which has a pretty bay window

■ An island, an extra large pantry and a built-in desk add increased efficiency to the gourmet Kitchen

■ The sunny Breakfast area and Family Room are in an open layout for an illusion of more space

■ The Master Suite includes a private bath with two vanities, a whirlpool tub, a shower and a linen closet

■ The three additional bedrooms are roomy in size and share the full family bath in the hall

■ There is no material list available for this plan

First floor — 1,337 sq. ft.
Second floor — 1,326 sq. ft.
Width — 53'-10"
Depth — 43'-10"

Total living area 2,663 sq. ft. ■ *Price Code E*

FIRST FLOOR

SECOND FLOOR

Two Story-Brick Colonial

No. 92671

■ **This plan features:**

— Four bedrooms

— Three full and one half baths

■ A covered front Porch and Foyer with lovely staircase greet you

■ The Living Room flows freely into the Dining Room for carefree entertaining

■ The Hearth Room has a twelve foot ceiling, fireplace, and entertainment center

■ The unique Kitchen design is a cook's delight and it adjoins the Breakfast nook and a Screen Porch

■ Upstairs find four large bedrooms with ample closet space, and three full baths

■ An oversized three car garage, rear deck and gazebo round out this magnificent home

■ There is no materials list available for this plan

First floor — 1,666 sq. ft.
Second floor — 1,036 sq. ft.
Mid floor — 743 sq. ft.

Total living area 3,445 sq. ft. ■ *Price Code F*

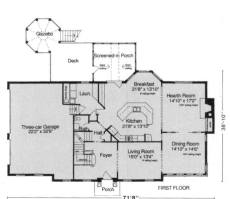

Loft Overlooks Foyer

No. 10583

■ **This plan features:**

— Four bedrooms

— Three full baths

■ Enormous rooms and two Garages

■ An island Kitchen with an eating peninsula for informal dining

■ A sun-filled Great Room with a massive fireplace and open-beamed ceiling

■ A large wrap-around deck to expand the outdoor living area

■ A Master Bedroom suite with a private deck, two large walk-in closets, and a lavish sky-lit tub

■ A large Recreation Room on the lower floor with access to the rear patio

First floor — 2,367 sq. ft.
Lower floor — 1,241 sq. ft.
Basement (unfinished) — 372 sq. ft.
Loft — 295 sq. ft.
Garage (upper) — 660 sq. ft.
Garage (lower) — 636 sq. ft.

FIRST FLOOR

LOWER FLOOR

An
EXCLUSIVE DESIGN
By Karl Kreeger

■ *Total living area 3,903 sq. ft.* ■ *Price Code F* ■

Whimsical Two-story Farmhouse

© 1993 Donald A. Gardner Architects, Inc.

■ *Total living area 2,182 sq. ft.* ■ *Price Code D* ■

No. 96442

■ **This plan features:**

— Four bedrooms

— Three full and one half baths

■ Double gable with palladian, clerestory window and wraparound Porch provide country appeal

■ First floor enjoys nine foot ceilings throughout

■ Palladian windows flood two-story Foyer and Great Room with natural light

■ Both Master Bedroom and Great Room access covered, rear Porch

■ One upstairs bedroom offers private bath and walk-in closet

First floor — 1,346 sq. ft.
Second floor — 836 sq. ft.

FIRST FLOOR PLAN

SECOND FLOOR PLAN

■ *Total living area 1,003 sq. ft.* ■ *Price Code A* ■

No. 35009

■ This plan features:

— One bedroom

— One full bath

■ A front Deck area to relax on

■ A U-shaped Kitchen with an efficient layout, double sink and ample work as a storage space

■ A Dining area that views the front deck and yard

■ A Living Room with a built-in entertainment center and view of the front deck and yard

■ A large Bedroom that includes a double closet

■ A Loft overlooking the Dining and Living Room, that can be expanded as future needs arrive

First floor — 763 sq. ft.
Second floor — 240 sq. ft.

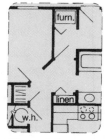

Slab/ Crawl Space Option

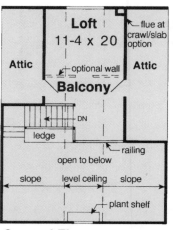

Second Floor

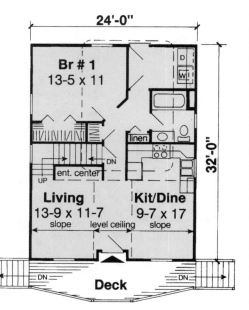

First Floor

Stately Manor

■ *Total living area 2,380 sq. ft.* ■ *Price Code D* ■

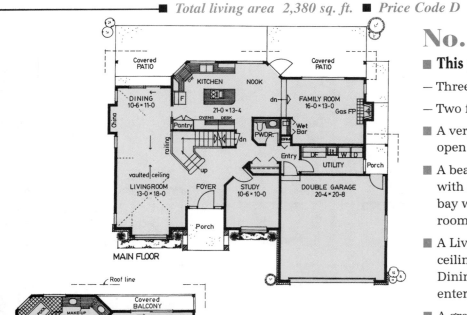

MAIN FLOOR

SECOND FLOOR

No. 90966

■ **This plan features:**

— Three bedrooms

— Two full and one half baths

■ A very spacious Foyer with an open staircase and lots of angles

■ A beautiful Kitchen equipped with a cooktop island and a full bay window wall that includes a roomy Breakfast Nook

■ A Living Room with a vaulted ceiling that flows into the formal Dining Room for ease in entertaining

■ A grand Master Suite equipped with a walk-in closet and five-piece private bath

Main floor — 1,383 sq. ft.
Second floor — 997 sq. ft.
Basement — 1,374 sq. ft.
Garage — 420 sq. ft.
Width — 54'-0"
Depth — 47'-0"

An **EXCLUSIVE DESIGN**
By Westhome Planners, Ltd.

Room to Grow

No. 90838

This plan features:

— Three bedrooms

— Three full baths

■ A corner gas fireplace in the spacious Living Room

■ A Master Suite including a private Bath with a whirlpool tub, separate shower and a double vanity

■ An island Kitchen that is well-equipped to efficiently serve both formal Dining Room and informal Nook

■ Two additional bedrooms sharing a full bath on the second floor

First floor — 1,837 sq. ft.
Second floor — 848 sq. ft.
Basement — 1,803 sq. ft.
Bonus room — 288 sq. ft.

An EXCLUSIVE DESIGN
By Westhome Planners, Ltd.

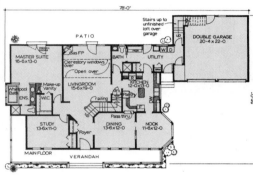

■ Total living area 2,685 sq. ft. ■ Price Code E ■

SECOND FLOOR

Attractive Curb Presence

No. 93334

This plan features:

— Four bedrooms

— Three full and one half baths

■ A distinctive roofline with brick and wood siding and a floor-to-ceiling bay window

■ A Porch entrance leading into an open Foyer area with a Balcony and window seat above

■ An unusual Living Room featuring a half-circle of windows topped by a stepped ceiling, and French doors into a Sun Room

■ A stepped ceiling and a large bay window adding charm to the formal Dining Room

■ An informal Family Room, with a massive fireplace, convenient built-ins, and a wall of windows, opening to Dinette/Kitchen area

■ An island Kitchen with a double sink, built-in desk and a sky-lit Dinette area leading to the formal Dining Room, and a walk-in pantry

■ Master Suite with a tray ceiling and a whirlpool, corner window tub, double vanity and an extra large walk-in closet

■ No materials list is available for this plan

First floor — 1,970 sq. ft.
Second floor — 1,638 sq. ft.
Bonus room — 587 sq. ft.

■ Total living area 3,608 sq. ft. ■ Price Code F ■

An EXCLUSIVE DESIGN
By Patrick Morabito, A.I.A. Architect

Wrap-Around Porch Adds a Touch of Country

■ **Total living area 2,647 sq. ft.** ■ **Price Code E** ■

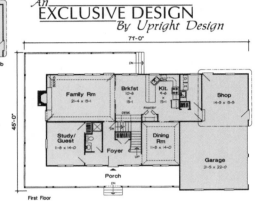

An **EXCLUSIVE DESIGN** *By Upright Design*

No. 24403

■ **This plan features:**

— Three or four bedrooms

— Two full and one three-quarter baths

■ A large welcoming, wrap-around porch adding an old-fashioned country feel

■ A study/guest room with convenient access to a full, hall bath

■ An elegant Dining Room topped by a decorative ceiling treatment

■ An expansive Family Room equipped with a massive fireplace with built-in bookshelves

■ An informal Breakfast Room conveniently enhanced by a built-in planning desk

■ Peninsula counter/eating bar, a built-in pantry, double sink and ample counter and cabinet space in the efficient Kitchen

■ A cathedral ceiling crowning the Master Suite

■ Two additional bedrooms sharing a full, compartmented hall bath

First floor — 1,378 sq. ft.
Second floor — 1,269 sq. ft.
Basement — 1,378 sq. ft.
Garage — 717 sq. ft.
Porch — 801 sq. ft.

Polished & Poised

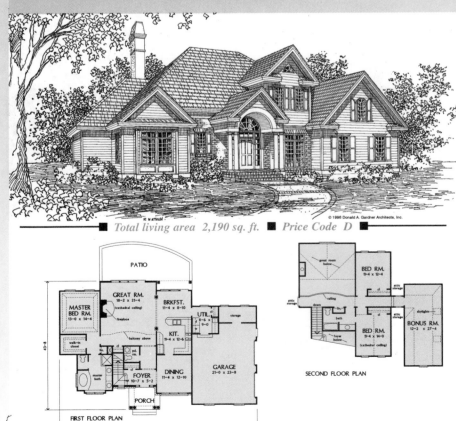

■ **Total living area 2,190 sq. ft.** ■ **Price Code D** ■

No. 96471

■ **This plan features:**

— Three bedrooms

— Two full and one half baths

■ Hip roof, gables and brick accents add poise and polish to this traditional home

■ Curved transom window and sidelights illuminate the gracious Foyer

■ A curved balcony overlooks the Great Room which has a cathedral ceiling, fireplace and a wall of windows overlooking the Patio

■ Hub Kitchen easily serves the Dining Room, Breakfast area and the Patio beyond

■ Master Bedroom wing is enhanced by a tray ceiling, walk-in closet and a deluxe bath

First floor — 1,577 sq. ft.
Second floor — 613 sq. ft.
Bonus room — 390 sq. ft.
Garage & storage — 634 sq. ft.

Modest Tudor with a Massive Look

■ *Total living area 2,209 sq. ft.* ■ *Price Code D* ■

No. 90012

■ This plan features:

— Three bedrooms

— Two full and one half baths

■ A large log-burning fireplace centrally located on the far wall of the Living Room

■ A formal Dining Room with access to either the screen porch, terrace, or Kitchen

■ A Kitchen with a cooktop island and a built-in Breakfast Nook

■ A Family Room with French door access to another porch

■ A Master Suite with lounge area, private Master Bath, and a walk-in closet

■ Two additional bedrooms with access to the full hall bath

First floor — 1,078 sq. ft.
Second floor — 1,131 sq. ft.

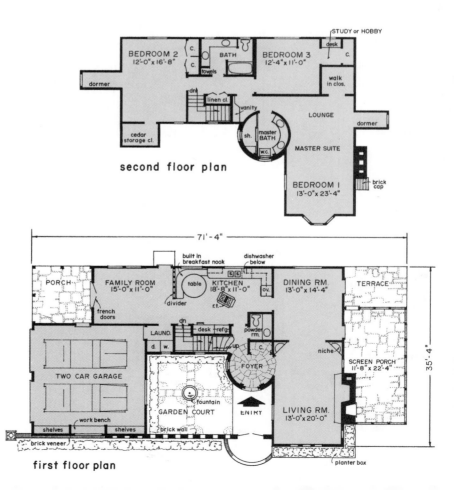

second floor plan

first floor plan

Eye-Catching Turret Adds to Master Suite

Total living area 2,403 sq. ft. ■ *Price Code D* ■

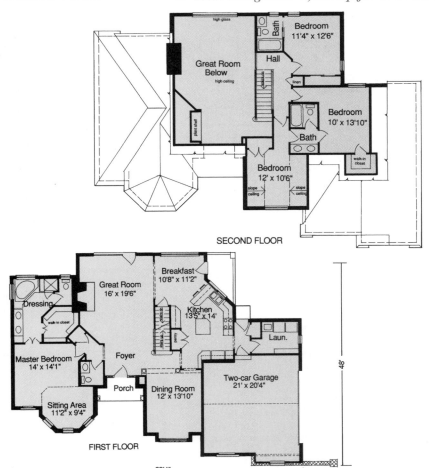

SECOND FLOOR

- Great Room Below
- high ceiling
- high glass
- Bath
- Bedroom 11'4" x 12'6"
- Hall
- linen
- Bedroom 10' x 13'10"
- Bath
- walk-in closet
- Bedroom 12' x 10'6"
- slope ceiling
- plant shelf

FIRST FLOOR

- Dressing
- walk-in closet
- Master Bedroom 14' x 14'1"
- Sitting Area 11'2" x 9'4"
- Foyer
- Porch
- Great Room 16' x 19'6"
- Breakfast 10'8" x 11'2"
- Kitchen 13'5" x 14'
- Laun.
- Dining Room 12' x 13'10"
- Two-car Garage 21' x 20'4"
- 63'4"
- 48'

No. 92651

■ **This plan features:**

— Four bedrooms

— Three full and one half baths

■ Sheltered entry surrounded by glass leads into open Foyer and Great Room with high ceiling, hearth fireplace and atrium door to back yard

■ Columns frame entrance to Dining Room

■ Kitchen with built-in pantry, work island and bright Breakfast area

■ Master Bedroom wing with sitting area, walk-in closet and private bath with corner window tub and double vanity

■ Three bedrooms, one with a private bath

First floor — 1,710 sq. ft.
Second floor — 693 sq. ft.
Basement — 1,620 sq. ft.
Garage — 467 sq. ft.

Spectacular Stucco and Stone

No. 94401 ®

■ This plan features:

— Three bedrooms

— Two full and one half baths

■ Two-story glass entry opens to expansive Great Room with an inviting fireplace between bookcases and French doors to back yard

■ Convenient Dining Room opens to Great Room and adjoins Kitchen

■ Open Kitchen and Morning Room with pantry, cooktop island, fireplace and skylights, provides efficiency and relaxation

■ Secluded Master Bedroom offers lovely bay window, two walk-in closets and a luxurious bath

■ Two second floor bedrooms with walk-in closets and vanities, have private access to a full bath

■ Optional second floor plan adds another bedroom, bath and Bonus Room

■ An optional basement or crawl space foundation — please specify when ordering

■ No materials list available

First floor — 1,719 sq. ft.
Second floor — 608 sq. ft.
Bonus space — 630 sq. ft.

■ Total living area 2,327 sq. ft. ■ Price Code E ■

SECOND FLOOR PLAN

FIRST FLOOR PLAN

Magnificent Elevation

No. 94940 ✕

■ This plan features:

— Four bedrooms

— Two full and one half baths

■ Impressive elevation masterfully combines brick and wood

■ The highlight of the sixteen-foot high Entry is an angled staircase

■ Formal Living and Dining rooms ideal for entertaining with tapered columns and decorative windows

■ Ideal Kitchen with a work island, adjoins the Breakfast bay and is open to the Family Room with a beamed ceiling and a fireplace

■ Double door entrance into the Master Bedroom suite that features a tiered ceiling, walk-in closet and a plush bath

First floor — 1,369 sq. ft.
Second floor — 1,111 sq. ft.
Basement — 1,369 sq. ft.
Garage — 716 sq. ft.

■ Total living area 2,480 sq. ft. ■ Price Code D ■

FIRST FLOOR

SECOND FLOOR

© design basics, inc.

An Air of Refinement

© 1993 Donald A. Gardner Architects, Inc.

■ Total living area 2,130 sq. ft. ■ Price Code D ■

FIRST FLOOR PLAN

SECOND FLOOR PLAN

No. 96438

■ This plan features:

— Four bedrooms

— Three full baths

■ Hip roof, brick veneer and arched windows catch attention

■ Foyer, flanked by Dining Room and Bedroom/Study, opens to great Room with cozy fireplace and wall of windows

■ Cathedral ceilings and arched windows bathe Dining Room and Breakfast area in natural light

■ Private Master Bedroom suite has cathedral ceiling and sumptuous bath with whirlpool tub, shower and dual vanity

■ Two more bedrooms and Bonus Room share third full bath

■ Specify basement or crawl space foundation when ordering this plan

First floor — 1,694 sq. ft.
Second floor — 436 sq. ft.
Bonus room — 345 sq. ft.
Garage & storage — 567 sq. ft.

Sensational Entry

■ Total living area 4,362 sq. ft. ■ Price Code F ■

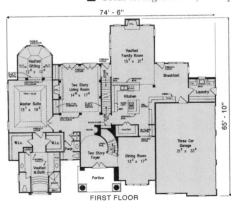

FIRST FLOOR

SECOND FLOOR

No. 98404

■ This plan features:

— Four bedrooms

— Three full and one half baths

■ Grand columns frame two-story Portico leading into a gracious Foyer with a curved staircase

■ Two-story Living Room accented by columns, a massive fireplace and French doors to the rear yard

■ Vaulted Family Room highlighted by outdoor views and a cozy fireplace, opens to Kitchen/Breakfast area

■ Ideal Kitchen with a cooktop island/serving bar, walk-in pantry, Breakfast area and nearby Laundry and Garage entry

■ Secluded Master Suite offers a vaulted Sitting area with radius windows and decorative columns, two walk-in closets, and a lavish bath

■ Three second floor bedrooms with walk-in closets and private access to full baths

■ An optional basement or crawl space foundation — please specify when ordering

First floor — 2,764 sq. ft.
Second floor — 1,598 sq. ft.
Garage — 743 sq. ft.

Master Suite Crowns Plan

■ *Total living area 1,778 sq. ft.* ■ *Price Code B* ■

No. 10394

■ **This plan features:**

— Three bedrooms

— Two full baths

■ A Master Bedroom which occupies the entire second level

■ A passive solar design

■ A Living Room which rises two stories in the front

■ Skylights in the sloping ceilings of the Kitchen and Master Bath

First floor — 1,306 sq. ft.
Second floor — 472 sq. ft.
Garage — 576 sq. ft.

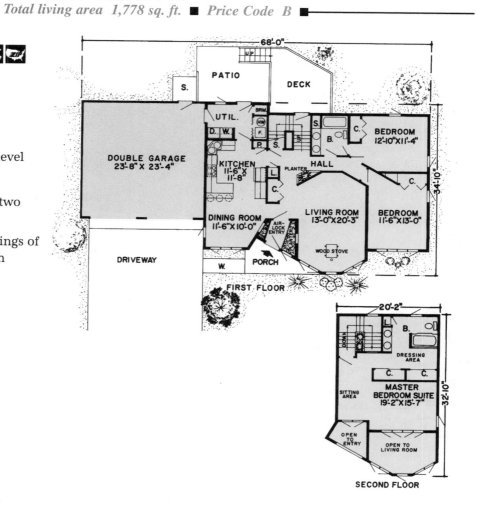

68'-0"

PATIO   DECK

UTIL.   BRM   S.   C.   BEDROOM
D.W.   HW   12'-10"X11'-4"
F.
P.   S.   S.   B.

DOUBLE GARAGE
23'-8" X 23'-4"   KITCHEN   PLANTER   HALL
11'-6" X   C.
11'-8"   L

DINING ROOM   LIVING ROOM   BEDROOM
11'-6"X10'-0"   13'-0"X20'-3"   11'-6"X13'-0"

AIR-
LOCK
ENTRY   PLANTER

DRIVEWAY   W.   PORCH   WOOD STOVE

FIRST FLOOR

34'-10"

20'-2"

DOWN   L   B.

DRESSING
AREA

SITTING   C.   C.
AREA
MASTER
BEDROOM SUITE
19'-2"X15'-7"

OPEN   OPEN
TO   TO
ENTRY   LIVING ROOM

32'-10"

SECOND FLOOR

Country Style For Today

■ *Total living area 2,406 sq. ft.* ■ *Price Code D* ■

No. 91700

■ **This plan features:**

— Three bedrooms

— Two full and one half baths

■ A wide wrap-around porch for a farmhouse style

■ A spacious Living Room with double doors and a large front window

■ A garden window over the double sink in the huge, country Kitchen with two islands, one a butcher block, and the other an eating bar

■ A corner fireplace in the Family Room enjoyed throughout the Nook and Kitchen, thanks to an open layout

■ A Master Suite with a spa tub, and a huge walk-in closet as well as a shower and double vanity

First floor — 1,785 sq. ft.
Second floor — 621 sq. ft.

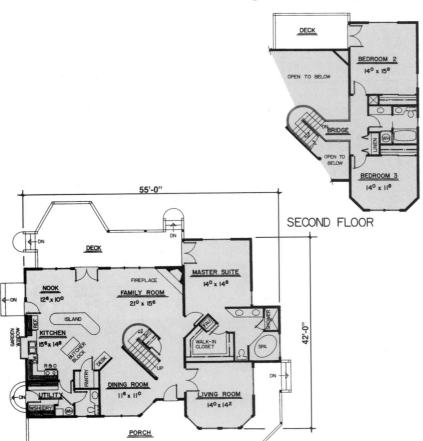

SECOND FLOOR

FIRST FLOOR

Comfortable, Easy Living

No. 96444

This plan features:

— Five bedrooms

— Three full and one half baths

■ Great Room is overlooked by a curved balcony and features a fireplace with built-ins on either side

■ Spacious and efficient Kitchen equipped with a cooktop island has direct access to Breakfast Room and Dining Room

■ Swing Room, Bedroom/Study, with private full bath and closet

■ Master Suite pampered by lavish bath and large walk-in closet

■ Three additional second floor bedrooms, each with ample storage, share a full bath in the hall

First floor — 2,176 sq. ft.
Second floor — 861 sq. ft.
Bonus room — 483 sq. ft.
Garage — 710 sq. ft.

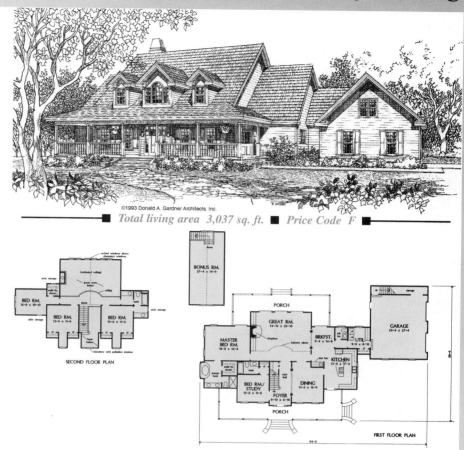

©1993 Donald A. Gardner Architects, Inc.

■ *Total living area 3,037 sq. ft.* ■ *Price Code F* ■

Covered Porch Shelters Entry

No. 98422

This plan features:

— Three bedrooms

— Two full and one half baths

■ There is a convenient pass-through from the Kitchen into the Family Room

■ An easy flow into the Dining Room enhances the interaction of the Living Spaces on the first floor

■ A fireplace highlights the spacious Family Room

■ The Kitchen opens to the Breakfast Room which has a French door that accesses the rear yard

■ Decorative Ceiling treatment highlights the Master Bedroom while a vaulted ceiling tops the Master Bath

■ Two additional bedrooms share the use of the full bath in the hall

■ Please specify a basement or crawl space foundation when ordering

First floor — 719 sq. ft.
Second floor — 717 sq. ft.
Basement — 719 sq. ft.
Garage — 480 sq. ft.

■ *Total living area 1,436 sq. ft.* ■ *Price Code A* ■

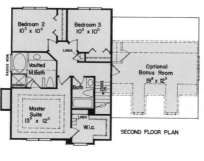

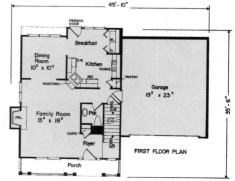

Brick Beauty

Total living area 2,685 sq. ft. ■ Price Code E ■

No. 98525

■ **This plan features:**

— Four bedrooms

— Three full and one half baths

■ Living Room and the Dining Room are each distinguished by their impressive front windows

■ Kitchen with center island opens into the Breakfast Nook which has sliding doors to the backyard patio

■ Enormous Family Room with fireplace, will be the central location of family activities

■ First floor Master Bedroom is removed from high traffic areas, and is complimented by a spacious bath and walk-in closet

■ Connected by the upstairs hallway are three bedrooms and two full baths

■ No materials list is available for this plan

First floor — 1,842 sq. ft.
Second floor — 843 sq. ft.
Width — 60'-0"
Depth — 48'-9"

Sprawling Two-Story

Total living area 2,702 sq. ft. ■ Price Code E ■

No. 99143

■ **This plan features:**

— Three bedrooms

— Two full and one half baths

■ Two-story Entry hall with dramatic staircase

■ Den highlighted by bright windows and a cathedral ceiling

■ Spacious floor plan includes Great Room with fireplace and Nook opening to a Screen Porch

■ L-shaped Kitchen equipped with a center island

■ Luxurious Master Suite tucked away on the first floor

■ Located upstairs are a loft, a full bath and two bedrooms, one with a cathedral ceiling

■ A three-car Garage completes this plan

■ There is no materials list available for this plan

First floor — 2,032 sq. ft.
Second floor — 670 sq. ft
Basement — 2,032 sq. ft.

An
EXCLUSIVE DESIGN
By Ahmann Design Inc.

■ *Total living area 3,029 sq. ft.* ■ *Price Code E* ■

No. 93604

■ **This plan features:**

— Four bedrooms

— Three full and one half bath

■ A two story Foyer

■ A formal Living Room and Dining Room perfect for entertaining

■ A two-story Grand Room with a focal point fireplace

■ A gourmet Kitchen with a work island, walk-in pantry, built-in planning desk, double sink and more than ample cabinet and counter space

■ A first floor Master Suite with a decorative ceiling and a luxurious Master Bath

■ No materials list available

■ This plan is not to be built within a 50 mile radius of Atlanta, GA

First floor — 2,115 sq. ft.
Second floor — 914 sq. ft.
Basement — 2,115 sq. ft.
Garage — 448 sq. ft.

FIRST FLOOR

SECOND FLOOR

An
EXCLUSIVE DESIGN
By *Garrell Associates Inc.*

Country Brick

■ *Total living area 2,443 sq. ft.* ■ *Price Code D* ■

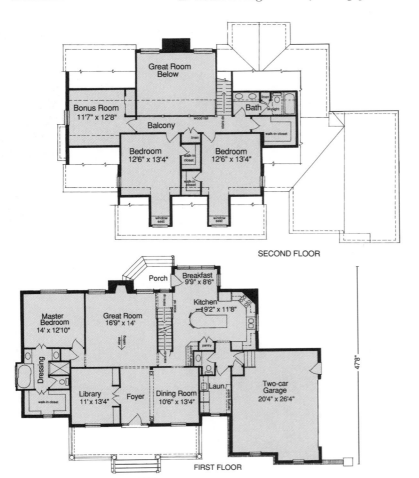

SECOND FLOOR

FIRST FLOOR

Great Room Below

Bonus Room
11'7" x 12'8"

Balcony

Bath

Bedroom
12'6" x 13'4"

Bedroom
12'6" x 13'4"

walk-in closet

window seat

window seat

Master Bedroom
14' x 12'10"

Dressing

walk-in closet

Library
11' x 13'4"

Foyer

Great Room
16'9" x 14'

Dining Room
10'6" x 13'4"

Laun.

Porch

Breakfast
9'9" x 8'6"

Kitchen
9'2" x 11'8"

pantry

Two-car Garage
20'4" x 26'4"

78'4"

47'8"

No. 92653

■ **This plan features:**

— Three or four bedrooms

— Two full and one half baths

■ Friendly front porch leads into a gracious open Foyer

■ Secluded Library offers a quiet space with built-in shelves

■ Great Room with a focal point fireplace topped by sloped ceiling

■ Kitchen with island snack bar, bright Breakfast area, pantry and nearby Laundry/Garage entry

■ Master Bedroom offers a deluxe bath and spacious walk-in closet

■ Two additional bedrooms with walk-in closets and window seats, share a double vanity bath, and Bonus Room

First floor — 1,710 sq. ft.
Second floor — 733 sq. ft.
Bonus — 181 sq. ft.
Basement — 1,697 sq. ft.
Garage — 499 sq. ft.

No. 92673

■ This plan features:

— Four bedrooms

— Three full and two half baths

■ Covered porch and open Foyer with magnificent staircase welcome you home

■ Living Room which has a fireplace flows into the Dining Room

■ A butler's pantry connects the Dining Room to the Breakfast and Kitchen areas

■ The sunken Hearth Room has a cozy fireplace and accesses the rear deck

■ The Master Suite encompasses much of the second floor and contains many luxuries

■ There are also three more bedrooms and two full baths located upstairs

■ A three car garage completes this home

■ No materials list is available for this plan

First floor — 2,094 sq. ft.
Second floor — 2,169 sq. ft.
Basement — 2,049 sq. ft.

■ Total living area 4,263 sq. ft. ■ Price Code F ■

Traditional with a Dramatic Entry

No. 93052

■ This plan features:

— Four bedrooms

— Two full and one half baths

■ An open Kitchen, Breakfast Room and Family Room with a two-sided fireplace, visible from all areas

■ An efficient, gourmet Kitchen with a peninsula counter and a built-in pantry

■ A first floor, amenities packed, Master Suite with his-and-her vanities, a whirlpool tub and a shower

■ Three additional bedrooms on the second floor, all have walk-in closets, and share a full bath with a double vanity

■ A small television loft that adds to the relaxation space and completes the second floor

■ No materials list is available for this plan

First floor — 1,774 sq. ft.
Second floor — 844 sq. ft.
Garage — 520 sq. ft.

■ Total living area 2,618 sq. ft. ■ Price Code E ■

FIRST FLOOR

SECOND FLOOR

Simple Elegance

Total living area 2,217 sq. ft. ■ Price Code D

No. 92622

■ **This plan features:**

— Three bedrooms

— Two full and one half baths

■ A sunken Great Room, large enough for family gatherings, that is enhanced by a fireplace

■ A bay window in the Dining Room that has direct access to the Kitchen

■ A Master Bedroom Suite with a garden bath and walk-in closet

■ A second floor Library that can double as a fourth bedroom

■ Two additional bedrooms share a full hall bath

■ No materials list is available for this plan

First floor — 1,134 sq. ft.
Second floor — 1,083 sq. ft.
Basement — 931 sq. ft.
Garage — 554 sq. ft.

A Touch of Victorian Styling

Total living area 1,764 sq. ft. ■ Price Code B

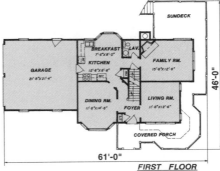

No. 93230

■ **This plan features:**

— Three bedrooms

— Two full and one half baths

■ A covered porch and a pointed roof on the sitting alcove of the Master Suite giving this home a Victorian look

■ A formal Living Room directly across from the Dining Room for ease in entertaining

■ An efficient Kitchen with a bright bayed Breakfast area

■ The Family Room has a cozy fireplace nestled in a corner

■ A large Master Suite with a cozy sitting alcove and double vanity bath

■ Two additional bedrooms serviced by a full hall bath

■ No materials list is available for this plan

First floor — 887 sq. ft.
Second floor — 877 sq. ft.
Basement — 859 sq. ft.
Garage — 484 sq. ft.

An EXCLUSIVE DESIGN
By Jannis Vann & Associates, Inc.

■ *Total living area 3,098 sq. ft.* ■ *Price Code E* ■

No. 94403 ℞

■ This plan features:

— Three bedrooms

— Three full and one half baths

■ Great Room accented by hearth fireplace between built-in shelves

■ Formal Dining Room highlighted by a lovely bay window and dropped tray ceiling

■ Glass Breakfast area extends from Kitchen and opens to Great Room

■ Cooktop island/snack bar, loads of counter and storage space and walk-in pantry in Kitchen

■ Luxurious Master Bedroom wing with Patio access, vaulted ceiling, walk-in closet and lavish bath

■ An optional basement or crawl space foundation — please specify when ordering

■ No materials list available

First floor — 2,214 sq. ft.
Second floor — 884 sq. ft.
Bonus — 330 sq. ft.
Garage — 525 sq. ft.

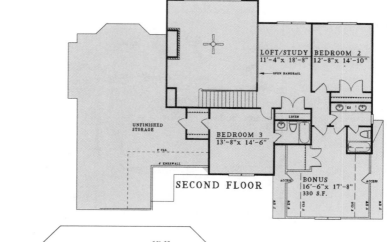

LOFT/STUDY
11'-4" x 18'-8"

BEDROOM 2
12'-8" x 14'-10"

UNFINISHED
STORAGE

BEDROOM 3
13'-8" x 14'-6"

LINEN

SECOND FLOOR

BONUS
16'-6" x 17'-8"
330 S.F.

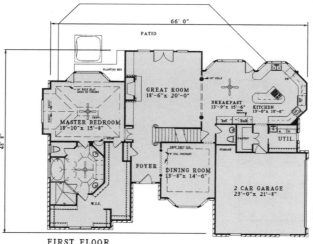

66' 0"

PATIO

GREAT ROOM
18'-6" x 20'-0"

BREAKFAST
13'-9" x 15'-6"

KITCHEN
13'-0" x 15'-6"

MASTER BEDROOM
18'-10" x 15'-8"

48' 8"

UTIL.

PANTRY

FOYER

DINING ROOM
13'-8" x 14'-6"

2 CAR GARAGE
23'-0" x 21'-8"

W.I.C.

FIRST FLOOR

Rich Classic Lines

■ *Total living area 2,212 sq. ft.* ■ *Price Code D* ■

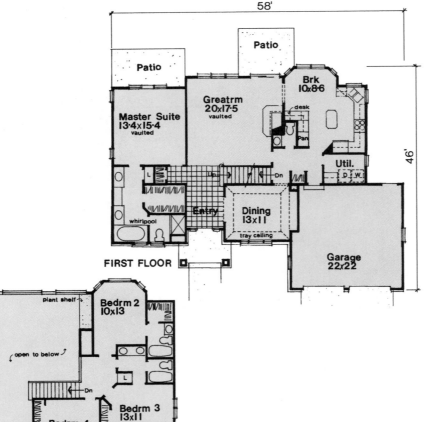

FIRST FLOOR

SECOND FLOOR

No. 91901

■ This plan features:

— Four bedrooms

— Three full and one half baths

■ A two-story Foyer flooded by light through a half-round transom

■ A corner fireplace in the Great Room with French doors to the Breakfast/Kitchen area

■ A center island in the Kitchen with an angled sink

■ A tray ceiling and recessed hutch area in the formal Dining Room

■ A Master Suite with a walk-in closet, a whirlpool tub, and a double vanity

■ No materials list is available for this plan

First floor — 1,496 sq. ft.
Second floor — 716 sq. ft.
Basement — 1,420 sq. ft.
Garage — 460 sq. ft.

No. 93207

■ This plan features:

— Four bedrooms

— Two full and one half baths

■ Foyer entrance divides the formal Living and Dining Rooms

■ Efficient Kitchen is set between the Breakfast Nook that accesses the sundeck and the laundry room

■ Large Family Room with a cozy fireplace

■ Luxurious Master Suite includes a walk-in closet, a sitting area and private bath with stall shower, oval tub and double vanity

■ Three additional bedrooms each have a walk-in closet and share the full hall bath

■ No materials list available

First floor — 1,075 sq. ft.
Second floor — 1,353 sq. ft.
Basement — 977 sq. ft.
Garage — 462 sq. ft.

■ *Total living area 2,428 sq. ft.* ■ *Price Code D* ■

SECOND FLOOR

FIRST FLOOR

An
EXCLUSIVE DESIGN
By Jannis Vann & Associates, Inc.

A Tasteful Elegance

No. 93321

■ This plan features:

— Four bedrooms

— Two full and one half baths

■ A Foyer with a vaulted ceiling, giving a great first impression

■ A Kitchen with a cooktop island and many built-in amenities

■ A Dinette with sliding glass doors to a wooden deck

■ A large Family Room with a beamed ceiling, bay window and a cozy fireplace

■ A tray ceiling as the crowning touch to the formal Living Room, which also has a terrific fireplace

■ A Master Bedroom with a stepped ceiling, double vanity private bath and a huge walk-in closet

■ Three additional bedrooms, with ample closet space, share use of a full hall Bath

■ No materials list is available for this plan

First floor — 1,947 sq. ft.
Second floor — 1,390 sq. ft.
Basement — 1,947 sq. ft.
Garage — 680 sq. ft.
Deck — 322 sq. ft.

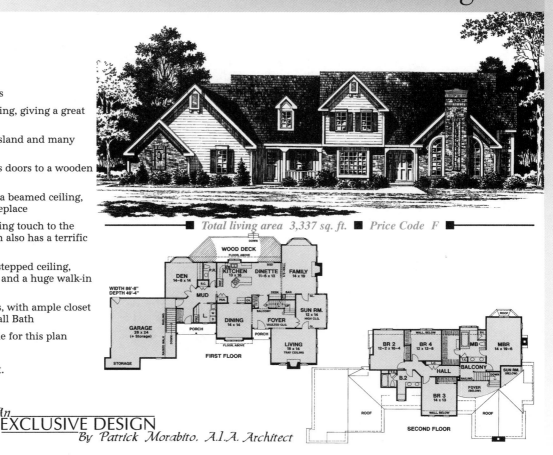

■ *Total living area 3,337 sq. ft.* ■ *Price Code F* ■

FIRST FLOOR

SECOND FLOOR

An
EXCLUSIVE DESIGN
By Patrick Morabito, A.I.A. Architect

53

Open Plan is Full of Air & Light

■ *Total living area 1,505 sq. ft.* ■ *Price Code B* ■

No. 98463

■ **This plan features:**

—Three bedrooms

—Two full and one half baths

■ Foyer open to the Family Room and highlighted by a fireplace

■ Dining Room, with a sliding glass door to rear yard adjoins Family Room

■ Kitchen and Nook in an efficient open layout

■ Second floor Master Suite topped by tray ceiling over the bedroom and a vaulted ceiling over the lavish bath

■ Two additional bedrooms share a full bath in the hall

■ An optional basement or crawl space foundation — please specify when ordering

■ No materials list available

First floor — 767 sq. ft.
Second floor — 738 sq. ft.
Bonus room — 240 sq. ft.
Basement — 767 sq. ft.

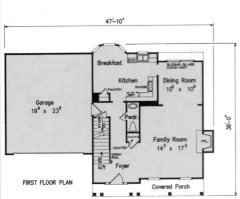

Relaxing Retreat

■ *Total living area 1,012 sq. ft.* ■ *Price Code A* ■

No. 94306

■ **This plan features:**

— Three bedrooms

— Two three quarter baths

■ A wood Deck, expanding living space, leads into a tiled Entry and the open layout of the Living/Dining area and Kitchen

■ A central fireplace warming both temperature and atmosphere in the Living/Dining area

■ An efficient Kitchen with a side entry and a convenient closet

■ A roomy Master Bedroom with a private bath and second floor Deck

■ A first floor bedroom next to the full bath

■ A Loft Bedroom with clerestory windows and an oversized closet

■ No materials list is available for this plan

First floor — 598 sq. ft.
Second floor — 414 sq. ft.

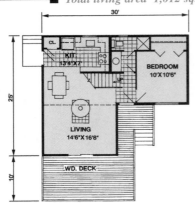

An EXCLUSIVE DESIGN
By Marshall Associates

54

■ *Total living area 2,306 sq. ft.* ■ *Price Code D* ■

No. 93704

■ **This plan features:**

— Three bedrooms

— Two full and one half baths

■ Front Porch shelters entrance into Foyer, Great Room and Study

■ Great Room with inviting fireplace opens to formal Dining Room

■ Spacious Kitchen with work island, built-in pantry and serving/snack bar for Breakfast area and Porch

■ Master Bedroom adjoins Study, pampering bath and Utility area

■ Two second floor bedrooms with double closets, share a double vanity bath and study alcove

■ No materials list is available for this plan

Main level — 1,748 sq. ft.
Upper level — 558 sq. ft.
Garage — 440 sq. ft.

An
EXCLUSIVE DESIGN
By Building Science Associates

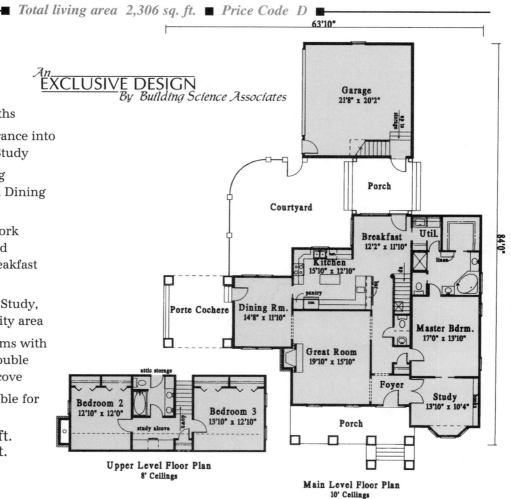

Upper Level Floor Plan
8' Ceilings

Main Level Floor Plan
10' Ceilings

Lovely Second Home

■ *Total living area 1,096 sq. ft.* ■ *Price Code A* ■

No. 91002

■ **This plan features:**

— Three bedrooms

— One full and one half baths

■ Fireplace warms both entryway and Living Room

■ Dining and Living Rooms opening onto the deck, which surrounds the house on three sides

Main floor — 808 sq. ft.
Upper floor — 288 sq. ft.

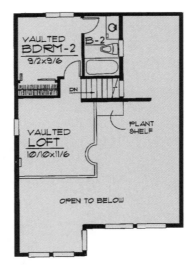

VAULTED BDRM-2
9/2x9/6

B-2

DN

VAULTED LOFT
10/10x11/6

PLANT SHELF

OPEN TO BELOW

UPPER FLOOR PLAN

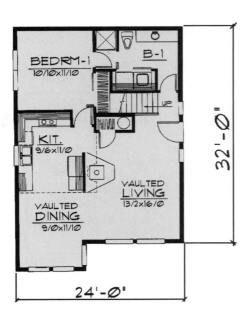

BEDRM-1
10/10x11/10

B-1

UP

KIT.
9/6x11/0

VAULTED LIVING
13/2x16/0

VAULTED DINING
9/0x11/10

32'-0"

24'-0"

MAIN FLOOR PLAN

Spacious Country Charm

No. 94107

■ **This plan features**

— Three Bedrooms

— Two full and one half baths

■ Comfortable front Porch leads into bright, two-story Foyer

■ Pillars frame entrance to formal Dining Room highlighted by bay window

■ Expansive Great Room accented by hearth fireplace and triple window opens to Kitchen/Dining area

■ Efficient Kitchen with loads of counter and storage space and Dining area with window access to rear yard

■ Corner Master Bedroom offers triple window and luxurious Master Bath

■ Two additional bedrooms with ample closets, share a full bath

■ No materials list is available for this plan

First floor — 961 sq. ft.
Second floor — 926 sq. ft.
Garage — 548 sq. ft.

■ *Total living area 1,887 sq. ft.* ■ *Price Code C* ■

Southern Styling

No. 94631

■ **This plan features:**

— Four bedrooms

— Three full baths

■ Porches and patios expand living space to the outdoors

■ Living Room includes a large fireplace with built-in cabinets and shelving

■ Efficient L-shaped Kitchen has a work island and enjoys easy access to both dining areas

■ The Master Suite includes a five-piece bath and a walk-in closet

■ Two additional bedrooms share a full bath

■ A fourth bedroom on the second floor has a full bath and is the perfect guest room

■ An optional slab or crawl space foundation — please specify when ordering

■ No materials list available

First floor — 2,346 sq. ft.
Second floor — 386 sq. ft.

■ *Total living area 2,732 sq. ft.* ■ *Price Code E* ■

WIDTH 60'-10"
DEPTH 73'-5"

SECOND FLOOR

FIRST FLOOR

A Hint of Victorian Nostalgia

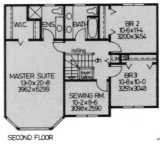

■ *Total living area 2,175 sq. ft.* ■ *Price Code C* ■

MAIN FLOOR

SECOND FLOOR

No. 90909

■ **This plan features:**

— Three bedrooms

— Two full and one half baths

■ A classic center stairwell

■ A Kitchen with full bay window and built-in eating table

■ A spacious Master Suite including a large walk-in closet and full bath

Main floor — 1,206 sq. ft.
Second floor — 969 sq. ft.
Garage — 471 sq. ft.
Basement — 1,206 sq. ft.
Width — 61'
Depth — 44'

An
EXCLUSIVE DESIGN
By Westhome Planners, Ltd.

Appealing Front Porch

■ *Total living area 1,842 sq. ft.* ■ *Price Code C* ■

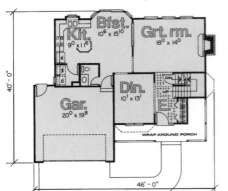

FIRST FLOOR

SECOND FLOOR

No. 94935

■ **This plan features:**

— Four bedrooms

— Two full and one half baths

■ Appealing wrap-around Porch graces this home

■ Light and airy two-story entrance with a side-light, plant shelf and a closet

■ Wall of windows and fireplace featured in the Great Room

■ Open Kitchen with easy access to the Breakfast area, Dining room and the Garage

■ Lovely Master Bedroom suite with tiered ceiling, two walk-in closets and a deluxe bath

First floor — 919 sq. ft.
Second floor — 923 sq. ft.
Basement — 919 sq. ft.
Garage — 414 sq. ft.

■ *Total living area 2,759 sq. ft.* ■ *Price Code E* ■

No. 90443

■ This plan features:

— Three bedrooms

— Three full and two half baths

■ A Master Suite with two closets and bath with separate shower, corner tub and dual vanity

■ A large Dining Room with a bay window, adjacent to the Kitchen

■ A formal Living Room for entertaining and a cozy Family Room with fireplace

■ Two upstairs bedrooms with walk-in closets and private baths

■ A Bonus Room to allow the house to grow with your needs

■ An optional basement or crawl space foundation — please specify when ordering

First floor — 1,927 sq. ft.
Second floor — 832 sq. ft.
Bonus room — 624 sq. ft.
Basement — 1,674 sq. ft.

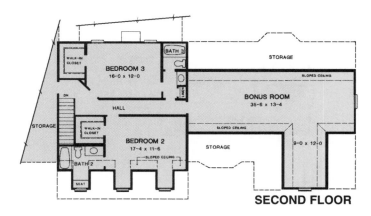

SECOND FLOOR

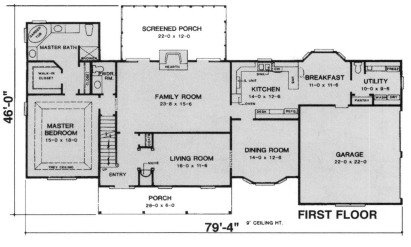

FIRST FLOOR

Unusual and Dramatic

— Total living area 3,500 sq. ft. ■ Price Code F ■

No. 92048

■ **This plan features:**

— Four bedrooms

— Three full and one half baths

■ Elegant Entry with decorative windows, arched openings and a double curved staircase

■ Cathedral ceilings crown arched windows in the Den and Living Room

■ Family Room with a vaulted ceiling and a large fireplace

■ Hub Kitchen with a work island/serving counter, Breakfast alcove and nearby Garage entry

■ Secluded Master Suite with a lovely bay window, two walk-in closets and a plush bath

■ Three second floor bedrooms, one with a private bath

FIRST FLOOR — 2,646 SQ. FT.
SECOND FLOOR — 854 SQ. FT.
BASEMENT — 2,656 SQ. FT.

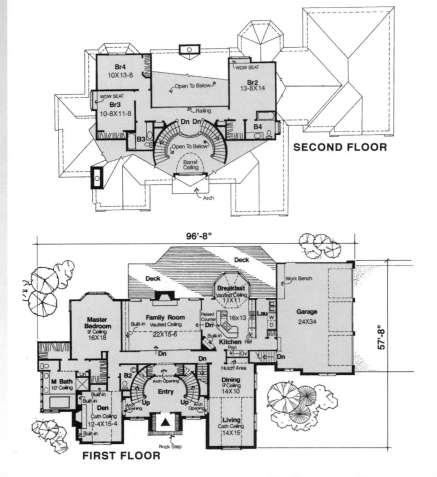

SECOND FLOOR

FIRST FLOOR

Comfortable Country Ease

No. 24405

This plan features:

— Three or four bedrooms

— Two full and two half baths

■ A sprawling front porch giving way to a traditional Foyer area with a half bath and a graceful staircase

■ A tray ceiling adding elegance to the Dining Room which directly accesses the Kitchen

■ A large country Kitchen with a center work island including plenty of storage and work space

■ A tray ceiling accenting the Family Room, also highlighted by a fireplace

■ A vaulted ceiling and a private bath enhancing the Master Suite

■ Two additional bedrooms served by a full hall bath

■ An optional fourth bedroom

First floor — 1,104 sq. ft.
Second floor — 960 sq. ft.

An
EXCLUSIVE DESIGN
By Upright Design

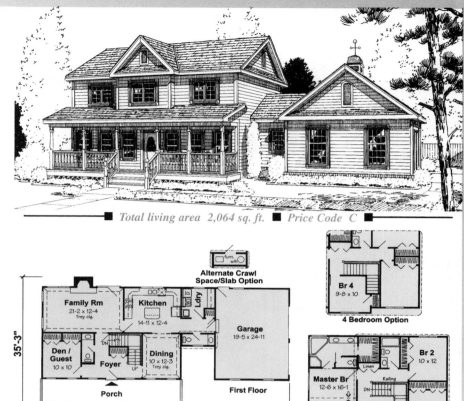

■ *Total living area 2,064 sq. ft.* ■ *Price Code C* ■

---

ttractive Elevation with Impressive Curb Appeal

No. 93117

This plan features:

— Four bedrooms

— Two full and one half baths

■ A cozy Study that is accented with one side of a double-sided fireplace

■ A wonderful layout between the Kitchen and Dining Room that encourages family interaction

■ An eating bar, double sink, and more than ample cabinet and counter space in the Kitchen

■ An expansive Family Room, enhanced by the other side of the double fireplace

■ An oval tub, separate shower, double sink and a large closet adding to the luxury and pampering of the Master Suite

■ Three additional bedrooms that share a full hall bath

■ No materials list is available for this plan

First floor — 1,737 sq. ft.
Second floor — 747 sq. ft.
Basement — 1,737 sq. ft.
Garage — 446 sq. ft.

An
EXCLUSIVE DESIGN
By Ahmann Design Inc.

■ *Total living area 2,484 sq. ft.* ■ *Price Code D* ■

WIDTH 50'-8"
DEPTH 60'-0"

61

Splendid Two-Story

Total living area 3,127 sq. ft. ■ Price Code D

No. 92689

■ **This plan features:**

– Four bedrooms

– Two full and one half baths

■ High ceilings in the foyer and Great Room with a wall of windows

■ Gourmet kitchen with island and large breakfast room adjoining cozy Hearth Room

■ Formal Dining Room and Library with built-in bookshelves

■ Master suite with exciting ceiling treatment and luxurious, private bath

■ Roomy second floor bedrooms share a full hall bath

■ No materials list is available for this plan

First floor — 2,297 sq. ft.
Second floor — 830 sq. ft.
Basement — 2,171 sq. ft.
Width — 74'-8"
Depth — 53'-0"

Distinctive Classic

Total living area 2,875 sq. ft. ■ Price Code E

No. 93248

■ **This plan features:**

– Four bedrooms

– Two full and one half baths

■ Classic home has perfect layout for older children

■ Living Room with vaulted ceiling above arched window opens to Dining Room for easy entertaining

■ Efficient Kitchen with angled cooktop/serving counter and walk-in pantry serves Breakfast bay, Patio, Family Room and Dining Room

■ Private Master Bedroom suite offers his-hers walk-in closets and vanities, and whirlpool tub

■ Three bedrooms, two with walk-in closets, on second floor share full bath

■ No materials list available for this plan

■ Specify basement, slab or crawl space foundation when ordering this plan

First floor — 1,995 sq. ft.
Second floor — 880 sq. ft.
Basement — 1,965 sq. ft.
Garage — 484 sq. ft.
Width — 52'-10"
Depth — 58'-5"

An EXCLUSIVE DESIGN
By Jannis Vann & Associates, Inc.

Classic Southern Colonial Style

■ *Total living area 2,490 sq. ft.* ■ *Price Code D* ■

No. 94407 ℞

■ **This plan features:**

— Three bedrooms

— Three full and one half baths

■ The two-story glass Entry is accented by the curved staircase

■ The Master Bedroom is appointed with his-n-her closets and a private Bath

■ Upstairs find two Bedrooms each with their own full bath, and a Bonus space

■ The Great Room with a fireplace is separated from the Dining Room by columns

■ The Kitchen and skylight Morning Room are each accented by bay windows

■ An optional basement or crawl space foundation — please specify when ordering

■ No materials list available

First floor — 1,822 sq. ft.
Second floor — 668 sq. ft.
Bonus — 448 sq. ft.
Garage — 400 sq. ft.

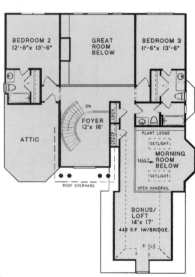

SECOND FLOOR

FIRST FLOOR

Victorian Details Add Visual Delight

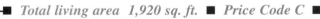
■ *Total living area 1,920 sq. ft.* ■ *Price Code C* ■

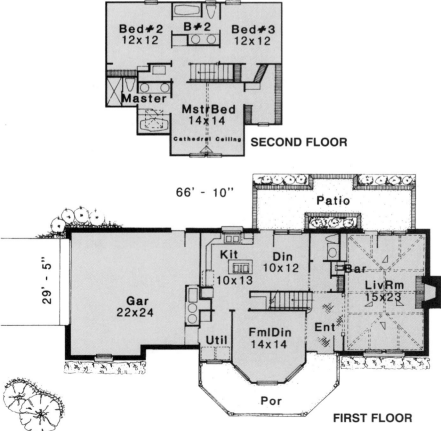

SECOND FLOOR

66' - 10"

29' - 5"

Patio

Kit 10x13

Din 10x12

Bar

LivRm 15x23

Gar 22x24

Util

FmlDin 14x14

Ent

Por

FIRST FLOOR

No. 92218

■ **This plan features:**

— Three bedrooms

— Two full and one half baths

■ Quaint country porch

■ Expansive Living Room with a cozy fireplace and beamed ceiling

■ Formal Dining Room highlighted by an alcove of windows

■ An open Kitchen with cooktop work island, and nearby Utility room with Garage entry

■ Master Bedroom suite offers a cathedral ceiling, huge walk-in closet and a pampering bath

■ Two secondary bedrooms with ample closets and private access to a full bath

First floor — 1,082 sq. ft.
Second floor — 838 sq. ft.
Garage — 500 sq. ft.

No. 92624

■ **This plan features:**

— Three bedrooms

— Three full baths

■ This home offers large rooms and lots of extra living space

■ The Foyer gives way to the elegant Dining Room and the sunken Living Room

■ A large Family Room is located in the rear of the home and is completed by a fireplace

■ The L-shaped Kitchen features a center island and opens into a screen porch and the Breakfast Nook

■ Upstairs includes a spacious Master Bedroom with it's own bath and an enormous closet

■ Two secondary bedrooms share a full bath on the second floor

■ There is no materials list available for this plan

First floor — 1,614 sq. ft.
Second floor — 1,158 sq. ft.
Garage — 420 sq. ft.
Basement — 1,358 sq. ft.
Width — 65'-8"
Depth — 37'-4"

■ *Total living area 2,772 sq. ft.* ■ *Price Code E* ■

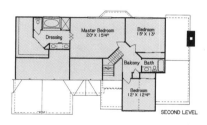

No. 96473 ⚒

■ **This plan features:**

— Four bedrooms

— Two full and one half baths

■ Barrel vaulted Foyer with an arched transom window invites all into this comfortable home

■ Master Bedroom retreat has a walk-in closet, double vanity and bath with a skylight

■ Family Room has a fireplace, built-ins and is topped by a cathedral ceiling

■ Efficient Kitchen with an island sink and easy access to Breakfast bay, Deck, Dining Room and the Utility/Garage area

■ A full bath is shared by three second floor bedrooms

First floor — 1,784 sq. ft.
Second floor — 657 sq. ft.
Bonus room — 332 sq. ft.
Garage & storage — 542 sq. ft.

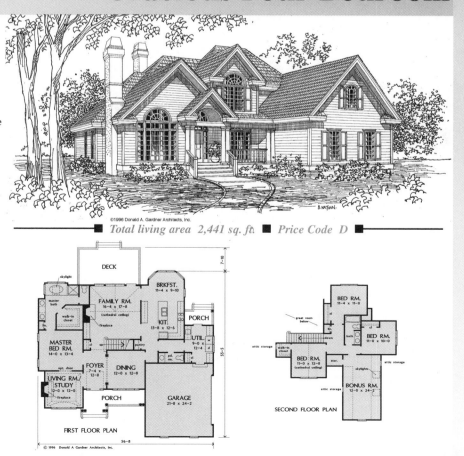

©1996 Donald A. Gardner Architects, Inc.

■ *Total living area 2,441 sq. ft.* ■ *Price Code D* ■

Master Suite Privacy

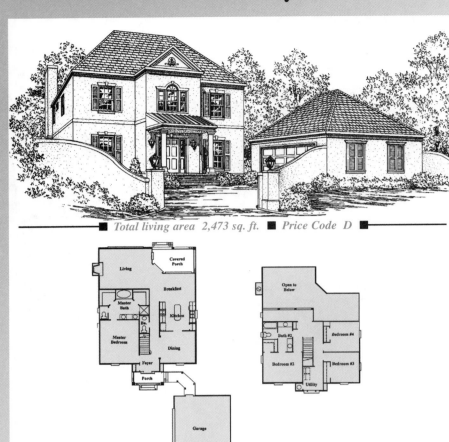

Total living area 2,473 sq. ft. ■ Price Code D

No. 94635

■ **This plan features:**

— Four bedrooms

— Two full and one half baths

■ Elegant, "Old World" styling outside with a modern floor plan on the inside

■ Private first floor Master Bedroom offers two walk-in closets, a double vanity and a whirlpool tub in the bath

■ Center island in Kitchen easily serves the Dining Room, the Breakfast area and the rear Porch

■ Spacious two-story Living Room has a cozy fireplace

■ Three additional bedrooms, a full bath and a Utility room on second floor round out this plan

■ No materials list is available for this plan

■ An optional crawl space or slab foundation — please specify when ordering

First floor — 1,504 sq. ft.
Second floor — 969 sq. ft.
Width — 36'-0"
Depth — 53'-0"

Classic Columns

Total living area 2,830 sq. ft. ■ Price Code E

No. 99145

■ **This plan features:**

— Four bedrooms

— Two full and one half baths

■ Two-story Family Room has a rear wall fireplace

■ Large Kitchen has a wrap-around counter, walk-in pantry and center island

■ The Master Bedroom is highlighted by a tray ceiling, a walk-in closet and a private bath

■ The Living Room and Den are set between a hall with a half-bath

■ Two upstairs bedrooms have window seats, while a third has a cathedral ceiling

■ A full bath with a dual vanity services the upstairs bedrooms

■ There is no materials list available for this plan

First floor — 2,082 sq. ft.
Second floor — 748 sq. ft.
Basement — 2,082 sq. ft.

An
EXCLUSIVE DESIGN
By Ahmann Design Inc.

■ *Total living area 2,099 sq. ft.* ■ *Price Code C* ■

No. 92672

■ **This plan features:**

— Four bedrooms

— Two full and one half baths

■ Open Foyer leads into the formal Living and Dining rooms

■ Multiple windows accentuate the open Family Room and Breakfast Nook

■ The L-shaped Kitchen is open and arranged for maximum convenience

■ The large Master Suite has it's own bath and a walk-in closet

■ Three additional bedrooms share a full bath on the second floor

■ A Bonus Room is located over the garage for future consideration

■ There is no materials list available for this plan

First floor — 1,095 sq. ft.
Second floor — 1,004 sq. ft
Bonus — 323 sq. ft.

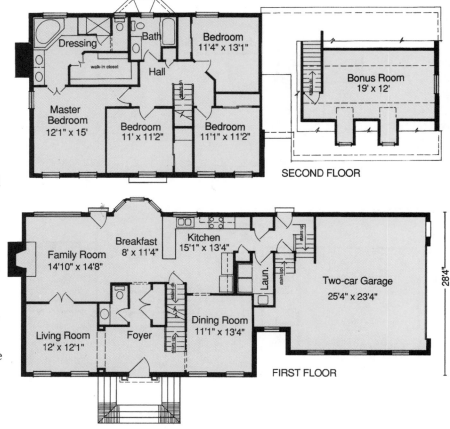

Dressing

Bath

Bedroom
11'4" x 13'1"

walk-in closet

Hall

Bonus Room
19' x 12'

Master
Bedroom
12'1" x 15'

Bedroom
11' x 11'2"

Bedroom
11'1" x 11'2"

SECOND FLOOR

Breakfast
8' x 11'4"

Kitchen
15'1" x 13'4"

Family Room
14'10" x 14'8"

Laun.

Two-car Garage
25'4" x 23'4"

28'4"

Living Room
12' x 12'1"

Foyer

Dining Room
11'1" x 13'4"

FIRST FLOOR

69'

Stucco and Stone

■ *Total living area 2,176 sq. ft.* ■ *Price Code C* ■

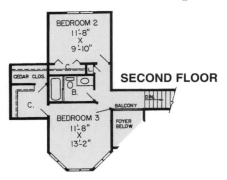

SECOND FLOOR

BEDROOM 2
11'-8"
X
9'-10"

CEDAR CLOS.

BALCONY

FOYER BELOW

BEDROOM 3
11'-8"
X
13'-2"

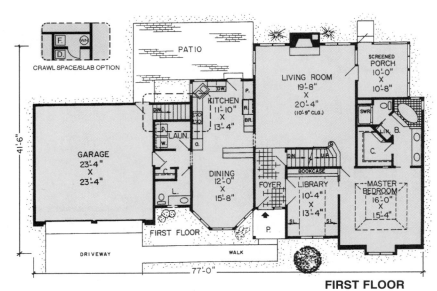

CRAWL SPACE/SLAB OPTION

PATIO

LIVING ROOM
19'-8"
X
20'-4"
(10'-9" CLG.)

SCREENED PORCH
10'-0"
X
10'-8"

KITCHEN
11'-10"
X
13'-4"

GARAGE
23'-4"
X
23'-4"

LAUN.

DINING
12'-0"
X
15'-8"

FOYER

LIBRARY
10'-4"
X
13'-4"

BOOKCASE

MASTER BEDROOM
16'-0"
X
15'-4"

FIRST FLOOR

DRIVEWAY

WALK

41'-6"

77'-0"

FIRST FLOOR

No. 10555

■ This plan features:

— Three bedrooms

— Two full and one half baths

■ A formal foyer leading through double doors into a well-designed library

■ A Master Bedroom offering vaulted ceilings and a huge bath area

■ An oversized Living Room with a fireplace

■ A utility room and half bath located next to the Garage

First floor — 1,671 sq. ft.
Second floor — 505 sq. ft.
Basement — 1,661 sq. ft.
Garage — 604 sq. ft.
Screened porch — 114 sq. ft.

An
EXCLUSIVE DESIGN
By Karl Kreeger

No. 98801

■ This plan features:

— Three bedrooms

— One full and one three-quarter baths

■ Appealing grade-level entry home is designed to capture a front view

■ Combined formal Living and Dining rooms create a feeling of space

■ A dream Kitchen with a peninsula counter, corner window and a Nook

■ The Master Bedroom suite boasts a walk-in closet and a private bath

■ The lower level offers future expansion ideas

Main floor — 1,388 sq. ft.
Lower floor — 169 sq. ft.
Basement — 930 sq. ft.
Garage — 453 sq. ft.

An
EXCLUSIVE DESIGN
By Weinmaster Home Design

■ *Total living area 1,557 sq. ft.* ■ *Price Code B*

MAIN FLOOR

LOWER FLOOR

No. 99116

■ This plan features:

— Four bedrooms

— Two full and one half baths

■ Unique Great Room has a rear window wall and a comfortable fireplace

■ In the front of the home the Den has a bay window and built in cabinets

■ Pass from the Dining Room into the Nook and Kitchen area for serving ease

■ The Kitchen comes complete with a pantry, double sink and a eating bar

■ The upstairs Master Bedroom has a private bath as well as a huge closet

■ Three more bedrooms and a full bath complete the second floor

■ There is no materials list available for this plan

First floor — 1,356 sq. ft.
Second floor — 1,060 sq. ft.
Basement — 1,356 sq. ft.

An
EXCLUSIVE DESIGN
By Ahmann Design Inc.

■ *Total living area 2,416 sq. ft.* ■ *Price Code D*

FIRST FLOOR

SECOND FLOOR

Impressive Brick

■ *Total living area 2,716 sq. ft.* ■ *Price Code E* ■

An EXCLUSIVE DESIGN
By Britt J. Willis

Second Floor

- M Br 15 x 16
- Br 2 13 x 11-1
- Br 3 12 x 11-1
- Br 4 13 x 11
- whirlpool

First Floor

- 74'-8"
- 42'-4"
- Garage 33-8 x 33-4
- Util.
- Kitchen 11-6 x 11
- Brkfst 12 x 13
- Family 15 x 18-4
- Dining 13 x 13
- Foyer
- Living 13 x 14
- ent. center
- see-thru fireplace

No. 24550

■ This plan features:

— Four bedrooms

— Two full and one half bath

■ Decorative facade of brick and windows, and a covered entrance leading into a two-story, raised Foyer with a splendid, curved staircase

■ A dramatic cathedral ceiling and a two-way fireplace in the Living Room

■ A formal Dining Room accented by a lovely bay window

■ A Family Room with the unique fireplace and built-in entertainment center opens to the Breakfast/Kitchen area

■ An efficient, island Kitchen with an atrium sink, walk-in pantry, built-in desk expanding to bright Breakfast area and outdoors as well as Utility room and Garage

■ A Master Suite with a vaulted ceiling, over-sized walk-in closet, and a plush Bath with a corner window tub, two vanities and an oversized shower

■ Three additional bedrooms, on second floor, sharing a full bath

First floor — 1,433 sq. ft.
Second floor — 1,283 sq. ft.
Basement — 1,433 sq. ft.
Garage — 923 sq. ft.

Tradition with a Twist

■ *Total living area 1,949 sq. ft.* ■ *Price Code C* ■

MAIN FLOOR

- Sunken FAMILY ROOM 15-6x13-3 4724x4038
- NOOK 8-0x11-10 2408x3606
- KITCHEN 10-0x11-10 3048x3606
- Storage/ Workshop
- LIVINGROOM 12-0x18-3 3657x5562
- DINING 11-6x12-10 3505x3911
- DOUBLE GARAGE
- FOYER UP
- PORCH
- WIDTH: 55'-0"
- DEPTH: 32'-0"

SECOND FLOOR

- BR 3 10-2x11-10 3098x3606
- BR 4 10-0x8-6 3048x2590
- W.I.C.
- Sundeck
- BR 2 10-2x10-6 3098x3200
- MBR 11-4x16-2 3454x4927
- Bath
- skylite

No. 90933

■ This plan features:

— Four bedrooms

— Two full and one half baths

■ A sky-lit foyer

■ A sunken Family Room warmed by a fireplace and separated by a railing from the Breakfast Nook

■ A well-appointed Kitchen which serves either the informal Breakfast Nook or the formal Dining Room with efficiency

■ A Master Suite with a walk-in closet, full bath and a private, hidden sun deck

First floor — 1,104 sq. ft.
Second floor — 845 sq. ft.
Garage & workshop — 538 sq. ft.
Basement — 1,098 sq. ft.

An EXCLUSIVE DESIGN
By Westhome Planners, Ltd.

Modern Design Highlighted by Split Roofline

■ *Total living area 1,540 sq. ft.* ■ *Price Code B* ■

No. 90028

■ **This plan features:**

— Three bedrooms

— Two baths

■ An energy efficient solar hot water system with solar flat-plate collector panels and double glazed windows

■ A Living/Dining area accentuated by massive stonefaced, heat-circulating fireplace

■ An upstairs bedrooms sharing a skylit full bath

First floor — 960 sq. ft.
Second floor — 580 sq. ft.
Wood deck — 460 sq. ft.

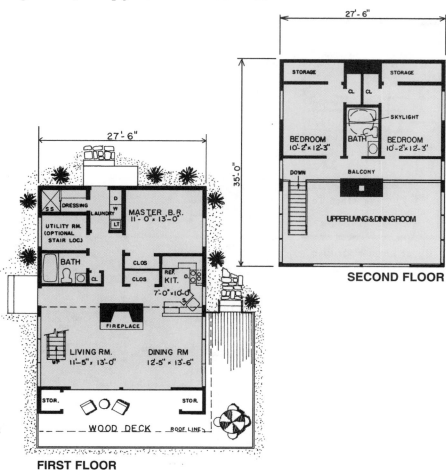

FIRST FLOOR

SECOND FLOOR

Dramatic Design

An
EXCLUSIVE DESIGN
By Building Science Associates

■ Total living area 2,607 sq. ft. ■ Price Code E ■

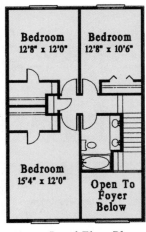

Bedroom
12'8" x 12'0"

Bedroom
12'8" x 10'6"

Bedroom
15'4" x 12'0"

Open To
Foyer
Below

Upper Level Floor Plan

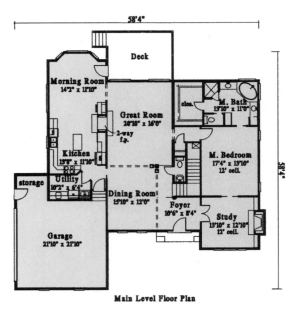

58'4"

Deck

Morning Room
14'2" x 11'10"

Great Room
20'10" x 16'0"

2-way
f.p.

M. Bath
13'10" x 11'0"

clos.

Kitchen
15'5" x 11'10"

M. Bedroom
17'4" x 13'10"
12' ceil.

Utility
10'2" x 8'4"

storage

Dining Room
15'10" x 12'0"

Foyer
10'6" x 8'4"

Study
13'10" x 12'10"
12' ceil.

Garage
21'10" x 21'10"

38'4"

Main Level Floor Plan

No. 93709

■ **This plan features:**

— Four bedrooms

— Two full and one half baths

■ Dramatic two-story foyer flows into the formal dining area which is defined by a cluster of columns

■ Great Room shares a two-way fireplace with the Morning Room that opens onto the deck

■ The Kitchen features a built-in pantry, island and a planning desk

■ The Master Bedroom has a private, double vanity bath and a walk-in closet

■ Three upstairs bedrooms contain abundant closet space and share an oversized bath

■ No materials list is available for this plan

First floor — 1,910 sq. ft.
Second floor — 697 sq. ft.

Perfect Home for Narrow Lot

No. 96487

This plan features:

— Three bedrooms

— Two full and one half baths

■ Wraparound Porch and two-car Garage features unusual for narrow lot floor plan

■ Alcove of windows and columns add distinction to Dining Room

■ Cathedral ceiling above inviting fireplace accent spacious Great Room

■ Efficient Kitchen with peninsula counter accesses side Porch and Deck

■ Master suite on first floor and two additional bedrooms and Bonus Room on second floor

■ This plan comes with crawl space foundation

First floor — 1,219 sq. ft.
Second floor — 450 sq. ft.
Bonus Room — 406 sq. ft.
Garage — 473 sq. ft.

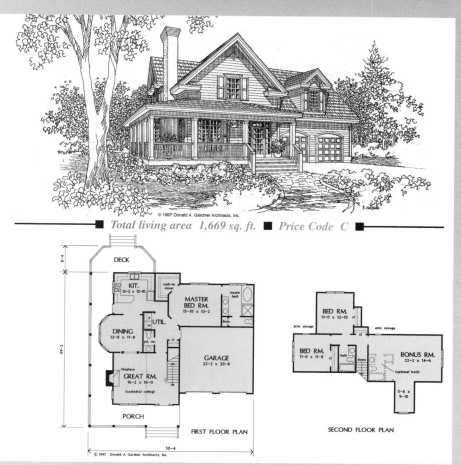

■ *Total living area 1,669 sq. ft.* ■ *Price Code C* ■

© 1997 Donald A. Gardner Architects, Inc.

Comfortable Country Porch

No. 99056

This plan features:

— Four bedrooms

— Two full and one half bath

■ Wrap-around Porch leads into two-story Foyer with a lovely banister staircase

■ Formal Living Room with arched opening into Family Room with hearth fireplace

■ Efficient, U-shaped Kitchen with a pantry, peninsula serving counter, bright Breakfast area, Garage entry and laundry facilities

■ Corner Master Bedroom offers two closets, a double vanity and jaccuzi

■ Three additional bedrooms convenient to a full bath

■ No materials list is available for this plan

First floor — 1,348 sq. ft.
Second floor — 1,137 sq. ft.
Basement — 1,348 sq. ft.

■ *Total living area 2,485 sq. ft.* ■ *Price Code D* ■

WIDTH 69'-0"
DEPTH 37'-0"

Simply Elegant Design

■ *Total living area 2,109 sq. ft.* ■ *Price Code C* ■

FIRST FLOOR

SECOND FLOOR

No. 99268

■ **This plan features:**

— Three bedrooms

— Two full and one half baths

■ Double door entry into Foyer and Living Room beyond

■ Formal Living Room with patio access, shares see-through fireplace with Family Room

■ Open and efficient Kitchen with pantry, peninsula snackbar, Dining Room and patio beyond, and nearby laundry/service entry

■ Private Master Bedroom pampered with two walk-in closets and a dressing area with a double vanity and whirlpool tub

■ Two additional bedrooms with arched windows, share a full bath

First floor — 1,182 sq. ft.
Second floor — 927 sq. ft.

Classic Family Living

■ *Total living area 2,137 sq. ft.* ■ *Price Code C* ■

FIRST FLOOR

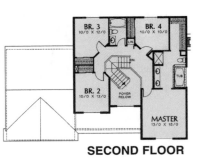

SECOND FLOOR

No. 91536

■ **This plan features:**

— Four Bedrooms

— Two full and one half baths

■ Sheltered Porch leads into two-story Foyer with a graceful angled staircase

■ Parlor enhanced by an elegant bay window

■ Open Family Room with a triple window and cozy fireplace

■ An efficient Kitchen with a work island/snackbar, eating Nook and nearby Dining Room and laundry/Garage entry

■ Corner Master suite offers a double vanity bath and a large, walk-in closet

■ Three additional bedrooms share a full bath

First floor — 1,157 sq. ft.
Second floor — 980 sq. ft.

Multiple Porches Provide Added Interest

■ *Total living area 3,149 sq. ft.* ■ *Price Code E* ■

No. 94622

■ **This plan features:**

— Four bedrooms

— Three full and one half baths

■ Great Room with large fireplace and French doors to Porch and Deck

■ Country-size Kitchen with cooktop work island, walk-in pantry and Breakfast area with Porch access

■ Pampering Master Bedroom offers a decorative ceiling, sitting area, porch and Deck access, a huge walk-in closet and lavish bath

■ Three second floor bedrooms with walk-in closets have private access to a full bath

■ An optional crawl space or slab foundation — please specify when ordering

■ No materials list available

First floor — 2,033 sq. ft.
Second floor — 1,116 sq. ft.

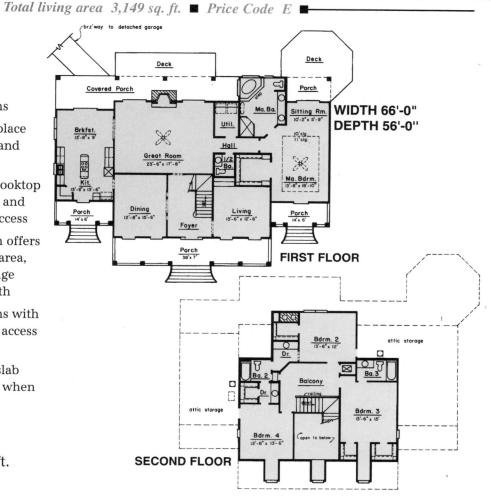

WIDTH 66'-0"
DEPTH 56'-0"

FIRST FLOOR

SECOND FLOOR

Elegance And A Relaxed Lifestyle

© 1994 Donald A. Gardner Architects, Inc.

■ *Total living area 2,436 sq. ft.* ■ *Price Code D* ■

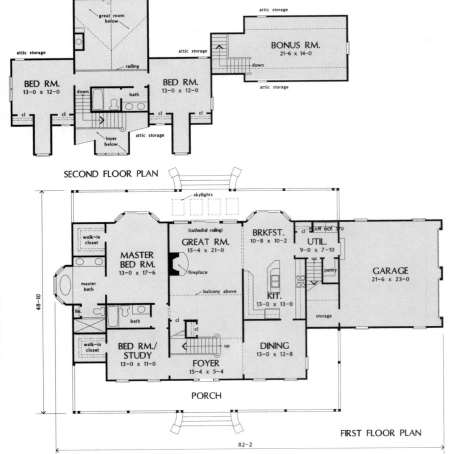

SECOND FLOOR PLAN

FIRST FLOOR PLAN

PORCH

No. 99895

■ This plan features:

— Four bedrooms

— Three full baths

■ This family home has combined elegance with a relaxed lifestyle in an open plan full of surprises

■ Open two-level Foyer has a palladian window which visually ties in the formal Dining area to the expansive Great Room

■ Windows all around, including bays in Master Bedroom suite and Breakfast area provide natural light, while nine foot ceilings create volume

■ Master Bedroom suite features a whirlpool tub, separate shower and his-n-her vanities

First floor — 1,841 sq. ft.
Second floor — 595 sq. ft.
Bonus room — 411 sq. ft.
Garage & storage — 596 sq. ft.

No. 96403

This plan features:

— Four bedrooms

— Two full baths

■ Columns between the foyer and living room/study hint at all the extras in this four bedroom country estate with a warm, welcoming exterior

■ Transom windows over French doors open up the living room/study to the front porch, while a generous family room accesses the covered back porch

■ Deluxe master suite is topped by a tray ceiling and includes a bath with a sunny garden tub bay and ample closet space

■ Bonus room is accessed from the second floor and ready to expand family living space for future needs

First floor — 1,483 sq. ft.
Second floor — 1,349 sq. ft.
Bonus — 486 sq. ft.
Garage — 738 sq. ft.

■ Total living area 2,832 sq. ft. ■ Price Code E ■

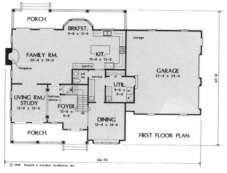

Contemporary Classic with a Custom Look

No. 99314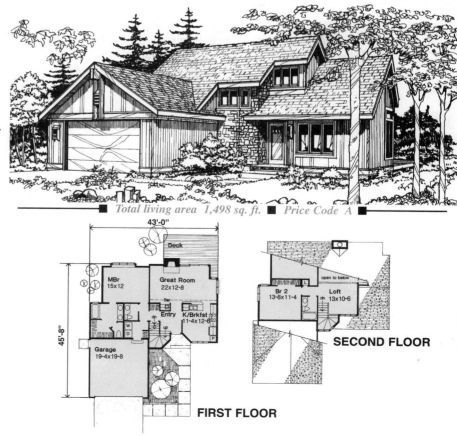

This plan features:

— Two bedrooms

— Two full and one half baths

■ A well-appointed Kitchen with an angular Nook

■ A two-story Great Room accentuated by a massive fireplace and glass sliders to the rear Deck

■ A bump-out window seat and private Bath with double vanity in the Master Suite

First floor — 1,044 sq. ft.
Second floor — 454 sq. ft.

■ Total living area 1,498 sq. ft. ■ Price Code A ■

Home Office Space

Total living area 3,073 sq. ft. ■ Price Code E

No. 99270 ✗

■ This plan features:

— Three or four bedrooms

— Three full and one half baths

■ Friendly front Porch adds country charm to practical design

■ Open Foyer with lovely landing staircase, flanked by Study and Living Room

■ Hub Kitchen with built-in pantry, peninsula eating bar, eating Nook and adjoining Dining Room

■ Comfortable Family Room with beamed ceiling, large fireplace and access to rear yard, Laundry and Office/Guest space

■ Corner Master Bedroom with Dressing area and his and her walk-in closets

■ Two additional bedrooms with double closets, share a double vanity batH

First floor — 1,762 sq. ft.
Second floor — 1,311 sq. ft.
Garage — 561 sq. ft.
Width — 66'-0"
Depth — 47'-6"

FIRST FLOOR

SECOND FLOOR

Striking Structure

Total living area 2,277 sq. ft. ■ Price Code D

No. 99431 ✗

■ This plan features:

— Four bedrooms

— Two full and one half baths

■ Wrap-around covered porch and windows create a striking appearance

■ Great Room features a cathedral ceiling, transom windows, and huge fireplace

■ Center-island kitchen has a lazy Susan and an ample pantry

■ Double doors access the Master Bedroom which is enhanced by a decorative boxed ceiling

■ Upstairs are three more bedrooms and a full bath

First floor — 1,570 sq. ft.
Second floor — 707 sq. ft.
Basement — 1,570 sq. ft.
Garage — 504 sq. ft.

SECOND FLOOR

FIRST FLOOR

■ *Total living area 4,532 sq. ft.* ■ *Price Code F* ■

No. 99373

■ This plan features:

— Four bedrooms

— Three full and one half baths

■ A high impact two story, double door transom Entry

■ A two story Family Room with a wall consisting of a fireplace and windows

■ A spacious Master Suite with unique curved glass block behind the tub in the Master Bath and a semi-circular window wall with see-through fireplace in sitting area

■ A gourmet Kitchen and Breakfast area opening to a Lanai

■ A Guest Suite with private deck and walk-in closet

Main floor — 3,158 sq. ft.
Upper floor — 1,374 sq. ft.

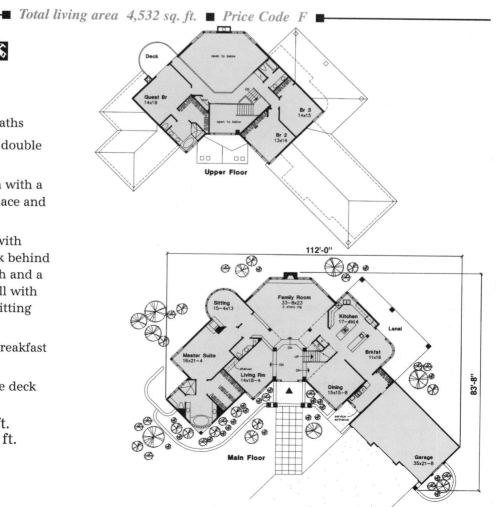

Grand Country Porch

■ *Total living area 2,665 sq. ft.* ■ *Price Code E* ■

No. 94615

■ This plan features:

— Four bedrooms

— Three full baths

■ Large front Porch provides shade and Southern hospitality

■ Spacious Living Room with access to Covered Porch and Patio, and a cozy fireplace between built-in shelves

■ Country Kitchen with a cooktop island, bright Breakfast bay, Utility Room and Garage entry

■ Corner Master Bedroom with a walk-in closet and private bath

■ First floor bedroom with private access to a full bath

■ Two second floor bedrooms with dormers, walk-in closets and separate vanities, share a full bath

■ An optional crawl space or slab foundation — please specify when ordering

■ No materials list available

First floor — 1,916 sq. ft.
Second floor — 749 sq. ft.
Garage — 479 sq. ft.

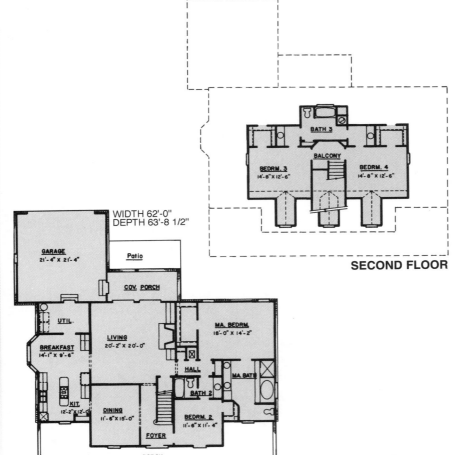

SECOND FLOOR

WIDTH 62'-0"
DEPTH 63'-8 1/2"

FIRST FLOOR

Country Victorian

No. 93283

This plan features:

— Four bedrooms

— Two full and one half baths

■ Victorian accent on a country porch with an octagonal sitting area

■ A central Foyer area highlighted by a decorative staircase and a convenient coat closet

■ An elegant bay window enhancing the formal Dining Room

■ A formal Living Room viewing the porch and front yard

■ A large country Kitchen with a central work island and an open layout into the cheery Breakfast Bay

■ An expansive Family Room equipped with a cozy fireplace and two sets of French doors leading to the Sun deck

■ A grand Master Suite with a sitting alcove, a walk-in closet, a bath and a private balcony

■ Three additional bedrooms, one with an attractive bay, sharing use of a full bath in the hall

■ Convenient second floor laundry area

First floor — 1,155 sq. ft.
Second floor — 1,209 sq. ft.

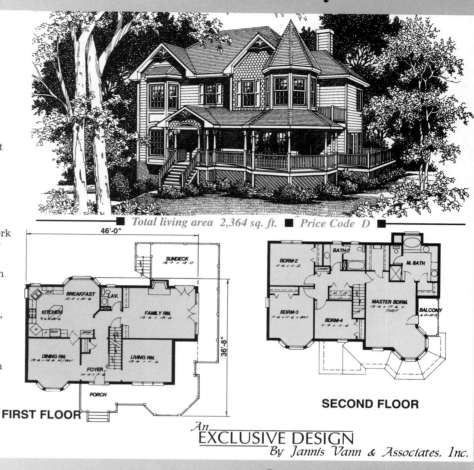

■ Total living area 2,364 sq. ft. ■ Price Code D ■

FIRST FLOOR

SECOND FLOOR

An
EXCLUSIVE DESIGN
By Jannis Vann & Associates, Inc.

Grand Balcony

No. 94633

This plan features:

— Three bedrooms

— Two full and one half baths

■ Front Porch and grand Balcony invite one and all to this gracious home

■ Traditional Foyer placement between the Living and Dining rooms

■ Family Room features inviting fireplace and direct access to the Breakfast nook

■ Efficient U-shaped Kitchen has an island counter and a walk-in pantry

■ An optional slab or a crawl space foundation — please specify when ordering

■ No materials list available

First floor — 1,261 sq. ft.
Second floor — 1,065 sq. ft.

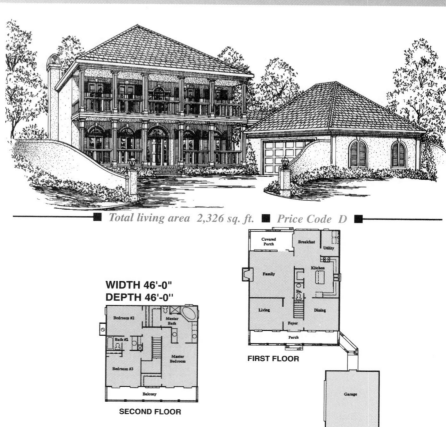

■ Total living area 2,326 sq. ft. ■ Price Code D ■

WIDTH 46'-0"
DEPTH 46'-0''

FIRST FLOOR

SECOND FLOOR

An Impressive and Dynamic House

Total living area 2,250 sq. ft. ■ Price Code D

No. 92627

■ **This plan features:**

— Three or four bedrooms

— Two full and one half baths

■ Multiple gables and brick trim and a recessed Entry

■ A Great Room with a high ceiling, fireplace and transom windows

■ An abundance of counter space and cabinets in the Kitchen

■ A Breakfast Bay with a built-in pantry

■ A luxurious first floor Master Suite with a whirlpool tub, double vanities and shower

■ Two upstairs bedrooms that share a full hall bath

■ A Bonus Room to accommodate future needs

■ No materials list is available for this plan

First floor — 1,670 sq. ft.
Second floor — 580 sq. ft.
Bonus room — 227 sq. ft.
Basement — 1,590 sq. ft.
Garage — 616 sq. ft.

Distinguished Look

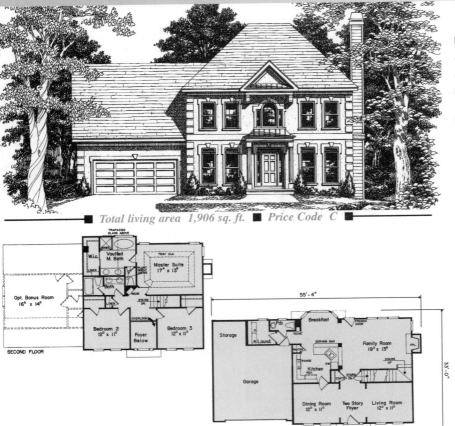

Total living area 1,906 sq. ft. ■ Price Code C

No. 98429

■ **This plan features:**

— Three bedrooms

— Two full and one half baths

■ The Family Room, Breakfast Room and the Kitchen are presented in an open layout

■ A fireplace in the Family Room provides a warm atmosphere

■ The plush Master Suite pampers the owner and features a trapezoid glass above the tub

■ Two additional bedrooms share the use of the double vanity bath in the hall

■ An optional basement, crawl space or slab foundation — please specify when ordering

First floor — 1,028 sq. ft.
Second floor — 878 sq. ft.
Bonus room — 315 sq. ft.
Garage — 497 sq. ft.

Three Porches Offer Outdoor Charm

■ *Total living area 1,274 sq. ft.* ■ *Price Code A* ■

No. 90048

■ **This plan features:**

— Three bedrooms

— Two full baths

■ An oversized log burning fireplace in the spacious Living/Dining area which is two stories high with sliding glass doors

■ Three porches offering the maximum in outdoor living space

■ A private bedroom located on the second floor

■ An efficient Kitchen including an eating bar and access to the covered Dining Porch

First floor — 974 sq. ft.
Second floor — 300 sq. ft.

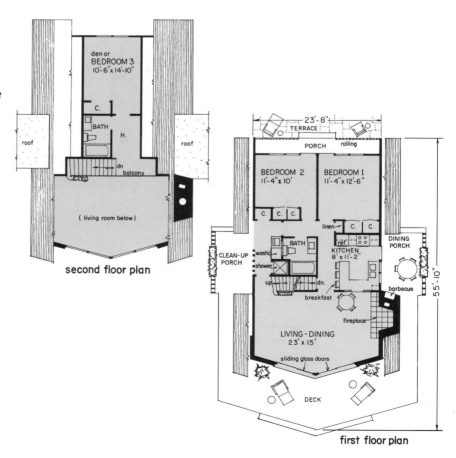

second floor plan

first floor plan

Charming Country Style

■ *Total living area 1,596 sq. ft.* ■ *Price Code B* ■

© design basics, inc.

FIRST FLOOR

SECOND FLOOR

First floor — 1,191 sq. ft.
Second floor — 405 sq. ft.
Basement — 1,191 sq. ft.
Garage — 454 sq. ft.

No. 99404

■ This plan features:

— Three bedrooms

— Two full and one half baths

■ Specious Great Room enhanced by a fireplace and transom windows

■ Breakfast Room with a bay window and direct access to the Kitchen

■ Snack bar extending work space in the Kitchen

■ Master Suite enhanced by a crowning in a boxed nine foot ceiling, a compartmental whirlpool bath and a large walk-in closet

■ Second floor balcony overlooking the U-shaped stairs and Entry

■ Two second floor bedrooms share a full hall bath

Designed for Sloping Lot

No. 91517

- This plan features:
- — Three bedrooms
- — Two full and one half baths
- An impressive elevation accented by palladium windows and a raised entrance
- Two-story Living Room with corner fireplace opens to Dining area and Kitchen for ease in entertaining
- Expansive Dining area with atrium door to rear yard
- Efficient Kitchen with built-in pantry and angled serving counter
- Comfortable Family Room with French doors to raised Deck and easy access to laundry and half bath
- Secluded Master suite with arched window below a vaulted ceiling, walk-in closet and double vanity bath
- Two additional bedrooms with ample closets share a full bath

First floor — 1,022 sq. ft.
Second floor — 813 sq. ft.
Garage — 1077 sq. ft.

■ Total living area 1,835 sq. ft. ■ Price Code C ■

◄ 36' ►

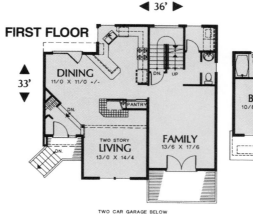

FIRST FLOOR

▲ 33' ▼

DINING
11/0 X 11/0 +/-

PANTRY

DN. UP

TWO STORY LIVING
13/0 X 14/4

FAMILY
13/6 X 17/6

TWO CAR GARAGE BELOW

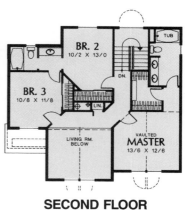

BR. 2
10/2 X 13/0

TUB

BR. 3
10/8 X 11/8

LIN.

DN.

LIVING RM. BELOW

VAULTED MASTER
13/6 X 12/6

SECOND FLOOR

Coastal Delight

No. 94202

- **This plan features:**
- — Three bedrooms
- — Two full baths
- Living area above the Garage and Storage/Bonus areas offering a "piling" design for coastal, waterfront or low-lying terrain
- Three sets of double doors below a vaulted ceiling in the Great Room offer lots of air, light and easy access to both the Sun Deck and Veranda
- A Dining Room convenient to the Great Room and Kitchen featuring vaulted ceilings and decorative windows
- A glassed Nook adjacent to the efficient Kitchen with an island work center
- Two secondary bedrooms, a full bath and a Utility room on the first floor
- A second floor Master Suite with a vaulted ceiling, double door to a private Deck, his-n-her closets and a plush bath

First floor — 1,736 sq. ft.
Second floor — 640 sq. ft.
Lower floor — 840 sq. ft.
Bonus room — 253 sq. ft.
Garage — 840 sq. ft

■ Total living area 3,216 sq. ft. ■ Price Code F ■

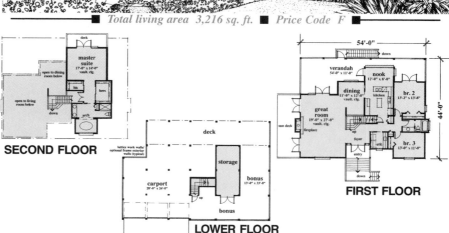

deck

master suite
17'-0" x 14'-0"
vault. clg.

open to dining room below

his   hers

open to living room below

down   arch

SECOND FLOOR

lattice work walls
optional frame exterior
walls (typical)

deck

storage

carport
28'-0" x 26'-0"

bonus
13'-4" x 33'-4"

bonus

LOWER FLOOR

54'-0"

verandah
54'-0" x 11'-0"

nook
12'-0" x 11'-0"

dining
11'-0" x 12'-0"
vault. clg.

kitchen

br. 2
13'-2" x 13'-8"

great room
19'-0" x 27'-0"
vault. clg.

sun deck

fireplace

foyer

up

entry

br. 3
13'-0" x 11'-0"

down

44'-0"

FIRST FLOOR

Curved Stairway Highlights Plan

No. 10587

■ **This plan features:**

— Three bedrooms

— Two and one half baths

■ A Family Room with vaulted ceilings and a wood-burning fireplace

■ A sunken Living Room with a fireplace and an open view of the Dining Room

■ A Laundry room surrounded by the bedrooms for convenience

First floor — 2,036 sq. ft.
Second floor — 1,554 sq. ft.
Garage — 533 sq. ft.

Total living area 3,590 sq. ft. ■ *Price Code F*

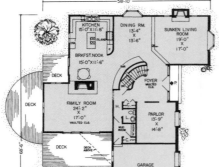

Notable Windows

No. 94950

■ **This plan features:**

— Four bedrooms

— Two full and one half baths

■ Gables accenting arches enhance this brick and wood home

■ Open Entry between formal Living and Dining rooms provide ease in entertaining

■ Comfortable Family Room offers a fireplace, a wet bar, and a wall of windows

■ Kitchen includes an island counter and adjoins the Breakfast bay with the laundry/garage nearby

■ Luxurious Master Bedroom suite has a bath with a skylight

■ Three secondary bedrooms, two with window seats, share full bath

First floor — 1,179 sq. ft.
Second floor — 1,019 sq. ft.
Basement — 1,179 sq. ft.
Garage — 466 sq. ft.

Total living area 2,198 sq. ft. ■ *Price Code C*

© design basics, inc.

FIRST FLOOR

SECOND FLOOR

Double Decks Adorn Luxurious Master Suite

■ *Total living area* 2,700 sq. ft. ■ *Price Code* E ■

No. 91022 ✕

■ **This plan features:**

— Three bedrooms

— Two full and one half baths

■ Abundant windows, indoor planters and three decks uniting every room with the outdoors

■ An efficient Kitchen with direct access to the Nook and the formal Dining Room

■ A wood stove warming the spacious Family Room

■ A secluded Master Suite with private deck, Den and master Bath

■ An optional basement, slab or crawl space foundation — please specify when ordering

Main floor — 1,985 sq. ft.
Upper floor — 715 sq. ft.

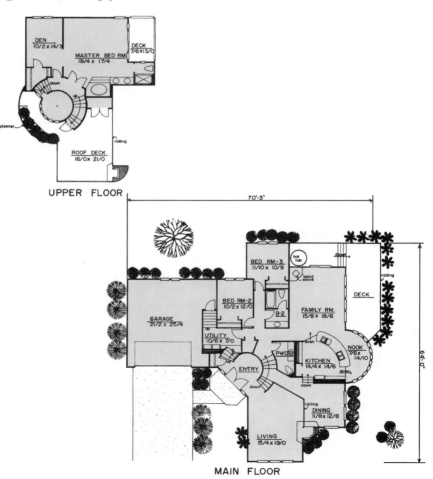

DEN
10/2 x 14/3

MASTER BED RM.
18/4 x 17/4

DECK
7/6 x 13/0

planter

railing

ROOF DECK
16/0 x 21/0

UPPER FLOOR

70'-3"

BED RM.-3
11/10 x 10/9

hot tub

wood stove

DECK

railing

GARAGE
21/2 x 25/4

BED RM.-2
10/2 x 12/0

B-2

FAMILY RM.
15/8 x 18/6

64'-0"

UTILITY
10/6 x 7/0

NOOK
7/6 x 14/10

PWDR

KITCHEN
14/4 x 14/6

ENTRY

DINING
11/8 x 12/8

railing

LIVING
15/4 x 19/0

MAIN FLOOR

Classic Exterior with Modern Interior

■ *Total living area 1,876 sq. ft.* ■ *Price Code C* ■

WIDTH 56'-2"
DEPTH 48'-0"

Master Bedroom 14'1" x 15'1"

Great Room 16'8" x 15'4"

Dining Area 10'1" x 14'1"

Bath

Laun.

Dressing

Foyer

Kitchen 13'2" x 11'8"

pantry

Porch

Two-car Garage 20' x 27'5"

Screened-in Porch

FIRST FLOOR

Bedroom 10'5" x 12'

Bedroom 11'6" x 11'5"

Foyer Below

Hall

Bath

Bonus Bedroom 10' x 18'2"

SECOND FLOOR

No. 92674

■ **This plan features:**

— Three or four bedrooms

— Two full and one half baths

■ Front Porch leads into an open Foyer and Great Room beyond accented by a sloped ceiling, corner fireplace and multiple windows

■ An efficient Kitchen with a cooktop island, walk-in pantry, a bright Dining Area and nearby Screened Porch, Laundry and Garage entry

■ Deluxe Master Bedroom wing with a decorative ceiling, large walk-in closet and plush bath

■ Three or four bedrooms on the second floor share a double vanity bath

■ No materials list available

First floor — 1,348 sq. ft.
Second floor — 528 sq. ft.
Bonus — 195 sq. ft.
Basement — 1,300 sq. ft.

Inviting Front Porch

No. 93298

■ **This plan features:**

— Three bedrooms

— Two full and one half baths

■ Detailed gables and inviting front porch create a warm welcoming facade

■ Open foyer features an angled staircase, a half-bath and a coat closet

■ The expansive, informal living area at the rear of the home features a fireplace and opens onto the sundeck

■ The efficient Kitchen has easy access to both the formal and informal dining areas

■ Master Bedroom includes a walk-in closet and compartmented private bath

■ Two secondary bedrooms share a bath with a double vanity

■ No materials list is available for this plan

First floor — 797 sq. ft.
Second floor — 886 sq. ft.
Basement — 797 sq. ft.

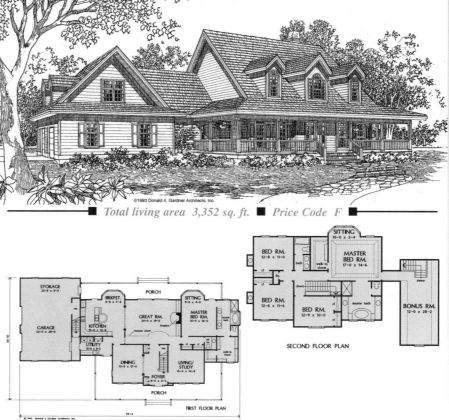

■ *Total living area 1,683 sq. ft.* ■ *Price Code B* ■

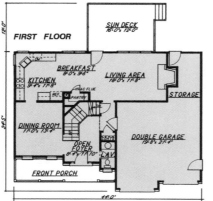

An EXCLUSIVE DESIGN
By Jannis Vann & Associates, Inc.

Impressive Spaces Prevail

No. 96443 ⚒

■ **This plan features:**

— Four bedrooms

— Three full and one half baths

■ Two-level Foyer with a clerestory window and a curved balcony above the Great Room

■ Family Kitchen is convenient to the Breakfast bay, rear Porch, Dining Room and the Utility/Garage

■ Master Bedroom retreat offers a sitting area, walk-in closet and a double vanity bath

■ Three additional bedrooms on the second floor share a full bath

■ The Bonus Room and ample storage space provide additional space for a growing family

First floor — 2,357 sq. ft.
Second floor — 995 sq. ft.
Bonus room — 545 sq. ft.
Garage & storage — 975 sq. ft.

Total living area 3,352 sq. ft. ■ *Price Code F* ■

Outstanding Appeal

■ *Total living area 3,949 sq. ft.* ■ *Price Code F* ■

No. 98437

■ **This plan features:**

— Five bedrooms

— Four full and one half baths

■ The Formal Dining and Living Rooms are off the two-story Foyer

■ A Butler pantry located between the Kitchen and formal Dining Room for convenience

■ An Island Kitchen with a walk-in pantry and a peninsula counter/serving bar highlight this room

■ The Breakfast room accesses the rear yard through a French door

■ The second floor Master Suite is topped by a tray ceiling in the bedroom and by a vaulted ceiling above the Sitting Room and Bath

■ Three additional bedrooms with private access to full baths and closet space

■ Please specify a basement or crawl space foundation when ordering

First floor — 2,002 sq. ft.
Second floor — 1,947 sq. ft.
Basement — 2,002 sq. ft.
Garage — 737 sq. ft.

Elegant High Ceiling

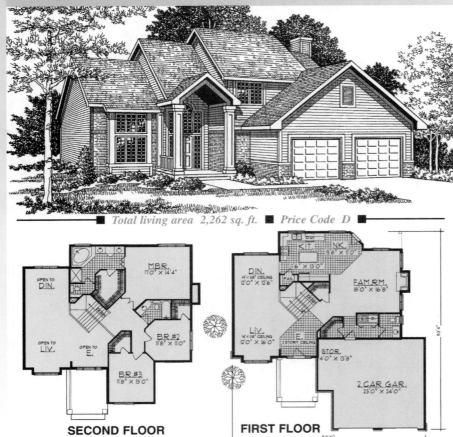

■ *Total living area 2,262 sq. ft.* ■ *Price Code D* ■

SECOND FLOOR   **FIRST FLOOR**

No. 99127

■ **This plan features:**

— Three bedrooms

— Two full and one half baths

■ The open Family Room features a fireplace and large windows

■ The spacious Kitchen features a center island, walk-in pantry and adjoins the Breakfast Nook

■ An open U-shaped staircase leads upstairs to the Master Bedroom with large closet and private bath

■ Two additional bedrooms both with walk-in closets share a full bath on the second floor

■ There is no materials list available for this plan

First floor — 1,271 sq. ft.
Second floor — 991 sq. ft.
Basement — 1,271 sq. ft.

An EXCLUSIVE DESIGN
By Ahmann Design Inc.

■ *Total living area 1,869 sq. ft.* ■ *Price Code C* ■

No. 93904

An
EXCLUSIVE DESIGN
By Independent Designs

■ **This plan features:**

— Three bedrooms

— Two full and one half baths

■ A two-story Foyer illuminated by an arched window above

■ Formal Living Room adjoined to the Dining Room by an arched opening

■ A second arched opening into the Family Room highlighted by a gas fireplace

■ Kitchen equipped with an island and a bayed breakfast area

■ A lavish Master Bath with a garden tub and a walk-in closet

■ A bonus room for future expansion

■ No materials list available

First floor — 1,121 sq. ft.
Second floor — 748 sq. ft.

WIDTH 61'-0"
DEPTH 32'-0"

FIRST FLOOR

SECOND FLOOR

Every Luxurious Feature One Could Want

■ *Total living area 3,276 sq. ft.* ■ *Price Code F* ■

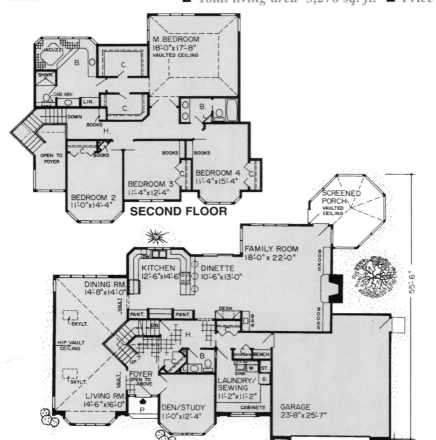

SECOND FLOOR

M. BEDROOM
18'-0" x 17'-8"
VAULTED CEILING

JACUZZI

SHWR.

BEDROOM 2
11'-0" x 14'-4"

BEDROOM 3
11'-4" x 12'-4"

BEDROOM 4
11'-4" x 15'-4"

OPEN TO FOYER

FIRST FLOOR

FAMILY ROOM
18'-0" x 22'-0"

KITCHEN
12'-6" x 14'-6"

DINETTE
10'-6" x 13'-0"

DINING RM.
14'-8" x 14'-0"

SCREENED PORCH
VAULTED CEILING

HIP VAULT CEILING

LIVING RM.
14'-6" x 16'-0"

FOYER OPEN TO ABOVE

DEN/STUDY
11'-0" x 12'-4"

LAUNDRY/ SEWING
11'-2" x 11'-2"

GARAGE
23'-8" x 25'-7"

DRIVEWAY

69'-0"

55'-6"

No. 10686

■ **This plan features:**

— Four bedrooms

— Two and one half baths

■ An open staircase leading to the bedrooms and dividing the space between the vaulted Living and Dining Rooms

■ A wide family area including the Kitchen, Dinette and Family Room complete with built-in bar, bookcases, and fireplace

■ A Master Bedroom with a vaulted ceiling, spacious closets and Jacuzzi

First floor — 1,786 sq. ft.
Second floor — 1,490 sq. ft.
Basement — 1,773 sq. ft.
Garage — 579 sq. ft.

Expansive Inside and Out

No. 94996 ⚒

■ **This plan features:**

— Four bedrooms

— Two full and one half baths

■ Dramatic Entry opens to Dining Room with built-in hutch, and the Great Room with a fireplace set between decorative windows

■ Convenient Kitchen has an island snack bar, Breakfast area, built-in desk and a pantry

■ Master Bedroom wing with arched window, skylit dressing area, whirlpool tub and a walk-in closet

■ Three second floor bedrooms, one with an arched window, share a full bath

First floor — 1,505 sq. ft.
Second floor — 610 sq. ft.
Basement — 1,505 sq. ft.
Garage — 693 sq. ft.

■ *Total living area 2,115 sq. ft.* ■ *Price Code C* ■

SECOND FLOOR

FIRST FLOOR

© design basics, inc.

Stately Two-Story Portico Entrance

No. 99213 ⚒

■ **This plan features:**

— Four bedrooms

— Four full and one half baths

■ Two-story portico entrance leads into formal Foyer with a grand, landing staircase

■ Gallery leads into immense Gathering Room highlighted by an inviting fireplace and glass all around with Terrace access

■ Bow window, built-ins and a hearth fireplace accent private Study

■ Ideal Kitchen with cooktop/serving island, snackbar, Breakfast area with Terrace access, and nearby Laundry, Garage entry and Dining Room

■ Spacious Master Bedroom offers a cozy fireplace, cathedral ceiling, a wall of windows, two walk-in closets and vanities, and an over-sized whirlpool tub

■ Three additional and spacious bedrooms with private baths

First floor — 3,116 sq. ft.
Second floor — 1,997 sq. ft.
Garage — 792 sq. ft.

■ *Total living area 5,113 sq. ft.* ■ *Price Code F* ■

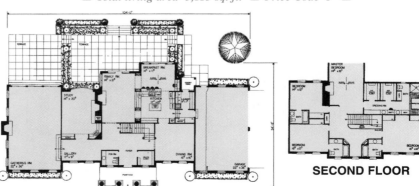

FIRST FLOOR

SECOND FLOOR

Southern Breeze

■ Total living area 2,801 sq. ft. ■ Price Code E ■

No. 94636

■ **This plan features:**

— Five bedrooms

— Three full baths

■ Southern styled front Porch

■ Living Room ideal for entertaining with a cozy fireplace for warmth and hospitality

■ Spacious, first floor Master Bedroom suite features a luxurious bath

■ Secondary bedroom on the first floor, has a walk-in closet

■ Upstairs are three additional bedrooms with walk-in closets, a Game Room and a full bath

■ An optional slab or crawl space foundation — please specify when ordering

■ No materials list available

First floor — 1,651 sq. ft.
Second floor — 1,150 sq. ft.

WIDTH 46'-4"
DEPTH 79'-1"

Country Style for Today

■ Total living area 2,212 sq. ft. ■ Price Code D ■

No. 99620

■ **This plan features:**

— Four bedrooms

— Two full and one half baths

■ Two bay windows in the formal Living Room with a heat-circulating fireplace to enhance the mood and warmth

■ A spacious formal Dining Room with a bay window and easy access to the Kitchen

■ An octagon-shaped Dinette defined by columns, dropped beams and a bay window

■ An efficient island Kitchen with ample storage and counter space

■ A Master Suite equipped with a large whirlpool tub plus a double vanity

■ Three additional bedrooms that share a full hall bath

First floor — 1,132 sq. ft.
Second floor — 1,020 sq. ft.
Basement — 1,026 sq. ft.
Garage & storage — 469 sq. ft.
Laundry/mudroom — 60 sq. ft.

Livin

© 1992 Donald A. Gardner Architects, Inc.

■ *Total living area 2,561 sq. ft.* ■ *Price Code E* ■

No. 99891 ✖

■ This plan features:

— Four bedrooms

— Two full and one half baths

■ Double gables, wrap-around Porch and custom window details add appeal to farmhouse

■ Formal Living and Dining rooms connected by Foyer in front , while casual living areas expand rear

■ Efficient Kitchen with island cooktop and easy access to all eating areas

■ Fireplace, wetbar and rear Porch and Deck provide great entertainment space

■ Spacious Master bedroom suite features walk-in closet and pampering bath

First floor — 1,357 sq. ft.
Second floor — 1,204 sq. ft.
Garage & storage — 546 sq. ft.

SECOND FLOOR PLAN

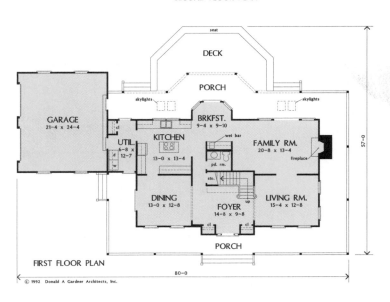

FIRST FLOOR PLAN

© 1992 Donald A Gardner Architects, Inc.

Total living area 1,246 sq. ft. ■ Price Code A

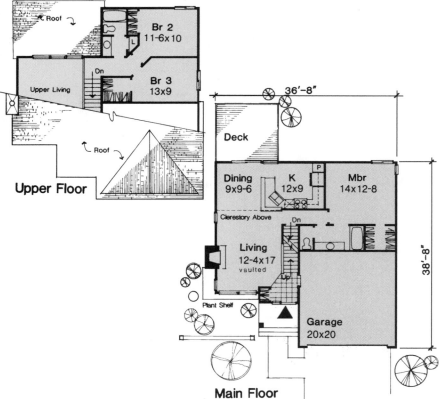

Upper Floor

Br 2
11-6x10

Br 3
13x9

Upper Living

Roof

Dn

Roof

Main Floor

36'-8"

Deck

Dining
9x9-6

K
12x9

P

Mbr
14x12-8

Clerestory Above

Living
12-4x17
vaulted

Dn

Up

Plant Shelf

Garage
20x20

38'-8"

No. 90353

■ This plan features:

— Three bedrooms

— Two full baths

■ A vaulted ceiling in the Living Room and the Dining Room, with a clerestory above

■ A Master Bedroom with a walk-in closet and private full bath

■ An efficient Kitchen, with a corner double sink and peninsula counter

■ A Dining Room with sliding doors to the deck

■ A Living Room with a fireplace that adds warmth to open areas

■ Two additional bedrooms that share a full hall bath

Main floor — 846 sq. ft.
Upper floor — 400 sq. ft.

Comfortable with Style

No. 91547

■ This plan features:

— Three bedrooms

— Two full and one half baths

■ A quaint front porch providing a sheltered entrance into the small Entry hall with a convenient coat closet

■ A vaulted ceiling crowning the formal Living Room and Dining Room with a fireplace further enhancing the Living Room area

■ An efficient and well-appointed Kitchen with only a peninsula counter separating it from the informal Nook

■ An expansive Family Room with an optional second fireplace, open to both the Nook and the Kitchen for a spacious feel

■ A roomy Master Suite topped by a vaulted ceiling contains an ultra bath with spa tub, double vanity and a compartment water closet and step-in shower

■ Two additional bedrooms share the full bath in the hall

First floor — 913 sq. ft.
Second floor — 813 sq. ft.

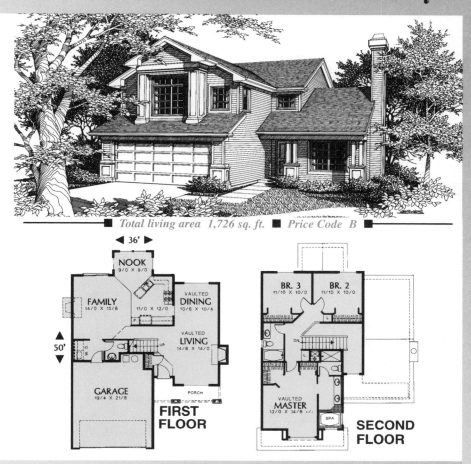

■ Total living area 1,726 sq. ft. ■ Price Code B ■

Perfect for Entertaining

No. 96407

■ This plan features:

— Four bedrooms

— Three full and one half baths

■ Front dormers and wrap-around Porch

■ Dramatic Great Room boasts a cathedral ceiling and a fireplace nestled between built-in shelves

■ French doors expand living space to full length rear Porch

■ Center island and peninsula counter create an efficient Kitchen/Breakfast area

■ First floor Master Bedroom Suite features a walk-in closet and spacious Master Bath

First floor — 1,831 sq. ft.
Second floor — 941 sq. ft.
Bonus room — 539 sq. ft.
Garage & storage — 684 sq. ft.

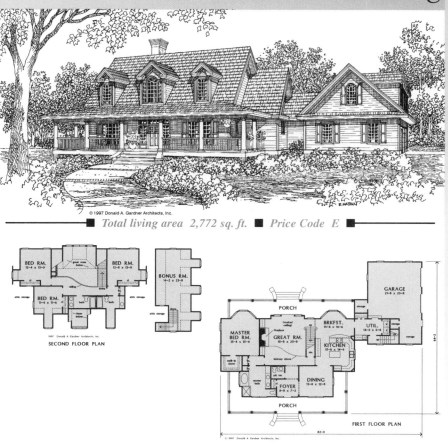

© 1997 Donald A. Gardner Architects, Inc.

■ Total living area 2,772 sq. ft. ■ Price Code E ■

Colonial Home with All the Traditional Comforts

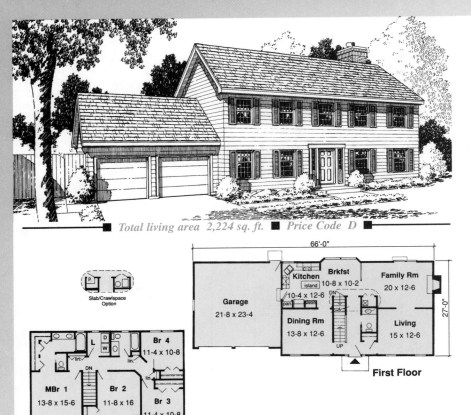

■ *Total living area 2,224 sq. ft.* ■ *Price Code D* ■

No. 34705

■ This plan features:

— Four bedrooms

— Two and one half baths

■ A formal Living Room and Dining Room flanking a spacious entry

■ Family areas flowing together into an open space at the rear of the home

■ An island Kitchen with a built-in pantry centrally located for easy service to the Dining Room and Breakfast area

■ A Master Suite including large closets and double vanities in the bath

First floor — 1,090 sq. ft.
Second floor — 1,134 sq. ft.
Basement — 1,090 sq. ft.
Garage — 576 sq. ft.

Gracious Entrance

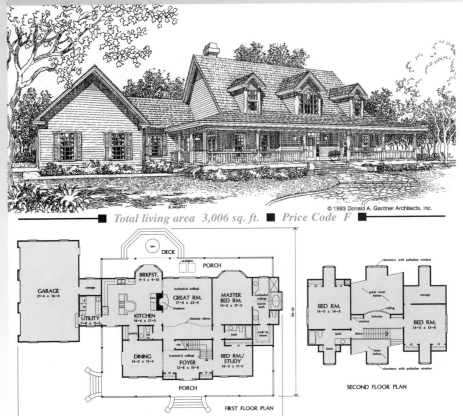

■ *Total living area 3,006 sq. ft.* ■ *Price Code F* ■

No. 99888

■ This plan features:

—Four bedrooms

—Three full and one half baths

■ Cathedral ceilings in the Foyer, Master Bath and Great Room.

■ Spacious Kitchen enhanced by an island with a built-in stove and a windowed Breakfast area overlooking a Porch with Sp

■ Main level Master Suite with a walk-in closet, overlooking the back Porch

■ Utility/Laundry room between the oversized Garage and Kitchen.

■ Two bedrooms, a bathroom and a balcony overlooking the Great Room from the second floor

First floor — 2,238 sq. ft.
Second floor — 768 sq. ft.
Garage — 865 sq. ft.

Grand Columned Entrance

■ *Total living area 3,335 sq. ft.* ■ *Price Code F* ■

No. 92219

■ This plan features:

— Four bedrooms

— Three full and one half baths

■ Entry hall with a graceful landing staircase, flanked by formal areas

■ Fireplaces highlight the Living Room/Parlor and Dining Room

■ Kitchen with an island cooktop, built-in pantry and Breakfast area

■ Cathedral ceiling crowns Family Room and is accented by a fireplace

■ Lavish Master Bedroom wing with plenty of storage space

■ Three bedrooms, one with a private bath

First floor — 2,432 sq. ft.
Second floor — 903 sq. ft.
Basement — 2,432 sq. ft.

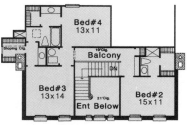

Upper Floor

Main Floor

Elegant and Inviting

■ *Total living area 2,744 sq. ft.* ■ *Price Code E* ■

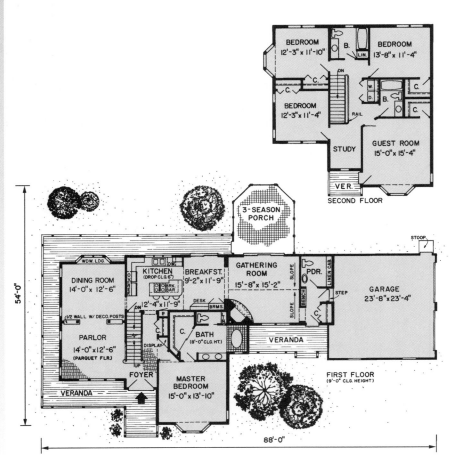

BEDROOM
12'-3" x 11'-10"

BEDROOM
13'-8" x 11'-4"

BEDROOM
12'-3" x 11'-4"

STUDY

GUEST ROOM
15'-0" x 15'-4"

VER.

SECOND FLOOR

3-SEASON PORCH

DINING ROOM
14'-0" x 12'-6"

KITCHEN
(DROP CLG. 6")

BREAKFST.
9'-2" x 11'-9"

GATHERING ROOM
15'-8" x 15'-2"

PDR.

GARAGE
23'-8" x 23'-4"

PARLOR
14'-0" x 12'-6"
(PARQUET FLR.)

BATH
(8'-0" CLG. HT.)

VERANDA

FOYER

MASTER BEDROOM
15'-0" x 13'-10"

VERANDA

FIRST FLOOR
(9'-0" CLG. HEIGHT)

54'-0"

88'-0"

No. 10689

■ **This plan features:**

— Five bedrooms

— Three and one half baths

■ Wrap-around verandas and a three-season porch

■ An elegant Parlor with a parquet floor and a formal Dining Room separated by a half-wall

■ An adjoining Kitchen with a Breakfast bar and nook

■ A Gathering Room with a fireplace, soaring ceilings and access to the porch

First floor — 1,580 sq. ft.
Second floor — 1,164 sq. ft.
Basement — 1,329 sq. ft.
Garage — 576 sq. ft.

No. 24563

■ This plan features:

— Four bedrooms

— Two full and one half baths

■ Stone and columns accenting the wrap-around front porch

■ A formal Living Room and Dining Room adjoining with columns at their entrances

■ An island Kitchen with a double sink, plenty of cabinet and counter space and a walk-in pantry

■ A Breakfast Room flowing into the Family Room and the Kitchen

■ A corner fireplace and a built-in entertainment center in the Family Room

■ A lavish Master Suite topped by a decorative ceiling and an ultra bath

■ Three roomy, additional bedrooms sharing a full hall bath

First floor — 1,584 sq. ft.
Second floor — 1,277 sq. ft.
Garage — 550 sq. ft.
Basement — 1,584 sq. ft.

An
EXCLUSIVE DESIGN
By Britt J. Willis

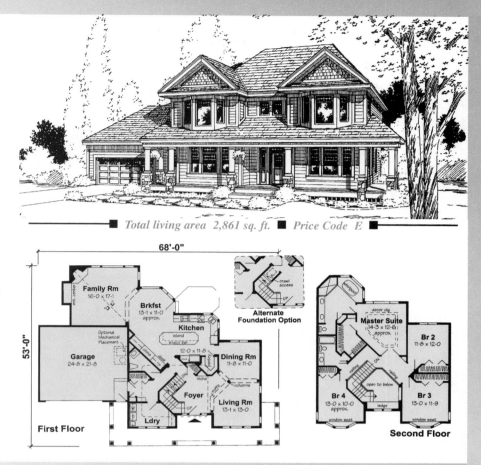

■ Total living area 2,861 sq. ft. ■ Price Code E ■

No. 99664

■ This plan features:

— Four bedrooms

— Two full and one half baths

■ Columns outline the entry to the formal Dining Room

■ The Great Room has a built-in fireplace with adjacent log storage

■ The Kitchen has a center work island and opens to the Dinette

■ A Study and a half bath are located off the Great Room

■ The secluded Master Suite has dual walk-in closets and a private bath

■ Located upstairs are three additional bedrooms and a full bath

■ An optional basement, slab or crawl space foundation — please specify when ordering

First floor — 1,522 sq. ft.
Second floor — 683 sq. ft.
Basement — 1,522 sq. ft.
Garage — 489 sq. ft.

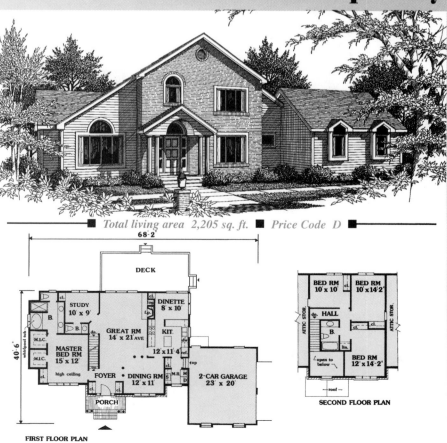

■ Total living area 2,205 sq. ft. ■ Price Code D ■

Unique Brick Facade

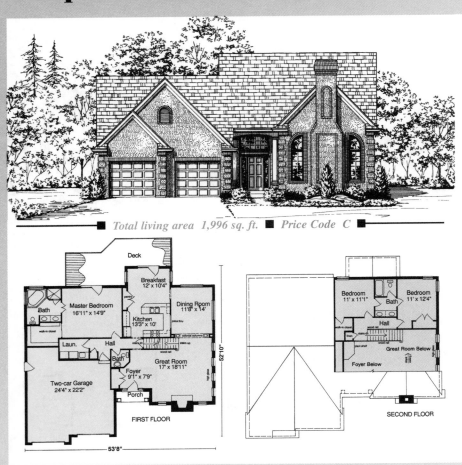

■ *Total living area 1,996 sq. ft.* ■ *Price Code C* ■

FIRST FLOOR

SECOND FLOOR

No. 92641

■ **This plan features:**

— Three bedrooms

— Two full and one half bath

■ Sheltered entry leads into open Foyer and Great Room

■ High glass windows brighten Great Room with focal point fireplace

■ Colonial columns lead into formal Dining Room with large windows

■ Efficient, U-shaped Kitchen with pass-thru counter, built-in pantry and glass Breakfast area with atrium door to Deck

■ Secluded Master Bedroom with atrium door to Deck, walk-in closet , double vanity and corner, garden tub

■ Two additional bedrooms on second floor share double vanity bath

■ No materials list available

First floor —1,516 sq. ft.
Second floor — 480 sq. ft.
Basement — 1,477 sq. ft.

Life's Simple Pleasures

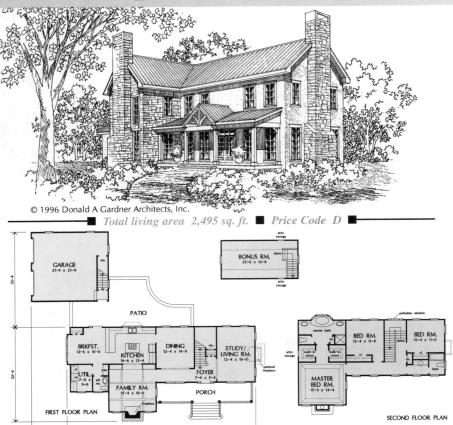

© 1996 Donald A Gardner Architects, Inc.

■ *Total living area 2,495 sq. ft.* ■ *Price Code D* ■

FIRST FLOOR PLAN

SECOND FLOOR PLAN

No. 99816

■ **This plan features:**

— Three bedrooms

— Two full and one half baths

■ Living Room/Study with an optional fireplace

■ Large Dining Room is convenient to the Kitchen

■ Kitchen is well equipped with a cooktop island

■ Sunny Breakfast Room with a window wall also access the patio

■ Family Room has a beamed ceiling and a fireplace

■ Located upstairs are three large bedrooms and two full baths

First floor — 1,428 sq. ft.
Second floor — 1,067 sq. ft.
Bonus — 342 sq. ft.
Garage — 584 sq. ft.

Snug Retreat With A View

■ *Total living area 880 sq. ft.* ■ *Price Code A* ■

No. 91031 ✂

■ **This plan features:**

— One bedroom plus loft

— One full bath

■ A large front Deck providing views and an expansive entrance

■ A two-story Living/Dining area with double glass doors leading out to the Deck

■ An efficient, U-shaped Kitchen with a pass through counter to the Dining area

■ A first floor Bedroom, with ample closet space, located near a full shower bath

■ A Loft/Bedroom on the second floor offering multiple uses

Main floor — 572 sq. ft.
Loft — 308 sq. ft.

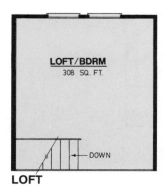

LOFT/BDRM
308 SQ. FT.

← DOWN

LOFT

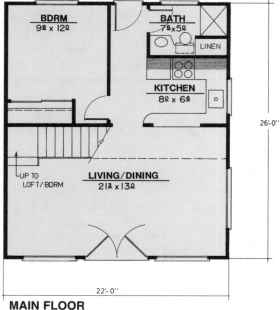

BDRM
9⁰ x 12⁰

BATH
7⁰ x 5⁰

LINEN

KITCHEN
8⁰ x 6⁰

26'-0"

UP TO
LOFT/BDRM

LIVING/DINING
21³ x 13⁰

22'-0"

MAIN FLOOR

Detailed Brick and Fieldstone Facade

Total living area 2,205 sq. ft. ■ *Price Code D* ■

SECOND FLOOR

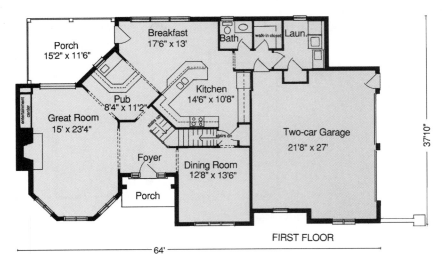

FIRST FLOOR

64'

No. 92675

■ **This plan features**

— Three bedrooms

— Two full and one half baths

■ Open Foyer enhanced by a graceful, banister staircase

■ Great Room highlighted by a twelve foot ceiling topping an alcove of windows, fireplace, built-in entertainment center and Porch access

■ Spacious Kitchen and Breakfast area with extended counter/snack bar and nearby Pub, walk-in closet, Laundry and Garage

■ Comfortable Master Bedroom with a large walk-in closet and double vanity bath

■ Two additional bedrooms share a double vanity bath

■ No materials list available

First floor — 1,192 sq. ft.
Second floor — 1,013 sq. ft.
Basement — 1,157 sq. ft.

Traditional Transom Windows Add Appeal

No. 90396 ⚒

■ This plan features:

— Three bedrooms

— Two full and one half baths

■ A vaulted ceiling in both the Living and adjoining Dining Rooms, accentuated by a fireplace

■ A well-appointed, sky-lit Kitchen which easily serves the Dining Room

■ A first floor Master Suite with a dramatic vaulted ceiling and private patio access

■ A private Master Bath with double vanity and walk-in closet

Main floor — 1,099 sq. ft.
Upper floor — 452 sq. ft.

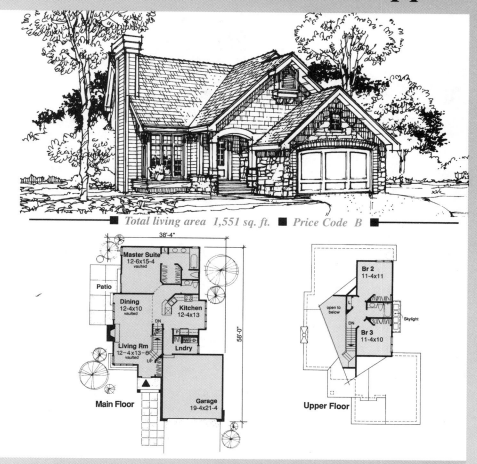

■ *Total living area 1,551 sq. ft.* **■** *Price Code B* **■**

Arched Windows Add Natural Light

No. 94609

■ This plan features:

— Four bedrooms

— Three full baths

■ Welcoming porch shelters entry into Foyer

■ Dining Room highlighted by alcove of windows

■ Spacious Living Room enhanced by a hearth fireplace, built-in shelves and glass access to Covered Porch

■ Efficient, U-shaped Kitchen with a peninsula serving, nearby laundry and bright Breakfast area with access to Porch

■ Pampering Bedroom one offers a large walk-in closet and double vanity bath

■ Three additional bedrooms with walk-in closets, have access to full baths

■ No materials list is available for this plan

■ An optional crawl space or slab foundation— please specify when ordering

First floor — 1,505 sq. ft.
Second floor — 555 sq. ft.
Garage — 400 sq. ft.

■ *Total living area 2,060 sq. ft.* **■** *Price Code C* **■**

Perfect for a Hillside

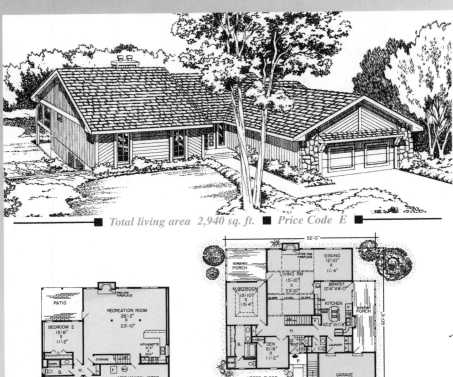

Total living area 2,940 sq. ft. ■ *Price Code E* ■

LOWER FLOOR

FIRST FLOOR

No. 10595

■ **This plan features:**

— Three bedrooms

— Two and one half baths

■ An island Kitchen with a breakfast area leading onto one of two screened porches

■ A huge Recreation Room with a Kitchenette and fireplace

■ A sloping ceiling and fireplace in the spacious Living Room

■ A central staircase directing traffic to all areas of the house

First floor — 1,643 sq. ft.
Lower floor — 1,297 sq. ft.
Garage — 528 sq. ft.

An
EXCLUSIVE DESIGN
By Karl Kreeger

Genteel Country Home

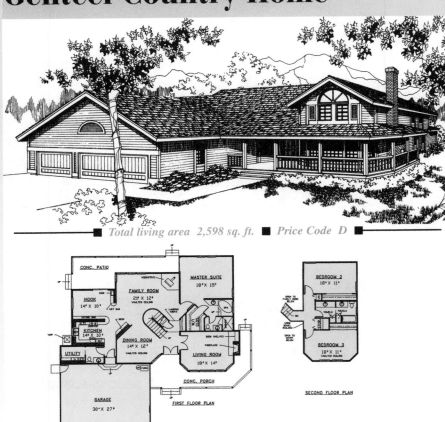

Total living area 2,598 sq. ft. ■ *Price Code D* ■

No. 99796

■ **This plan features:**

— Three bedrooms

— Two full and one half bath

■ A wrap-around porch and numerous Windows enhance the facade of the home

■ A double door entry

■ A classic formal Living Room with a fireplace, built-in shelves and double doors for privacy

■ Vaulted ceilings in the Dining Room, Living Room and one Bedroom

■ A large first floor Master Suite with a lavish bath and a walk-in closet

■ A corner wood stove adding a cozy touch to the Family Room

■ A built-in wetbar dividing the Family Room from the Nook area and a peninsula counter/eating bar dividing the Kitchen from the Nook area

■ Two additional bedrooms on the second floor sharing the use of a compartmented bath with two basins

First floor — 1,923 sq. ft.
Second floor — 675 sq. ft.
Garage — 858 sq. ft.
Width — 62 sq. ft.
Depth — 67 sq. ft.

Distinctive Brick with Room to Expand

■ Total living area 2,645 sq. ft. ■ Price Code E ■

No. 93206

■ This plan features:

— Four bedrooms

— Two full and one half baths

■ Arched entrance with decorative glass leads into two-story Foyer

■ Formal Dining Room with tray ceiling above decorative window

■ Efficient Kitchen with island cooktop, built-in desk and pantry

■ Master Bedroom topped by tray ceiling with French door to Patio, huge private bath with garden tub and two walk-in closets

■ Three additional bedrooms with ample closets share laundry and full bath

■ Optional space for Storage and Future Bedroom with full bath

■ An optional basement, crawl space or slab foundation — please specify when ordering

First Floor — 2,577 sq. ft.
Future Second Floor — 619 sq. ft.
Bridge — 68 sq. ft.
Basement — 2,561 sq. ft.
Garage — 560 sq. ft.

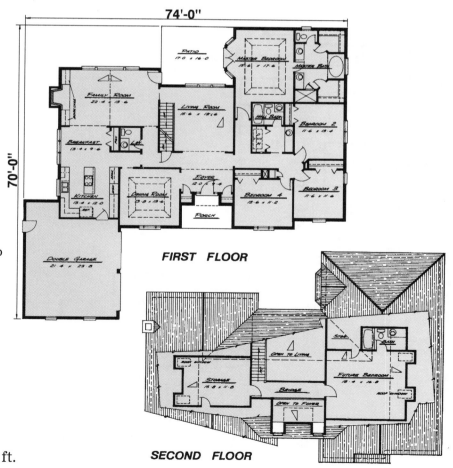

FIRST FLOOR

SECOND FLOOR

An EXCLUSIVE DESIGN
By Jannis Vann & Associate

Country Elegance

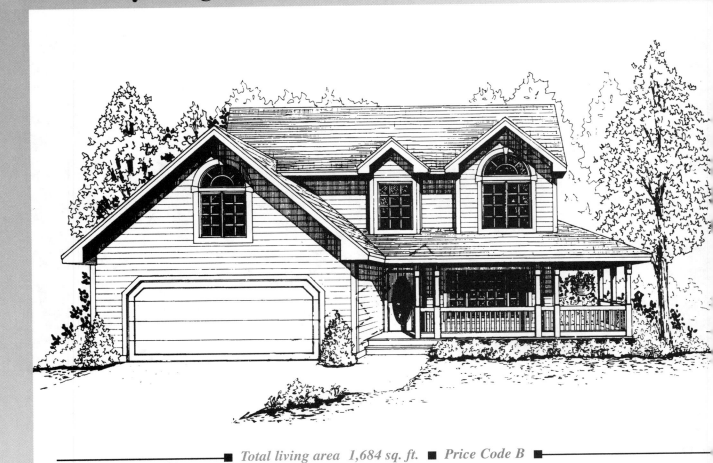

■ *Total living area 1,684 sq. ft.* ■ *Price Code B* ■

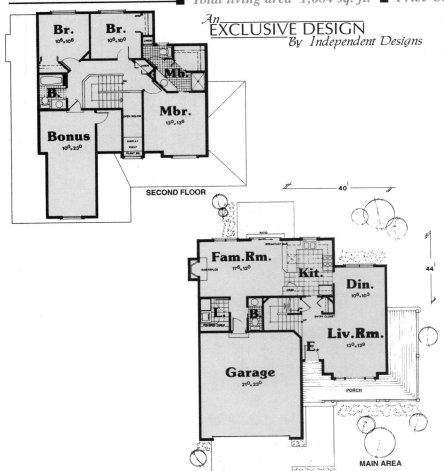

An
EXCLUSIVE DESIGN
By Independent Designs

SECOND FLOOR

Br.
10⁶x10⁶

Br.
10⁶x10⁰

Mb.

Mbr.
13⁰x13⁶

B.

Bonus
10⁰x23⁰

40'

44'

Fam.Rm.
17⁶x12⁰

Kit.

Din.
10⁶x10³

Liv.Rm.
13⁰x12⁹

E.

Garage
21⁰x23⁰

MAIN AREA

No. 93905

■ **This plan features:**

— Three bedrooms

— Two full and one half baths

■ Welcoming front Porch leads into open Entry with landing staircase and convenient closet

■ Comfortable Family Room with gas fireplace and sliding glass door to Patio

■ Efficient U-shaped Kitchen with built-in desk and eating bar

■ Private Master Bedroom with an arched window, plush bath and walk-in closet

■ Bonus Room with another arched window and storage space

■ No materials list available

First floor — 913 sq. ft.
Second floor — 771 sq. ft.
Garage — 483 sq. ft.

Comfort and Convenience

No. 20363

This plan features:

— Three bedrooms

— Two and one half baths

■ Transom windows, skylights, and an open plan combining to make this brick classic a sun-filled retreat

■ Soaring ceilings in the foyer

■ A Family Room including a fireplace and open access to the Kitchen and Breakfast area

■ An island Kitchen with a built-in bar to make mealtime preparation a breeze

■ A luxurious Master Suite with a vaulted bath area including a garden spa

■ Two good-size bedrooms on the second floor, sharing a full bath

First floor — 1,859 sq. ft.

Second floor — 579 sq. ft.

Basement — 1,859 sq. ft.

Garage — 622 sq. ft.

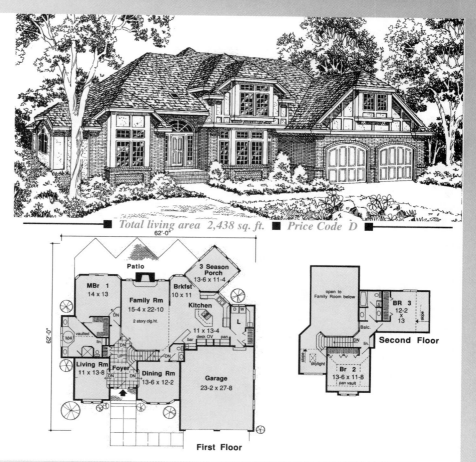

■ Total living area 2,438 sq. ft. ■ Price Code D ■

Wrapping Front Porch and Gabled Dormers

No. 96411

This plan features:

— Four bedrooms

— Three full baths

■ Great Room with a fireplace, cathedral ceiling, and a balcony above

■ Flexible bedroom/study having a walk-in closet and an adjacent full bath

■ First floor Master Suite with a sunny bay window and a private bath topped by a cathedral ceiling and highlighted by his-n-her vanities, and a separate tub and shower

■ Two additional bedrooms, each with dormer windows, sharing a full bath with a cathedral ceiling, palladian window and a double vanity

■ Bonus room over the garage for future expansion

First floor — 1,939 sq. ft.

Second floor — 657 sq. ft.

Garage & Storage — 526 sq. ft.

Bonus room — 386 sq. ft.

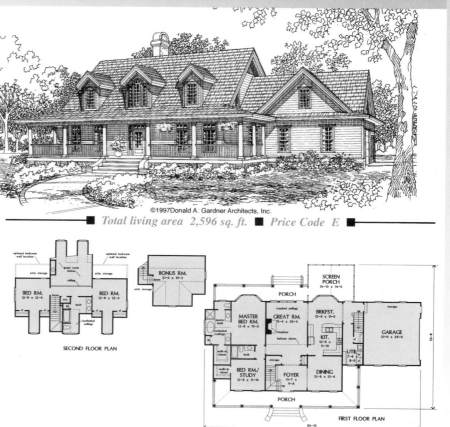

©1997 Donald A. Gardner Architects, Inc.

■ Total living area 2,596 sq. ft. ■ Price Code E ■

Charming, Compact and Convenient

■ *Total living area 1,752 sq. ft.* ■ *Price Code B* ■

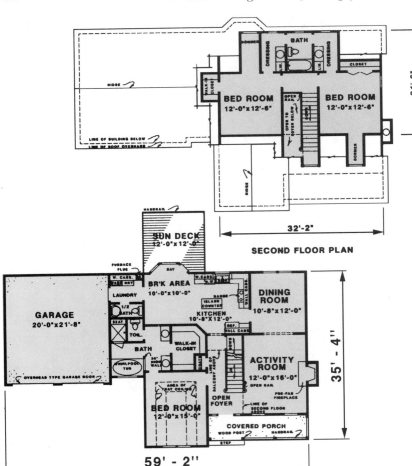

SECOND FLOOR PLAN

No. 94803

■ **This plan features:**

— Three bedrooms

— Two full and one half bath

■ Spacious Activity Room with a pre-fab fireplace opens to formal Dining Room

■ Country-size Kitchen/ Breakfast area with island counter and access to Sun Deck and Laundry/Garage entry

■ First floor bedroom highlighted by lovely arched window below a tray ceiling and a pampering bath

■ Two upstairs bedrooms share a twin vanity bath

■ An optional basement or crawl space foundation — please specify when ordering

First floor — 1,165 sq. ft.
Second floor — 587 sq. ft.
Garage — 455 sq. ft.

Stately Exterior with an Open Interior

■ *Total living area 2,655 sq. ft.* ■ *Price Code E* ■

No. 99424

■ This plan features:

— Four bedrooms

— Two full and one half baths

■ Open Entry accented by a lovely landing staircase and access to Study and formal Dining Room

■ Central Family Room with an inviting fireplace and a cathedral ceiling extending into Kitchen

■ Spacious Kitchen offers a work island/snackbar, built-in pantry, glass Breakfast area and nearby Porch, Utilities and Garage entry

■ Secluded Master Bedroom enhanced by a large walk-in closet and lavish bath

■ Three second floor bedrooms share a double vanity bath

First floor — 1,906 sq. ft.
Second floor — 749 sq. ft.
Basement — 1,906 sq. ft.
Garage — 682 sq. ft.

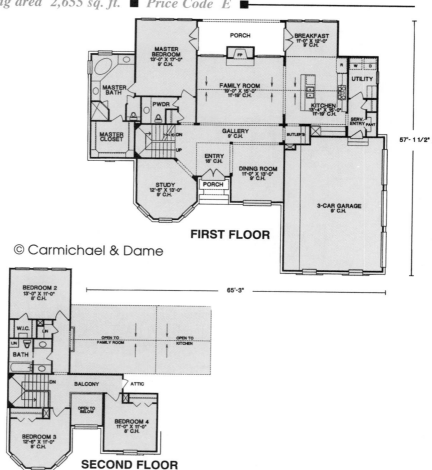

© Carmichael & Dame

FIRST FLOOR

SECOND FLOOR

Dormers and Porch Spell Country Atmosphere

■ *Total living area 3,072 sq. ft.* ■ *Price Code E* ■

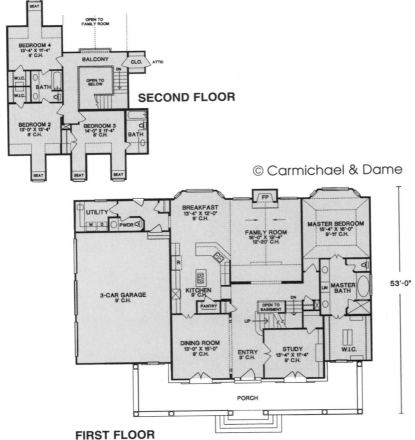

© Carmichael & Dame

SECOND FLOOR

SEAT

BEDROOM 4
13'-4" X 11'-4"
8' C.H.

OPEN TO FAMILY ROOM

BALCONY

OPEN TO BELOW

CLO. ATTIC

W.I.C.

BATH

DN

BEDROOM 2
13'-0" X 13'-4"
8' C.H.

BEDROOM 3
14'-0" X 11'-4"
8' C.H.

BATH

SEAT   SEAT   SEAT

FIRST FLOOR

UTILITY   W   D

PWDR

BREAKFAST
13'-4" X 12'-0"
9' C.H.

FP

FAMILY ROOM
16'-0" X 19'-4"
12'-20' C.H.

MASTER BEDROOM
15'-4" X 16'-0"
9'-11" C.H.

3-CAR GARAGE
9' C.H.

R

KITCHEN
9' C.H.

PANTRY

DINING ROOM
13'-0" X 15'-0"
9' C.H.

OPEN TO BASEMENT

UP

ENTRY
9' C.H.

STUDY
13'-4" X 11'-4"
9' C.H.

DN

LIN

MASTER BATH

W.I.C.

53'-0"

PORCH

67'-8"

No. 99425

■ **This plan features:**

— Four bedrooms

— Three full and one half baths

■ French doors lead from both the Dining Room and the Study onto the front Porch

■ The center island Kitchen also has a walk in pantry

■ The bayed Breakfast Nook opens into the Family Room which features a fireplace

■ The Master Bedroom has a bay window, private bath, and walk in closet

■ Upstairs there are three Bedrooms with windows seat in the dormers, and two full Baths

■ There is no materials list available for this plan

First floor — 2,116 sq. ft.
Second floor — 956 sq. ft.
Basement — 2,116 sq. ft.
Garage — 675 sq. ft.

Comfortable and Relaxed Environment

No. 92639

This plan features:

- Three bedrooms
- Two full and one half baths
- A covered porch and boxed window enhancing the exterior
- An easy flow traffic pattern creates step saving convenience
- An open stairway adds elegance to the Foyer
- A spacious Great Room and Breakfast Area forming an area large enough for real family enjoyment
- A U-shaped Kitchen highlighted by a corner sink and ample counter and storage space
- A half bath and a Laundry Room rounding out the first floor
- A Master Suite with a walk-in closet plus a compartmented bath
- Two additional bedrooms sharing use of a bath with skylight
- A full basement providing the option of creating expanded play area in the lower level
- No materials list is available for this plan

First floor — 748 sq. ft.
Second floor — 705 sq. ft.

■ *Total living area 1,453 sq. ft.* ■ *Price Code A* ■

Distinctive French Door Entrance

No. 93210

This plan features:

- Four bedrooms
- Two full and one half baths
- French Doors open into a two-story foyer topped by a beautiful arched window
- Both the formal Living and Dining Rooms enjoy plenty of natural light through their bay windows
- Well-appointed Kitchen includes a peninsula counter and easy access to both dining areas
- Expansive Family Room has a fireplace and opens onto the rear sundeck
- Large Master Suite has a private bath with double vanity and a walk-in closet
- Three second floor bedrooms share a full hall bath with double vanity
- No materials list is available for this plan

First floor — 1,560 sq. ft.
Second floor — 834 sq. ft.
Basement — 772 sq. ft.

■ *Total living area 2,394 sq. ft.* ■ *Price Code D* ■

An
EXCLUSIVE DESIGN
By Jannis Vann & Associates, Inc.

113

Four Bedroom Country Classic

© 1994 Donald A. Gardner Architects, Inc.

B. NATHAN

Total living area 2,164 sq. ft. ■ *Price Code D* ■

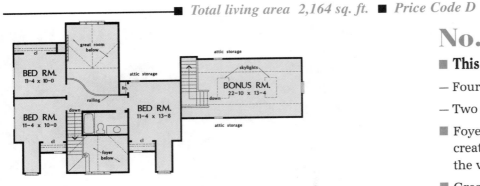

SECOND FLOOR PLAN

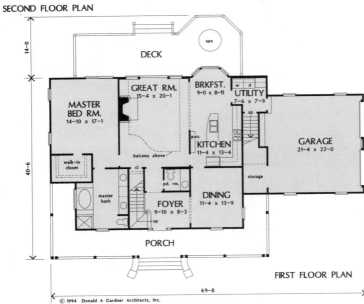

FIRST FLOOR PLAN

No. 96408

■ This plan features:

— Four bedrooms

— Two full and one half baths

■ Foyer open to the dining room creating a hall with a balcony over the vaulted Great Room

■ Great Room opens to the deck and to the island Kitchen with convenient pantry

■ Nine foot ceilings on the first floor expand volume

■ Master Suite pampered by a whirlpool tub, double vanity, separate shower, and access to the deck

■ Bonus room to be finished now or later

First floor — 1,499 sq. ft.
Second floor — 665 sq. ft.
Garage & storage — 567 sq. ft.
Bonus room — 380 sq. ft.

© 1994 Donald A Gardner Architects, Inc.

Compact and Complete Design

■ *Total living area 1,991 sq. ft.* ■ *Price Code C* ■

No. 94004

■ This plan features:

— Four bedrooms

— Two full and one half baths

■ Covered Porch leads into two-story Entry with angled staircase

■ Vaulted bay window and cozy fireplace enhance Living Room and Dining area with decorative ceiling

■ Efficient Kitchen with cooktop island, adjacent laundry, Breakfast bay with access to Deck, and Family Room

■ Master Bedroom with walk-in closet, double vanity and Jacuzzi

■ Three additional bedrooms with ample closet space, share a full bath

■ No materials list is available for this plan

Main floor — 1,026 sq. ft.
Second floor — 965 sq. ft.
Garage — 594 sq. ft.

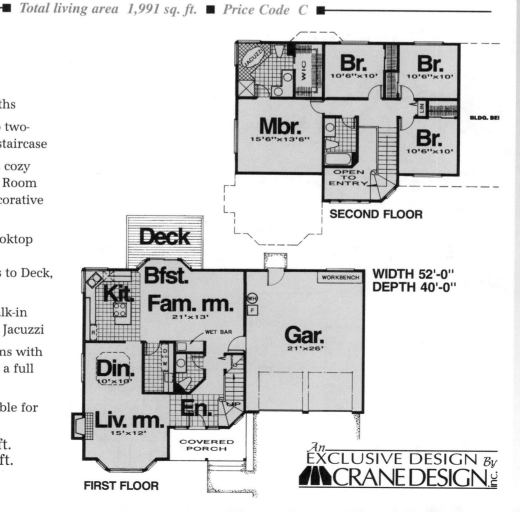

SECOND FLOOR

Br. 10'6"x10'
Br. 10'6"x10'
Mbr. 15'6"x13'6"
WIC
JACUZZI
LIN
BLDG. BEI
Br. 10'6"x10'
OPEN TO ENTRY

FIRST FLOOR

Deck
Bfst.
Kit.
Fam. rm. 21'x13'
WET BAR
WORKBENCH
Gar. 21'x26'
WH
F
Din. 10'x10'
En.
UP
Liv. rm. 15'x12'
COVERED PORCH

WIDTH 52'-0"
DEPTH 40'-0"

An EXCLUSIVE DESIGN *By* CRANE DESIGN inc.

115

Three Bedroom Features Cathedral Ceilings

■ *Total living area 1,775 sq. ft.* ■ *Price Code B* ■

No. 20051 ✕

■ **This plan features:**

— Three bedrooms

— Two and a half baths

■ A Kitchen with central island, built-in desk, pantry and adjacent Breakfast Nook

■ A fireplaced Living Room with built-in book case that combines with the Dining Room

■ A Master Suite with private full bath

First floor — 1,285 sq. ft.
Second floor — 490 sq. ft.
Basement — 1,285 sq. ft.
Garage — 495 sq. ft.

An
EXCLUSIVE DESIGN
By Karl Kreeger

Functional Floor Plan

No. 94600

■ **This plan features:**

— Four bedrooms

— Three full baths

■ Columns accent front Porch and entrance into two-story Foyer

■ Expansive Living Room with hearth fireplace between French doors leading to Covered Porch and Patio

■ Efficient Kitchen with peninsula counter, bright Breakfast area and adjoining Utility, Dining Room and Garage entry

■ Private Master Bedroom wing with a large walk-in closet and plush bath with two vanities

■ First floor bedroom with another walk-in closet and full bath access, offers multiple uses

■ Two additional bedrooms on second floor with dormers and large closets, share a full bath with separate vanities

■ No materials list is available for this plan

■ An optional crawl space or slab foundation —please specify when ordering

First floor — 1,685 sq. ft.
Second floor — 648 sq. ft.
Garage — 560 sq. ft.

■ *Total living area 2,333 sq. ft.* ■ *Price Code D* ■

© 1991 Donald A. Gardner Architects, Inc.

■ *Total living area 1,898 sq. ft.* ■ *Price Code C* ■

No. 99852 ✄

■ This plan features:

— Three bedrooms

— Two full and one half baths

■ Ready, set, grow with this lovely country home enhanced by wraparound Porch and rear Deck

■ Palladian window in clerestory dormer bathes two-story Foyer in natural light

■ Private Master Bedroom suite offers everything: walk-in closet, whirlpool tub, shower, and double vanity

■ Two upstairs bedrooms with dormers and storage access, share a full bath

■ An optional basement or crawl space foundation — please specify when ordering

First floor — 1,356 sq. ft.
Second floor — 542 sq. ft.
Bonus room — 393 sq. ft.
Garage & storage — 543 sq. ft.

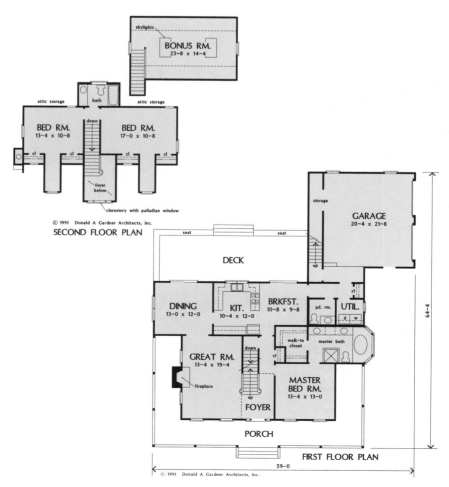

SECOND FLOOR PLAN
© 1991 Donald A Gardner Architects, Inc.

FIRST FLOOR PLAN
© 1991 Donald A Gardner Architects, Inc.

Contemporary Plan With Old World Charm

Total living area 2,600 sq. ft. ■ *Price Code D* ■

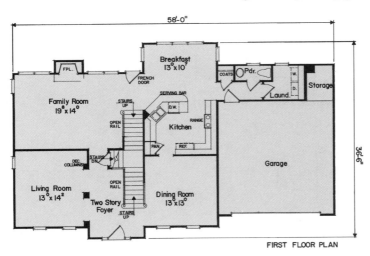

FIRST FLOOR PLAN

SECOND FLOOR PLAN

No. 98417

■ This plan features:

— Four bedrooms

— Two full and one half baths

■ Entrance to Living Room is accented by three decorative columns

■ The Pantry and extended counter/serving bar highlight the Kitchen which is open to the Breakfast Area

■ Master Suite is enhanced by a two-sided fireplace, a sitting room with a bay window, and a luxurious private bath crowned by a vaulted ceiling

■ Located upstairs, three additional bedrooms share the full hall bath

■ Please specify a basement or slab foundation when ordering

First floor — 1,252 sq. ft.
Second floor — 1,348 sq. ft.
Basement — 1,252 sq. ft.
Garage — 483 sq. ft.

Opulent Luxury

■ *Total living area 3,783 sq. ft.* ■ *Price Code F* ■

No. 92237

- This plan features:

– Four bedrooms

– Three full and one half baths

■ A stone hearth fireplace and built-in book shelves enhance the Living Room

■ Family Room with a huge fireplace, cathedral ceiling and access to Covered Veranda

■ Spacious Kitchen with cooktop island/snackbar, built-in pantry and Breakfast Room

■ Master Bedroom with a pullman ceiling, sitting area, private Covered Patio, two walk-in closets and a whirlpool tub

■ Three additional bedrooms with walk-in closets and private access to a full bath

First floor — 2,804 sq. ft.
Second floor — 979 sq. ft.
Basement — 2,804 sq. ft.

Upper Level

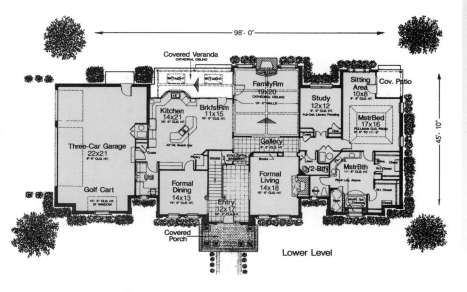

Lower Level

Exquisite Detail

■ *Total living area 3,262 sq. ft.* ■ *Price Code F* ■

No. 98400

■ This plan features:

— Four bedrooms

— Three full and one half baths

■ Two-story Foyer between formal Living and Dining rooms

■ Formal Living Room with access to Covered Porch

■ Radius windows and arches, huge fireplace enhance spacious Family Room

■ Kitchen has a pantry, cooktop/serving bar and a two-story Breakfast area

■ Expansive Master Bedroom offers a tray ceiling, a cozy Sitting Room a luxurious bath and huge walk-in closet

■ An optional basement or crawl space foundation — please specify when ordering

First floor — 1,418 sq. ft.
Second floor — 1,844 sq. ft.
Garage — 820 sq. ft.

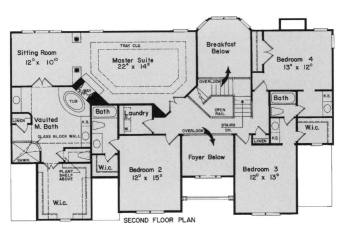

SECOND FLOOR PLAN

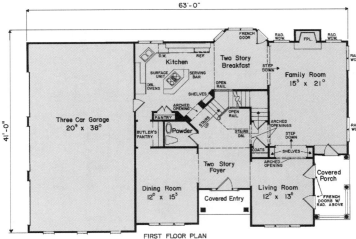

FIRST FLOOR PLAN

Mountain Retreat

No. 34625

This plan features:

- Two bedrooms
- Two full baths
- A Deck entrance through double sliding glass doors into a spacious Living Room with a cozy fireplace and a sloped ceiling
- An efficient, U-shaped Kitchen with an open counter to the Living Room and a view
- A Master Bedroom with a double closet, full bath and a laundry
- An upper level with a Bedroom and a Loft sharing a full bath

First floor — 780 sq. ft
Second floor — 451 sq. ft.
Basement — 780 sq. ft.

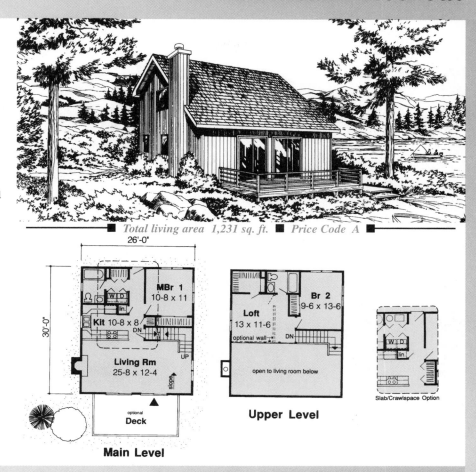

■ *Total living area 1,231 sq. ft.* ■ *Price Code A* ■

Easy Family Living

No. 91549

This plan features:

- Three bedrooms
- Two full and one half baths
- Sheltered entry leads into bright foyer with a lovely, angled staircase
- Two-story Great Room with hearth fireplace and atrium door to back yard
- Convenient Kitchen with serving counter/snackbar, bright Dining area, built-in pantry and desk, and nearby laundry and Garage entry
- Quiet Master suite with a walk-in closet and double vanity bath
- Two additional bedrooms with ample closets, share a full bath

First floor — 663 sq. ft.
Second floor — 740 sq. ft.

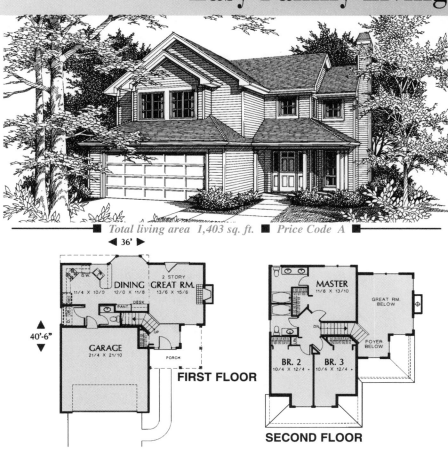

■ *Total living area 1,403 sq. ft.* ■ *Price Code A* ■

Magnificent Presence

■ *Total living area 4,500 sq. ft.* ■ *Price Code F* ■

No. 99410

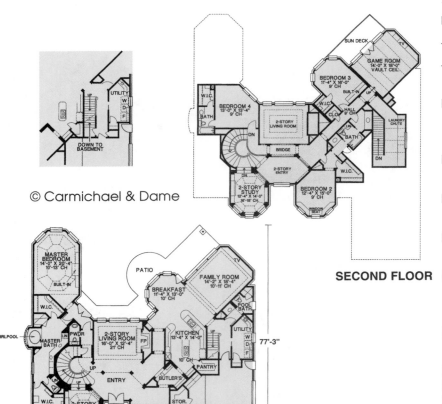

© Carmichael & Dame

SECOND FLOOR

FIRST FLOOR

74'-7"

77'-3"

■ **This plan features:**

— Four bedrooms

— Three full, one three quarter, and one half baths

■ Curved staircase leads to elevated two-story Study and the Master Suite

■ Dining Room is connected to the Kitchen by a butler's pantry

■ Two-story Living Room has a fireplace and distinctive windows

■ Breakfast Bay adjoins family room with built-in entertainment center

■ Three bedrooms, a Game Room, and two full baths on the upper level

■ Three-car garage has an adjoining Storage Room

First floor — 2,897 sq. ft.
Second floor — 1,603 sq. ft.
Basement — 2,897 sq. ft.
Garage — 793 sq. ft.

Balcony Overlooks Living Room Below

■ *Total living area 1,351 sq. ft.* ■ *Price Code A* ■

No. 90356 ⚒

■ **This plan features:**

— Three bedrooms

— Two full and one half baths

■ A vaulted ceiling Living Room with a balcony above and a fireplace

■ An efficient, well-equipped Kitchen with stovetop island and easy flow of traffic into the Dining Room

■ A deck accessible from the Living Room

■ A luxurious Master Suite with a bay window seat, walk-in closet, dressing area, and a private shower

■ Two additional bedrooms that share a full hall bath

First floor — 674 sq. ft.
Second floor — 677 sq. ft.

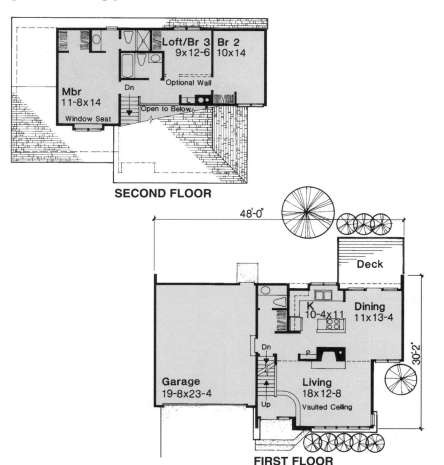

Old-Fashioned Charm

■ *Total living area 2,050 sq. ft.* ■ *Price Code C* ■

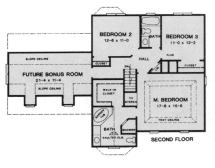

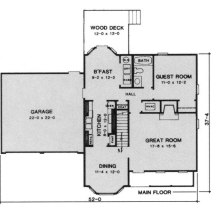

No. 90445

■ **This plan features:**

— Four bedrooms

— Three full baths

■ A large Master Suite with a trayed ceiling and a vaulted ceiling in the lavish, private bath

■ Two additional bedrooms sharing the full hall bath

■ A Great Room with a cozy fireplace focal point

■ A bayed formal Dining Room convenient to the galley Kitchen

■ A sunny Breakfast Nook with a convenient laundry area

■ An optional basement, slab or crawl space foundation — please specify when ordering

Main floor — 1,030 sq. ft.
Second floor — 1,020 sq. ft.
Bonus room — 284 sq. ft.

Elegant Family Home

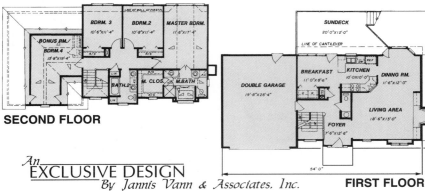

■ *Total living area 1,842 sq. ft.* ■ *Price Code C* ■

SECOND FLOOR

FIRST FLOOR

An EXCLUSIVE DESIGN
By Jannis Vann & Associates, Inc.

No. 93217

■ **This plan features:**

— Three bedrooms

— Two full and one half baths

■ Living Room has a fireplace with built-in bookshelves set between it

■ Formal Dining Room is adjacent to the Living Room creating an open atmosphere

■ Efficient Kitchen has a peninsula counter and adjoins the Breakfast Room

■ Expansive Master Suite has a walk-in closet and luxurious private bath

■ Two additional bedrooms share a full hall bath with a double vanity

■ Large Bonus Room can be used as a fourth bedroom or additional family living space

■ An optional basement or slab foundation — please specify when ordering

First floor — 850 sq. ft.
Second floor — 904 sq. ft.
Finished stairs — 88 sq. ft.
Bonus Room — 235 sq. ft.
Basement — 740 sq. ft.

Sprawling Wrap-Around Porch

■ *Total living area 1,985 sq. ft.* ■ *Price Code D* ■

No. 94812

■ This plan features:

- Three bedrooms

- Two full and one half baths

■ Old-fashioned quality with dormers and a Covered Porch leading into this modern floor plan

■ Activity Room has a fireplace for warmth and comfort

■ Efficient, U-shaped Kitchen has a work island, a snack bar and a vaulted Breakfast room with Sun Deck access

■ First floor Master Bedroom suite enjoys a plush bath and a walk-in closet

■ Two additional bedrooms on the second floor each have dormer windows and access to a full bath

First floor — 1,426 sq. ft.
Second floor — 559 sq. ft.
Basement — 1,426 sq. ft.
Garage — 500 sq. ft.

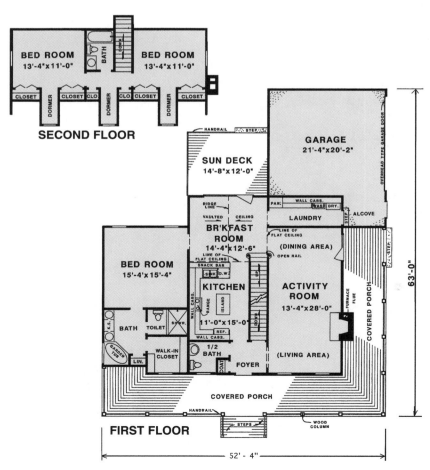

Luxurious Yet Cozy

■ *Total living area 3,395 sq. ft.* ■ *Price Code F* ■

SECOND FLOOR

FIRST FLOOR

No. 98403

■ **This plan features:**

— Four bedrooms

— Three full and one half baths

■ Living Room is enhanced by a fieldstone fireplace and vaulted ceiling

■ Inviting fireplace between windows, and a vaulted ceiling enhance Great Room

■ Kitchen with a work island, serving bar, bright Breakfast area and walk-in pantry

■ Corner Master Suite includes a cozy fireplace, a vaulted Sitting Room and a lavish dressing area

■ Optional basement, crawl space or slab foundation — please specify when ordering

First floor — 2,467 sq. ft.
Second floor — 928 sq. ft.
Bonus — 296 sq. ft.
Garage — 566 sq. ft.

■ *Total living area 2,425 sq. ft.* ■ *Price Code E* ■

No. 98419

■ **This plan features:**

– Three bedrooms

– Two full and one half baths

■ Vaulted Great Room is highlighted by a fireplace and French doors to the rear yard

■ Decorative columns define the Dining Room

■ A built-in pantry and a radius window above the double sink in the Kitchen

■ The Breakfast Bay is crowned by a vaulted ceiling

■ A tray ceiling over the Master Bedroom and Sitting Area and a vaulted ceiling crowns the Master Bath

■ Two additional bedrooms, each with a walk-in closet, share the full, double vanity bath in the hall

■ Please specify a basement, crawl space or slab foundation when ordering

■ No material list is available for this plan

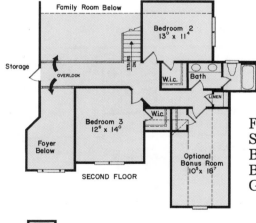

First floor — 1,796 sq. ft.
Second floor — 629 sq. ft.
Bonus room — 208 sq. ft.
Basement — 1,796 sq. ft.
Garage — 588 sq. ft.

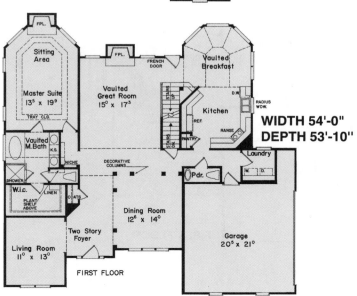

WIDTH 54'-0"
DEPTH 53'-10"

Brick and Wood Highlighted by Sunbursts

■ *Total living area 1,813 sq. ft.* ■ *Price Code C* ■

No. 94104

■ **This plan features:**

— Three bedrooms

— Two full and one half baths

■ Sheltered Porch entrance leads into two-story Foyer with lovely landing staircase

■ Beautiful bay window brightens Living Room opening into formal Dining Room

■ L-shaped Kitchen with a built-in pantry and Dining area with sliding glass door to rear yard

■ Comfortable Family Room with focal point fireplace topped by cathedral ceiling

■ Corner master Bedroom offers two closets and a private bath

■ Two additional bedrooms with large closets share a full bath

■ No materials list is available for this plan

First floor — 1,094 sq. ft.
Second floor — 719 sq. ft.
Garage — 432 sq. ft.

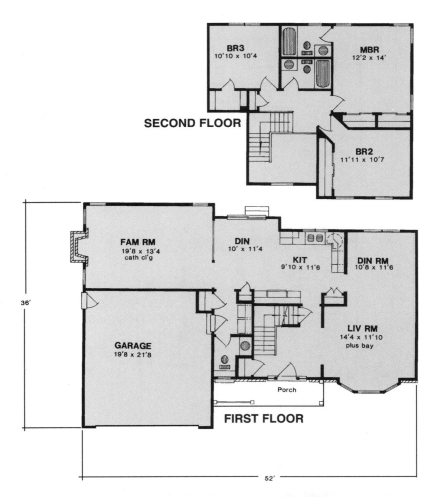

Unique Ceilings

No. 91672

This plan features:

- Four bedrooms
- Three full and one half baths
- A elegant covered entrance leading into a Great Hall with direct access to all living areas
- A unusually shaped Living Room accented by magnificent front windows, a vaulted ceiling and a warm, hearth fireplace
- A formal Dining Room with a built-in alcove flowing from the Living Room into the Kitchen
- An efficient Kitchen equipped with a cooktop island/snackbar, a corner window sink and a bright eating Nook
- A private Master Suite with a tray ceiling highlighted by a bay window and leading to a lavish Bath with a spa tub and double vanity
- A secondary bedroom on the first floor with a built-in desk could double as a den
- On the second floor, two additional bedrooms with walk-in closets sharing a full hall bath and a huge Bonus Room
- No materials list available

First floor — 1,928 sq. ft.
Second floor — 504 sq. ft.
Bonus — 335 sq. ft.

Total living area 2,432 sq. ft. ■ *Price Code D* ■

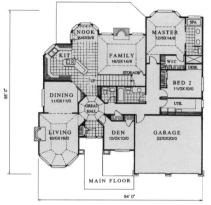

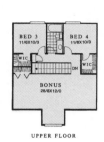

Plenty of Room to Grow

No. 92647

This plan features:

- Three bedrooms
- Two full and one half baths
- Fieldstone and wood siding accent Porch entrance into open Foyer with lovely landing staircase
- Sunken Great Room with large fireplace, built-in entertainment center and access to rear yard
- Hub Kitchen with built-in pantry, serving counter, bright Breakfast area and adjoining Dining Room, Laundry and Garage entry
- Corner Master bedroom with walk-in closet, pampering bath with double vanity and whirlpool tub topped by sloped ceiling
- Two or three additional bedrooms share a full bath and a study/computer area
- No materials list available

First floor — 1,065 sq. ft.
Second floor — 833 sq. ft.
Bonus Room — 254 sq. ft.
Garage — 652 sq. ft.

Total living area 1,898 sq. ft. ■ *Price Code C* ■

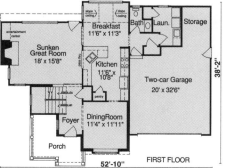

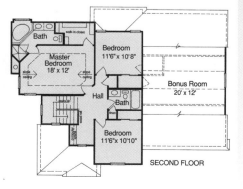

Luxury That You Deserve

■ Total living area 3,238 sq. ft. ■ Price Code E ■

© design basics, inc.

SECOND FLOOR

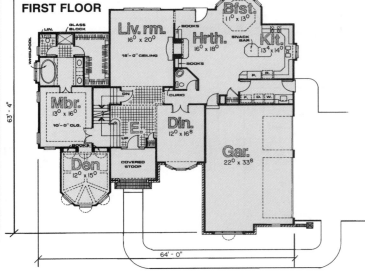

FIRST FLOOR

No. 99430

■ This plan features:

— Four bedrooms

— Two full, one three quarter and one half baths

■ Enter the bayed formal Dining Room from the grand Entry Hall

■ The warm hearth room and bright bayed Nook compliment the fully appointed Kitchen

■ The Living Room has a see through fireplace and a wall of windows overlooking the backyard

■ French doors leading into the Master Suite feature a private Den, Bath with whirlpool tub, an a glass block shower

■ Upstairs are three more Bedrooms, two full Baths, and a Bonus Room

First floor — 2,235 sq. ft.
Second floor — 1,003 sq. ft.
Garage — 740 sq. ft.
Basement — 2,235 sq. ft.

Four Bedroom 1-1/2 Story Design

■ *Total living area 1,531 sq. ft.* ■ *Price Code B* ■

No. 90358 ✕

■ **This plan features:**

- Three bedrooms

- Two full baths

■ A vaulted ceiling in the Great Room and a fireplace

■ An efficient Kitchen with a peninsula counter and double sink

■ A Family Room with easy access to the wood Deck

■ A Master Bedroom with private bath entrance

■ Convenient laundry facilities outside the Master Bedroom

■ Two additional bedrooms upstairs with walk-in closets and the use of the full hall bath

Main floor — 1,062 sq. ft.
Upper floor — 469 sq. ft.

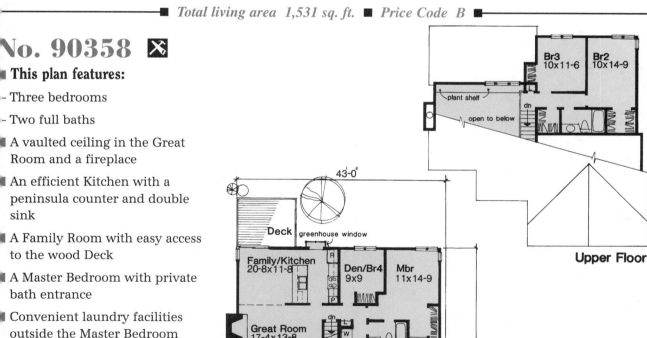

Br3 10x11-6
Br2 10x14-9
plant shelf
open to below
dn

Upper Floor

43'-0"

Deck greenhouse window

Family/Kitchen 20-8x11-8

Den/Br4 9x9

Mbr 11x14-9

Great Room 17-4x13-8 vaulted ceiling

43'-0"

dn

up

Garage 21-4x21-8

Main Floor

Call This Home

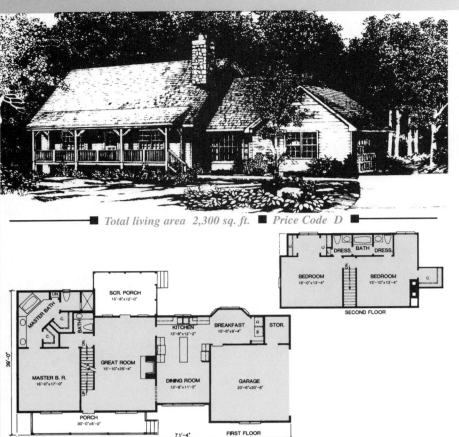

■ Total living area 2,300 sq. ft. ■ Price Code D ■

No. 90424

■ **This plan features:**

— Three bedrooms

— Two full and one half baths

■ A covered porch in the front and a screened porch in the back to take advantage of seasonal weather

■ A Great Room with a stone fireplace that occupies the center of the home

■ An island Kitchen that flows directly into the Dining Room and the Breakfast Bay

■ A secluded Master Bedroom with a five-piece bath and his-n-her walk-in closets

■ Two upstairs bedrooms, each with plenty o closet space and private access to a shared bath

■ An optional basement or crawl space foundation — please specify when ordering

First floor — 1,535 sq. ft.
Second floor — 765 sq. ft.
Basement — 1,091 sq. ft.

Dine On The Deck

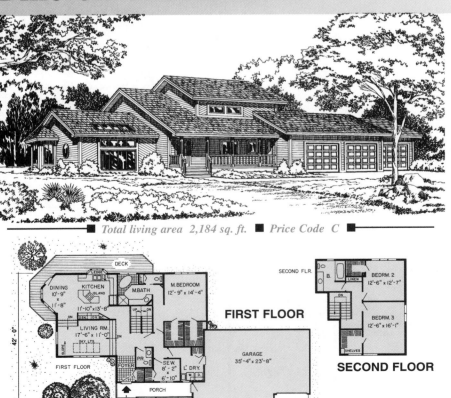

■ Total living area 2,184 sq. ft. ■ Price Code C ■

No. 10679

■ **This plan features:**

— Three bedrooms

— Two full and one half baths

■ A rear-facing Master Suite with his-n-her walk-in closets and a luxurious bath overlooking the deck

■ A sunken Living Room with expansive stacked windows and sloping ceilings

■ A range-top island Kitchen open to the Dining area

■ A Sewing Room, Laundry Room and large Garage

First floor — 1,445 sq. ft.
Second floor — 739 sq. ft.
Basement — 1,229 sq. ft.
Garage — 724 sq. ft.

An Old-Fashioned Country Feel

■ *Total living area 2,091 sq. ft.* ■ *Price Code C* ■

No. 93212

■ This plan features:

— Three bedrooms

— Two full and one half baths

■ Living Room with a cozy fireplace

■ A formal Dining Room with a bay window and direct access to the Sun Deck

■ U-shaped Kitchen efficiently arranged with ample work space

■ Master Suite with an elegant private bath complete with jacuzzi and a step-in shower

■ Two additional bedrooms, with ample closet space, share a full hall bath

■ A future Bonus Room to finish, tailored to your needs

■ An optional basement, crawl space or slab foundation — please specify when ordering

First floor — 1,362 sq. ft.
Second floor — 729 sq. ft.
Bonus room — 384 sq. ft.
Basement — 988 sq. ft.
Garage — 559 sq ft

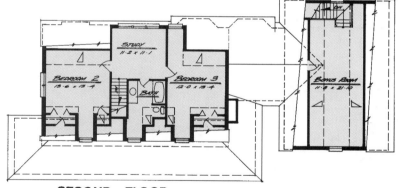

SECOND FLOOR

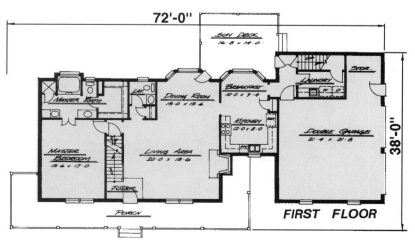

FIRST FLOOR

An EXCLUSIVE DESIGN
By Jannis Vann & Associates, Inc.

133

Balcony Offers Sweeping Views

■ *Total living area 3,746 sq. ft.* ■ *Price Code F* ■

DECK

SITTING
10'-6"
x
14'-6"

MASTER SUITE
22'-6"
x
18'-0"

OPEN TO BELOW

PAN. VAULT CLG.

DESK
BR. 2
12'-8"
x
12'-0"

BALCONY

BATH

VAN.

BR. 3
13'-8"
x
12'-3"
SEAT

RAILING

OPEN TO BELOW

SEAT

GUEST RM.
11'-3"
x
12'-6"
SEAT

SPA

BOOKS

SLOPE   SLOPE

SECOND FLOOR

DECK

3-SEASON PORCH
17'-4"
x
11'-8"

BRKFAST.
10'-8"
x
17'-8"

DN

GREAT RM.
14'-8"
x
21'-6"

KITCHEN
ISLAND

EATING BAR
11'-8" x 16'-8"

GARAGE
36'-8"
x
31'-4"

STUDY
12'-8"
x
12'-6"

2 STORY CLG. HT.

DESK
CHINA

L'DRY.

LIVING ROOM
13'-8"
x
15'-6"

DINING RM.
13'-8"
x
13'-9"

P.R.

BALC. ABOVE
FOYER

UP

FIRST FLOOR

93'-0"

54'-0"

No. 10778

■ **This plan features:**

— Three bedrooms

— Three and one half baths

■ A Living Room and a formal Dining Room located off the foyer

■ A convenient island Kitchen steps away from both the Dining Room and the Three Season Porch

■ A cozy Master Suite including a fireplace and large a bath area

First floor — 1,978 sq. ft
Second floor — 1,768 sq. ft.
Basement — 1,978 sq. ft.

Brick Opulence and Grandeur

■ *Total living area 3,921 sq. ft.* ■ *Price Code F* ■

No. 92248

■ This plan features:

- Four bedrooms

- Three full and one half baths

■ Dramatic two-story glass Entry with a curved staircase

■ Both Living and Family rooms offer high ceilings, decorative windows and large fireplaces

■ Large, but efficient Kitchen with a cooktop serving island, walk-in pantry, bright Breakfast area and Patio access

■ Lavish Master Bedroom with a cathedral ceiling, two walk-in closets, and large bath

■ Two additional bedrooms with ample closets, share a double vanity bath

First floor — 2,506 sq. ft.
Second floor — 1,415 sq. ft.
Garage — 660 sq. ft.

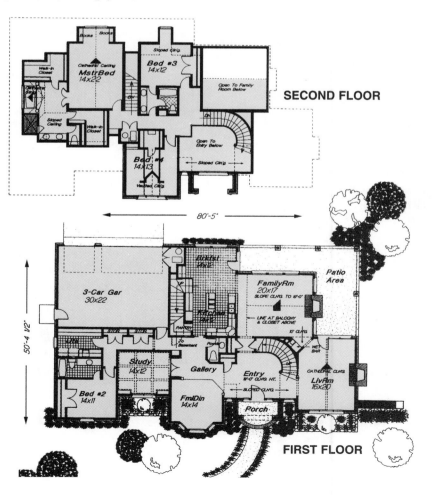

Appealing Farmhouse Design

© 1995 Donald A. Gardner Architects, Inc.

■ *Total living area 1,792 sq. ft.* ■ • *Price Code C* ■

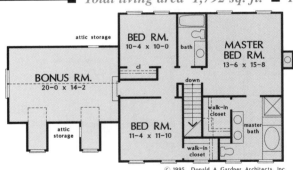

© 1995 Donald A Gardner Architects, Inc.

SECOND FLOOR PLAN

First floor — 959 sq. f.t
Second floor — 833 sq. ft.
Bonus room — 344 sq. ft.
Garage & storage — 500 sq. ft.

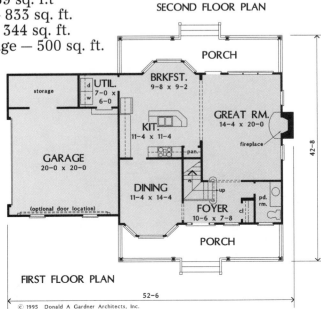

FIRST FLOOR PLAN

© 1995 Donald A Gardner Architects, Inc.

No. 99836

■ **This plan features:**

— Three bedrooms

— Two full and one half baths

■ Comfortable farmhouse features
an easy to build floor plan with all
the extras

■ Active families will enjoy the
Great Room which is open to the
Kitchen and Breakfast bay, as well
as expanded living space provided
by the full back porch

■ For narrower lot restrictions, the
Garage can be modified to open
in front

■ Second floor Master Bedroom
suite contains a walk-in closet and
a private bath with a garden tub
and separate shower

■ Two more bedrooms on the
second floor, one with a walk-in
closet, share a full bath

Double Gables and Exciting Entry

No. 92692

■ This plan features:

— Four bedrooms

— Two full and one half baths

■ Impressive exterior features double gables and arched window

■ Spacious foyer separates the formal Dining Room and Living Room

■ Roomy Kitchen and Breakfast Bay are adjacent to the large Family Room which has a fireplace and accesses the rear deck

■ Spacious Master Bedroom Suite features private bath with dual vanity, shower stall and whirlpool tub

■ Three additional bedroom share a full hall bath

■ No materials list is available for this plan

First floor — 1,207 sq. ft.
Second floor — 1,181 sq. ft.
Basement — 1,207 sq. ft.

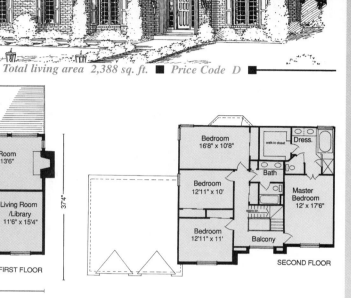

■ Total living area 2,388 sq. ft. ■ Price Code D ■

Year Round Indoor/Outdoor Living

No. 94204

■ This plan features:

— Three bedrooms

— Two full baths

■ A "piling" design with a Garage and Storage/Bonus area below the Living area for coastal, waterfront or low-lying terrain

■ An Entry Porch into an expansive Great Room with a hearth fireplace, a vaulted ceiling and double door to a Sundeck

■ An inviting Dining area with a vaulted ceiling and double door leading to the screened Veranda and Sundeck

■ An efficient Kitchen with a peninsula counter and adjacent Laundry

■ An airy Master Suite with a walk-in closet, double vanity and direct access to the outdoors

■ Another bedroom and a bedroom/loft area on the second floor sharing a full bath

■ No materials list is available for this plan

First floor — 1,189 sq. ft.
Second floor — 575 sq. ft.
Bonus room — 581 sq. ft.
Garage — 658 sq. ft.

■ Total living area 1,764 sq. ft. ■ Price Code B ■

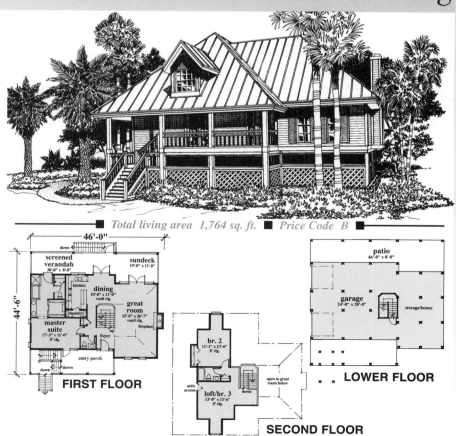

Regal Residence

Total living area 3,039 sq. ft. ■ *Price Code F* ■

No. 98405

■ **This plan features:**

— Five bedrooms

— Four full baths

■ Keystone, arched windows accent entrance into two-story Foyer

■ Spacious two-story Family Room enhanced by a fireplace

■ Kitchen with a cooktop island/serving bar and a walk-in pantry,

■ First floor Guest Room/Study with roomy closet and adjoining full bath

■ Luxurious Master Suite offers a tray ceiling, Sitting Area, a huge walk-in closet and a vaulted bath

■ Optional basement or crawl space foundation — please specify when ordering

First floor — 1,488 sq. ft.
Second floor — 1,551 sq. ft.
Garage — 667 sq. ft.

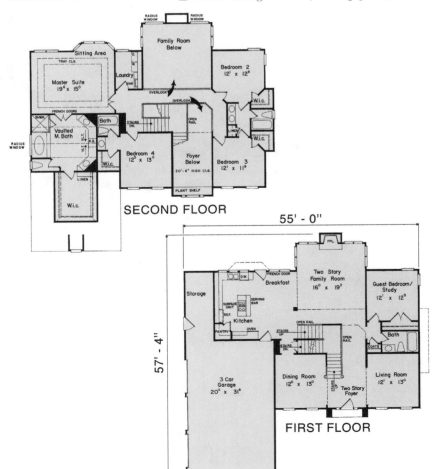

SECOND FLOOR

FIRST FLOOR

■ *Total living area 2,099 sq. ft.* ■ *Price Code C* ■

No. 91053

This plan features:

- Three bedrooms
- Two full and one half baths

■ A classic Victorian exterior design accented by a wonderful turret room and second floor covered porch above a sweeping veranda

■ A spacious formal Living Room

■ An efficient, U-shaped Kitchen with a peninsula snackbar, opens to an eating Nook and Family Room for informal gatherings

■ An elegant Master Suite with a unique, octagon Sitting area, a private Porch, an oversized, walk-in closet and private Bath with a double vanity and a window tub

■ Two bedrooms with ample closets sharing a full hall bath

First floor — 1,150 sq. ft.
Second floor — 949 sq. ft.
Garage — 484 sq. ft.

SECOND FLOOR

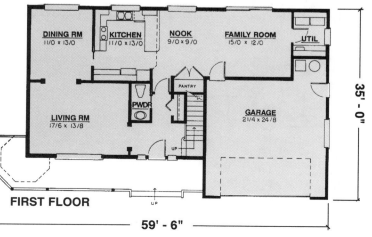

FIRST FLOOR

59' - 6"

35' - 0"

Soft Arches Accent Country Design

No. 94233

■ Total living area 2,527 sq. ft. ■ Price Code D ■

■ **This plan features:**

— Four or five bedrooms

— Two full and one half baths

■ Entry Porch with double dormers and doors enhances country charm

■ Pillared arches frame Foyer, Dining Room and Great Room

■ Open Great Room with optional built-ins and sliding glass doors to Verandah

■ Compact Kitchen with walk-in pantry and a counter/snackbar which opens to eating Nook and Great Room

■ Comfortable Master Suite with his-n-her closets and vanities and a garden tub

■ Corner Study/Bedroom with Lanai access offers multiple uses

■ An optional basement or slab foundation — please specify when ordering

■ No materials list is available for this plan

First floor — 1,676 sq. ft.
Second floor — 851 sq. ft.
Garage — 304 sq. ft.

Stature and Dignity

No. 96490

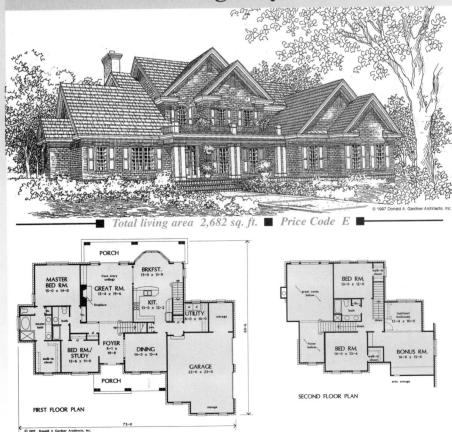

■ Total living area 2,682 sq. ft. ■ Price Code E ■

■ **This plan features:**

— Four bedrooms

— Three full baths

■ Multiple columns and gables add appeal to traditional style

■ Foyer and Great Room both have two-story ceilings and clerestory windows

■ Great Room highlighted by fireplace, built-in shelves and French doors to back Porch

■ Bright Breakfast bay accesses efficient Kitchen and back stairway to bedrooms and Bonus Room

■ Bedroom/Study and full bath near Master Bedroom suite offers multiple uses

■ This plan comes with a crawl space foundation

First floor — 2,067 sq. ft.
Second floor — 615 sq. ft.
Bonus room — 433 sq. ft.
Garage & storage — 729 sq. ft.

■ *Total living area 3,423 sq. ft.* ■ *Price Code F* ■

No. 98536

■ **This plan features:**

– Four bedrooms

– Two full and one half baths

■ Vaulted Master Bedroom has a private skylight bath and large walk in closet with a built in chest of drawers

■ Three more bedrooms (one possibly a Study) have walk-in closets and share a full bath

■ A loft and bonus room above the Living Room

■ Family Room has built-in book shelves, a fireplace, and overlooks the covered verandah in the backyard

■ The huge three car garage has a separate shop area

■ An optional slab or a crawl space foundation — please specify when ordering

First floor — 2,787 sq. ft.
Second floor — 636 sq. ft.

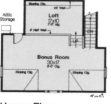

Upper Floor
Optional Bonus Room & Loft

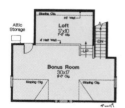

Upper Floor

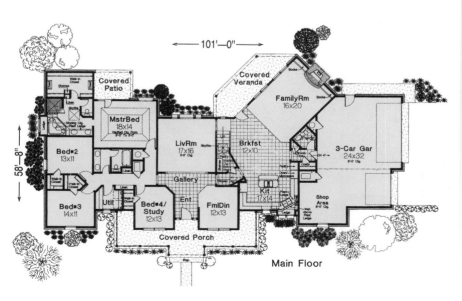

Main Floor

Comfortable Vacation Living

■ *Total living area 2,017 sq. ft.* ■ *Price Code C* ■

SECOND FLOOR

DECK
12⁰ x 22⁰

LOFT
11¹⁰ x 20⁶

ATTIC ACCESS

WALK-IN CLOSET

DN

OPEN TO BELOW

WIDTH 58'-0"
DEPTH 48'-0"

CARPORT
22⁰ x 12⁰

KITCHEN

WSH DRY

UTILITY

SINK

FAU

WALK-IN CLOSET

WALK-IN CLOSET

SHOWER

SHOWER

EATING BAR

BEDROOM
15⁸ x 15⁰

BEDROOM
15⁸ x 15⁰

DINING
9⁶ x 10⁶

UP

UP

UP FIREPLACE
RAISED HEARTH

LIVING ROOM
25⁰ x 16⁶

DECK

FIRST FLOOR

No. 98714 ⌧

■ **This plan features:**

— Three bedrooms

— Three full and one half baths

■ A wrap-around Deck offering views and access into the Living Room

■ A sunken Living Room with a vaulted ceiling, and a raised-hearth fireplace adjoining the Dining area

■ An open Kitchen with a corner sink and windows, an eating bar and a walk-in storage/pantry

■ Two private Bedroom suites with sliding glass doors leading to a Deck, walk-in closets and plush baths

■ A Loft area with a walk-in closet, attic access, and a private bath and a Deck

First floor — 1,704 sq ft
Second floor — 313 sq. ft.

Economical Vacation Home With Viewing Deck

■ *Total living area 1,288 sq. ft.* ■ *Price Code A* ■

No. 99238 ☒

■ **This plan features:**

– Three bedrooms

– Two full baths

■ A large rectangular Living Room with a fireplace at one end and plenty of room for separate activities at the other end

■ A galley-style Kitchen with adjoining Dining area

■ A second-floor Master Bedroom with a children's dormitory across the hall

■ A second-floor deck outside the Master Bedroom

First floor — 784 sq. ft.
Second floor — 504 sq. ft.

SECOND FLOOR

FIRST FLOOR

Compact and Convenient Colonial

■ *Total living area 1,248 sq. ft.* ■ *Price Code A* ■

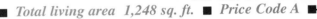

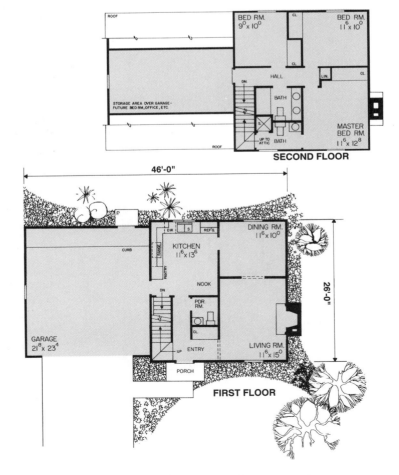

No. 99255

■ **This plan features:**

— Three bedrooms

— Two full and one half baths

■ Traditional Entry with landing staircase, closet and powder room

■ Living Room with focal point fireplace opens to formal Dining Room for ease in entertaining

■ Efficient, L-shaped Kitchen with built-in pantry, eating Nook and Garage entry

■ Corner Master Bedroom with private bath and attic access

■ Two additional bedrooms with ample closets share a double vanity bath

First floor — 624 sq. ft.
Second floor — 624 sq. ft.
Garage — 510 sq. ft.

Luxuriously Styled Exterior

No. 92691

■ This plan features:

— Four bedrooms

— Three full and one half baths

■ Stylish exterior with wood and stone trim and an octagonal tower

■ Great Room has high windows, a fireplace and a volume ceiling

■ Formal Dining Room adjacent to the Kitchen

■ Spacious Breakfast Room opens to the charming Hearth Room

■ Master Suite has a sitting alcove and a deluxe bath

■ Second floor features a bedroom suite with private bath and two additional bedrooms share a third full bath

■ No materials list is available for this plan

First floor — 1,915 sq. ft.
Second floor — 823 sq. ft.
Basement — 1,915 sq. ft.

■ Total living area 2,738 sq. ft. ■ Price Code D ■

Beautiful Arched Windows

No. 93920

■ This plan features:

— Three bedrooms

— Two full and one half baths

■ Tiled foyer leads into the Den and formal Living Room featuring a bay window

■ Efficient Kitchen has an island and easily accesses the formal Dining Room

■ Family Room with a fireplace, and the Breakfast Room are open to the Kitchen creating a wide open area

■ Master Suite includes a walk-in closet and five piece bath

■ Two additional bedrooms share a full hall bath

■ No materials list is available for this plan

First floor — 1,261 sq. ft.
Second floor — 818 sq. ft.
Basement — 1,184 sq. ft.

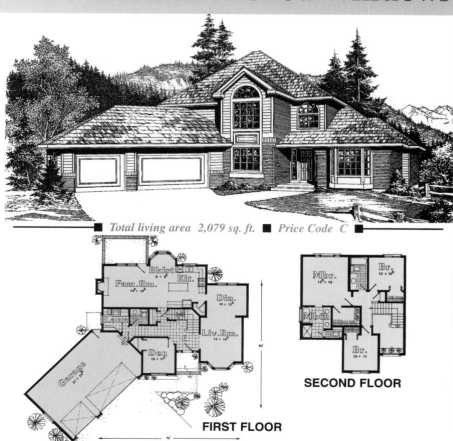

■ Total living area 2,079 sq. ft. ■ Price Code C ■

An
EXCLUSIVE DESIGN
By Independent Designs

Arches Enhance Style

■ *Total living area 3,393 sq. ft.* ■ *Price Code F* ■

Second floor

© Carmichael & Dame

Optional Basement Access

First floor

79'-9 1/2"

53'-11'

No. 99442

■ This plan features:

— Four bedrooms

— Three full and one half baths

■ Open layout of rooms separated by arched openings

■ Living Room is graced by a fireplace and adjoins the Dining Room

■ Family Room has a second fireplace and is open to the Breakfast Nook and Kitchen

■ A mid level Study is brightened by a large front window

■ This plan has four huge Bedrooms and three full Baths upstairs

First floor — 1,786 sq. ft.
Second floor — 1,607 sq. ft
Garage — 682 sq. ft.

146

■ *Total living area 2,483 sq. ft.* ■ *Price Code D* ■

No. 99269

■ This plan features:

– Three bedrooms

– Two full and one half baths

■ Imposing columns highlight entrance into central Foyer

■ Expansive Drawing Room with huge fireplace and access to Garden Terrace

■ Open Family Room with a sliding glass door to Terrace, conveniently located

■ Efficient Kitchen with serving counter/snackbar, Laundry and Garage entry

■ Corner Master Bedroom offers a double vanity bath with a whirlpool window tub

■ Two additional bedrooms share a double vanity bath

First floor — 1,507 sq. ft.
Second floor — 976 sq. ft.
Garage — 454 sq. ft.

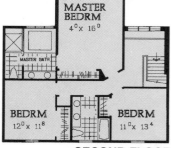

SECOND FLOOR

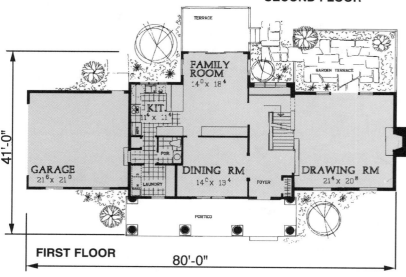

FIRST FLOOR

Spacious Kitchen Completes Special Design

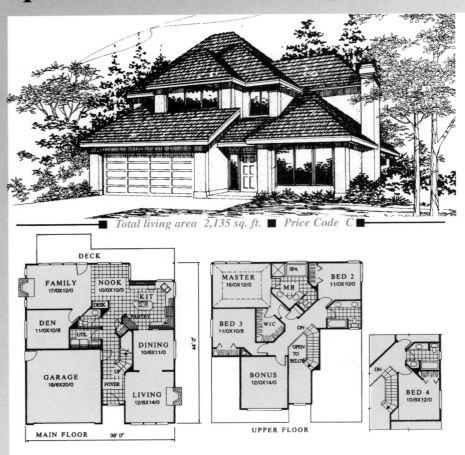

Total living area 2,135 sq. ft. ■ Price Code C

MAIN FLOOR 39' 0"

UPPER FLOOR

No. 91654

■ This plan features:

— Three or four bedrooms

— Two or three full baths and one half bath

■ A picture window and fireplace accent the Living Room

■ An island Kitchen with a built-in pantry, corner double sink, built-in desk and a sunny eating Nook

■ A spacious Family Room with a cozy fireplace and direct access to the deck

■ A Master Suite with a decorative ceiling, walk-in closet, and a private Master Bath

■ Two (optional three) additional bedrooms with easy access to a full hall bath

First floor — 1,233 sq. ft.
Second floor — 902 sq. ft.
Bonus room — 168 sq. ft.

Impressive Family Home

Total living area 3,674 sq. ft. ■ Price Code F

WIDTH 100'-7"
DEPTH 67'-10"

FIRST FLOOR

SECOND FLOOR

No. 92656

■ This plan features:

— Four bedrooms

— Three full and one half baths

■ Expansive Foyer with steps leading to Gallery and Great Room framed with pillar

■ Both the Library and Dining Room highlighted by decorative windows

■ Circular Kitchen with walk-in pantry, snackbar, spacious Breakfast area with Deck access and nearby Hearth Room, Laundry and Garage

■ Cozy Hearth Room highlighted by second fireplace, furniture alcove and sloped ceiling

■ Master Bedroom wing offers a sloped ceiling, luxurious bath and a large, walk-in closet

■ Three second floor bedrooms with ample closets and private access to a full bath

■ No materials list is available for this plan

First floor — 2,710 sq. ft.
Second floor — 964 sq. ft.
Basement — 2,700 sq. ft.

Spacious Elegance

■ *Total living area 2,349 sq. ft.* ■ *Price Code D* ■

No. 98455

■ This plan features:

- Four bedrooms

- Three full baths

- ■ The two-story Foyer with palladian window illuminates a lovely staircase and the Dining Room entry way

- ■ The Family Room has a vaulted ceiling and an inviting fireplace

- ■ Vaulted ceiling and a radius window highlight the Breakfast area and the efficient Kitchen

- ■ The Master Bedroom suite boasts a tray ceiling, luxurious bath and a walk-in closet

- ■ An optional basement or crawl space foundation — please specify when ordering

First floor — 1,761 sq. ft.
Second floor — 588 sq. ft.
Bonus Room — 267 sq. ft.
Garage — 435 sq. ft.

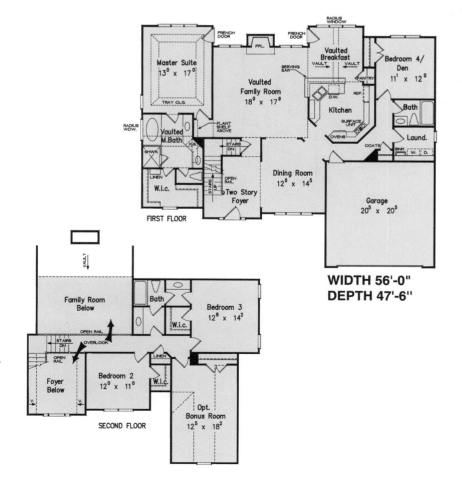

WIDTH 56'-0"
DEPTH 47'-6"

Family-Sized Accommodations

■ *Total living area 1,874 sq. ft.* ■ *Price Code C* ■

No. 98454

■ This plan features:

— Four bedrooms

— Two full and one half baths

■ A spacious feeling provided by a vaulted ceiling in Foyer

■ A fireplace is nestled by an alcove of windows in the Family Room

■ An angled Kitchen with a work island and a pantry easily serves the Breakfast area and the Dining Room

■ The Master Bedroom is accented by a tray ceiling, a lavish bath and a walk-in closet

■ An optional basement or crawl space foundation — please specify when ordering

First floor — 1,320 sq. ft.
Second floor — 554 sq. ft.
Bonus room — 155 sq. ft.
Garage — 406 sq. ft.

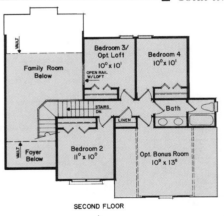

SECOND FLOOR

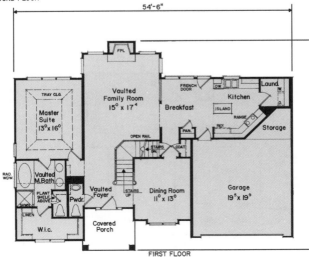

FIRST FLOOR

■ *Total living area 3,381 sq. ft.* ■ ● *Price Code F* ■

No. 98514

■ This plan features:

- Five bedrooms

- Three full and one half baths

■ The Entry/Gallery features a grand spiral staircase

■ The Study has built in book cases centered between a window

■ Formal Living and Dining rooms each have palladian windows

■ The large Family Room has a fireplace

■ The first floor Master Bedroom has a bath with a cathedral ceiling

■ An optional slab or crawl space foundation — please specify when ordering

First floor — 2,208 sq. ft.
Second floor — 1,173 sq. ft.
Bonus — 224 sq. ft.
Garage — 520 sq. ft.

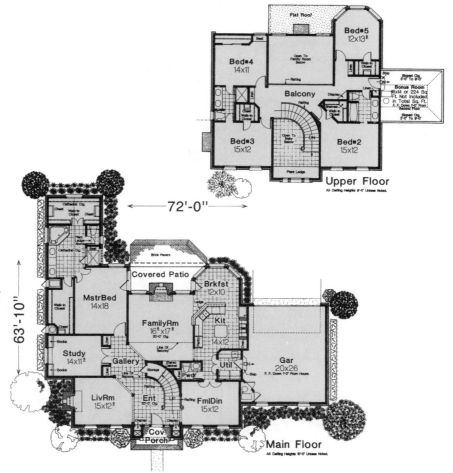

Impressive Fieldstone Facade

■ *Total living area 3,110 sq. ft.* ■ *Price Code E* ■

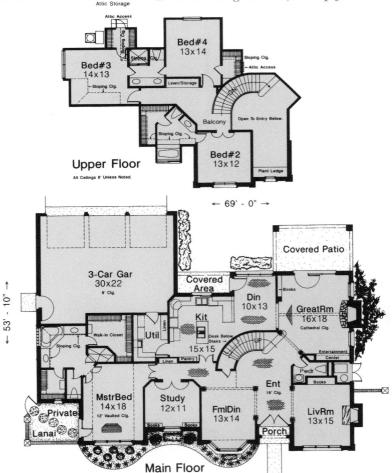

Attic Storage

Attic Access

Bed#4
13x14

Bed#3
14x13

Sloping Clg.

Attic Access

Linen/Storage

Sloping Clg.

Balcony

Open To Entry Below.

Sloping Clg.

Bed#2
13x12

Plant Ledge

Upper Floor

All Ceilings 8' Unless Noted.

← 69' - 0" →

← 53' - 10" →

3-Car Gar
30x22
8' Clg.

Covered Patio

Covered Area

Din
10x13

Books

GreatRm
16x18
Cathedral Clg.

Kit
15x15

Walk-In Closet

Util

Desk Below Stairs

Sloping Clg

Linen

Pantry

Entertainment Center

MstrBed
14x18
12' Vaulted Clg.

Study
12x11

FmlDin
13x14

Ent
19' Clg.

Pwdr

Books

Private

Lanai

LivRm
13x15

Books

Porch

Main Floor

No. 92277

■ **This plan features:**

— Four bedrooms

— Three full and one half baths

■ Double door leads into two-story entry with an exquisite curved staircase

■ Formal Living Room features a marble hearth fireplace, triple window and built-in book shelves

■ Formal Dining Room defined by columns and a lovely bay window

■ Expansive Great Room with entertainment center, fieldstone fireplace, cathedral ceiling

■ Vaulted ceiling crowns Master Bedroom suite offering a plush bath and two walk-in closets

■ Three more bedrooms, one with private bath, have walk-in closets

Main floor — 2,190 sq. ft.
Upper floor — 920 sq. ft.
Garage — 624 sq. ft.

Roof Garden Delight

No. 94304

This plan features:

- Three bedrooms

- Two full baths

- A tiled Entry Court leading into the Foyer and setting a southwestern theme

- A Living/Dining area with a corner fireplace, window walls and access to a Patio

- An efficient, U-shaped Kitchen with an eating bar and laundry area

- Two first floor bedrooms sharing a full bath

- A second floor Master Bedroom with a double closet, built-in shelves, a private bath and direct access to the Roof Garden

- No materials list is available for this plan

First floor — 981 sq. ft.

Second floor — 396 sq. ft.

An EXCLUSIVE DESIGN *By Marshall Associates*

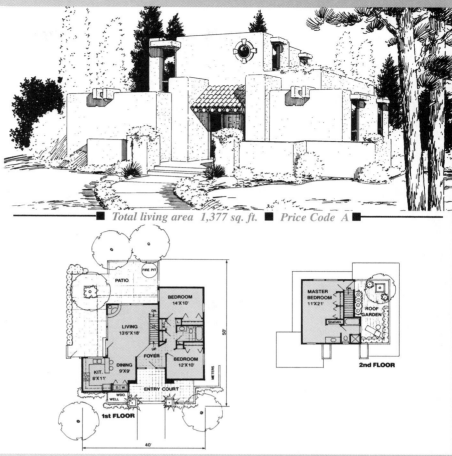

■ *Total living area 1,377 sq. ft.* ■ *Price Code A* ■

Isolated Master Suite

No. 90420

This plan features:

- Three bedrooms

- Two full and one half baths

- A spacious, sunken Living Room with a cathedral ceiling

- An isolated Master Suite with a private bath and walk-in closet

- Two additional bedrooms with a unique bath-and-a-half and ample storage space

- An efficient U-shaped Kitchen with a double sink, ample cabinets, counter space and a Breakfast area

- A second floor Studio overlooking the Living Room

- An optional basement, slab or crawl space foundation — please specify when ordering

First floor — 2,213 sq. ft.

Second floor — 260 sq. ft.

Basement — 2,213 sq. ft.

Garage — 422 sq. ft.

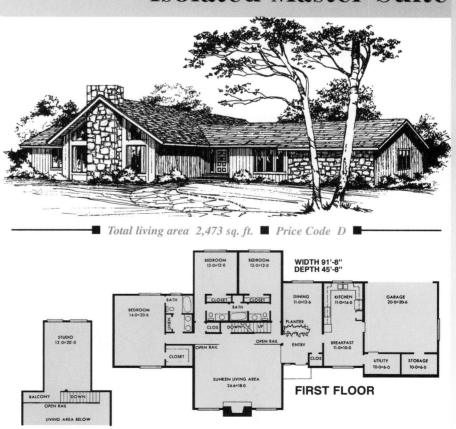

■ *Total living area 2,473 sq. ft.* ■ *Price Code D* ■

Lots of Space in this Small Package

■ *Total living area 1,283 sq. ft.* ■ *Price Code A* ■

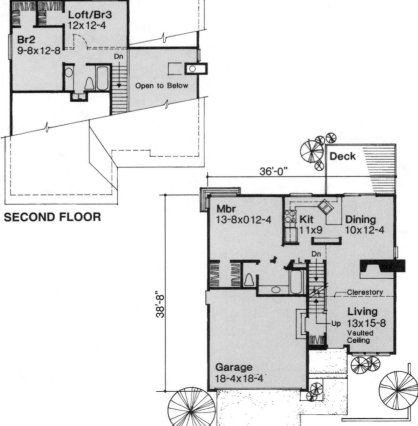

SECOND FLOOR

Loft/Br3
12x12-4

Br2
9-8x12-8

Dn

Open to Below

36'-0"

Deck

38'-8"

Mbr
13-8x012-4

Kit
11x9

Dining
10x12-4

Dn

Clerestory

Living
13x15-8
Vaulted Ceiling

Up

Garage
18-4x18-4

FIRST FLOOR

No. 90378

■ **This plan features:**

— Two bedrooms with possible third bedroom/loft

— Two full baths

■ A Living Room with dynamic, soaring angles and a fireplace

■ A first floor Master Suite with full bath and walk in-closet

■ Walk-in closets in all bedrooms

First floor — 878 sq. ft.
Second floor — 405 sq. ft.

Veranda Mirrors Two-Story Bay

■ *Total living area 4,217 sq. ft.* ■ *Price Code F* ■

No. 10780

■ **This plan features:**

- Four bedrooms

- Two and one half baths

■ A huge foyer flanked by the formal Parlor and Dining Room

■ An island Kitchen with an adjoining pantry

■ A Breakfast bay and sunken Gathering Room located at the rear of the home

■ Double doors opening to the Master Suite and the book-lined Master Retreat

■ An elegant Master Bath including a raised tub and adjoining cedar closet

First floor — 2,108 sq. ft.
Second floor — 2,109 sq. ft.
Basement — 1,946 sq. ft.
Garage — 764 sq. ft.

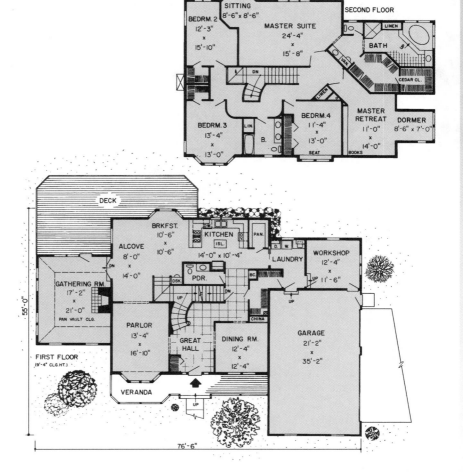

Welcoming Style

No. 94001

■ This plan features:

— Four bedrooms

— Two full and one half baths

■ Tiled Entry accented by an angled staircase

■ Beautiful bay windows illuminate sunken Living Room and formal Dining Room

■ Well-designed Kitchen with built-in pantry, serving bar and Bistro

■ Family Room offers a cozy fireplace and sliding glass doors to Deck

■ Master Bedroom enhanced by window seat, private bath and a large walk-in closet

■ No materials list available

■ An optional basement or crawl space foundation — please specify when ordering

First floor — 947 sq. ft.
Second floor — 752 sq. ft.
Garage — 440 sq. ft.

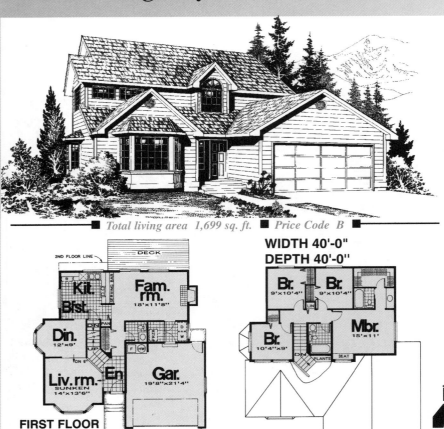

Total living area 1,699 sq. ft. ■ *Price Code B* ■

WIDTH 40'-0"
DEPTH 40'-0"

FIRST FLOOR

SECOND FLOOR

An **EXCLUSIVE DESIGN** *By* **CRANE DESIGN** inc.

Vaulted Ceilings Make Every Room Special

No. 10698

■ This plan features:

— Five bedrooms

— Five full baths

■ An enjoyable view from the island Kitchen which is separated from the Morning Room by only a counter

■ Access to the pool from the covered patio or from the Living and Family Rooms

■ The Living and Family Rooms with beamed ten-foot ceilings and massive fireplaces

■ A Master Suite with a raised tub, built-in dressing tables and a fireplaced Sitting room with vaulted ceiling

First floor — 4,014 sq. ft.
Second floor — 727 sq. ft.
Garage — 657 sq. ft.

Total living area 4,741 sq. ft. ■ *Price Code F* ■

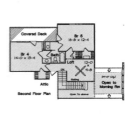

■ *Total living area 1,792 sq. ft.* ■ *Price Code B* ■

No. 94105

■ **This plan features:**

- Three bedrooms

- Two full and one half bath

■ Covered Entry into two-story Foyer with a dramatic landing staircase brightened by decorative window

■ Spacious Living/Dining Room combination with hearth fireplace and decorative windows

■ Hub Kitchen with built-in pantry and informal Dining area with sliding glass door to rear yard

■ First floor Master Bedroom offers a walk-in closet, dressing area and full bath

■ Two additional bedrooms on second floor share a full bath

■ No materials list is available for this plan

First floor — 1,281 sq. ft.
Second floor — 511 sq. ft.
Garage — 467 sq. ft.

WIDTH 58'-0"
DEPTH 44'-0"

DIN RM
11'8 x 11'11

KIT
9'8 x 11'7

DW

DIN
8'8 x 11'5

MBR
15'8 x 13'5

MBATH

PANTRY

REF

Dress'g

LIV RM
15' x 13'8

Mud Rm/Entry

Lav

WI Closet

Two-Story
FOYER

W
D

Laun

COUNTER

GARAGE
21'4 x 21'8

Covered Entry

FIRST FLOOR

BR3
11' x 11'7

BATH 2

Foyer Below

BR2
11'4 x 11'11

SECOND FLOOR

Eye Catching Tower

■ *Total living area 3,323 sq. ft.* ■ *Price Code E* ■

© Carmichael & Dame

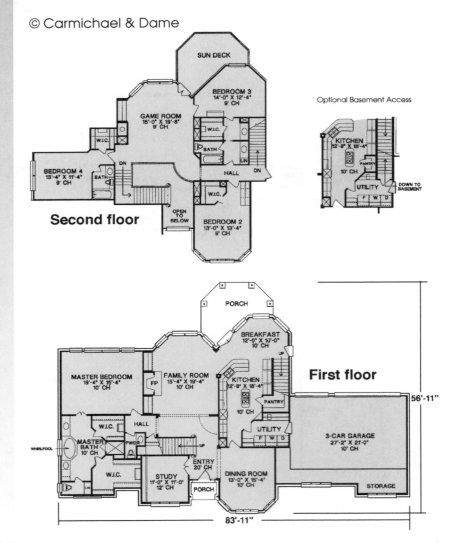

SUN DECK

BEDROOM 3
14'-0" X 12'-4"
9' CH

GAME ROOM
15'-0" X 19'-8"
9' CH

W.I.C.

BATH

BEDROOM 4
13'-4" X 11'-4"
9' CH

BATH

W.I.C.

DN

HALL

LIN

DN

W.I.C.

Second floor

OPEN TO BELOW

BEDROOM 2
13'-0" X 13'-4"
9' CH

Optional Basement Access

KITCHEN
12'-8" X 18'-4"

PANTRY

10' CH

UTILITY

DOWN TO BASEMENT

F W D

PORCH

BREAKFAST
12'-0" X 10'-0"
10' CH

UP

MASTER BEDROOM
19'-4" X 15'-4"
10' CH

FP

FAMILY ROOM
15'-4" X 19'-4"
10' CH

KITCHEN
12'-8" X 18'-4"

First floor

PANTRY

10' CH

W.I.C.

HALL

PWDR

UP

UTILITY

F W D

3-CAR GARAGE
27'-2" X 21'-0"
10' CH

56'-11"

MASTER BATH
10' CH

WHIRLPOOL

W.I.C.

LIN

STUDY
11'-0" X 11'-0"
12' CH

ENTRY
20' CH

DINING ROOM
13'-0" X 15'-4"
10' CH

STORAGE

PORCH

83'-11"

No. 99438

■ **This plan features:**

— Four bedrooms

— Four full and one half baths

■ Dining Room with bay perfect for special dinner parties

■ Study with high ceiling and windows

■ Family Room with fireplace is open to the Breakfast Bay and gourmet Kitchen

■ First floor Master Bedrooms span the width of the home and contains every luxury imaginable

■ Located upstairs are three bedrooms, a Game Room, a Sun Deck and two full baths

■ This plan has a three car garage with storage space

First floor — 2,117 sq. ft.
Second floor — 1,206 sq. ft.
Garage — 685 sq. ft.

■ *Total living area 3,480 sq. ft.* ■ *Price Code F* ■

No. 98508

■ This plan features:

- Four bedrooms

- Three full and one half baths

■ Formal Living and Dining rooms gracefully defined with columns and decorative windows

■ Wood plank flooring and a massive fireplace accent the Great Room

■ Hub Kitchen with brick pavers, extended serving counter, bright Breakfast area

■ Private Master Bedroom offers a Private Lanai and plush dressing area

■ Three second floor bedrooms with walk-in closets and private access to a full bath

Main floor — 2,441 sq. ft.
Upper floor — 1,039 sq. ft.
Bonus — 271 sq. ft.
Garage — 660 sq. ft.

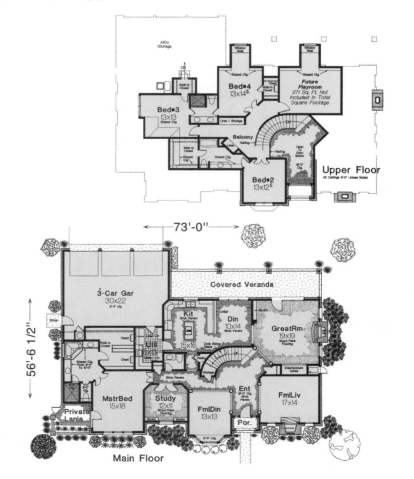

Imposing and Practical Design

■ *Total living area 2,085 sq. ft.* ■ *Price Code C* ■

FIRST FLOOR

SECOND FLOOR

No. 93213

■ **This plan features:**

— Three bedrooms

— Two full and one half baths

■ Bay windows illuminate formal Dining and Living Rooms

■ Family Room with cozy fireplace and a wall of windows

■ Efficient, U-shaped Kitchen

■ Private Master Bedroom crowned by decorative ceiling, features a walk-in closet, two vanities and garden tub bath

■ Two additional bedrooms, full bath and convenient laundry closet complete second floor

■ An optional basement or slab foundation — please specify when ordering

■ No materials list available

First floor — 1,126 sq. ft.
Second floor — 959 sq. ft
Basement — 458 sq. ft.
Garage — 627 sq. ft.

An
EXCLUSIVE DESIGN
By Jannis Vann & Associates, Inc.

Stately Elegance

No. 92603

This plan features:

- Four bedrooms

- Two full and one half baths

- Varied roof line, brick, and window details add to the stately elegance of this home

- Two-story Foyer opens into the Dining Room and the sunken Living Room

- First floor Master Suite has a unique ceiling and a private bath illuminated by a skylight

- The second floor has a balcony that is open to the Foyer and Family Room below it

- The second floor also contains three large bedrooms and a full bath

- A two car garage is connected to the home by a hallway that also leads to the Laundry Room

- No materials list is available for this plan

First level — 2,017 sq. ft.
Second level — 772 sq. ft.

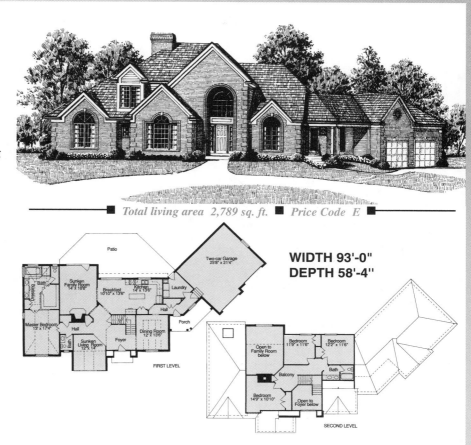

■ *Total living area* 2,789 *sq. ft.* ■ *Price Code* E ■

WIDTH 93'-0"
DEPTH 58'-4"

Reminiscent of the Deep South

No. 94713 ✕

This plan features:

- Three bedrooms

- Two full and one half baths

- Victorian Porch leads into Foyer and two-story Great Room with a focal point fireplace

- Efficient, U-shaped Kitchen opens to Great Room and Dining Room

- Private Master Suite with triple windows, walk-in closet and luxurious bath with a double vanity and garden window tub

- Two second floor bedrooms with large closets, share a full bath and Loft

First floor — 1,350 sq. ft.
Second floor — 589 sq. ft.

■ *Total living area* 1,939 *sq. ft.* ■ *Price Code* C ■

SECOND FLOOR

FIRST FLOOR

Traditional Elegance

■ *Total living area 3,813 sq. ft.* ■ *Price Code F* ■

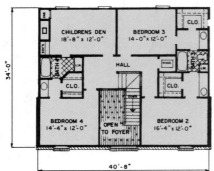

SECOND FLOOR PLAN

FIRST FLOOR PLAN

No. 92504

■ This plan features:

— Four bedrooms

— Three full and one half baths

■ A elegant entrance leading into a two story Foyer

■ Floor to ceiling windows in the formal Living and Dining Rooms

■ A spacious Den with a hearth fireplace, built-in book shelves, a wetbar and a wall of windows

■ A Kitchen equipped with a bright Breakfast area and a walk-in pantry

■ A grand Master Suite with decorative ceilings, a private Porch, and two walk-in closets

■ An optional crawl space or slab foundation — please specify whe ordering

First floor — 2,553 sq. ft.
Second floor — 1,260 sq. ft.
Garage — 714 sq. ft.

Distinguished Dwelling

■ *Total living area 2,733 sq. ft.* ■ *Price Code E* ■

No. 94112

This plan features:

- Four bedrooms

- Two full and one half baths

- Grand two-story Entry into Foyer with a lovely landing staircase

- Living Room with a decorative window and a vaulted ceiling

- Beautiful bay window highlights formal Dining Room

- Convenient Kitchen with cooktop work island, pantry, octagon Dining area, and nearby Study, Laundry and Garage entry

- Luxurious Master Bedroom offers a glass alcove, walk-in closet and pampering bath with a corner tub

- Three bedrooms with decorative windows, share a full bath

- No materials list available

First floor — 1,514 sq. ft.
Second floor — 1,219 sq. ft.

First Floor Master Suite

No. 94613

■ **This plan features:**

— Four bedrooms

— Three full and one half baths

■ Welcoming country porch adds to appeal and living space

■ Central Foyer provides ventilation and access to all areas of home

■ Spacious Living Room enhanced by fireplace and access to Covered Porch

■ Efficient Kitchen with work island, built-in pantry, Utility room, Garage entry and Breakfast area

■ Spacious Master Bedroom suite with a pampering, private bath

■ Three second floor bedrooms with walk-in closets, share two full baths and a Game Room

■ An optional crawl space or slab foundation — please specify when ordering

■ No materials list is available for this plan

First floor — 1,492 sq. ft.
Second floor — 865 sq. ft.
Bonus — 303 sq. ft.
Garage — 574 sq. ft.

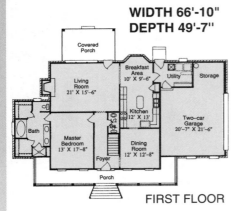

■ *Total living area 2,357 sq. ft.* ■ *Price Code D* ■

WIDTH 66'-10"
DEPTH 49'-7"

FIRST FLOOR

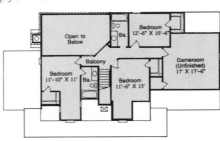

SECOND FLOOR

Flowing Floor Plan

No. 96415

■ **This plan features:**

— Four bedrooms

— Three full baths

■ Welcoming Foyer leads into the Living Room that is topped by a tray ceiling

■ Columns define the Great Room and the Dining Room for an elegant look

■ Balcony overlooks the Great Room with a volume ceiling and an inviting fireplace

■ Spacious Kitchen with a cooktop work island, a Breakfast bay and a nearby Utility/Garage

■ Corner Master Bedroom suite offers a tray ceiling, walk-in closet and a deluxe bath

■ Second floor bedrooms share a full bath

First floor — 2,184 sq. ft.
Second floor — 678 sq. ft.
Bonus Room — 353 sq. ft.
Garage & Storage — 578 sq. ft.

■ *Total living area 2,862 sq. ft.* ■ *Price Code E* ■

FIRST FLOOR PLAN

SECOND FLOOR PLAN

Updated Tudor

■ *Total living area 3,063 sq. ft.* ■ *Price Code E* ■

No. 20076 ✕ *An* EXCLUSIVE DESIGN *By Karl Kreeger*

■ **This plan features:**

- Four bedrooms

- Two full and one three-quarter baths

■ Two-story Foyer with a lovely, landing staircase

■ Formal rooms enhanced by decorative windows and ceilings

■ Expansive Family Room with a high ceiling, and a fireplace

■ Kitchen with a cooktop island/snackbar, walk-in pantry, and nearby Utility/Garage entry

■ Master Bedroom offers decorative windows, a walk-in closet, double vanity and whirlpool tub

■ Three bedrooms with walk-in closets and private bath access

First floor — 2,030 sq. ft.

Second floor — 1,033 sq. ft.

Basement — 2,030 sq. ft.

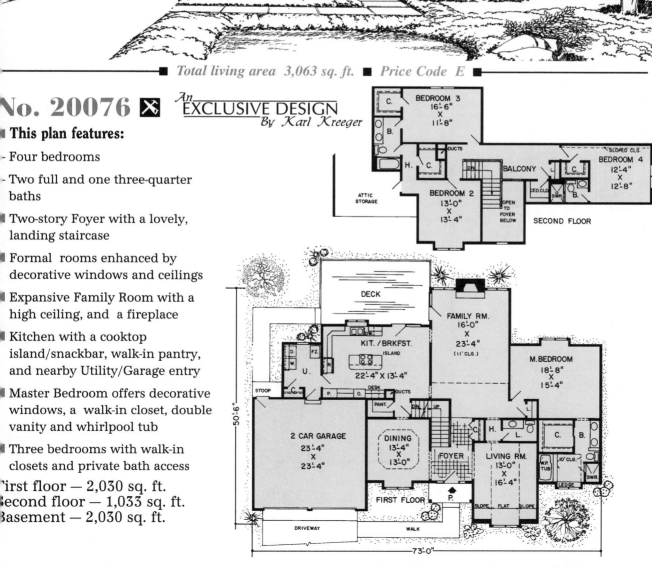

Compact Victorian Ideal for Narrow Lot

■ *Total living area 1,737 sq. ft.* ■ *Price Code B* ■

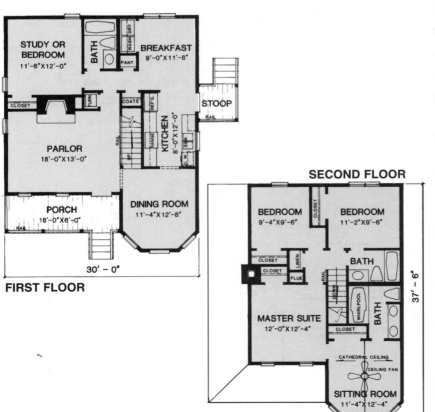

FIRST FLOOR

STUDY OR BEDROOM 11'-6"X12'-0"

BATH

BREAKFAST 9'-0"X11'-8"

CLOSET

FURN.

COATS

REFG.

STOOP

RAIL

PARLOR 18'-0"X13'-0"

KITCHEN 8'-0"X12'-0"

RANGE

SINK

UP

PORCH 18'-0"X6'-0"

DINING ROOM 11'-4"X12'-8"

30' - 0"

SECOND FLOOR

BEDROOM 9'-4"X9'-6"

BEDROOM 11'-2"X9'-6"

CLOSET

CLOSET

CLOSET

LINEN

BATH

FLUE

MASTER SUITE 12'-0"X12'-4"

WHIRLPOOL

BATH

CLOSET

37' - 6"

CATHEDRAL CEILING

CEILING FAN

SITTING ROOM 11'-4"X12'-4"

No. 90406

■ This plan features:

— Three bedrooms

— Three full baths

■ A large, front Parlor with a raised hearth fireplace

■ A Dining Room with a sunny bay window

■ An efficient galley Kitchen serving the formal Dining Room and informal Breakfast Room

■ A beautiful Master Suite with two closets, an oversized tub and double vanity, plus a private sitting room with a bayed window and vaulted ceiling

■ An optional basement, slab or crawl space foundation — please specify when ordering

First floor — 954 sq. ft.
Second floor — 783 sq. ft.

■ *Total living area 1,772 sq. ft.* ■ *Price Code B* ■

No. 94203

■ This plan features:

- Two bedrooms

- Two full baths

■ A covered Entry Porch leading into a spacious Great Room

■ Great Room with a vaulted ceiling, cozy fireplace and double door to the Veranda

■ An efficient, L-shaped Kitchen with a work island and Dining area with a double door to the Sundeck

■ Study and secondary bedroom with ample closet space share a full bath

■ A private, second floor Master Suite with an oversized walk-in closet and luxurious bath

■ No materials list is available for this plan

First floor — 1,136 sq. ft.
Second floor — 636 sq. ft.
Garage — 526 sq. ft.

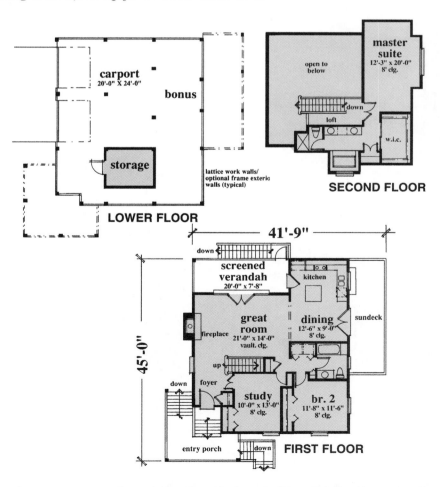

Classic Country Farmhouse

© 1992 Donald A Gardner Architects, Inc.

■ *Total living area 1,663 sq. ft.* ■ *Price Code C* ■

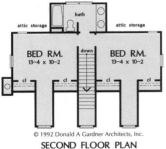

© 1992 Donald A Gardner Architects, Inc.
SECOND FLOOR PLAN

First floor — 1,145 sq. ft.
Second floor — 518 sq. ft.
Bonus room — 380 sq. ft.
Garage & storage — 509 sq. ft.

No. 99800 ✕

■ **This plan features:**

— Three bedrooms

— Two full and one half baths

■ Covered Porch gives classic country farmhouse look, and includes multiple dormers, a grea[t] layout for entertaining, and a Bonus Room

■ Clerestory dormer window bathe[s] the two-story Foyer in natural light

■ Large Great Room with fireplace opens to the Dining/Breakfast/Kitchen space, which leads to a spacious Deck with optional spa and seating for easy indoor/outdoor entertaining

■ First floor Master Bedroom suite offers privacy and luxury with a separate shower, whirlpool tub, and a double vanity

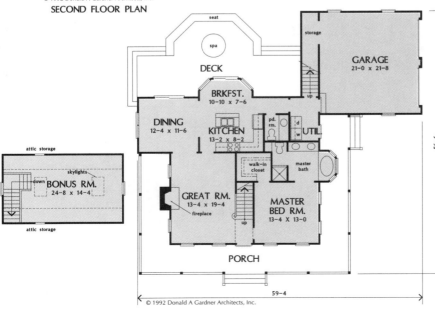

© 1992 Donald A Gardner Architects, Inc.
FIRST FLOOR PLAN

A Spacious Abode with Plenty of Growing Room

No. 10802

This plan features:

– Three bedrooms

– Two full and one half baths

■ A central foyer creating a dazzling impression for entering guests

■ Formal Living and Dining Rooms overlooking the front yard for elegant entertaining

■ A Family Room with a fireplace, built in bar, and bookcases

■ An island Kitchen designed for the modern two-cook family

■ An adjoining rear deck as a great place for a barbecue

■ A Master Suite with a sunny well-appointed bath, walk-in closet, and sky-lit secret room over the three car Garage

First floor — 1,522 sq. ft.
Second floor — 1,545 sq. ft.

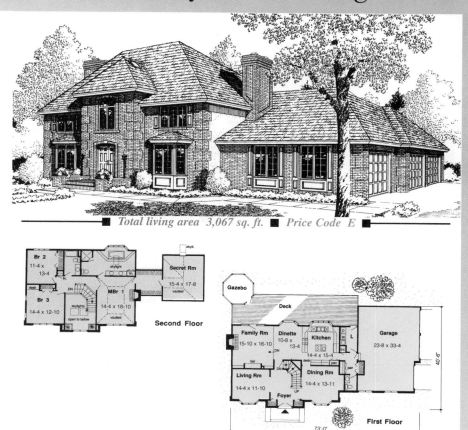

■ *Total living area 3,067 sq. ft.* ■ *Price Code E* ■

Country Living in a Doll House

No. 90410

This plan features:

– Three bedrooms

– Two full and one half baths

■ An eat-in country Kitchen with an island counter and bay window

■ A spacious Great Room with a fireplace flowing easily into the Dining area

■ A first floor Master Suite including a walk-in closet and a private compartmentalized bath

■ Two additional bedrooms sharing a full bath with a double vanity

■ An optional basement or crawl space foundation — please specify when ordering

First floor — 1,277 sq. ft.
Second floor — 720 sq. ft.

■ *Total living area 1,997 sq. ft.* ■ *Price Code C* ■

Fashionable Country Style

■ *Total living area 2,695 sq. ft.* ■ *Price Code E* ■

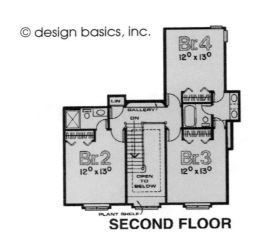

© design basics, inc.

SECOND FLOOR

Br. 4
12⁰ x 13⁰

LIN

GALLERY

DN

Br. 2
12⁰ x 13⁰

Br. 3
12⁰ x 13⁰

OPEN TO BELOW

PLANT SHELF

No. 99450

■ **This plan features:**

— Four bedrooms

— Two full, one three quarter, and one half baths

■ The large covered front Porch adds old fashioned appeal to this modern floor plan

■ The Dining Room features a decorative ceiling and a built in hutch

■ The Kitchen has a center island and is adjacent to the gazebo shaped Nook

■ The Great Room is accented by transom windows and a fireplace with bookcases on either side of it

■ The Master Bedroom has a cathedral ceiling, a door to the front porch, and a large bath with a whirlpool tub

■ Upstairs are three additional Bedrooms and two full baths

■ This plan is available with a basement or a crawl space foundation, please specify when ordering this plan

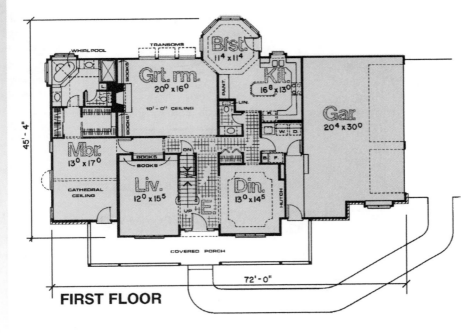

WHIRLPOOL

TRANSOMS

Bfst.
11⁴ x 11⁴

Grt. rm.
20⁰ x 16⁰

Kit
16⁸ x 13⁰

10'-0" CEILING

PANT.

Gar.
20⁴ x 30⁰

45'-4"

Mbr.
13⁰ x 17⁰

CATHEDRAL CEILING

BOOKS

Liv.
12⁰ x 15⁵

DN

Din.
13⁰ x 14⁵

UP

HUTCH

COVERED PORCH

72'-0"

FIRST FLOOR

First floor — 1,881 sq. ft.
Second floor — 814 sq. ft.
Garage — 534 sq. ft.

Elegant Victorian

■ *Total living area 2,455 sq. ft.* ■ *Price Code D* ■

No. 98518

This plan features:

- Three bedrooms

- Two full and one half baths

■ Serve guests dinner in the bayed Dining Room and then gather in the Living Room which features a cathedral ceiling

■ The Family Room which is accented by a fireplace

■ The Master Bedroom has a sitting area, walk in closet, and a private bath

■ There is a Bonus Room upstairs for future expansion

■ This plan features a three car Garage with space for storage

■ An optional basement or slab foundation — please specify when ordering

First floor — 1,447 sq. ft.
Second floor — 1,008 sq. ft.
Garage — 756 sq. ft.

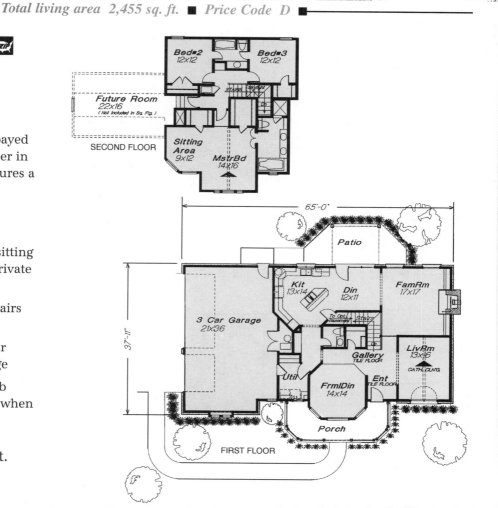

Impressive Contemporary

Total living area 1,770 sq. ft. ■ *Price Code B*

COVED MASTER 13/9 X 15/0

SPA

BONUS 14/0 X 14/0

DN

BED 2 10/0 X 11/0

BED 3 10/0 X 10/0

UPPER FLOOR

FAMILY 15/0 X 12/0

NOOK 9/3 X 8/0

KIT

GARAGE 28/0 X 22/0

DINING 11/8 X 10/9

LIVING 12/0 X 14/0

UP

DEN 10/0 X 11/6

MAIN FLOOR

40' 6"

62'0"

No. 91673

■ **This plan features:**

— Three bedrooms

— Two full and one half baths

■ An octagon shaped Dining Room with windows on five sides

■ An open layout between the Kitchen, Nook and Family Room

■ An efficient, well-appointed Kitchen with a double sink and a peninsula counter, that may double as an eating bar

■ A Family Room with a fireplace

■ A formal Living Room with a view of the front yard

■ A coved ceiling topping the Master Bedroom with full bath containing a spa tub, double vanity, separate shower and walk-in closet

■ Two additional bedrooms sharing the full hall bath

■ A Bonus Room for future expansion

■ No materials list is available for this plan

Main floor— 1,007 sq. ft.
Upper floor— 763 sq. ft.
Bonus— 280 sq. ft.

Livable with a Touch of Drama

Total living area 1,933 sq. ft. ■ *Price Code C*

Deck

Breakfast 11-10 x 10-8

Dining Room 11-8 x 12-6

pass thru

Kitchen 13-4 x 9-9

Master Bedroom 16 x 13-2

Bath

WIDTH 52'-0"
DEPTH 50'-0"

stairs up

stairs dn

entertainment center

walk-in closet

Laundry

Sunken Great Room 17 x 19

Bath

Foyer

12' ceiling

Two-car Garage 23-4 x 20-2

Porch

FIRST FLOOR

Bedroom 11 x 12-4

Bath

Bedroom 11 x 11

Balcony

Great Room Below

Foyer Below

plant shelf

slope ceiling

stairs dn

SECOND FLOOR

No. 92612

■ **This plan features:**

— Three bedrooms

— Two full and one half baths

■ A dramatic facade created by a natural sto... chimney, decorative windows and pillar entrance

■ A two-story, sunken Great Room with a 12" ceiling accenting the large, stone fireplace framed by curved floor-to-ceiling windows

■ A formal Dining Room stepping from the Great Room and the Kitchen with a pass-thru and a wall of windows to the backyar...

■ An efficient, U-shaped Kitchen with a built-in pantry, a peninsula counter/snackbar and a bright, glassed Breakfast area with atrium door to the Deck

■ A plush Master Bedroom Suite with a larg... walk-in closet and a private Bath with a double vanity and corner window tub

■ Two additional bedrooms, on the second floor, sharing a full bath with a double vanity

■ No materials list is available for this plan

First floor — 1,448 sq. ft.
Second floor — 485 sq. ft.

■ *Total living area 1,768 sq. ft.* ■ *Price Code B* ■

No. 94907

This plan features:

- Three bedrooms

- Two full and one half baths

■ Covered porch and double doors lead into Entry accented by a window seat and curved banister stair case

■ Decorative windows overlooking back yard and a large fireplace highlight Great Room

■ A hub Kitchen with an island/snack bar and large pantry access formal Dining Room, Breakfast area and covered side Porch

■ Powder room, laundry area, Garage entry and storage nearby Kitchen

■ Master Bedroom has two walk-in closets, two vanities and a whirlpool tub

■ Two additional bedrooms, one with a vaulted ceiling above a window seat, share a full bath

First floor — 905 sq. ft.
Second floor — 863 sq. ft.
Basement — 905 sq. ft.
Garage — 487 sq. ft.

© design basics, inc.

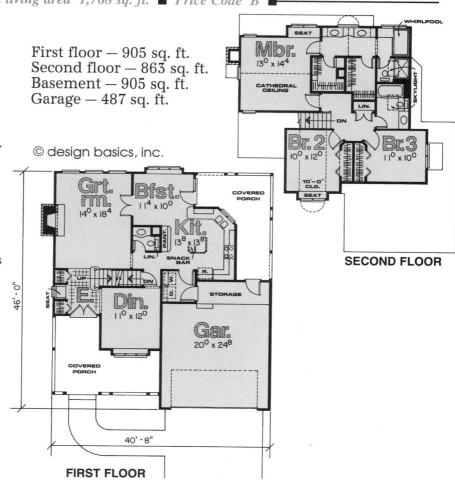

SECOND FLOOR

FIRST FLOOR

■ *Total living area 3,511 sq. ft.* ■ *Price Code E* ■

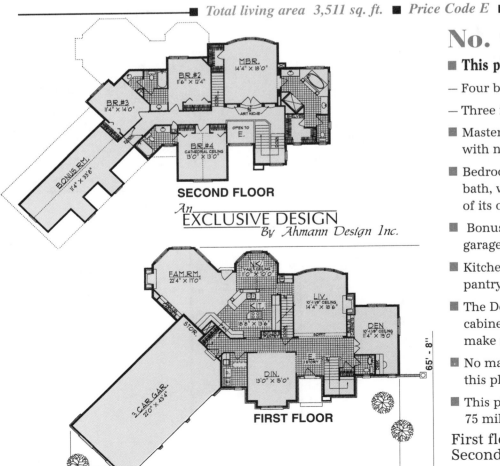

BR.#3
11'4" X 14'0"

BR.#2
11'6" X 12'4"

MBR.
14'4" X 18'0"

ART NICHE

OPEN TO E.

BR.#4
CATHEDRAL CEILING
13'0" X 13'0"

BONUS RM.
11'4" X 33'6"

SECOND FLOOR

An **EXCLUSIVE DESIGN**
By Ahmann Design Inc.

FAM. RM.
22'4" X 11'0"

NK.
10'0" X 10'0"

KIT.
18'0" X 13'6"

LIV.
14'4" X 18'6"

DEN
11'4" X 19'0"

STOR.

3 CAR GAR.
22'0" X 43'4"

DIN.
13'0" X 15'0"

FIRST FLOOR

65' - 8"

90' - 3"

No. 99118

■ **This plan features:**

— Four bedrooms

— Three full and one half baths

■ Master Bedroom has French doors with niches on either side

■ Bedrooms 2 and 3 share a full bath, while bedroom 4 has a bath of its own and a cathedral ceiling

■ Bonus Room over the three car garage

■ Kitchen has ample counter space, pantry and a center island

■ The Den with built in desk and cabinets is the perfect place to make a great home Office

■ No materials list is available for this plan

■ This plan is not to be built within 75 mile radius of Cedar Rapids, IA

First floor — 2,751 sq. ft.
Second floor — 1,185 sq. ft.

B. NATHAN

© 1993 Donald A. Gardner Architects, Inc.

■ *Total living area 1,713 sq. ft.* ■ *Price Code C* ■

No. 96440

This plan features:

- Three bedrooms

- Two full baths

■ Covered porches front and back with an open interior capped by a cathedral ceiling

■ Cathedral ceiling timing the Great Room, Kitchen/Dining and loft/study into an impressive living space

■ Kitchen equipped with an island cooktop and counter opening to both the Great Room and the Dining Room

■ A cathedral ceiling topping the front bedroom/study,

■ A large bay cozies up the rear bedroom

■ Luxurious Master Suite located upstairs for extra privacy

irst floor — 1,146 sq. ft.
econd floor — 567 sq. ft.

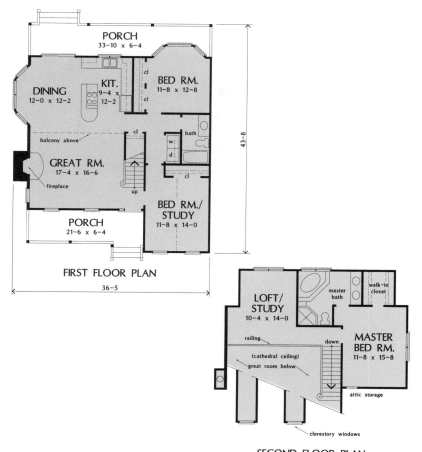

FIRST FLOOR PLAN

SECOND FLOOR PLAN

Distinctive Design

■ *Total living area 1,998 sq. ft.* ■ *Price Code C* ■

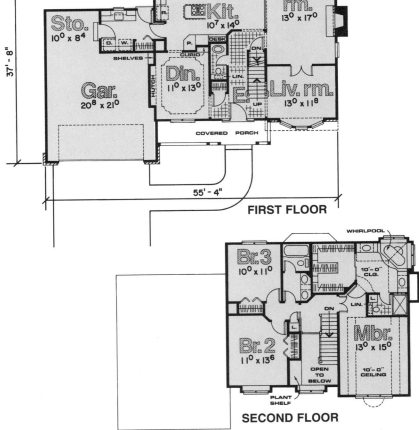

© design basics, inc.

Sto.
10⁰ x 8⁴

Gar.
20⁸ x 21⁰

37' - 8"

Bfst.
10⁰ x 11⁸

Kit.
10⁷ x 14⁰

Fam. rm.
13⁰ x 17⁰

SHELVES

DESK

CURIO

P.

Din.
11⁰ x 13⁰

HUTCH

LIN.

DN

UP

Liv. rm.
13⁰ x 11⁸

COVERED   PORCH

55' - 4"

FIRST FLOOR

WHIRLPOOL

Br. 3
10⁰ x 11⁰

10'-0" CLG.

DN

LIN.

L.

Br. 2
11⁰ x 13⁶

L

OPEN TO BELOW

Mbr.
13⁰ x 15⁰

10'-0" CEILING

PLANT SHELF

SECOND FLOOR

No. 94904

■ **This plan features:**

— Three bedrooms

— Two full and one half baths

■ Living Room is distinguished by warmth of bayed window and French doors leading to Family Room

■ Built-in curio cabinet adds interest to formal Dining Room

■ Well-appointed Kitchen with island cook top and Breakfast are designed to save you steps

■ Family Room with focal point fireplace for informal gatherings

■ Spacious Master Bedroom suite with vaulted ceiling over decorative window and plush dressing area

■ Secondary bedrooms share a double vanity bath

First floor — 1,093 sq. ft.
Second floor — 905 sq. ft.
Basement — 1,093 sq. ft.
Garage — 527 sq. ft.

Symmetrical Southern Beauty

No. 94611

This plan features:

- Four bedrooms
- Three full and one half baths
- Inviting front porch shades arched windows in warm climate
- Spacious Family Room with cozy fireplace and access to Covered Porch and Patio
- Open Dining Room accented by columns conveniently located
- Peninsula counter/eating bar and adjoining Breakfast area, Garage entry and Utility room in efficient Kitchen
- Corner Master Bedroom with large walk-in closet and double vanity bath
- First floor bedroom with a walk-in closet and private bath
- Two additional bedrooms on second floor with walk-in closets, share a full bath and balcony
- An optional crawl space or slab foundation — please specify when ordering
- No materials list available

First floor — 1,796 sq. ft.
Second floor — 610 sq. ft.
Garage — 570 sq. ft.

■ *Total living area 2,406 sq. ft.* ● *Price Code D* ■

WIDTH 65'-8.5"
DEPTH 64'-8.5"

SECOND FLOOR

FIRST FLOOR

Today's Amenities, Yesterday's Charm

No. 10805

This plan features:

- Three bedrooms
- Two full and one half baths
- Wide corner boards, clapboard siding, and a full-length covered porch lending a friendly air to this classic home
- A central entry opening to a cozy Den on the right, a sunken Living Room with adjoining Dining Room on the left
- An informal Dining Nook accented by bay windows
- A Master Suite spanning the rear of the home including a huge, walk-in closet, a private bath with double vanity, and a whirlpool tub

First floor — 1,622 sq. ft.
Second floor — 1,156 sq. ft.

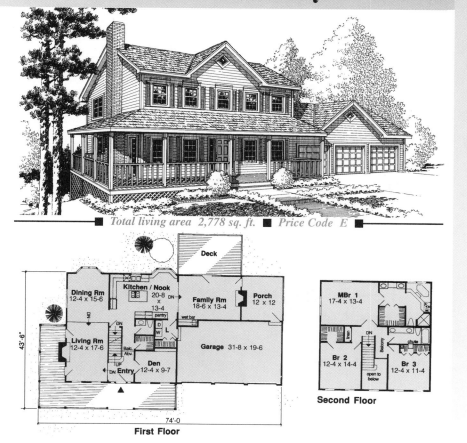

■ *Total living area 2,778 sq. ft.* ● *Price Code E* ■

First Floor

Second Floor

Traditional Home

© design basics inc.

■ Total living area 2,979 sq. ft. ■ ■ Price Code E ■

FIRST FLOOR

SECOND FLOOR

No. 99452

■ **This plan features:**

— Four bedrooms

— Two full and one half baths

■ Dining Room has a built-in hutch and a bay window

■ Cozy Den and Great Room have high ceilings and transom windows

■ Conveniently arranged Kitchen adjoins the Breakfast Nook

■ The warm Gathering Room features a fireplace and a cathedral ceiling

■ The secluded Master Bedroom is world away from the busy areas of the home

■ Upstairs are three bedrooms and two full baths

First floor — 2,158 sq. ft.
Second floor — 821 sq. ft.
Basement — 2,158 sq. ft.
Garage — 692 sq. ft.

Modern Luxury

■ Total living area 2,686 sq. ft. ■ Price Code E ■

No. 98457 ✖

■ **This plan features:**

- Four bedrooms

- Three full and one half baths

■ A feeling of spaciousness is created by the two-story Foyer in this home

■ Arched openings and decorative windows enhance the Dining and Living Rooms

■ The efficient Kitchen has a work island, pantry and a Breakfast area

■ The plush Master Suite features a tray ceiling above, an alcove of windows and a whirlpool bath

■ An optional basement or a crawl space foundation — please specify when ordering

First floor — 1,883 sq. ft.
Second floor — 803 sq. ft.
Garage — 495 sq. ft.

Charming Exterior

No. 92611

■ **This plan features:**

— Four bedrooms

— Two full and one half baths

■ The Foyer features a grand staircase and opens into the Dining Room punctuated by columns

■ The Great Room has a unique shape that adds plenty of usable living space to the home

■ The Kitchen has a center island and flows openly into the Breakfast Room

■ The second floor Master Suite has a walk-in closet and a private bath

■ Three additional bedrooms have ample closet space and share a full bath

■ No materials list is available for this plan

First floor — 1,069 sq. ft.
Second floor — 1,015 sq. ft.
Width — 44'-4"
Depth — 45'-4"

■ *Total living area 2,084 sq. ft.* ● *Price Code C* ■

FIRST FLOOR

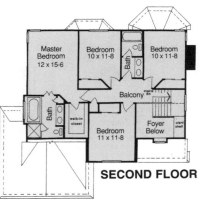

SECOND FLOOR

The Royal Treatment

No. 91687

■ **This plan features:**

— Four bedrooms

— Three full and one half baths

■ Enter from the covered porch into the tiled front Foyer with a spectacular curved staircase

■ The Living Room has a fireplace and bay with bright windows

■ The Kitchen also features a bay of windows as well as a cozy nook

■ In the Family Room is another fireplace and access to the deck

■ The spacious Master Suite also has a fireplace and a luxurious bath

■ Upstairs find three bedrooms, two full baths, and a bonus room

■ No materials list is available for this plan

First floor — 2,930 sq. ft.
Second floor — 1,265 sq. ft.
Bonus — 325 sq. ft.
Garage — 974 sq. ft.

■ *Total living area 4,195 sq. ft.* ■ *Price Code F* ■

■ *Total living area 1,576 sq. ft.* ■ *Price Code C* ■

No. 94138

This plan features:

- Three bedrooms
- One full and one half baths
- Country, homey feeling with wrap-around Porch
- Adjoining Living Room and Dining Rooms
- Efficient Kitchen easily serves Dining area with extended counter and a built-in pantry
- Spacious Family Room with optional fireplace and access to Laundry/Garage entry
- Large Master Bedroom with a walk-in closet and access to a full bath, offers a private bath option
- Two additional bedrooms with ample closets and full bath access
- No materials list available

First floor — 900 sq. ft.
Second floor — 676 sq. ft.
Basement — 900 sq. ft.
Garage — 448 sq. ft.

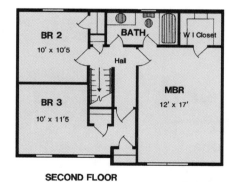

SECOND FLOOR

WIDTH 58'-0"
DEPTH 34'-0"

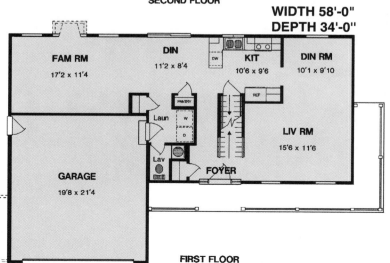

FIRST FLOOR

181

Eye Catching Style

■ Total living area 2,439 sq. ft. ■ Price Code D ■

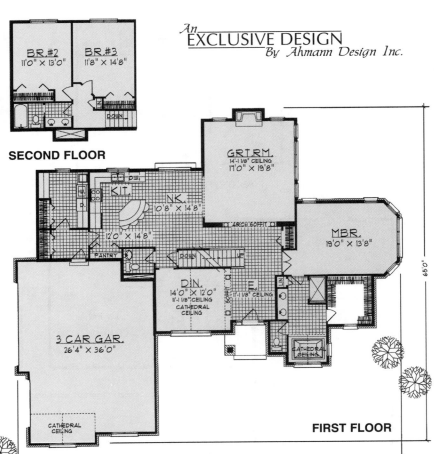

BR.#2
11'0" X 13'0"

BR.#3
11'8" X 14'8"

SECOND FLOOR

An
EXCLUSIVE DESIGN
By Ahmann Design Inc.

GRT.RM.
14'-1 1/8" CEILING
17'0" X 19'8"

KIT.

NK.
10'8" X 14'8"

12'0" X 14'8"

ARCH. SOFFIT

MBR.
19'0" X 13'8"

PANTRY

DOWN   UP

DIN.
14'0" X 12'0"
11'-1 1/8" CEILING
CATHEDRAL
CEILING

11'-1 1/8" CEILING

3 CAR GAR.
26'4" X 36'0"

CATHEDRAL
CEILING

CATHEDRAL
CEILING

65'0"

FIRST FLOOR

72'8"

No. 99138

■ **This plan features:**

— Three bedrooms

— Two full and one half baths

■ Dining Room has a cathedral ceiling and distinctive front windows

■ The Master Bedrooms has a bay and a bath with a cathedral ceiling

■ Enter the Great Room through an arched soffit to view the rear wall fireplace

■ An L-shaped Kitchen with adjacent nook and a curved snack bar

■ Two bedrooms and a full bath are located on the second floor

■ There is no materials list available for this plan

First floor — 1,944 sq. ft.
Second floor — 495 sq. ft.
Basement — 1,944 sq. ft.

Excellent Choice for First Time Buyer

■ *Total living area 1,766 sq. ft.* ■ *Price Code B* ■

No. 91055 ⊠

This plan features:

- Three bedrooms

- Two full and one half baths

- A Living Room with an expansive floor-to-ceiling triple window

- A comfortable Family Room with a sliding glass door, a Utility Closet with washer and dryer and access to the Kitchen

- Kitchen with a peninsula counter/snackbar

- A cozy Master Bedroom with a recessed dormer window and an oversized, walk-in closet

- Two additional bedrooms, on the second floor sharing a full hall bath, and a Playroom that could be a fourth bedroom

First floor — 805 sq. ft.
Second floor — 961 sq. ft.
Garage — 540 sq. ft.

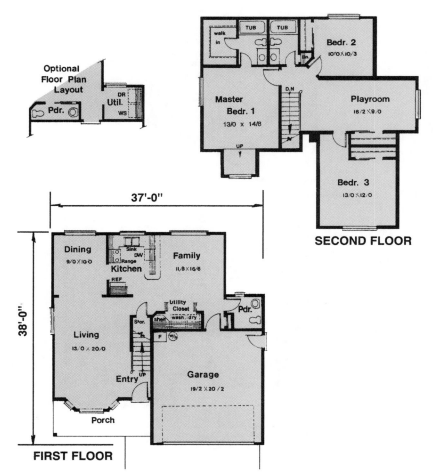

Captivating Colonial

© design basics inc.

■ *Total living area 2,585 sq. ft.* ■ *Price Code D* ■

SECOND FLOOR

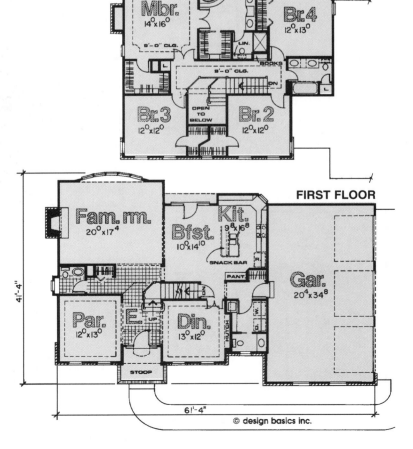

FIRST FLOOR

© design basics inc.

No. 99454 ✕

■ This plan features:

— Four bedrooms

— Two full and one half baths

■ Decorative windows and brick detailing

■ Dining room highlighted by decorative ceiling, French doors, and hutch space

■ The Family Room has a fireplace and a bow window

■ The Breakfast Nook and Kitchen are perfectly set up for meals on the run

■ Upstairs find the Master Bedroom and bath fully complemented

■ Three more bedrooms and a bath completed the second floor plan

■ This plan is available with a basement or slab foundation — please specify when ordering

First floor — 1,362 sq. ft.
Second floor — 1,223 sq. ft.
Garage — 734 sq. ft.

No. 20144

This plan features:

Four bedrooms

Three full and one half bath

A sprawling front porch

A two-way fireplace warming the Hearth Room and the Living Room

A formal, bayed Dining Room with decorative ceiling

An efficient, well-appointed Kitchen with peninsula counter and double sinks

A vaulted ceiling in the Master Suite which is equipped with a private Master Bath

Three additional bedrooms each with adjoining full baths

First floor — 1,737 sq. ft.

Second floor — 826 sq. ft.

Basement — 1,728 sq. ft.

An EXCLUSIVE DESIGN
By Karl Kreeger

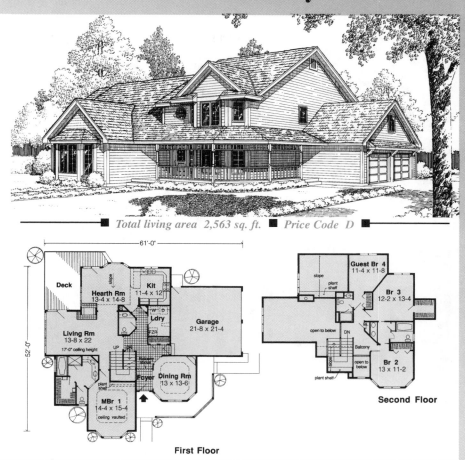

■ *Total living area 2,563 sq. ft.* ■ *Price Code D* ■

First Floor

Second Floor

Window Design Highlights Plan

No. 90348

This plan features:

Two bedrooms plus loft

Two full baths

An airy Living Room with glass on three sides and a fireplace tucked into corner

An efficient Kitchen serving the Living and Dining Rooms easily

First floor Bedrooms featuring a private bath and a walk-in closet connected to Storage area

A landing staircase leading to a second bedroom with a walk-in closet, a Laundry and a full Bath

A ladder to top-of-the-tower Loft with loads of light and multiple uses

First floor — 729 sq. ft.

Second floor — 420 sq. ft.

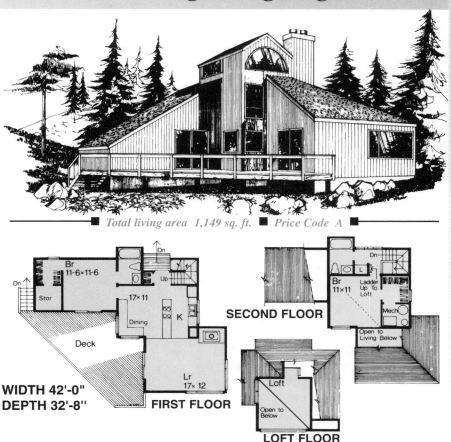

■ *Total living area 1,149 sq. ft.* ■ *Price Code A* ■

WIDTH 42'-0"
DEPTH 32'-8"

FIRST FLOOR

SECOND FLOOR

LOFT FLOOR

Rear of Home as Attractive as Front

■ *Total living area 2,440 sq. ft.* ■ *Price Code D* ■

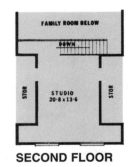

FAMILY ROOM BELOW

DOWN

STOR | STUDIO 20·8 x 13·6 | STOR

SECOND FLOOR

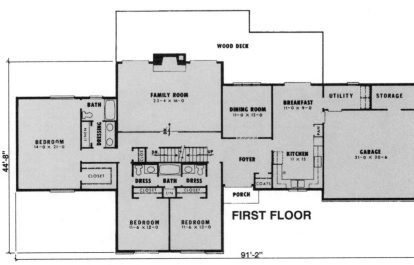

FIRST FLOOR

No. 90413

■ **This plan features:**

— Three bedrooms

— Two full and one half baths

■ A sunken Family Room with a cathedral ceiling and a stone fireplace

■ Two front bedrooms sharing a unique bath-and-a-half arrangement

■ A Master Bedroom with a compartmentalized bath, a doub vanity and linen closet

■ A U-shaped Kitchen, serving the Breakfast Nook and the formal Dining Room with ease

■ A second floor with a large Studi

■ An optional basement or crawl space foundation — please specif when ordering

First floor — 2,192 sq. ft.
Second floor — 248 sq. ft.

■ *Total living area 1,950 sq. ft.* ■ *Price Code C* ■

No. 99757 ✕

This plan features:

Three bedrooms

Two full and one half baths

Front Porch invites visiting and leads into an open Entry with an angled staircase

Living Room with a wall of windows and an island fireplace

Kitchen with a work island, walk-in pantry, garden window over sink, skylit Nook and nearby Deck

Corner Master Suite enhanced by Deck access, vaulted ceiling, a large walk-in closet and spa bath

Guest/Utility Room offers a pullman bed and laundry

Two second floor bedrooms with large closets, share a full bath

First floor —1,472 sq. ft.
Second floor — 478 sq. ft.
Garage — 558 sq. ft.

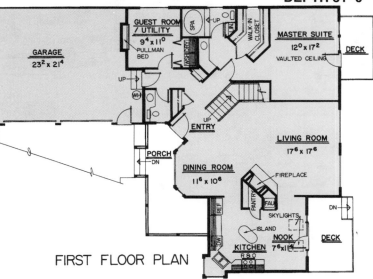

SECOND FLOOR PLAN

WIDTH 62'-0"
DEPTH 51'-0"

FIRST FLOOR PLAN

Tudor Grandeur for the Budget-Minded

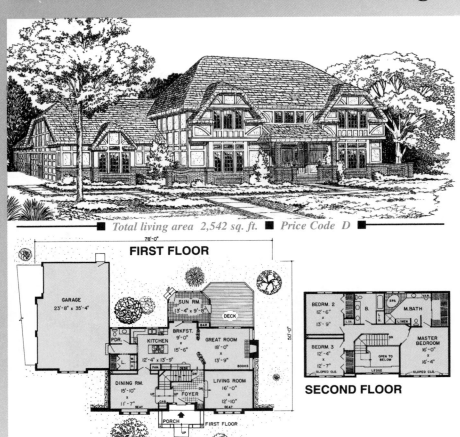

■ Total living area 2,542 sq. ft. ■ Price Code D ■

No. 20354 ✕📖

■ **This plan features:**

— Three bedrooms

— Two full and one half baths

■ A two-story foyer

■ Window seats in both the Living Room and the Dining Room

■ A convenient range-top island in the spacious Kitchen with built-in pantry and planning desk

■ An open arrangement between the Kitchen, Breakfast area, and the Great Room

■ A Master Suite with sloped ceiling and private Master Bath with spa tub and walk-in closet

■ Two additional bedrooms that share a full hall bath

First floor — 1,346 sq. ft.
Second floor — 1,196 sq. ft.
Basement — 1,346 sq. ft.
Garage — 840 sq. ft.

Unique Exterior

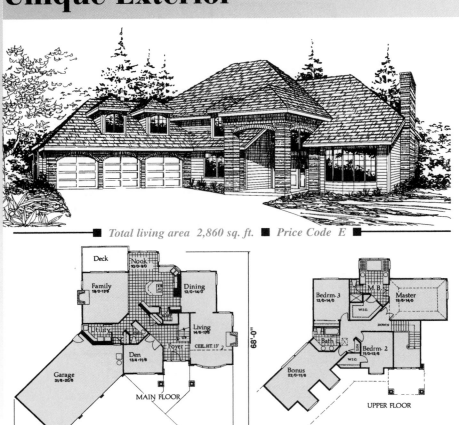

■ Total living area 2,860 sq. ft. ■ Price Code E ■

No. 91694

■ **This plan features:**

— Three bedrooms

— Two full and one half baths

■ Wood and brick exterior provides eye-catching design

■ Tile creating easy-care Foyer continues into Kitchen, Utility and Nook

■ Spacious Living Room enhanced by volume ceiling and curved window, opens to bright formal Dining area

■ Hub Kitchen with cooktop work island and walk-in pantry easily serves Dining Room, Nook and Deck beyond

■ Master suite pampered by tray ceiling, luxurious bath and walk-in closet

■ No materials list is available for this plan

First floor — 1,660 sq. ft.
Second floor — 1,200 sq. ft.
Bonus room — 356 sq. ft.
Garage — 672 sq. ft.

■ *Total living area 1,749 sq. ft.* ■ *Price Code B* ■

No. 93220

This plan features:

- Three bedrooms

- Two full and one half baths

- Open layout between Kitchen/ Breakfast area and Family Room

- Efficient Kitchen with cooktop peninsula, built-in pantry and a glassed Breakfast area

- Family Room with a focal point fireplace and access to Sundeck

- Master Bedroom enhanced by decorative ceiling and French doors leading into a private bath and walk-in closet

- Two additional bedrooms, full bath, laundry closet and Bonus Room complete second floor

- An optional basement, crawl space or slab — please specify when ordering

First floor — 902 sq. ft.
Second floor — 819 sq. ft.
Staircase — 28 sq. ft.
Bonus room — 210 sq. ft.
Garage — 400 sq. ft.

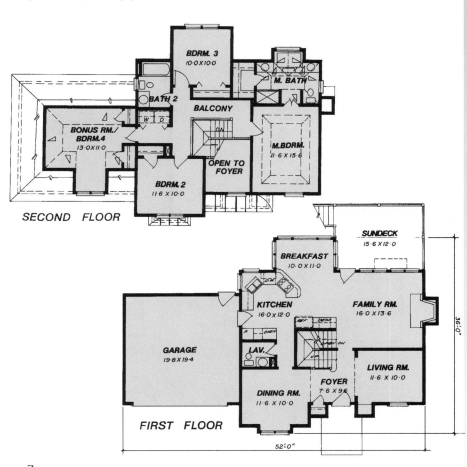

An EXCLUSIVE DESIGN
By Jannis Vann & Associates, Inc.

Executive Two-Story

■ *Total living area 2,116 sq. ft.* ■ *Price Code C* ■

An
EXCLUSIVE DESIGN
By Weinmaster Home Design

FIRST FLOOR

SECOND FLOOR

No. 98800

■ This plan features:

— Three bedrooms

— Two full and one half baths

■ Gracefully curving staircase dominating the Foyer

■ Kitchen and Breakfast Nook separated from the Family Room by only a railing and a step down

■ Built-ins and a fireplace in the sunken Family Room

■ Formal Living Room and Dining Room adjoin and include a fireplace and a built-in china cabinet area

■ Lavish Master Suite boasts a sitting room and a deluxe five piece bath

■ Bonus Room to be finished for future needs

First floor — 1,258 sq. ft.
Second floor — 858 sq. ft.
Garage — 441 sq. ft.

■ *Total living area 2,124 sq. ft.* ■ *Price Code C* ■

No. 99112 ✕

This plan features:

Three bedrooms

Two full and one half baths

Covered front porch and vaulted entry provide a warm welcome

Living room has a vaulted ceiling and a corner fireplace

The dining room has sliding doors to the backyard

U-shaped kitchen has a pantry, serving bar and a double sink

Master suite spans includes a private bath

Upstairs, two bedrooms, one with a massive closet and a full bath

First floor — 1,498 sq. ft.

Second floor — 626 sq. ft.

Basement — 1,485 sq. ft.

An
EXCLUSIVE DESIGN
By Ahmann Design Inc.

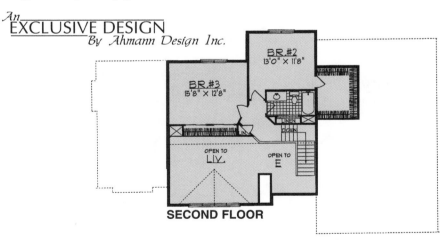

SECOND FLOOR

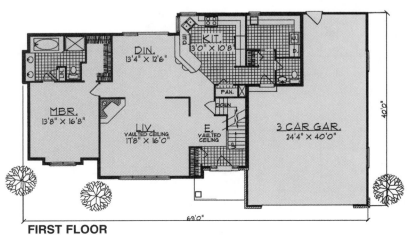

FIRST FLOOR

Stately Entrance Adds to Home's Exterior

■ *Total living area 2,244 sq. ft.* ■ *Price Code D* ■

An
EXCLUSIVE DESIGN
By Energetic Enterprises

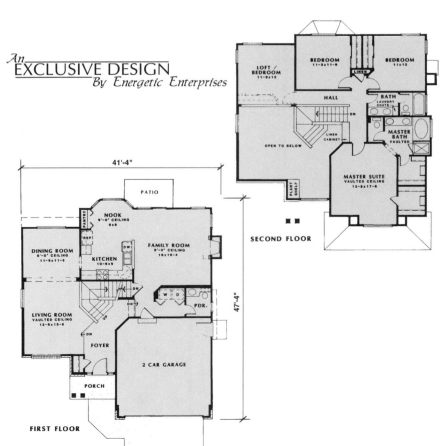

SECOND FLOOR

41'-4"

47'-4"

FIRST FLOOR

No. 24268

■ This plan features:

— Three or four bedrooms

— Two full and one half baths

■ A vaulted ceiling in the Living Room adding to its spaciousness

■ An efficient Kitchen with double sinks, and ample storage and counter space

■ An informal Eating Nook with a built-in pantry

■ A large Family Room with a fireplace

■ A plush Master Suite with a vaulted ceiling and luxurious Master Bath plus two walk-in closets

■ Two additional bedrooms share full bath with a convenient laundry chute

First floor — 1,115 sq. ft.
Second floor — 1,129 sq. ft.
Basement — 1,096 sq. ft.
Garage — 415 sq. ft.

No. 92156 ✖

This plan features:

Four bedrooms

Two full and one three quarter baths

Creates an indoor/outdoor relationship with terrific decks and large glass expanses

Family Room and Living Room enjoy glassed walls taking in the vistas

Living room enhanced by a cathedral ceiling and a warm fireplace

Dining room and Kitchen are in an open layout and highlighted by a center cooktop island/snack bar in the kitchen and large window in the Dining Room

Master Bedroom enhanced by floor to ceiling windowed area allowing natural light to filter in

Secondary bedroom in close proximity to full bath on first floor

Located on the lower level are two additional bedrooms, a three-quarter bath and a Family Room

First floor — 1,707 sq. ft.

Basement floor — 901 sq. ft.

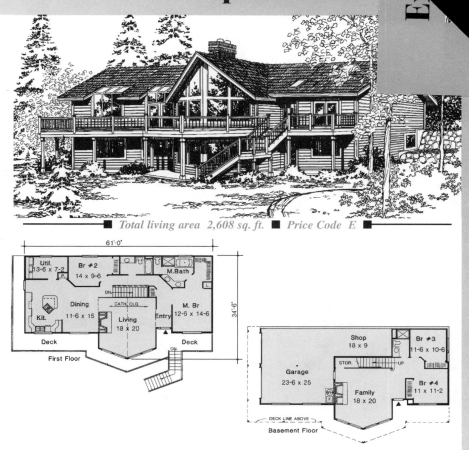

Total living area 2,608 sq. ft. ■ *Price Code E* ■

First Floor

Basement Floor

No. 35002 ✖ Я

This plan features:

Three Bedrooms

Two full and one half baths

A wonderful big front porch creating a homey welcome

A formal Living Room, with a picture window that views the porch and front yard

A formal Dining Room directly across from the Living Room, allowing for a smooth transition from room to room when entertaining

A well-appointed Kitchen with ample storage and counter space and a double sink

A first floor private Master Suite with a double vanity, compartmented bath and a large walk-in closet

Two secondary bedrooms that share a double vanity, full hall bath

Main floor — 1,120 sq. ft.

Second floor — 592 sq. ft.

Garage — 528 sq. ft.

Total living area 1,712 sq. ft. ■ *Price Code B* ■

SECOND FLOOR

FIRST FLOOR

Crawl Space / Slab Option

■ *Total living area 1,814 sq. ft.* ■ *Price Code B* ■

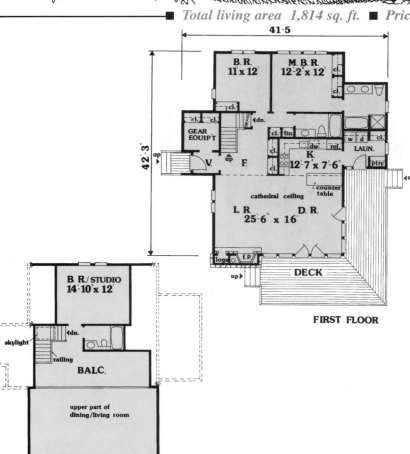

B. R.
11 x 12

M. B. R.
12-2 x 12

GEAR
EQUIP'T

LAUN.

K.
12-7 x 7-6

counter
table

cathedral ceiling

L. R.   D. R.
25-6 x 16

logs   f p.

DECK

41-5

42-3

FIRST FLOOR

B. R./STUDIO
14-10 x 12

skylight

railing

BALC.

upper part of
dining/living room

LOFT FLOOR

No. 99645

■ This plan features:

— Three bedrooms

— Three full baths

■ Wrap-around Deck expands Livi
outdoors

■ Impressive fieldstone fireplace
with log holder warms
Living/Dining Room

■ Efficient L-shaped Kitchen with
built-in counter table and
Laundry with built-in pantry

■ Master Bedroom suite with
aplush, double vanity bath

■ Second bedroom on first floor an
another bedroom on second floo
each have access to full baths

■ Side entrance into Vestibule wit
Gear Equipment area and Foyer
with two closet

First floor — 1,361 sq. ft.
Loft floor — 453 sq. ft.
Basement — 694 sq. ft.

Two-Story Foyer Adds to Elegance

■ *Total living area 2,454 sq. ft.* ■ *Price Code D* ■

No. 93240

■ **This plan features:**

- Four bedrooms

- Two full and one half bath

■ Two-story entrance with lovely, curved staircase

■ Family Room enhanced by fireplace and access to Sundeck

■ Country-sized Kitchen with bright Breakfast area, adjoins Dining Room and Utility/Garage entry

■ French doors lead into plush Master Bedroom with decorative ceiling and large Master Bath

■ Three additional bedrooms with ample closets share a full bath and Bonus Room

■ An optional basement, crawl space or slab foundation — please specify when ordering

First floor — 1,277 sq. ft.
Second floor — 1,177 sq. ft.
Bonus room — 392 sq. ft.
Basement — 1,261 sq. ft.
Garage — 572 sq. ft.

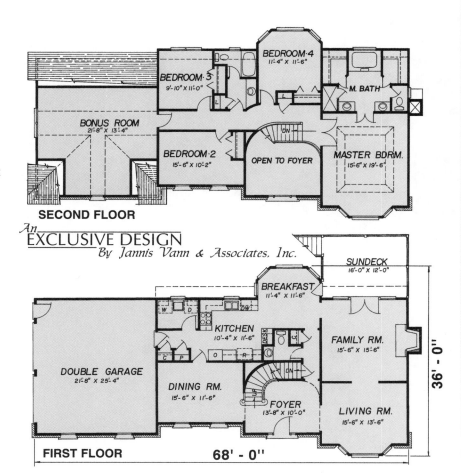

SECOND FLOOR

An EXCLUSIVE DESIGN
By Jannis Vann & Associates, Inc.

FIRST FLOOR

Classic Beauty

■ *Total living area 2,483 sq. ft.* ■ *Price Code D* ■

46'-0"

45'-0"

First Floor

Deck

Breakfast Area

Hearth Rm
18-4 x 13-4

Kit
11-10 x 11

Den / Office
Br 4
12-4 x 13-4

Dining Rm
13 x 13-8

1-1/2" clg. reveal

L'dry

DN

Garage
21-4 x 21-4

Living Rm
13 x 15-4

UP

Foyer

Second Floor

Br 3
11 x 11

skylt.
10'-0" clg. ht.

Balcony   DN

Br 2
13-6 x 11

MBr 1
21 x 15-6

foyer below

Sitting Area
15 x 7-8

No. 20134

■ **This plan features:**

— Three bedrooms

— Two and one half baths

■ Generous, well-placed windows and angular ceilings giving every room a cheery atmosphere

■ The Living and Dining Rooms flowing together off the foyer

■ Family areas at the rear of the home including a cozy Hearth Room adjoining the efficient Kitchen

■ A Master Suite located over the Garage, enhanced by a sky-lit bath, cozy sitting area, and a room-size closet

First floor — 1,361 sq. ft.
Second floor — 1,122 sq. ft.
Basement — 1,361 sq. ft.
Garage — 477 sq. ft.

An
EXCLUSIVE DESIGN
By Karl Kreeger

Unique A-Frame

■ *Total living area 1,309 sq. ft.* ■ *Price Code A* ■

FIRST FLOOR PLAN

26'-0"

CLOSET
RM.
LAUR.

BATH

CLOS.

HALL

UP

KITCHEN
9'-0" x 10'-0"

PNTY.

DINETTE
10'-0" x 12'-0"

LIVING ROOM
12'-0" x 15'-0"

DECK

PLANTER

BEDROOM
12'-0" x 12'-0"

SECOND FLOOR PLAN

13'-0"

BEDROOM
10'-0" x 12'-2"

CL.

BATH

CL.

BEDROOM
(OPT)
9'-8" x 12'-2"

BALCONY

No. 90025

■ **This plan features:**

— Three bedrooms

— Two full baths

■ Exterior highlighted by fieldstone chimney, red cedar roof, vertical siding and a redwood sun deck

■ Open Living Room, Dining and Kitchen layout provides a spacious feeling

■ Efficient, U-shaped Kitchen with built-in pantry and serving bar

■ Spacious first floor bedroom convenient to full bath and laundry

■ Two second floor bedrooms with ample closet space share a full bath

First floor — 867 sq. ft.
Second floor — 442 sq. ft.
Deck — 364 sq. ft.

Country Living in Any Neighborhood

■ *Total living area 2,181 sq. ft.* ■ *Price Code C* ■

No. 90436

This plan features:

Three bedrooms

Two full and two half baths

An expansive Family Room with fireplace

A Dining Room and Breakfast Nook lit by flowing natural light from bay windows

A first floor Master Suite with a double vanity bath that wraps around his-n-her closets

An optional basement, slab or crawl space foundation — please specify when ordering

First floor — 1,477 sq. ft.
Second floor — 704 sq. ft.
Basement — 1,374 sq. ft.

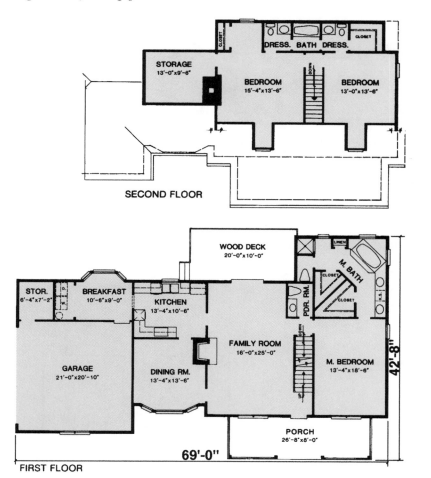

SECOND FLOOR

FIRST FLOOR

Letting the Light In

■ *Total living area 1,525 sq. ft.* ■ *Price Code B* ■

No. 91081

■ **This plan features:**

— Four bedrooms

— Two full baths

■ Covered Porch leads into easy-ca
tile Entry with angled staircase

■ Vaulted ceiling tops corner
windows and wood stove in
Living Room

■ Kitchen with built-in pantry, pas
through counter and plant shelf
window

■ Two first floor bedrooms share
full bath and Utility area

■ French doors lead into Master
Bedroom with skylight bath

■ Loft/Bedroom overlooking Livir
Room offers many options

■ No materials list is available for
this plan

First floor — 1076 sq. ft.
Second floor — 449 sq. ft.

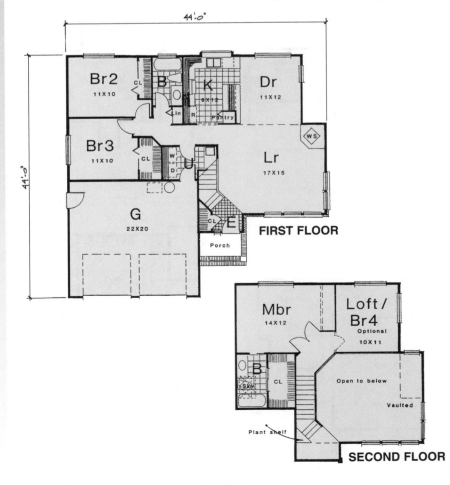

Sunny Character

■ *Total living area 1,819 sq. ft.* ■ *Price Code C* ■

No. 20158

This plan features:

- Three bedrooms

- Two full and one half baths

- A Kitchen with easy access to screened porch

- A Master suite including walk-in closet and luxury bath

- A second story balcony linking two bedrooms

First floor — 1,293 sq. ft
Second floor — 526 sq. ft.
Basement — 1,286 sq. ft.
Garage — 484 sq. ft.

An EXCLUSIVE DESIGN
By Karl Kreeger

Second Floor

- Br 3 10-8 x 12
- Balcony
- DN
- open to below
- Br 2 12 x 13-4
- plant shelf

First Floor

- MBr 1 14-8 x 13-4 decor. ceiling
- Deck
- skylight
- Living Rm 20 x 13-4
- slope
- Ldry
- W D
- ov
- pan.
- Balcony above
- DN
- Garage 21-4 x 21-4
- Screened Porch
- Kitchen 15-6 x 13-4
- Foyer
- UP
- decor. ceiling
- Dining Rm 11 x 12

44'-0"

68'-0"

Windows Distinguish Design

■ *Total living area 3,525 sq. ft.* ■ *Price Code F* ■

FIRST FLOOR

SECOND FLOOR

No. 98438

■ This plan features:

— Five bedrooms

— Four full and one half baths

■ Light shines into the Dining Room and the Living Room through their respective elegant windows

■ A hall through the Butler's Pantry leads the way into the Breakfast Nook

■ The two-story Family Room has a fireplace with built in bookcases on either side

■ The upstairs Master Suite has a sitting room and a French door that leads into the vaulted master bath

■ An optional basement or crawl space foundation — please specify when ordering

First floor — 1,786 sq. ft.
Second floor — 1,739 sq. ft.
Garage — 704 sq. ft.

No. 94715

This plan features:

Four bedrooms

Three full and one half baths

Old southern architecture incorporates today's open floor plan

Gracious two-story Foyer between formal Living and Dining rooms

Comfortable Great Room with a fireplace is nestled between French doors to the rear Decks

Hub Kitchen offers a cooktop island, an eating bar and a Breakfast area

Master Bedroom suite is enhanced by a fireplace and a plush bath

First floor — 2,094 sq. ft.

Second floor — 918 sq. ft.

Garage — 537 sq. ft.

Width — 71'-10"

Depth — 46'-0"

Total living area 3,012 sq. ft. ■ Price Code E

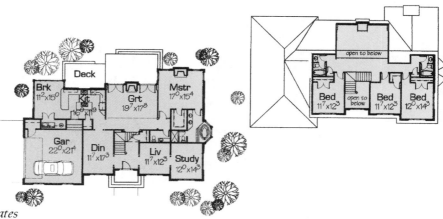

EXCLUSIVE DESIGN
By United Design Associates

Window-Studded Brick Facade Equals Success

No. 20353

This plan features:

Three bedrooms

Three full and one half bath

A sky-lit Foyer with a balcony above

A formal Dining Room made spacious by a vaulted ceiling

A large island Kitchen with peninsula counter that serves a glass-walled Breakfast area equipped with an adjoining pantry

A built-in bar in the huge Family Room with a cozy fireplace that is just steps away from the elegant Parlor

A magnificent Master Suite with pan vault ceiling, fireplace, circular spa, two-way access to a private deck and large walk-in closet

Two additional bedrooms each with a full bath

First floor — 1,807 sq. ft.

Second floor — 1,359 sq. ft.

Basement — 1,807 sq. ft.

Garage — 840 sq. ft.

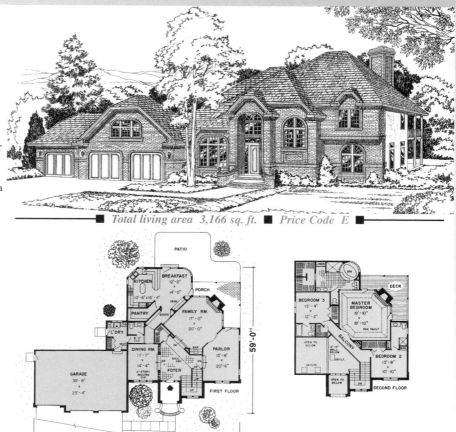

Total living area 3,166 sq. ft. ■ Price Code E

Farmhouse Charm

B. NATHAN.

■ *Total living area 1,846 sq. ft.* ■ *Price Code C* ■

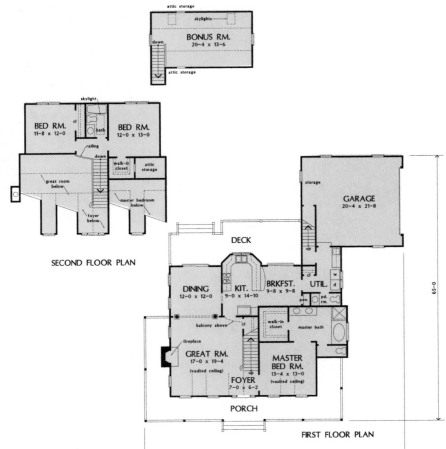

attic storage

BONUS RM.
20-4 x 13-6

skylights

down

attic storage

BED RM.
11-8 x 12-0

BED RM.
12-0 x 13-0

skylight

cl

bath

railing

walk-in closet

attic storage

down

great room below

master bedroom below

foyer below

SECOND FLOOR PLAN

storage

GARAGE
20-4 x 21-8

up

DECK

DINING
12-0 x 12-0

KIT.
9-0 x 14-10

BRKFST.
9-8 x 9-8

UTIL.

w
d

pen.

pd. rm.

cl

balcony above

cl

walk-in closet

master bath

fireplace

GREAT RM.
17-0 x 19-4
(vaulted ceiling)

MASTER BED RM.
13-4 x 13-0
(vaulted ceiling)

FOYER
7-0 x 6-2

up

PORCH

65-0

FIRST FLOOR PLAN

61-8

No. 96462 ⚒

■ **This plan features:**

— Three bedrooms

— Two full and one half baths

■ Nine foot ceilings and vaulted ceilings in Great Room and Master Bedroom add spaciousne

■ Dining Room accented by columns and accesses Deck for outdoor living

■ Efficient Kitchen features peninsula counter with serving bar for Breakfast area

■ Master Bedroom suite includes walk-in closet, garden tub, show and double vanity

■ Two bedrooms,.one with walk-i closet, share full, skylit bath

First floor — 1,380 sq. ft.
Second floor — 466 sq. ft.
Bonus room — 326 sq. ft.
Garage — 523 sq. ft.

Spectacular Sophistication

■ *Total living area 1,933 sq. ft.* ■ *Price Code C* ■

No. 94944

This plan features:

Four bedrooms

Two full and one half baths

Open Foyer with circular window and a plant shelf leads into the Dining Room

Great Room with an inviting fireplace and windows front and back

Open Kitchen has a work island and accesses the Breakfast area

Bedroom suite features a nine-foot boxed ceiling, a walk-in closet and whirlpool bath

Three additional bedrooms share a full bath with a double vanity

First floor — 941 sq. ft.
Second floor — 992 sq. ft.
Basement — 941 sq. ft.
Garage — 480 sq. ft.

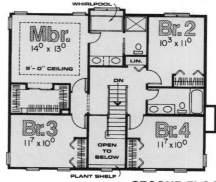

SECOND FLOOR

© design basics, inc.

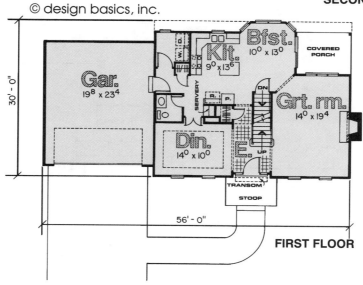

FIRST FLOOR

The Essence of Elegance

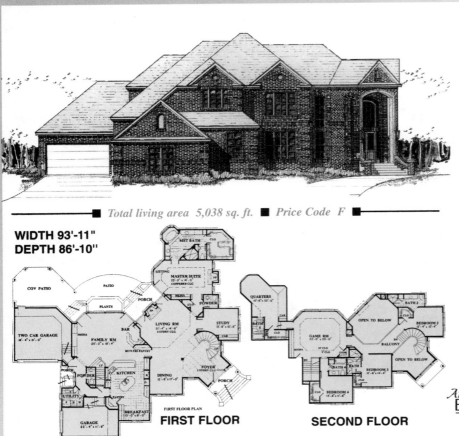

Total living area 5,038 sq. ft. ■ **Price Code F**

WIDTH 93'-11"
DEPTH 86'-10"

FIRST FLOOR

SECOND FLOOR

No. 92915

■ **This plan features:**

— Five bedrooms

— Five full and two half baths

■ With a two-story Foyer and curved staircase, the entrance to this home provides for every convenience and whim

■ Open Living and Dining rooms provide entertaining ease and access to Covered Porch and Patio

■ Central Family Room offers media center, bar, butlers pantry, and access to the Kitchen

■ Master Suite pampers with coffered ceiling above, also a fireplace, sitting area and media center

■ Second floor boasts three bedrooms with private baths and a Game Room

■ No materials list is available for this plan

First floor — 3,224 sq. ft.
Second floor — 1,814 sq. ft.
Bonus — 461 sq. ft.
Garages — 826 sq. ft.

An
EXCLUSIVE DESIGN
By Kent & Kent, Inc.

Traditional Two-Story Home

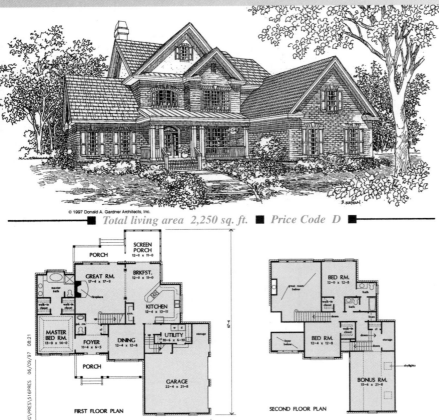

© 1997 Donald A. Gardner Architects, Inc.
Total living area 2,250 sq. ft. ■ **Price Code D**

FIRST FLOOR PLAN

SECOND FLOOR PLAN

No. 96491

■ **This plan features:**

— Three bedrooms

— Two full and two half baths

■ Facade handsomely accented by multiple gables, keystone arches and transom windows

■ Arched clerestory window lights two-story Foyer for dramatic entrance

■ Two-story Great Room exciting with inviting fireplace, wall of windows and back Porch access

■ Great cooks will enjoy open Kitchen and easy access to Screen Porch and Dining Room

■ Private Master Bedroom suite offers two walk-in closets and deluxe bath

First floor — 1,644 sq. ft.
Second floor — 606 sq. ft.
Bonus room — 548 sq. ft.
Garage & storage — 657 sq. ft.

Stately Colonial Home

■ *Total living area 2,959 sq. ft.* ■ *Price Code E* ■

No. 98534

This plan features:

- Four bedrooms

- Three full and one half baths

■ Stately columns and lovely arched windows

■ The entry is highlighted by a palladian window, a plant shelf and an angled staircase

■ The formal Living and Dining Rooms located off the Entry for ease in entertaining

■ Great Room has a fireplace and opens to Kitchen/Breakfast area and the Patio

■ The Master Bedroom wing offers Patio access, a luxurious bath and a walk-in closet

First floor — 1,848 sq. ft.
Second floor — 1,111 sq. ft.
Garage & shop — 722 sq. ft.

WIDTH 73'-4"
DEPTH 44'-1"

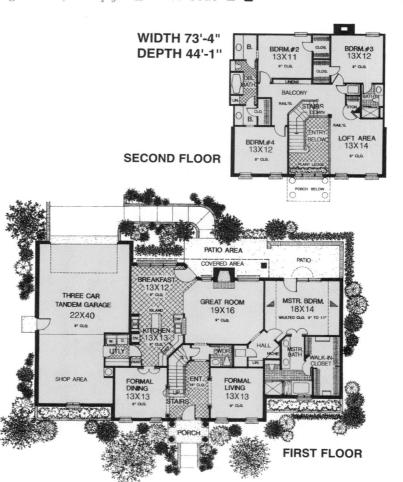

SECOND FLOOR

FIRST FLOOR

An Estate of Epic Proportion

Total living area 3,936 sq. ft. ■ **Price Code F** ■

No. 98539

■ This plan features

— Four bedrooms

— Three full and one half baths

■ Front door opening into a grand Entry way with a 20' ceiling and a spiral staircase

■ Living Room with cathedral ceiling and fireplace

■ Walk down the Gallery to the Study with a full wall built in bookcase

■ The enormous Master Bedroom has a walk in closet, sumptuous bath and a bayed Sitting area

■ Family Room has a wetbar and a fireplace

■ An optional basement or slab foundation — please specify when ordering

First floor — 2,751 sq. ft.
Second floor — 1,185 sq. ft.
Bonus — 343 sq. ft.
Garage — 790 sq. ft.

UPPER FLOOR

MAIN FLOOR

Brick Home of Distinction

■ *Total living area 3,023 sq. ft.* ■ *Price Code E* ■

An
EXCLUSIVE DESIGN
By Ahmann Design Inc.

No. 99109

This plan features:

Four bedrooms

Three full and one half baths

Past the covered front porch you step into a two-story Entry way

Voluminous two-story Family Room has a fireplace centered along the back wall, and the nook, while the Kitchen is in close proximity

Master bedroom has a private bath and a big walk-in closet

Two additional bedrooms upstairs with ample closet space that share a full bath

This plan has a three-car garage

No materials list is available for this plan

First floor — 1,873 sq. ft.
Second floor — 1,150 sq. ft.
Basement — 1,810 sq. ft.

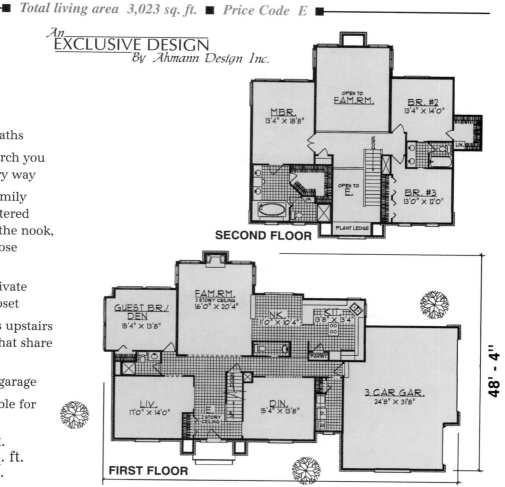

A Livab...

■ *Total living area 2,715 sq. ft.* ■ *Price Code E* ■

No. 94965

■ **This plan features:**

— Four bedrooms

— Two full, one three quarter and one half baths

■ The Master Bedroom is complete with a tray ceiling, two walk in closets, and a large bath

■ Three additional Bedrooms upstairs, all have ample closet space and share two full baths

■ The Dining and Living rooms both have decorative windows that let in plenty of light

■ The Family Room has a beamed ceiling and a fireplace

■ This home has a three car Garage with plenty of storage space

First floor — 1,400 sq. ft.
Second floor — 1,315 sq. ft.
Basement — 1,400 sq. ft.
Garage — 631 sq. ft.

SECOND FLOOR

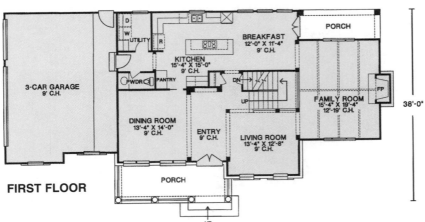

FIRST FLOOR

© Carmichael & Dame

Charm and Convenience

No. 92693

■ **This plan features:**

- Three bedrooms
- Two full and one half baths
■ Neo-traditional home features a large, charming front porch
■ Great Room has a fireplace and accesses the rear yard for indoor/outdoor living
■ Spacious Kitchen with a snack bar and access to both the breakfast area and formal Dining Room
■ Master Bedroom with a walk-in closet and a private bath
■ Two additional bedrooms share a full hall bath
■ No materials list is available for this plan

First floor — 924 sq. ft.
Second floor — 968 sq. ft.
Basement — 924 sq. ft.

■ *Total living area 1,892 sq. ft.* ■ *Price Code C* ■

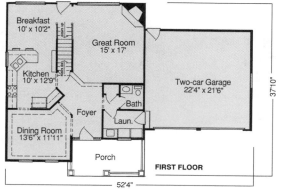

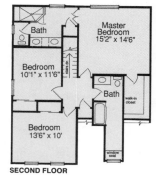

Eye-Catching Covered Entry

No. 94120 ✖

■ **This plan features:**

- Three bedrooms
- Two full and one half baths
■ Open layout gives this home a true sense of spaciousness
■ Great Room features a large fireplace and numerous windows for natural light
■ The efficient Kitchen has an extended counter/snack bar and accesses the Great Room and the Dinette
■ The formal Dining Room has a bay window and is conveniently located off the Kitchen and the foyer
■ The Master Bedroom has a walk-in closet and private bath with corner tub and double vanity
■ Two additional bedrooms share a full hall bath

First floor — 931 sq. ft.
Second floor — 942 sq. ft.
Basement — 895 sq. ft.
Width — 50'-0"
Depth — 38'-0"

■ *Total living area 1,873 sq. ft.* ■ *Price Code D* ■

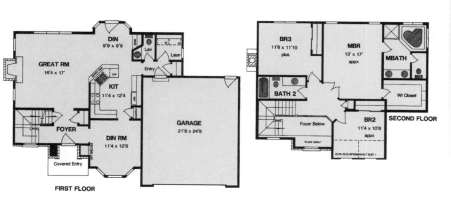

Fieldstone Facade and Arched Windows

Total living area 1,858 sq. ft. ■ *Price Code C* ■

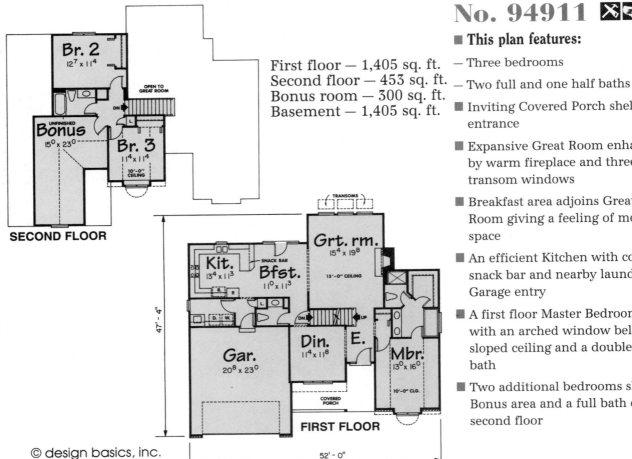

First floor — 1,405 sq. ft.
Second floor — 453 sq. ft.
Bonus room — 300 sq. ft.
Basement — 1,405 sq. ft.

No. 94911

■ This plan features:

— Three bedrooms

— Two full and one half baths

■ Inviting Covered Porch shelters entrance

■ Expansive Great Room enhanced by warm fireplace and three transom windows

■ Breakfast area adjoins Great Room giving a feeling of more space

■ An efficient Kitchen with counter snack bar and nearby laundry and Garage entry

■ A first floor Master Bedroom suite with an arched window below a sloped ceiling and a double vanity bath

■ Two additional bedrooms share a Bonus area and a full bath on the second floor

© design basics, inc.

Total living area 3,192 sq. ft. ■ **Price Code E** ■

No. 91319 ⚒

This plan features:

Three bedrooms

One full, one three quarter and one half baths

A wall of windows taking full advantage of the front view

A large, two-way staircase

A Master Bedroom with a private Master Bath and a walk-in wardrobe

An efficient Kitchen including a breakfast bar that opens into the Dining Area

A formal Living Room with a vaulted ceiling and a stone fireplace

First floor — 1,306 sq. ft.
Second floor — 598 sq. ft.
Lower level — 1,288 sq. ft.

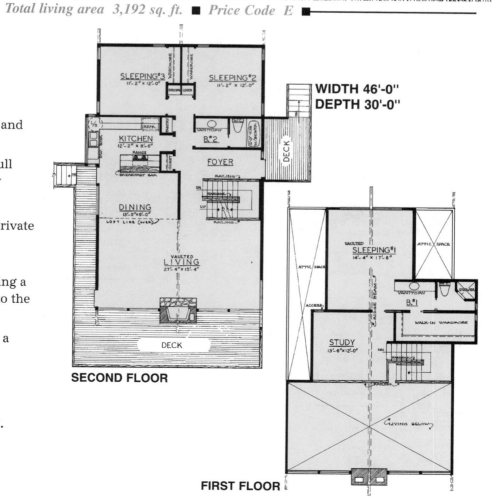

WIDTH 46'-0"
DEPTH 30'-0"

SECOND FLOOR

FIRST FLOOR

Great Style and Flexibility

Total living area 2,946 sq. ft. ■ Price Code E

FIRST FLOOR PLAN

SECOND FLOOR PLAN

No. 96445

■ This plan features:

— Four bedrooms

— Three full and one half baths

■ Bay windows, gables, a wrap-around Porch and the expansive Deck offer style and space

■ Balcony over the Foyer and the Great Room hosts a Loft/Study and accesses the second floor bedrooms

■ Central and spacious Kitchen easily serve the Breakfast area, Dining Room and the Deck

■ Great Room with a cozy fireplace accesse the rear Deck

■ Master Bedroom suite offers a walk-in closet, vanity and a private bath

First floor — 1,976 sq. ft.
Second floor — 970 sq. ft.

Family Living on Two Levels

Total living area 2,851 sq. ft. ■ Price Code E

FIRST FLOOR

SECOND FLOOR

Slab/Crawlspace Option

No. 20090

■ This plan features:

— Four bedrooms

— Two full and one half baths

■ A stacked window gracing the facade of t spacious, four-bedroom classic

■ A formal Parlor and Dining Room with decorative ceilings off the foyer

■ Family areas at the rear of the house arranged for convenient access to the Kitchen

■ A sky-lit Breakfast room with a surround outdoor deck

■ A cozy fireplace in the Family Room

■ A first floor Master Suite with double vanities, a walk-in closet, and an elegant recessed ceiling

First floor — 1,933 sq. ft.
Second floor — 918 sq. ft.
Basement — 1,888 sq. ft.
Garage— 475 sq. ft.

An

EXCLUSIVE DESIGN
By Karl Kreeger

■ Total living area 2,891 sq. ft. ■ Price Code E ■

No. 94231

This plan features:

Three bedrooms

Three full baths

Glass arch entrance into Foyer and Grand Room

Decorative windows highlight Study and formal Dining Room

Spacious Kitchen with walk-in pantry and peninsula serving counter easily serves Nook, Veranda and Dining Room

Luxurious Master suite with step ceiling, sitting area, his and hers closets and pampering bath

Two additional bedrooms, one with a private Deck, have bay windows and walk-in closets

No materials list available

First floor — 2,181 sq. ft.
Second floor — 710 sq. ft.
Garage —658 sq. ft.

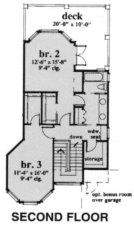

SECOND FLOOR

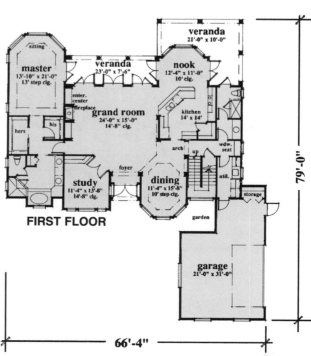

FIRST FLOOR

Elegant European Style

Total living area 2,039 sq. ft. ■ Price Code D ■

SECOND FLOOR PLAN

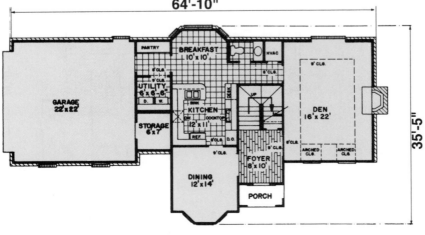

FIRST FLOOR PLAN

No. 92513

■ This plan features:

— Three bedrooms

— Two full and one half baths

■ Copper hood over double bay windows enhances facade of stucco, brick and arches

■ Balcony overlooks two-story Foyer highlighted by transom window

■ Spacious Den with focal point fireplace below decorative ceiling

■ Gourmet Kitchen with built-in desk, Breakfast bay, walk-in pantry and Utility area

■ Master Bedroom suite with decorative ceiling, oversized corner tub and vanity area

■ An optional crawl space or slab foundation — please specify when ordering

First floor — 1,065 sq. ft.
Second floor — 974 sq. ft.
Garage — 626 sq. ft.

■ *Total living area 1,567 sq. ft.* ■ *Price Code B* ■

No. 99641 ✕

■ This plan features:

- Three bedrooms

- Two full baths

■ The Living Room is enhanced by nine foot ceilings and a bookcase flanked fireplace

■ Two mullioned French doors from the Dining Room to the rear terrace

■ Laundry area serving as a Mudroom between the Garage and Kitchen

■ A Master Suite with a large walk-in closet and a compartmented Bath has a separate shower stall, whirlpool tub, double vanity and linen closet

■ Bonus area can be finished into a study or recreation room

First floor — 1,567 sq. ft.
Bonus area — 462 sq. ft.
Basement — 1,567 sq. ft.
Garage — 504 sq. ft.

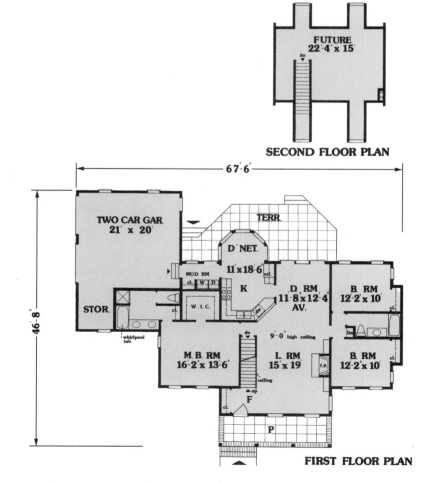

SECOND FLOOR PLAN

FIRST FLOOR PLAN

Home on a Hill

Total living area 1,908 sq. ft. ■ *Price Code C* ■

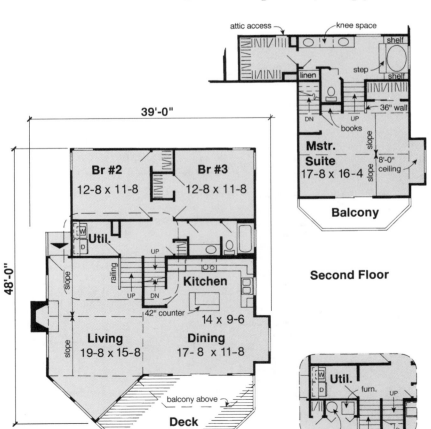

attic access — knee space

shelf

linen

step

shelf

36" wall

DN

UP

books

slope

8'-0"
ceiling

slope

**Mstr.
Suite**
17-8 x 16-4

Balcony

Second Floor

39'-0"

Br #2
12-8 x 11-8

Br #3
12-8 x 11-8

W
D
Util.

UP

railing

slope

UP DN

Kitchen

42" counter

14 x 9-6

Living
19-8 x 15-8

slope

Dining
17-8 x 11-8

48'-0"

balcony above

Deck

First Floor

W
D
Util.

furn.

UP

w.h.

UP

Pier/ Crawl Space Option

No. 20501

■ **This plan features:**

— Three bedrooms

— Two full baths

■ Window walls combining with
sliders to unite active areas with a
huge outdoor deck

■ Interior spaces flowing together
for an open feeling, that is
accentuated by the sloping
ceilings and towering fireplace in
the Living Room

■ An island Kitchen with easy
access to the Dining Room

■ A Master Suite complete with a
garden spa, abundant closet
space, and a balcony

First floor — 1,316 sq. ft.
Second floor — 592 sq. ft.

Compact Comfort

No. 10787

This plan features:

- Three bedrooms
- Two and one half baths
- Soaring ceilings and a wall of stacked windows
- A formal Dining Room perfect for entertaining
- A Kitchen/Family Room combination with a cozy fireplace
- An efficient Kitchen layout
- Three bedrooms upstairs and two full baths, including the luxury bath in the Master Bedroom

First floor — 1,088 sq. ft.
Second floor — 750 sq. ft.
Basement — 750 sq. ft.
Garage — 548 sq. ft.

Total living area 1,838 sq. ft. ■ Price Code C

Second Floor

First Floor

Perfect for a Woodland Setting

No. 35007

This plan features:

- Two bedrooms
- One full bath
- A Living Room and Dining Room/Kitchen located to the front of the house
- A sloped ceiling adding to the cozy feeling of the home
- A built-in entertainment center in the Living Room adding convenience
- An L-shaped Kitchen that includes a double sink and Dining area
- A full hall Bath easily accessible from either bedroom
- A Loft and Balcony that overlooks the Living Room and the Dining area
- Storage on either side of the Loft

First floor — 763 sq. ft.
Second floor — 264 sq. ft.

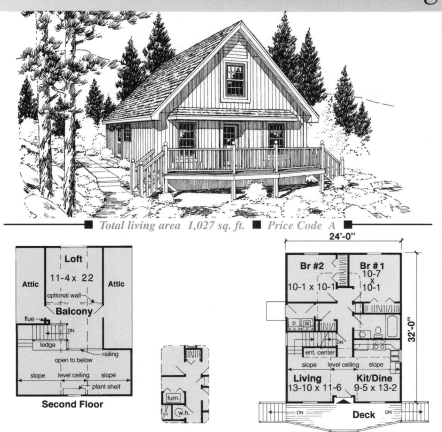

Total living area 1,027 sq. ft. ■ Price Code A

Second Floor

Slab/ Crawl Space Option

First Floor

Glorious Gables

■ *Total living area 3,306 sq. ft.* ■ *Price Code F* ■

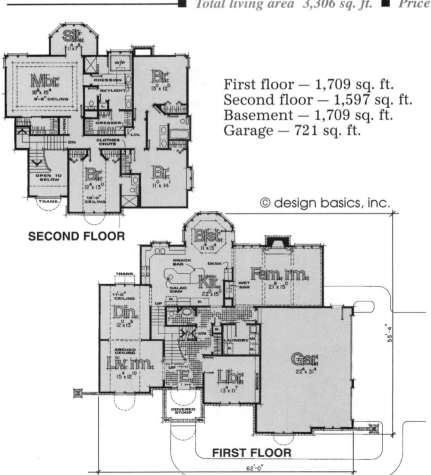

SECOND FLOOR

First floor — 1,709 sq. ft.
Second floor — 1,597 sq. ft.
Basement — 1,709 sq. ft.
Garage — 721 sq. ft.

© design basics, inc.

FIRST FLOOR

No. 94933

■ **This plan features:**

— Four bedrooms

— Two full, one three-quarter and one half baths

■ Arched windows and entry graciously greet one and all

■ Arched ceiling topping decorative windows highlights Living and Dining rooms

■ Double door leads into quiet Library with book shelves

■ Hub Kitchen with angled, work island/snackbar, built-in pantry and desk

■ Comfortable Family Room with hearth fireplace framed by decorative windows

■ Private Master Bedroom suite offers a Sitting area, two walk-in closets, and luxurious bath

■ Three additional bedrooms with ample closets and private access to a full bath

■ *Total living area 1,764 sq. ft.* ■ *Price Code B* ■

No. 90440 ⚒

This plan features:

Three bedrooms

Two full baths

A fireplaced Living Room with built-in bookshelves

A fully-equipped Kitchen with an island

A sunny Dining Room with glass sliders to a wood deck

A first floor Master Suite with walk-in closet and lavish Master Bath

An optional basement or crawl space foundation — please specify when ordering

Main floor — 1,100 sq. ft.
Second floor — 664 sq. ft.
Basement — 1,100 sq. ft.

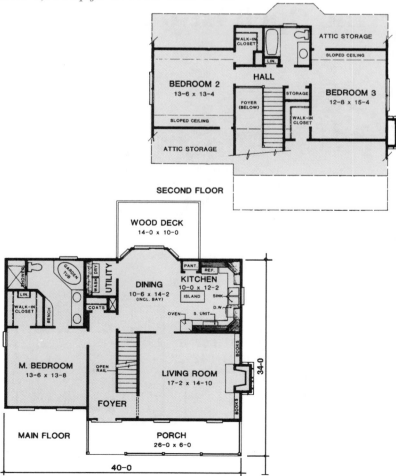

SECOND FLOOR

MAIN FLOOR

Compact, Yet Elegant

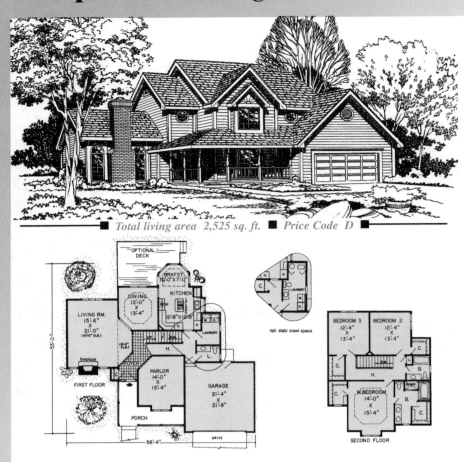

■ *Total living area 2,525 sq. ft.* ■ *Price Code D* ■

No. 34926

■ **This plan features:**

— Three bedrooms

— Two and one half baths

■ An angular plan giving each room an interesting shape

■ A wrap-around veranda

■ An entry foyer leading through the Living Room and Parlor

■ A Dining Room with a hexagonal, recesse ceiling

■ A sunny Breakfast room off the island Kitchen

■ A Master Suite with a bump-out window, walk-in closet, and double sinks in the private bath

First floor — 1,409 sq. ft.
Second floor — 1,116 sq. ft.
Basement — 1,409 sq. ft.
Garage — 483 sq. ft.

An
EXCLUSIVE DESIGN
By Karl Kreeger

Terrific Open Layout

■ *Total living area 1,995 sq. ft.* ■ *Price Code C* ■

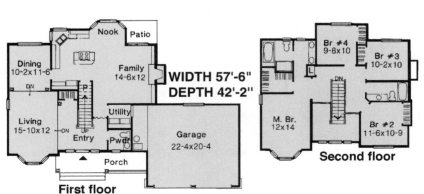

WIDTH 57'-6"
DEPTH 42'-2"

First floor

Second floor

No. 92160

■ **This plan features:**

— Four Bedrooms

— Two full and one half baths

■ An impressive entrance leads to an entry hall that has access to a powder room and both the formal and informal areas

■ Generous corner kitchen is open to the bayed nook bringing in an abundance of natural sunlight.

■ Family room including a focal point fireplace enjoyed from the nook and kitchen

■ Large master suite with a luxurious bath and a walk-in closet

■ Three additional bedrooms with a full ba located in proximity

First floor — 1,041 sq. ft.
Second floor — 954 sq. ft.

Quoins and Keystones Accent Stucco

■ *Total living area 3,840 sq. ft.* ■ *Price Code F* ■

No. 93247

This plan features:

Three bedrooms

Two full and four half baths

Living Room with a vaulted ceiling, Sundeck access and an inviting fireplace

Elegant Dining Room with decorative ceiling and corner built-ins

Kitchen with cooktop serving counter and Breakfast area

Palatial Master Bedroom with a fireplace, private Deck and a spectacular bath

Second floor offers three additional bedrooms, one and a half baths, Storage and space for future expansion

No materials list available

First floor — 2,656 sq. ft.
Second floor — 1,184 sq. ft.
Bonus — 508 sq. ft.
Basement — 2,642 sq. ft.
Garage — 528 sq. ft.

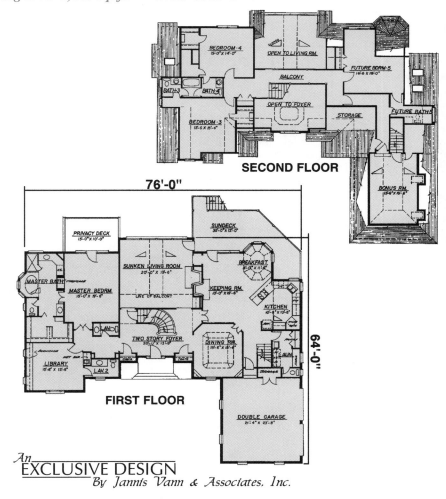

An
EXCLUSIVE DESIGN
By Jannis Vann & Associates, Inc.

Spacious Family Living

Total living area 2,303 sq. ft. ■ Price Code D ■

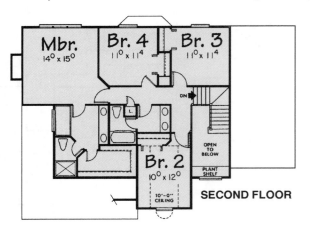

Mbr.
14⁰ x 15⁰

Br. 4
11⁰ x 11⁴

Br. 3
11⁰ x 11⁴

DN

OPEN TO BELOW

Br. 2
10⁰ x 12⁰

10'-0" CEILING

PLANT SHELF

SECOND FLOOR

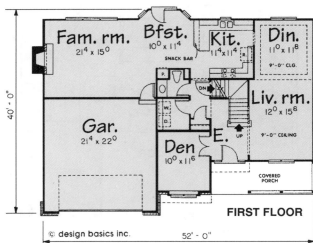

Fam. rm.
21⁴ x 15⁰

Bfst.
10⁰ x 11⁴

SNACK BAR

Kit.
11⁴ x 11⁴

Din.
11⁰ x 11⁸

9'-0" CLG.

P.

Gar.
21⁴ x 22⁰

40' - 0"

W. D.

DN

Liv. rm.
12⁰ x 15⁸

9'-0" CEILING

Den
10⁰ x 11⁶

E.

UP

COVERED PORCH

FIRST FLOOR

© design basics inc.

52' - 0"

No. 94956

■ This plan features:

— Four bedrooms

— Two full and one half baths

■ Front Porch welcomes friends a family home

■ Entry opens to spacious Living Room with a tiered ceiling and Dining Room beyond

■ Hub Kitchen easily serves the Dining Room, the Breakfast bay and the Family Room

■ Corner Master Bedroom has access to a private bath

■ Three additional bedrooms sha a double vanity bath

First floor — 1,269 sq. ft.
Second floor — 1,034 sq. ft.
Basement — 1,269 sq. ft.
Garage — 485 sq. ft.

■ *Total living area 1,675 sq. ft.* ■ *Price Code B* ■

No. 98431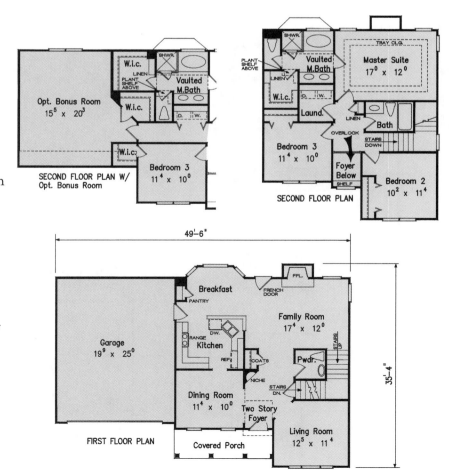

This plan features:

Three bedrooms

Two full and one half baths

An impressive two-story Foyer

The Kitchen is equipped with ample cabinet and counter space

Spacious Family Room flows from the Breakfast Bay and is highlighted by a fireplace and a French door to the rear yard

The Master Suite is topped by a tray ceiling and is enhanced by a vaulted, five-piece master bath

An optional basement or crawl space foundation — please specify when ordering

First floor — 882 sq. ft.

Second floor — 793 sq. ft.

Bonus room — 416 sq. ft.

Basement — 882 sq. ft.

Garage — 510 sq. ft.

Arches Add Ambiance

■ *Total living area 2,033 sq. ft.* ■ *Price Code D* ■

OPEN TO DEN

BEDROOM 2
11'-0" x 13'-0"

DOWN

LIN. LIN.

HVAC

OPEN TO FOYER

BEDROOM 3
11'-0" x 13'-0"

BEDROOM 4
14'-0" x 12'-0"

SECOND FLOOR

33'-0"

40'-0"

BOOKS

DEN
18'-0" x 16'-0"

BOOKS

BREAKFAST
11'-0" x 10'-0"

WASH DRY

STORAGE
12'-0" x 6'-0"

UP

PANT

SINK

KITCHEN
DW

RANGE

REF

HVAC

M. BATH

LIN

GARAGE
22'-0" x 22'-0"

DINING
11'-0" x 14'-0"

MASTER BED
14'-0" x 12'-0"

FOYER

PORCH

FIRST FLOOR

57'-0"

40'-0"

No. 92539

■ **This plan features:**

— Four bedrooms

— Two full and one half baths

■ Arched two-story entrance with lovely arched window

■ Den offers hearth fireplace between book shelves, raised ceiling and access to rear yard

■ Kitchen with peninsula counter, built-in pantry, Breakfast bay, Garage entry, and laundry acces

■ Private Master Bedroom with a walk-in closet and plush bath

■ Three bedrooms with walk-in closets share a double vanity bat

■ An optional slab or crawlspace foundation — please specify whe ordering

First floor — 1,250 sq. ft.
Second floor — 783 sq. ft
Garage and Storage —
555 sq. ft.

Beautiful Stucco & Stone

No. 98445

This plan features:

Three bedrooms

Two full and one half baths

This home is accented by keystone arches and a turret styled roof

The two story Foyer includes a half bath

The vaulted Family Room is highlighted by a fireplace and French doors to the rear yard

The Dining Room adjoins the Family Room which has access to the covered porch and the Kitchen

The Master Bedroom is crowned by a tray ceiling, while Master Bath has a vaulted ceiling

Two additional bedrooms share a full double vanity bath

A Balcony overlooks the Family Room and Foyer below

An optional basement or crawl space foundation — please specify when ordering

No materials list is available for this plan

First floor — 1,398 sq. ft.

Second floor — 515 sq. ft.

Basement — 1,398 sq. ft.

Garage — 421 sq. ft.

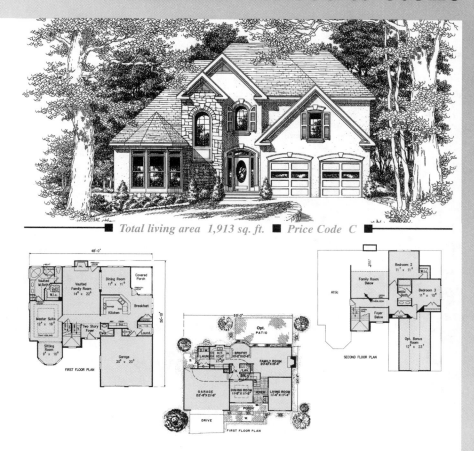

Total living area 1,913 sq. ft. ▪ Price Code C

Comfortable Family Home Leaves Room to Grow

No. 34827

This plan features:

Three bedrooms

Two full and one half baths

Formal Living and Dining Rooms off the central foyer for ease in entertaining

A Family Room with a large fireplace adjoining the Breakfast area with a bay window

A short hall leading past the powder room, linking the formal Dining Room with the Kitchen

Each bedroom containing a walk-in closet

A Master Suite including both a raised tub and a step-in shower

First floor — 1,212 sq. ft.

Second floor — 1,030 sq. ft.

Basement — 1,212 sq. ft.

Garage — 521 sq. ft.

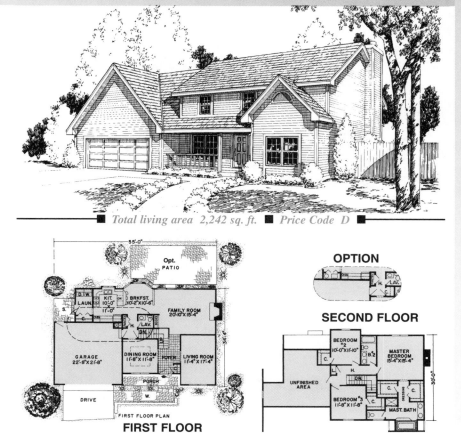

Total living area 2,242 sq. ft. ▪ Price Code D

225

Elegant Brick Two-Story

■ *Total living area 2,398 sq. ft.* ■ *Price Code D* ■

SECOND FLOOR PLAN

MAIN FLOOR PLAN

No. 90450

■ This plan features:

— Four bedrooms

— Two or three full and one half baths

■ A two-story Great Room with a fireplace and access to a deck

■ Master Suite with two walk-in closets and a private Master Bath

■ A large island Kitchen serving the formal Dining Room and the sunny Breakfast Nook with ease

■ Three additional bedrooms, two with walk-in closets, sharing a full hall bath

■ An optional Bonus Room with a private entrance from below

■ An optional basement or crawl space foundation — please specify when ordering

First floor — 1,637 sq. ft.
Second floor — 761 sq. ft.
Opt. bath & closet — 106 sq. ft.
Opt. bonus — 347 sq. ft.

■ *Total living area 2,162 sq. ft.* ■ *Price Code C* ■

No. 91343 ⚒

This plan features:

Three bedrooms

Two full and one half baths

A stone-faced fireplace and vaulted ceiling in the Living Room

An island food preparation center with a sink and a Breakfast bar in the Kitchen

Sliding glass doors leading from the Dining Room to the adjacent deck

A Master Suite with a vaulted ceiling, a Sitting Room, and a lavish Master Bath with a whirlpool tub, skylights, double vanity, and a walk-in closet

First floor — 1,338 sq. ft.
Second floor — 763 sq. ft.
Lower floor — 61 sq. ft.

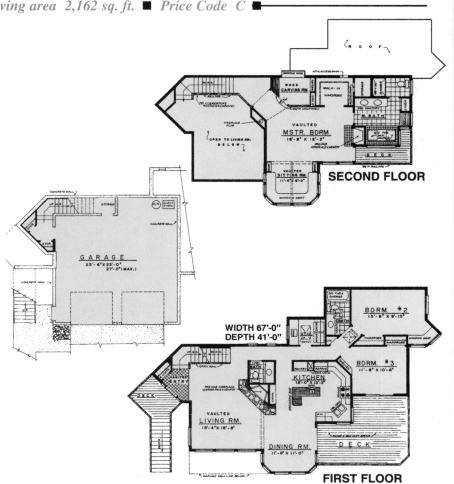

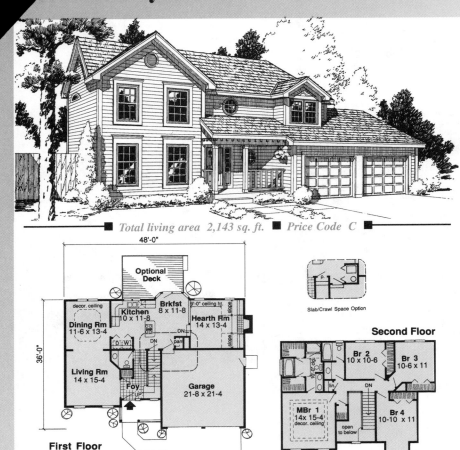

Total living area 2,143 sq. ft. ■ **Price Code C** ■

First Floor

48'-0"

36'-0"

Optional Deck

Brkfst 8 x 11-8

Kitchen 10 x 11-8

decor. ceiling

Dining Rm 11-6 x 13-4

Hearth Rm 14 x 13-4

9'-0" ceiling ht.

Living Rm 14 x 15-4

Foy UP

Garage 21-8 x 21-4

Slab/Crawl Space Option

Second Floor

Br 2 10 x 10-6

Br 3 10-6 x 11

MBr 1 14x 15-4 decor. ceiling

open to below

Br 4 10-10 x 11

No. 20179

■ **This plan features:**

— Four bedrooms

— Two full and one half baths

■ An efficient island Kitchen with ample storage and counter space, a laundry cen and a sunny Breakfast nook

■ A sunken Hearth Room with sloped ceili and cozy fireplace

■ A formal Living Room and Dining Room that flow conveniently into each other fo easy entertaining

■ A Master Suite with a decorative ceiling, private Master Bath and ample closet spa

■ Three additional bedrooms that share a f hall bath

First floor — 1,086 sq. ft.
Second floor — 1,057 sq. ft.
Basement — 881 sq. ft.
Garage — 484 sq. ft.

An
EXCLUSIVE DESIGN
By Karl Kreeger

Perfect for the Growing Family

Total living area 2,144 sq. ft. ■ **Price Code D** ■

spa

DECK

covered porch

covered porch

DINING 12-0 x 12-8

KIT. 10-6 x 16-4

BRKFST. 10-7 x 9-8

storage

GREAT RM. 15-4 x 19-8

walk-in closet

master bath

GARAGE 23-4 x 22-0

fireplace

MASTER BED RM. 15-4 x 14-4

FOYER 7-0 x 6-0

PORCH

72-8

FIRST FLOOR PLAN

bath

attic storage

attic storage

BED RM. 15-4 x 11-0

down

BED RM. 15-4 x 11-0

foyer below

SECOND FLOOR PLAN

down

BONUS RM. 13-4 x 25-8

No. 96446

■ **This plan features:**

— Three bedrooms

— Two full and one half baths

■ Natural light fills the two-story foyer through a palladian window in dormer above

■ Dining Room and Great Room adjoin for entertaining possibilities

■ U-shaped Kitchen with a curved counter opens to a large Breakfast Area

■ Master Suite, situated downstairs for privacy with generous walk-in closet, dou vanity, separate shower and a whirlpool

■ Please specify a basement or crawl space foundation when ordering

First floor — 1,484 sq. ft.
Second floor — 660 sq. ft.
Bonus room — 389 sq. ft.
Garage — 600 sq. ft.

■ *Total living area 897 sq. ft.* ■ *Price Code A* ■

No. 24309 ✕

This plan features:

- Two bedrooms

- One full bath

- A wrap-around deck equipped with a built-in bar-b-que for easy outdoor living

- An entry, in a wall of glass, opens the Living area to the outdoors

- A large fireplace in the Living area opens into an efficient Kitchen, with a built-in pantry, that serves the Nook area

- Two bedrooms share a centrally located full bath with a window tub

- A loft area ready for multiple uses

Main floor — 789 sq. ft.
Loft — 108 sq. ft.

An EXCLUSIVE DESIGN
By Marshall Associates

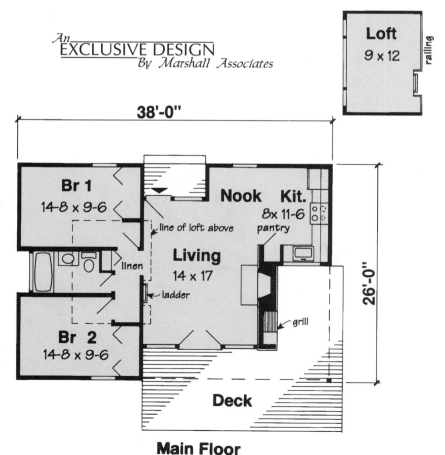

Loft
9 x 12
railing

38'-0"

Br 1
14-8 x 9-6

Nook   **Kit.**
8 x 11-6
pantry

line of loft above

linen

Living
14 x 17

26'-0"

ladder

grill

Br 2
14-8 x 9-6

Deck

Main Floor

Separate Guest Quarters

■ *Total living area 3,792 sq. ft.* ■ *Price Code F* ■

First floor — 2,853 sq. ft.
Second floor — 627 sq. ft.
Guest house — 312 sq. ft.
Garage — 777 sq. ft.

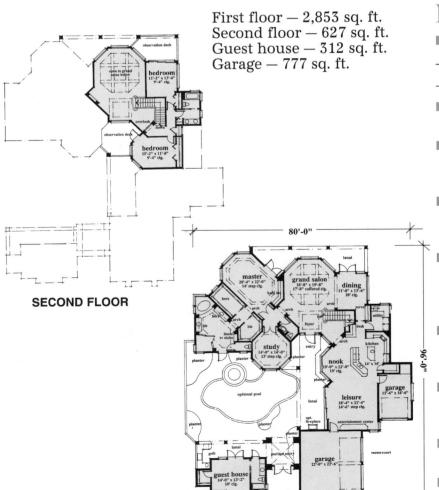

SECOND FLOOR

FIRST FLOOR

No. 94246

■ **This plan features:**

— Four bedrooms

— Three full and one half baths

■ Portico Entry way opens up to a unique courtyard plan

■ Octagon-shaped Grand Salon overlooks Lanai and opens to formal Dining area

■ An efficient Kitchen with a walk-in pantry, built-in desk, island sink and expansive snack bar

■ Open Leisure room with a high ceiling, offers an entertainment center, sliding glass doors to lanai and courtyard

■ Master wing has a large bedroom with a stepped ceiling, a bayed sitting area and lavish bath area

■ Two upstairs bedrooms with private decks, share a double vanity bath

■ Private Guest House offers luxurious accommodations

■ No materials list available

Cozy Front Porch

■ *Total living area 1,735 sq. ft.* ■ *Price Code B* ■

No. 93269

This plan features:

Three bedrooms

Two full and one half bath

A Living Room enhanced by a large fireplace

A formal Dining Room that is open to the Living Room

An efficient Kitchen that includes ample counter and cabinet space as well as double sinks and pass thru window

Breakfast Area with vaulted ceiling and a door to the sun deck

First floor Master Suite with separate tub & shower stall, plus a walk-in closet

Two additional bedrooms that share a full hall bath

First floor — 1,045 sq. ft.
Second floor — 690 sq. ft.
Basement — 465 sq. ft.
Garage — 580 sq. ft.

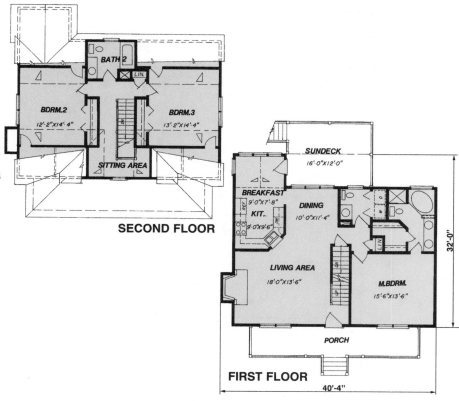

SECOND FLOOR

BATH 2

BDRM.2
12'-2"X14'-4"

BDRM.3
13'-2"X14'-4"

SITTING AREA

FIRST FLOOR

SUNDECK
16'-0"X12'-0"

BREAKFAST
9'0"X7'8"

KIT.
9'-0"X9'6"

DINING
10'-0"X11'-4"

LIVING AREA
18'-0"X13'-6"

M.BDRM.
15'-6"X13'-6"

PORCH

32'-0"

40'-4"

An
EXCLUSIVE DESIGN
By Jannis Vann & Associates, Inc.

Country-Style Home for Quality Living

■ *Total living area 2,466 sq. ft.* ■ *Price Code D* ■

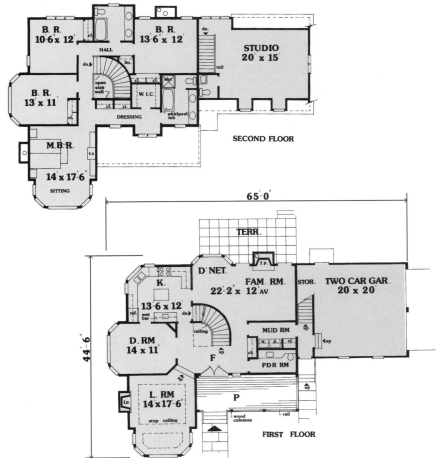

SECOND FLOOR

B. R.
10'-6 x 12'

HALL

B. R.
13'-6 x 12'

STUDIO
20' x 15'

B. R.
13' x 11'

open stair well

W. I.C.

DRESSING

whirlpool tub

M.B.R.
14 x 17'6

SITTING

FIRST FLOOR

65'-0"

44'-6'

TERR.

D' NET.

K.
13'-6 x 12'

FAM. RM.
22'-2" x 12' AV

STOR.

TWO CAR GAR.
20' x 20'

wet bar

D. RM
14 x 11'

railing

MUD RM

PDR RM

L. RM
14 x 17'-6

step ceiling

P

wood columns

rail

No. 99640 ⚒

■ **This plan features:**

— Four bedrooms

— Two full and two half baths

■ A spacious central Foyer which leads to all rooms

■ A sunken Living Room, enhanced by a focal point fireplace and a large windowed bay

■ An elegant formal Dining Room with interior corners angled to form an octagon

■ A fully equipped Kitchen with a center island

■ A luxurious Master Bedroom includes a dressing area, a walk closet and a deluxe bath

■ A Studio area above the garage that includes a half bath

First floor — 1,217 sq. ft.
Second floor — 1,249 sq. ft.
Basement — 1,249 sq. ft.
Garage — 431 sq. ft.

Classic Warmth

No. 34878

This plan features:

- Three bedrooms
- Two full baths
- Clapboard and brick exterior
- Cathedral ceilings gracing the Living and Dining Rooms lending an airy quality
- A Master Bedroom with private Master Bath and walk-in closet
- A spacious fireplaced Family Room
- Sliders leading from both Dining and Family Rooms to the rear patio adding to living space

First floor — 1,088 sq. ft.
Second floor — 750 sq. ft.
Basement — 750 sq. ft.
Garage — 517 sq. ft.

■ *Total living area 1,838 sq. ft.* ■ *Price Code C* ■

FIRST FLOOR

optional **Deck**

Dining
12-6 x 10-6

Kitchen
14-9 x 8-0

Family Rm
21-3 x 13-8

optional Fireplace

wood storage

Living Rm
12-6 x 14-6

W/D
DN

Foyer
UP

Garage
23-6 x 23-4

36'-8"

50'-0"

Slab/Crawlspace Option

SECOND FLOOR

MBr 1
12-4 x 12-8

DN

Br 3
9-10 x 11-4

Br 2
10-4 x 11-4

Casual Family Living

No. 96427

This plan features:

- Three bedrooms
- Two full baths
- Country styled front porch offering attractive curb appeal
- Spacious Great Room sporting a cathedral ceiling and a fireplace
- Dining room with a bay window and open layout with the Great room accessing the back porch directly
- Sunny and efficient Kitchen including a snack bar and bright Breakfast Bay
- First floor Master Suite with his and her walk-in closets and private access to a full bath
- Two additional bedrooms and a full bath on the second floor

First floor — 1,329 sq. ft.
Second floor — 465 sq. ft.
Garage — 513 sq. ft.

© 1997 Donald A. Gardner Architects, Inc.

■ *Total living area 1,794 sq. ft.* ■ *Price Code C* ■

GARAGE
21-0 x 23-0

PORCH

BRKFST.
10-0 x 9-9

PORCH

UTIL.

KIT.

DINING
13-8 x 8-0

GREAT RM.
20-0 x 16-0
(cathedral ceiling)

MASTER BED RM.
13-0 x 13-4

PORCH

FIRST FLOOR PLAN

BED RM.
12-0 x 12-0

great room below

BED RM.
12-0 x 12-8

SECOND FLOOR PLAN

233

French Flavor

Total living area 2,490 sq. ft. ■ *Price Code E* ■

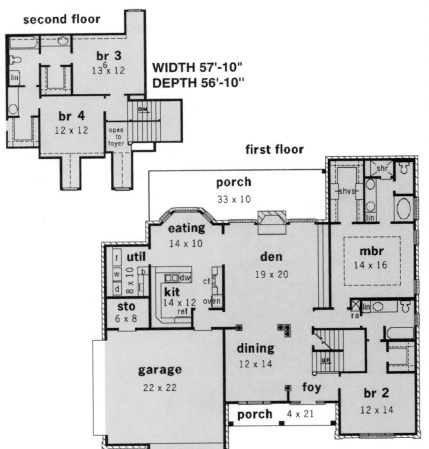

second floor

br 3 13⁶ x 12

WIDTH 57'-10"
DEPTH 56'-10"

br 4 12 x 12

open to foyer

first floor

porch 33 x 10

eating 14 x 10

util 8 x 10

kit 14 x 12

sto 6 x 8

den 19 x 20

mbr 14 x 16

garage 22 x 22

dining 12 x 14

foy

br 2 12 x 14

porch 4 x 21

No. 92549

■ **This plan features:**

— Four bedrooms

— Three full baths

■ Porch entry into open Foyer with a lovely, landing staircase

■ Elegant columns define Dining and Den area for gracious entertaining

■ Efficient, U-shaped Kitchen with serving counter, Eating bay, and nearby Utility and Garage

■ Decorative ceiling tops Master Bedroom offering a huge walk-in closet and plush bath

■ An optional crawl space or slab foundation — please specify whe ordering

First floor — 1,911 sq. ft.
Second floor — 579 sq. ft.
Garage — 560 sq. ft.

Country French Design

■ *Total living area 2,714 sq. ft.* ■ *Price Code E* ■

No. 90470 ✕

This plan features:

Three bedrooms

Two full and one half baths

Open Foyer receives light from the dormer above

Great Room features rear wall hearth fireplace and a built-in media center

Breakfast bay is open into the fully equipped U-shaped Kitchen

First floor Master Bedroom is in it's own wing of the home for privacy

An optional basement or a crawl space foundation — please specify when ordering

First floor — 1,997 sq. ft.
Second floor — 717 sq. ft.
Bonus room — 541 sq. ft.
Garage – 575 sq. ft.

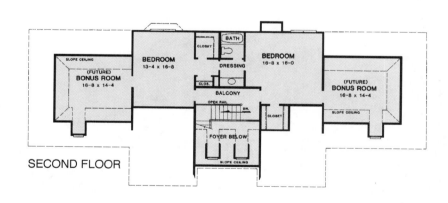

SECOND FLOOR

FIRST FLOOR

Turn Of The Century Charm

■ *Total living area 3,470 sq. ft.* ■ *Price Code F* ■

SECOND FLOOR

FIRST FLOOR

No. 93196

■ **This plan features:**

— Four bedrooms

— Three full and one half baths

■ Old fashioned turn of the century exterior blends well with contemporary floor plan

■ Bright two-story foyer framed by elegant formal Dining Room and a Study

■ Gourmet Kitchen is open to the Sun Room and the Breakfast Nook

■ Large Family Room features a cathedral ceiling and a cozy fireplace

■ Master Suite has a dramatic luxurious bath a walk-in closet and large sitting area

■ Three additional bedrooms on the second floor share two full baths

■ No materials list available

First floor — 2,470 sq. ft.
Second floor — 1,000 sq. ft.
Basement — 2,470 sq. ft.

An EXCLUSIVE DESIGN
By Ahmann Design In

Charming Two-Story

■ *Total living area 1,477 sq. ft.* ■ *Price Code A* ■

WIDTH 40'-0"
DEPTH 34'-0"

FIRST FLOOR

SECOND FLOOR

No. 94016

■ **This plan features:**

— Three bedrooms

— Two full and one half baths

■ Charming Covered Porch invites you into an open Living Room with a bay window

■ Large Family Room with fireplace and access to Deck and half bath with laundry area

■ Three ample bedrooms on second floor

■ A Master Bedroom with a box window, large closet and a private bath

■ Second and third bedrooms share a full bath and linen closet

■ No materials list is available for this plan

First floor — 778 sq. ft.
Second floor — 699 sq. ft.
Garage — 491 sq. ft.

An EXCLUSIVE DESIGN B

Southern Hospitality

■ *Total living area 1,771 sq. ft.* ■ *Price Code B* ■

No. 99285 ⚒

This plan features:

Three bedrooms

Two full and one half baths

Inviting atmosphere enhanced by Porch surrounding and shading home

Two-story Entry Hall graced by a landing staircase and arched window

Country Kitchen with cooktop island/snackbar, Eating alcove and archway to Family Room with cozy fireplace

First floor Master Suite with bay window, walk-in closet and pampering bath

Two double dormer bedrooms on second floor catch breezes and share a full bath

First floor — 1,171 sq. ft.
Second floor — 600 sq. ft.

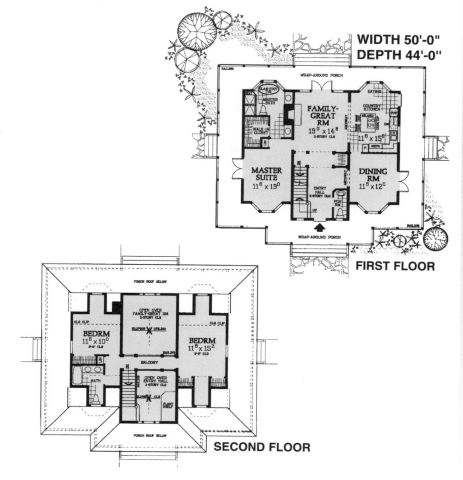

WIDTH 50'-0"
DEPTH 44'-0"

FIRST FLOOR

SECOND FLOOR

Timeless Beauty

Total living area 2,957 sq. ft. ■ Price Code E

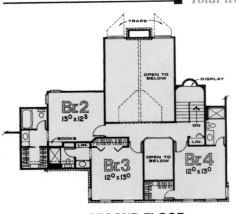

SECOND FLOOR

No. 94994

■ **This plan features:**

— Four bedrooms

— Two full, two three-quarter and one half baths

■ Two-story Entry hall accesses formal Dining and Living room

■ Spacious Great Room with cathedral ceiling, fireplace between floor to ceiling window and French doors into private D

■ Ideal Kitchen with built-in desk and pantry, work island, glass Breakfast area, and nearby laundry and Garage entry

■ Master Bedroom with a decorati ceiling, dressing/bath area with walk-in closet and whirlpool tub

■ Three second floor bedrooms w roomy closets and private baths

First floor — 2,063 sq. ft.
Second floor — 894 sq. ft.
Basement — 2,063 sq. ft.
Garage — 666 sq. ft.

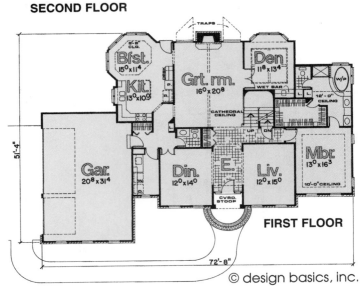

FIRST FLOOR

© design basics, inc.

Easy Living Plan

■ *Total living area 1,600 sq. ft.* ■ *Price Code B* ■

No. 98406

This plan features:

- Three bedrooms

- Two full and one half baths

- Kitchen, Breakfast Bay, and Family Room blend into a spacious open living area

- Convenient Laundry Center is tucked into the rear of the Kitchen

- Luxurious Master Suite is topped by a tray ceiling while a vaulted ceiling is in the bath

- Two roomy secondary bedrooms share the full bath in the hall

- Please specify a basement, crawl space or slab foundation when ordering

First floor — 828 sq. ft.
Second floor — 772 sq. ft.
Basement — 828 sq. ft.
Garage — 473 sq. ft.

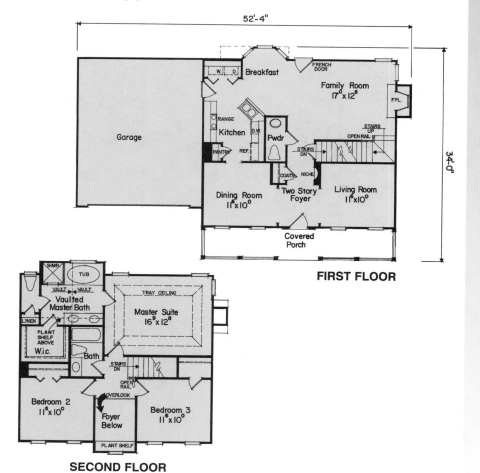

FIRST FLOOR

SECOND FLOOR

Split Bedroom Plan

■ *Total living area 2,051 sq. ft.* ■ *Price Code C* ■

No. 98427

■ This plan features:

— Three bedrooms

— Two full baths

■ Dining room is crowned by a tray ceiling

■ Living Room/Den privatized by double doors at its entrance, and is enhanced by a bay window

■ The Kitchen includes a walk-in pantry and a corner double sink

■ The Vaulted Breakfast Room flows naturally from the Kitchen

■ The Master Suite is topped by a tray ceiling, and contains a compartmental bath plus two walk-in closets

■ Two roomy additional bedrooms share a full bath in the hall

■ Please specify a basement or crawl space foundation when ordering

Main floor — 2,051 sq. ft.
Basement — 2,051 sq. ft.
Garage — 441 sq. ft.

WIDTH 56'-0"
DEPTH 60'-6"

MAIN FLOOR

Stately Three Bedroom Home

No. 93175

This plan features:

- Three bedrooms

- Two full and one half bath

- Columns astride the front door and window boxes for plants create a charming exterior

- Extensive use of windows that flood this home with natural light

- Great Room has a cathedral ceiling and a corner fireplace

- Efficient U-shaped Kitchen features a breakfast counter and access to the formal Dining Room

- First floor laundry area with storage and a half bath

- Master Bedroom boasts a cathedral ceiling and a private bath with a double vanity

- Two additional bedrooms share a full hall bath

- No materials list is available for this plan

First floor — 804 sq. ft.

Second floor — 746 sq. ft.

Basement — 804 sq. ft.

An
EXCLUSIVE DESIGN
By Ahmann Design Inc.

■ *Total living area 1,550 sq. ft.* ■ *Price Code B* ■

SECOND FLOOR PLAN

MAIN FLOOR PLAN

Family Room with a Fireplace

No. 93319

This plan features:

- Four bedrooms

- Two full and one half baths

- An island Kitchen with a built-in pantry, double sink and a convenient Dinette area

- A cozy fireplace enhancing the Family Room

- A formal Living Room and Dining Room

- A luxurious Master Suite with an ultra bath and walk-in closet

- Three additional bedrooms that share a full hall bath

- No materials list is available for this plan

First floor — 1,228 sq. ft.

Second floor — 1,191 sq. ft.

Basement — 1,228 sq. ft.

Garage — 528 sq. ft.

An
EXCLUSIVE DESIGN
By Patrick Morabito, A.I.A. Architect

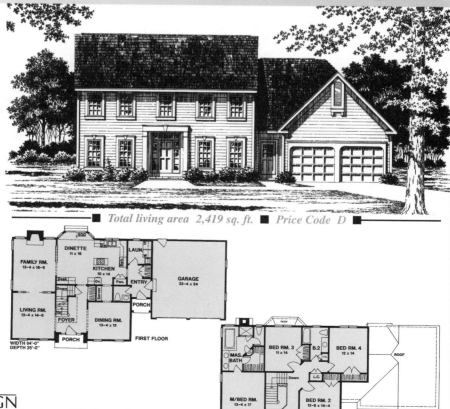

■ *Total living area 2,419 sq. ft.* ■ *Price Code D* ■

FIRST FLOOR

SECOND FLOOR

241

European Classic

Total living area 2,846 sq. ft. ■ **Price Code E** ■

First floor — 2,192 sq. ft.
Second floor — 654 sq. ft.
Bonus — 325 sq. ft.

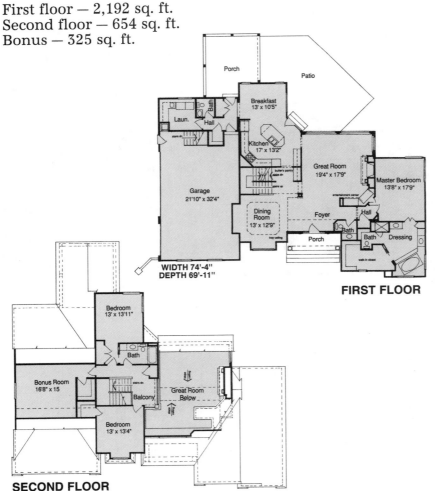

WIDTH 74'-4"
DEPTH 69'-11"

FIRST FLOOR

SECOND FLOOR

No. 92613

■ **This plan features:**

— Three bedrooms

— Two full and two half baths

■ Decorative stucco, keystone arch and boxed windows surroundin a broad, pillar entrance

■ A sloped ceiling in the Great Room accenting a wall of windows, a hearth fireplace and an entertainment center

■ An elegant formal Dining Room with a tray ceiling highlighting the decorative, boxed window

■ An efficient, island Kitchen opening to the Patio through atrium doors

■ Master Bedroom Suite with a luxurious Bath, walk-in closet, tv vanities and a raised, corner window tub

■ A second floor with two additional bedrooms sharing a full hall bath and a Bonus Room for future expansion

■ No materials list available

Unusual Contemporary Design

■ *Total living area 3,050 sq. ft.* ■ *Price Code E* ■

No. 98604

This plan features:

Three bedrooms

Two full and one half baths

Covered entrance framed by pillars opens to two-story Foyer with spectacular curved staircase

Elegant Living Room with bow window and twelve foot ceiling, opens to formal Dining area and covered Deck beyond

Open Kitchen with cooktop/serving island, eating Nook, and nearby Utility and Garage entry

Master suite with Sitting area, and huge walk-in closet

Two bedrooms share a double vanity bath and Bonus room

No materials list is available for this plan

First floor — 1,570 sq. ft.
Second floor — 1,480 sq. ft.

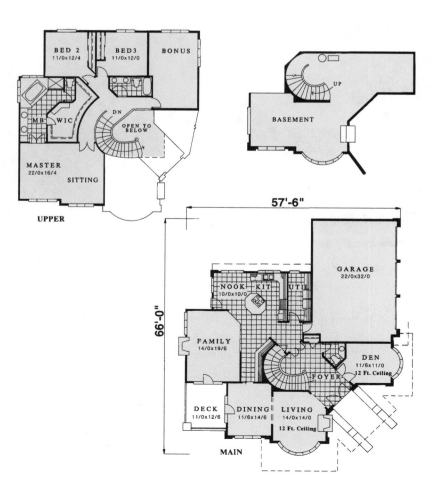

Uncommon Brickwork Enhances Facade

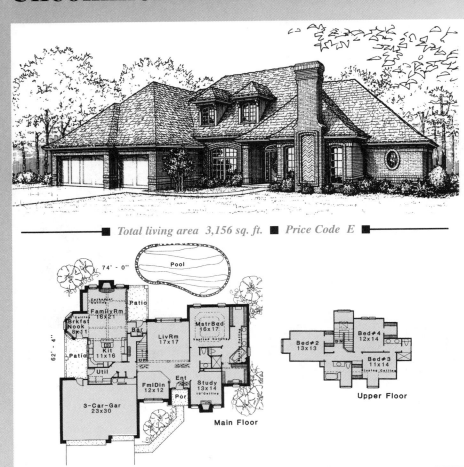

— Total living area 3,156 sq. ft. ■ Price Code E ■ —

Main Floor

Upper Floor

No. 92207

■ **This plan features:**

— Four bedrooms

— Three full and one half baths

■ Sheltered Porch leads into Entry and spacious Living Room with pool access

■ Quiet Study with focal point fireplace and open formal Dining Room

■ Expansive Kitchen with cooktop work island, efficiently serves Breakfast Nook, Patio and Dining Room

■ Master Bedroom wing offers a vaulted ceiling, two walk-in closets and a corner window tub

■ Three second floor bedrooms share two fu baths

■ No materials list is available for this plan

First floor — 2,304 sq. ft.
Second floor — 852 sq. ft.
Garage — 690 sq. ft.

Dignified Drama

— Total living area 2,617 sq. ft. ■ Price Code E ■ —

SECOND FLOOR

FIRST FLOOR

An EXCLUSIVE DESIGN
By Patrick Morabito, A.I.A. Architect

No. 93318

■ **This plan features:**

— Three bedrooms

— Two full and one half baths

■ A columned entrance into a bright, two-story Foyer

■ A Great Room with a vaulted ceiling and corner fireplace

■ Skylights above double sinks, brightening the island Kitchen that has a built-in pant and abundant cabinet and counter space

■ A Mudroom entrance with a convenient closet

■ A Master Bedroom that includes a windov seat, walk-in closet and an ultra Master B

■ Two additional bedrooms located on the second floor with private access to the fu bath

■ No materials list is available for this plan

First floor — 1,984 sq. ft.
Second floor — 633 sq. ft.
Basement — 1,984 sq. ft.
Garage — 884 sq. ft.

Old Fashioned With Contemporary Interior

■ *Total living area 2,052 sq. ft.* ■ *Price Code C* ■

No. 98407 ⚒

This plan features:

Four bedrooms

Three full baths

A two story Foyer is flanked by the Living Room and the Dining Room

The Family Room features a fireplace and a French door

The bayed Breakfast Nook and Pantry are adjacent to the Kitchen

The Master Suite with a trayed ceiling has an attached Bath with a vaulted ceiling

Upstairs are two additional Bedrooms, a full Bath, a laundry closet, and a Bonus room

An optional basement or a crawl space foundation — please specify when ordering

First floor — 1,135 sq. ft.
Second floor — 917 sq. ft.
Bonus — 216 sq. ft.

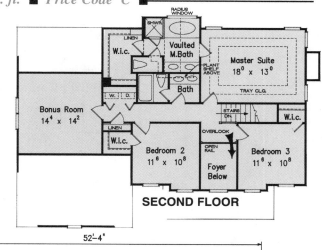

SECOND FLOOR

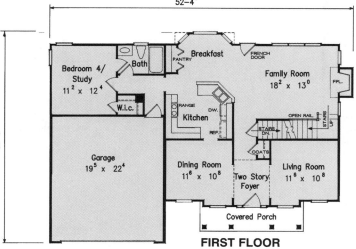

FIRST FLOOR

Fieldstone with Flexible Floor Plan

■ *Total living area 2,234 sq. ft.* ■ *Price Code D* ■

SECOND FLOOR

BED RM
12' x 10'

BED RM
11' x 10'

BED RM
13'-1" x 17'-0"

desk

GALLERY

BATH

STORAGE

FOYER BELOW

STORAGE

railing

lin.

vanity

dressing

LAV.

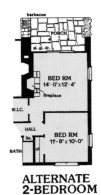

ALTERNATE 2-BEDROOM

barbecue

PORCH

sl. gl. dr.

BED RM
14'-0" x 12'-4"

fireplace

W.I.C.

HALL

lin.

BATH

cl.

BED RM
11'-8" x 10'-0"

FIRST FLOOR

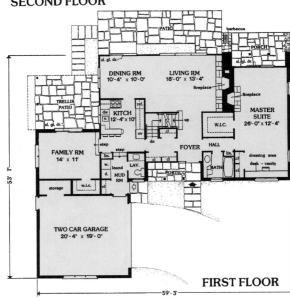

PATIO

barbecue

sl. gl. dr.

DINING RM
10'-4" x 10'-0"

LIVING RM
18'-0" x 13'-4"

PORCH

sl. gl. dr.

fireplace

TRELLIS PATIO

KITCH
12'-4" x 10'

ref.

dw
fk

ov

up

fireplace

MASTER SUITE
26'-0" x 12'-4"

W.I.C.

sl. gl. dr.

step

step

FOYER

HALL

dressing area

BATH

desk - vanity

FAMILY RM
14' x 11'

w.
laund
d.

LAV.

MUD RM

PORTICO

storage

w.i.c.

53' 1"

TWO CAR GARAGE
20'-4" x 19'-0"

59'-3"

No. 90600

■ **This plan features:**

— Four or five bedrooms

— Two full and two half baths

■ Design expands from a five room cottage to an eight room home

■ Portico leads into an open Foyer with a landing staircase

■ Spacious Living/Dining Room with a hearth fireplace

■ Hub Kitchen with peninsula snackbar and nearby

■ Master Suite offers a fireplace, Porch access and dressing area with built-in desk/vanity

■ Alternative floor plan offers two bedrooms on first floor, one with a fireplace

■ Three second floor bedrooms share one and a half baths

First floor — 1,409 sq. ft.
Second floor — 825 sq. ft.

■ *Total living area 1,505 sq. ft.* ■ *Price Code B* ■

No. 24326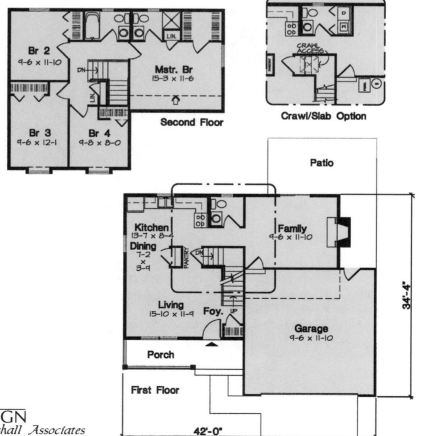

This plan features:

Four bedrooms

Two full and one half baths

A lovely front porch shading the entrance

A spacious Living Room that opens into the Dining Area which flows into the efficient Kitchen

A Family Room equipped with a cozy fireplace and sliding glass doors to a patio

A Master Suite with a large walk-in closet and a private bath with a step-in shower

Three additional bedrooms that share a full hall bath

First floor — 692 sq. ft.
Second floor — 813 sq. ft.
Basement — 699 sq. ft.
Garage — 484 sq. ft.

An EXCLUSIVE DESIGN
By Marshall Associates

Second Floor

Br 2 9-6 x 11-10
Mstr. Br 15-3 x 11-6
LIN.
DN
LIN
Br 3 9-6 x 12-1
Br 4 9-8 x 8-0

Crawl/Slab Option

CRAWL ACCESS

First Floor

Patio
Kitchen 13-7 x 8-4
Dining 7-2 x 3-9
PANTRY
DN
Family 9-6 x 11-10
Living 15-10 x 11-9
Foy.
UP
Garage 9-6 x 11-10
Porch

34'-4"
42'-0"

Western Farmhouse with Many Comforts

■ *Total living area 4,116 sq. ft.* ■ *Price Code F* ■

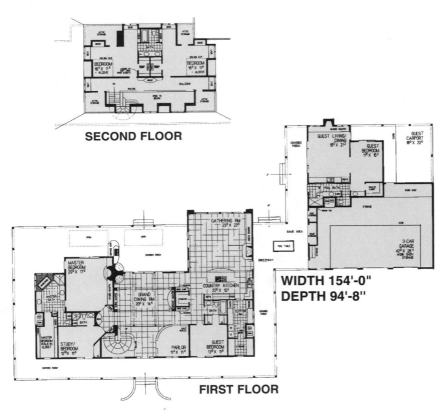

SECOND FLOOR

FIRST FLOOR

WIDTH 154'-0"
DEPTH 94'-8"

No. 99278

■ This plan features:

— Six bedrooms

— Five full baths

■ A Covered Porch surrounds hom

■ Central entrance enhanced by
circular stairway and curved wa
Parlor

■ Formal Dining Room offers a
built-in china alcove, service
counter and fireplace

■ Country Kitchen with a large co
top island overlooks expansive
Gathering Room

■ Master Bedroom highlighted by
raised hearth fireplace, porch
access and a plush bath

■ Separate Guest accommodation
include Living/Dining area,
bedroom and pool bath

Main floor — 3,166 sq. ft.
Second floor — 950 sq. ft.
Guest House/Carport —
680 sq. ft.

Beautiful Traditional Design

No. 94009

This plan features:

Three bedrooms

Two full and one half baths

Covered two-story porch with brick columns creates and exciting entrance

Open entry leads to the formal Living Room that has a fireplace

Family Room features a second fireplace and opens out to a backyard deck

Bright Kitchen has an island cooktop and is located adjacent to the Breakfast Room and the Dining Room

Master Suite features a walk-in closet and luxurious bath with a tub, separate toilet and double vanity

Two additional bedrooms share a full hall bath

No materials list is available for this plan

First floor — 1,240 sq. ft.

Second floor — 819 sq. ft.

An **EXCLUSIVE DESIGN** *By* **CRANE DESIGN** inc.

■ *Total living area* 2,059 sq. ft. ■ *Price Code* C ■

WIDTH 62'-0"
DEPTH 53'-0"

FIRST FLOOR

SECOND FLOOR

Luxury with Room to Expand

No. 34825

This plan features:

Three bedrooms

Two full and one half baths

A large unfinished area on the second floor which could be used as a hobby center or exercise room

A luxury Master Bedroom with two walk-in closets in the dressing area plus a convenient five-piece bath

A formal Dining Room and Living Room on either side of the tiled foyer

A cozy Family Room with a large fireplace

A Kitchen complete with a bump-out window over the sink and a snack bar

First floor — 1,212 sq. ft.

Second floor — 1,030 sq. ft.

Basement — 1,212 sq. ft.

Garage — 521 sq. ft.

An **EXCLUSIVE DESIGN** *By Karl Kreeger*

■ *Total living area* 2,242 sq. ft. ■ *Price Code* D ■

FIRST FLOOR PLAN

SECOND FLOOR PLAN

opt. slab/ crawl space

Designed for Entertaining

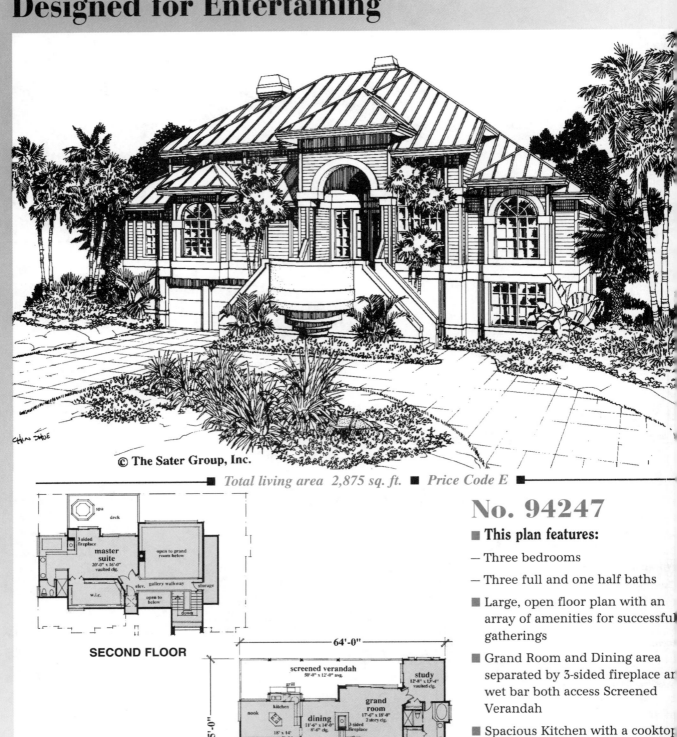

© The Sater Group, Inc.

■ *Total living area 2,875 sq. ft.* ■ *Price Code E* ■

SECOND FLOOR

FIRST FLOOR

LOWER FLOOR

No. 94247

■ **This plan features:**

— Three bedrooms

— Three full and one half baths

■ Large, open floor plan with an array of amenities for successful gatherings

■ Grand Room and Dining area separated by 3-sided fireplace and wet bar both access Screened Verandah

■ Spacious Kitchen with a cooktop island, eating Nook and access to Verandah and Dining Room

■ Secluded Master Suite enhanced by a private Spa Deck, huge walk-in closet and whirlpool tub

■ Study and two additional bedrooms have private access to full baths

■ No materials list available

First floor — 2,066 sq. ft.
Second floor — 809 sq. ft.
Garage — 798 sq. ft.

Spectacular Curving Stairway

■ *Total living area 3,172 sq. ft.* ■ *Price Code E* ■

No. 94995

This plan features:

Four bedrooms

Two full, one three-quarter and one half baths

Spacious formal entry with arched transom, is enhanced by curved staircase

Great Room is inviting with a cozy fireplace, a wetbar and triple arched windows

Open Kitchen, Breakfast and Hearth area combine efficiency and comfort for all

Master Bedroom retreat offers a private back door, a double walk-in closet and a whirlpool bath

Generous closets and baths enhance the three second floor bedrooms

First floor — 2,252 sq. ft.
Second floor — 920 sq. ft.
Basement — 2,252 sq. ft.
Garage — 646 sq. ft.

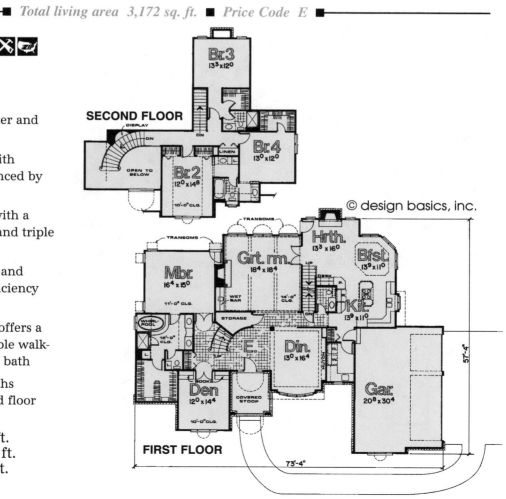

© design basics, inc.

Streetside Appeal

■ Total living area 2,157 sq. ft. ■ Price Code C ■

No. 20160

■ **This plan features:**

— Three bedrooms

— Two full and one half baths

■ An elegant Living and Dining Room combination that is divided by columns

■ A Family/Hearth Room with a two-way fireplace to the Breakfast room

■ A well-appointed Kitchen with built-in pantry, peninsula counter and double corner sink

■ A Master Suite with decorative ceiling, walk-in closet and private bath

■ Two additional bedrooms that share a full hall bath

First floor — 1,590 sq. ft.
Second floor — 567 sq. ft.
Basement — 1,576 sq. ft.
Garage — 456 sq. ft.

An EXCLUSIVE DESIGN
By Karl Kreeger

Elegant Residence

■ Total living area 3,870 sq. ft. ■ Price Code F ■

No. 92274

■ **This plan features:**

— Four bedrooms

— Three full and one half baths

■ Two-story glass Entry enhanced by a curved staircase

■ Open Living/Dining Room with decorative windows makes entertaining easy

■ Large, efficient Kitchen with cooktop/work island, huge walk-in pantry, Breakfast room, butler's pantry and Utility/Garage entry

■ Comfortable Family Room with hearth fireplace, built-ins and access to Covered Patio

■ Cathedral ceiling tops luxurious Master Bedroom offering a private Lanai, skylit bath, double walk-in closet, and adjoining Study

■ Three second floor bedrooms with walk-in closets and private access to full baths

■ No materials list is available for this plan

First floor — 2,807 sq. ft.
Second floor — 1,063 sq. ft.
Garage — 633 sq. ft.

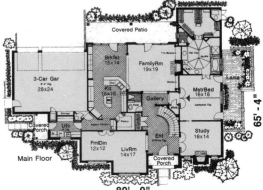

Master Suite with Private Sun Deck

■ *Total living area 2,139 sq. ft.* ■ *Price Code C* ■

No. 91411

This plan features:

Four bedrooms

Two full and one half baths

A sunken Living Room, formal Dining Room and island Kitchen enjoying an expansive view of the patio and backyard

A fireplaced Living Room

Skylights brightening the balcony and Master Bath

An optional basement, slab or crawl space foundation — please specify when ordering

Main level — 1,249 sq. ft.
Upper level — 890 sq. ft.
Garage — 462 sq. ft.

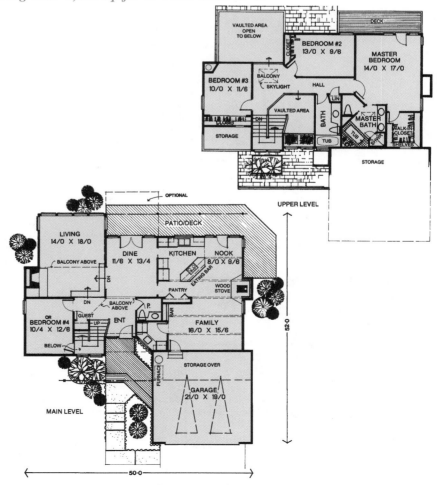

Three Bedroom Traditional Country Cape

■ *Total living area 1,494 sq. ft.* ■ *Price Code A* ■

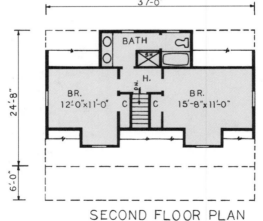

37'-0"

24'-8"

6'-0"

BATH

BR.
12'-0"x11'-0"

H.

BR.
15'-8"x11'-0"

C   C

SECOND FLOOR PLAN

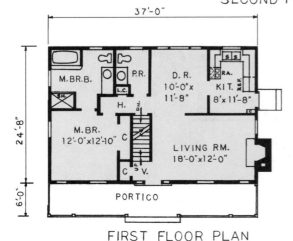

37'-0"

24'-8"

6'-0"

M.BR.B.   P.R.
L.C.

M.BR.
12'-0"x12'-10"

H.
DN.

C

C   V.

D. R.
10'-0"x
11'-8"

RA.

KIT.
8'x11'-8"

REF.

S   S

C

LIVING RM.
18'-0"x12'-0"

PORTICO

FIRST FLOOR PLAN

No. 99022

■ **This plan features:**

— Three bedrooms

— Two full and one half baths

■ Entry area with a coat closet

■ An ample Living Room with a fireplace

■ A Dining Room with a view of th[e] rear yard and located conveniently close to the Kitche[n] and Living Room

■ A U-shaped Kitchen with a double sink, ample cabinet and counter space and a side door t[o] the outside

■ A first floor Master Suite with a private Master Bath

■ Two additional, second floor bedrooms that share a full, doub[le] vanity bath with a separate shower

First floor — 913 sq. ft.
Second floor — 581 sq. ft.

■ *Total living area 1,767 sq. ft.* ■ *Price Code B* ■

No. 99045

This plan features:

Three bedrooms

Two full and one half baths

Full front Porch provides comfortable visiting and a sheltered entrance

Expansive Living Room with an inviting fireplace opens to bright Dining Room and Kitchen

U-shaped Kitchen with peninsula serving counter, Dining Room and nearby Pantry

Secluded Master Bedroom with two closets and a double vanity bath

Two second floor bedrooms share a full bath

No materials list is available for this plan

First floor — 1,108 sq. ft.
Second floor — 659 sq. ft.
Basement — 875 sq. ft.

SECOND FLOOR

FIRST FLOOR

WIDTH 67'-0"
DEPTH 30'-0"

Country Porch Topped by Dormer

■ *Total living area 1,470 sq. ft.* ■ *Price Code A* ■

No. 24706

■ **This plan features:**

— Three bedrooms

— Two full baths

■ Front Porch leads into tiled ent
and spacious Living Room with
focal point fireplace

■ Side entrance leads into Utility
Room and central Foyer with a
landing staircase

■ Kitchen with cooktop island, an
a bright Breakfast area

■ Second floor Master Bedroom
offers dormer window, vaulted
ceiling, walk-in closet and doub
vanity bath

■ Two additional bedrooms with
ample closets, share a full bath

First floor — 1,035 sq. ft.
Second floor — 435 sq. ft.
Basement — 1,018 sq. ft.

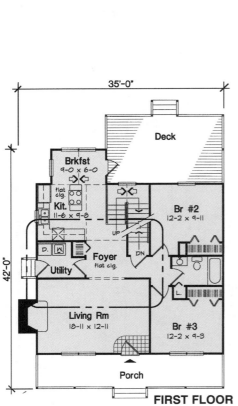

FIRST FLOOR

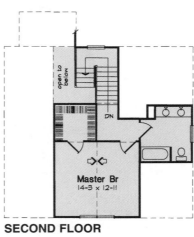

SECOND FLOOR

Alternate Foundation Plan

Out of the English Countryside

No. 98519

This plan features:

Four bedrooms

Three full and one half baths

From the Entry, is the Living Room/Study with a cozy fireplace, or left into the Dining Room, both rooms have lovely bay windows

The family Room has a fireplace and a door that leads out onto a covered patio

The Breakfast area is adjacent to the Family Room and the Kitchen which features a center island

The first floor Master Bedroom has two walk in closets and an attached bath with a spa tub

All of the upstairs Bedrooms have walk in closets, one has a full bath to itself, the other two share a full bath,

Also located upstairs is a Bonus Room that would be a perfect play room

There is no materials list available for this plan

First floor — 1,735 sq. ft.
Second floor — 789 sq. ft.
Bonus — 132 sq. ft.
Garage — 482 sq. ft.

■ *Total living area 2,524 sq. ft.* ■ *Price Code D* ■

Classic Colonial

No. 90469

This plan features:

Three bedrooms

Two full and one half baths

Colonial with room for expansion comes with an optional five bedrooms plan

Great Room features fireplace and access to the rear deck

Dining Room with a tray ceiling is convenient to the Kitchen

Breakfast bay adjoins L-shaped Kitchen which includes a center island

Second floor Master Suite has a luxurious bath with a garden tub

Two secondary bedrooms share a full bath

Please specify a basement or crawl space foundation when ordering

First floor — 1,098 sq. ft.
Second floor — 1,064 sq. ft.
Garage — 484 sq. ft.

■ *Total living area 2,162 sq. ft.* ■ *Price Code C* ■

A Grand Presence

■ *Total living area 3,620 sq. ft.* ■ *Price Code F* ■

An EXCLUSIVE DESIGN
By Patrick Morabito, A.I.A. Architect

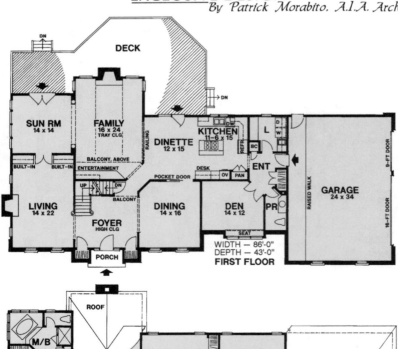

DECK

SUN RM 14 x 14

FAMILY 16 x 24 TRAY CLG

DINETTE 12 x 15

KITCHEN 11-6 x 15

BALCONY, ABOVE
ENTERTAINMENT

BUILT-IN   BUILT-IN

LIVING 14 x 22

UP   DN   BALCONY

POCKET DOOR

DESK   OV   PAN

ENT

FOYER HIGH CLG

DINING 14 x 16

DEN 14 x 12

PR

RAISED WALK

GARAGE 24 x 34

9-FT DOOR

16-FT DOOR

PORCH

SEAT

WIDTH — 86'-0"
DEPTH — 43'-0"
FIRST FLOOR

ROOF

M/B   TC

FAMILY (Below)

BR 2 15-3 x 13

BR 3 15-3 x 13

LIN

ROOF

BALCONY

HALL

TC

M/BR 14 x 18

DN   RAILING

FOYER (Below)

BR 4 14 x 14

B 2

PLANT SHELF

SECOND FLOOR

No. 93330

■ **This plan features:**

— Four bedrooms

— Two full and one half baths

■ A gourmet Kitchen with a cook island and built-in pantry and planning desk

■ A formal Living Room with a fireplace that can be seen from the Foyer

■ Pocket doors that separate the formal Dining Room from the informal Dinette area

■ An expansive Family Room with fireplace and a built-in entertainment center

■ A luxuriant Master Bath that highlights the Master Suite

■ Three bedrooms that share use a compartmented full hall bath

■ No materials list is available for this plan

First floor — 2,093 sq. ft.
Second floor — 1,527 sq. ft.
Basement — 2,093 sq. ft.
Garage — 816 sq. ft.

■ *Total living area 1,737 sq. ft.* ■ *Price Code B* ■

No. 91413 ⚒

This plan features:

Three bedrooms

Two full and one half baths

A spacious Family Room with a cozy fireplace and direct access to the patio

A well-appointed Kitchen with an eating bar peninsula, double sink and sunny eating Nook

A formal Living Room and Dining Room located at the front of the house

A Master Suite equipped with a walk-in closet, a double vanity and a full Master Bath

An optional basement, slab or crawl space foundation — please specify when ordering

First floor — 963 sq. ft.

Second floor — 774 sq. ft.

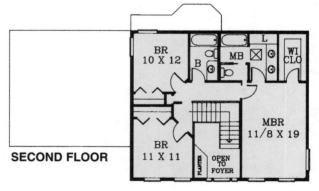

SECOND FLOOR

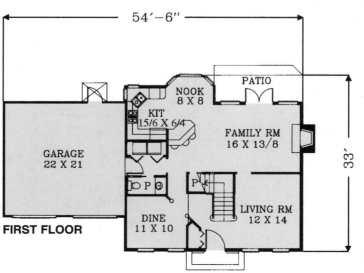

FIRST FLOOR

Clapboard Contemporary

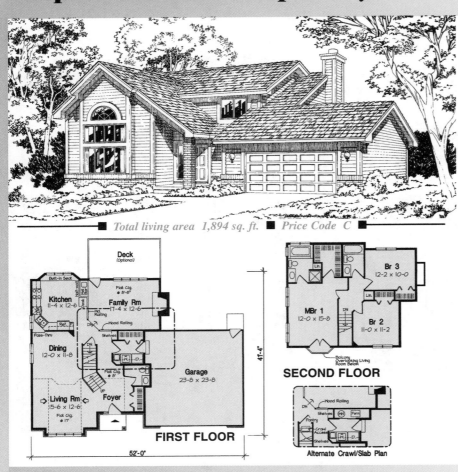

■ Total living area 1,894 sq. ft. ■ Price Code C ■

FIRST FLOOR

Deck (Optional)

Built-in Seat

Kitchen 11-4 x 12-6

Family Rm 17-4 x 12-6

Flat Clg. @ 8'-8"

Railing

Ref. Wood Railing

Pass-Thru

Dining 12-0 x 11-8

Shelves

Garage 23-8 x 23-8

Living Rm 15-6 x 12-6

Flat Clg. @ 11'

Foyer

Flat Clg. @ 8'

52'-0"

41'-4"

SECOND FLOOR

Lin.

Br 3 12-2 x 10-0

MBr 1 12-0 x 15-8

Lin.

Br 2 11-0 x 11-2

Balcony Overlooking Living Room Below

Alternate Crawl/Slab Plan

Wood Railing

Shelves

Pantry

Crawl Access

Shelves

No. 20367

■ **This plan features:**

— Three bedrooms

— Two full and one half baths

■ An exciting window wall gracing the dramatic two-story Living Room

■ A Kitchen with a double sink, built-in des and easy access to the Dining Room

■ A step down to the sunken Family Room with fireplace

■ A Master Bedroom with a luxurious Mast Bath and unique balcony

First floor — 1,108 sq. ft.
Second floor — 786 sq. ft.
Basement — 972 sq. ft.
Garage — 567 sq. ft.

Open Spaces

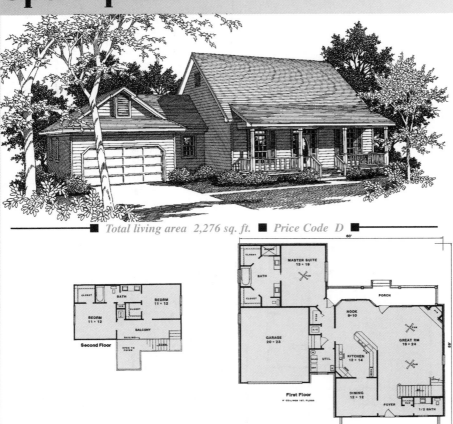

■ Total living area 2,276 sq. ft. ■ Price Code D ■

Second Floor

CLOSET

BATH

BEDRM 11 x 12

BEDRM 11 x 12

BALCONY

RAILING

OPEN TO FOYER

First Floor

60'

MASTER SUITE 13 x 19

BATH

CLOSET

PORCH

GARAGE 20 x 23

NOOK 9 x 10

A/C

UTIL

KITCHEN 12 x 14

GREAT RM 19 x 24

FAN

FAN

DINING 12 x 12

FOYER

1/2 BATH

PORCH

No. 96512

■ **This plan features:**

— Three bedrooms

— Two full and one half baths

■ Great Room opens to the Nook which adjoins the Kitchen creating a feeling of spaciousness

■ Cozy corner fireplace and two ceiling fan highlight the Great Room

■ The Kitchen is located between the Nook and the Dining Room for convenience in serving

■ Secluded Master Suite is enhanced by a f piece Master Bath and two walk-in closet

■ Two additional bedrooms on the second floor, each have a walk-in closet and acce to a full bath

First floor — 1,732 sq. ft.
Second floor — 544 sq. ft.
Garage — 460 sq. ft.

■ *Total living area 2,664 sq. ft.* ■ *Price Code E* ■

No. 92616

This plan features:

• Four bedrooms

• Two full and one half baths

• Central Foyer opens to formal Living and Dining rooms

• L-shaped Kitchen with work Island/snack bar, Breakfast area and access to Laundry, Den, and Garage

• Sunken Family Room with a cozy fireplace and access to rear yard

• Master Bedroom wing offers a plush bath with double vanity and whirlpool tub

• Three bedrooms with ample closets share a double vanity bath

First floor — 1,516 sq. ft.

Second floor — 1,148 sq. ft.

Garage — 440 sq. ft.

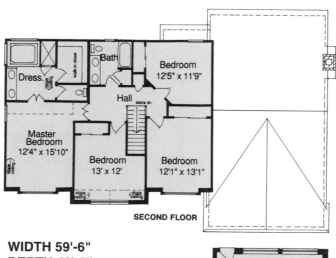

SECOND FLOOR

WIDTH 59'-6"
DEPTH 40'-0"

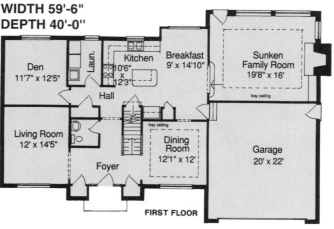

FIRST FLOOR

261

Yesteryear Flavor

■ *Total living area 2,356 sq. ft.* ■ *Price Code D* ■

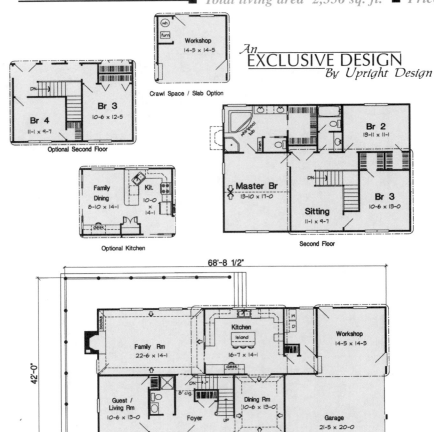

Workshop
14-5 x 14-5

Crawl Space / Slab Option

An
EXCLUSIVE DESIGN
By Upright Design

Br 3
10-6 x 12-5

Br 4
11-1 x 9-7

Optional Second Floor

Family
Dining
8-10 x 14-1

Kit.
10-0
x
14-1

desk

Optional Kitchen

Br 2
13-11 x 11-1

Master Br
13-10 x 17-0

Br 3
10-6 x 13-0

Sitting
11-1 x 9-7

Second Floor

68'-8 1/2"

42'-0"

Family Rm
22-6 x 14-1

Kitchen
Island
16-7 x 14-1

Workshop
14-5 x 14-5

desk

Guest /
Living Rm
10-6 x 13-0

Foyer

Dining Rm
10-6 x 13-0

Garage
21-5 x 20-0

Porch

First Floor

No. 24404

■ This plan features:

— Three or four bedrooms

— Three full baths

■ Wrap-around Porch leads to Foy
with a landing staircase

■ Formal Living Room doubles as
Guest Room

■ Huge Family Room highlighted
by a decorative ceiling, cozy
fireplace, and book shelves

■ Country-size Kitchen with islan
snackbar, built-in desk and nea
Dining Room, laundry/Worksh
and Garage access

■ Master Bedroom with a large
walk-in closet and a whirlpool t

■ Two additional bedrooms with
walk-in closets, share a full bath
and Sitting area

First floor — 1,236 sq. ft.
Second floor — 1,120 sq. ft.

Dual-Vanity Baths Ease Rush

■ Total living area 2,095 sq. ft. ■ Price Code C ■

No. 90622 ✖

This plan features:

Four bedrooms

Two full and one half baths

A wood beam ceiling in the spacious Family Room

An efficient, island Kitchen with a sunny bay window dinette

A formal Living Room with a heat-circulating fireplace

A large Master Suite with a walk-in closet and a private Master Bath

Three additional bedrooms sharing a full hall bath

First floor — 983 sq. ft.
Second floor — 1,013 sq. ft.
Mudroom — 99 sq. ft.
Garage — 481 sq. ft.

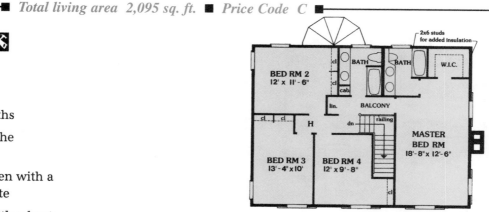

SECOND FLOOR

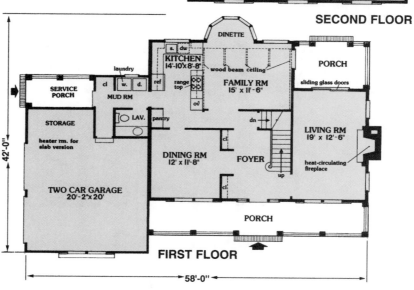

FIRST FLOOR

263

Quality and Diversity

■ *Total living area 2,022 sq. ft.* ■ *Price Code C* ■

SECOND FLOOR

Bedroom 11'0" x 11'2"
Bedroom 11'2" x 11'0"
Great Room Below
Hall
Bath
stairs dn
Bedroom 11'0" x 12'1"
Foyer Below

FIRST FLOOR

Breakfast 11' x 9'10"
Bath
Kitchen 13' x 10'5"
Laun. 9'6" x 8'1"
pantry
Great Room 16'5" x 16'8"
Master Bedroom 14'0" x 13'0"
stairs dn   stairs up
Foyer
Bath
Garage 20'0" x 21'3"
Dining Room 11'0" x 13'0"
Porch
walk-in closet
55'4"
47'8"

No. 92629

■ **This plan features:**

— Four bedrooms

— Two full and one half bath

■ Elegant arched entrance from Porch into Foyer

■ Corner fireplace and atrium do highlight Great Room

■ Hub Kitchen with walk-in pant and peninsula counter easily accesses glass Breakfast bay, ba yard, Great Room, Dining Room Laundry and Garage

■ Master Bedroom wing crowned tray ceiling offers plush bath ar walk-in closet

■ Three additional bedrooms wit decorative windows and large closets share a full bath

First floor — 1,401 sq. ft.
Second floor — 621 sq. ft.
Basement — 1,269 sq. ft.
Garage — 478 sq. ft.

Deck Surrounds House on Three Sides

No. 91304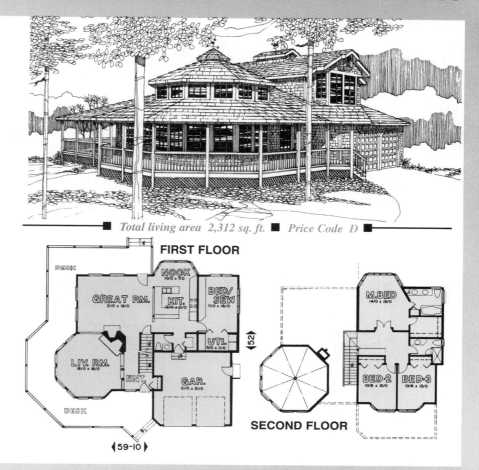

This plan features:

- Three bedrooms
- One full, one three-quarter and one half baths
- A sunken, circular Living Room with windows on four sides and a vaulted clerestory for a wide-open feeling
- Back-to-back fireplaces in the Living Room and the adjoining Great Room
- A convenient, efficient Kitchen with a sunny eating Nook
- A Master Suite with a walk-in closet and a private Master Bath
- Two additional bedrooms that share a full hall bath

First floor — 1,439 sq. ft.
Second floor — 873 sq. ft.

■ Total living area 2,312 sq. ft. ■ Price Code D ■

FIRST FLOOR

SECOND FLOOR

Style and Much More

No. 98446

This plan features:

- Three bedrooms
- Two full and one half baths
- The Foyer is accented by arched openings leading into the Dining and Living rooms
- The Dining Room has direct access to the Kitchen for ease in serving
- The Kitchen includes a serving bar to the family room and an easy flow into the breakfast Bay
- The Family Room is accented by fireplace and French door to the rear yard
- A tray ceiling decorates the Master Suite while a vaulted ceiling highlights the Master Bath
- Two additional bedrooms share the full bath in the hall
- No materials list is available for this plan

First floor — 1,039 sq. ft.
Second floor — 761 sq. ft.
Bonus area — 424 sq. ft.
Basement — 1,039 sq. ft.
Garage — 465 sq. ft.

■ Total living area 1,800 sq. ft. ■ Price Code B ■

Balanced Formal and Informal Areas

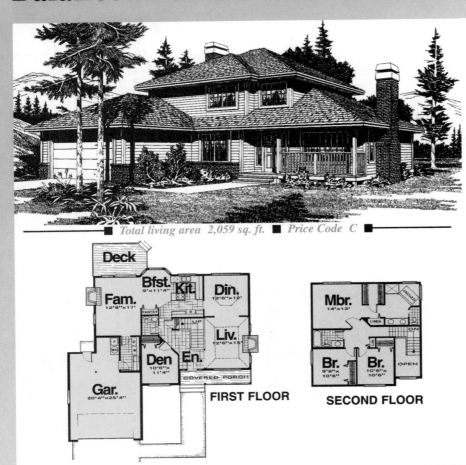

■ *Total living area 2,059 sq. ft.* ■ *Price Code C* ■

FIRST FLOOR

SECOND FLOOR

No. 94039

■ **This plan features:**

— Three bedrooms

— Two full and one half baths

■ Stylish exterior with covered porch leads a spacious and open foyer

■ Formal Living and Dining Rooms feature coffered ceilings and the Living Room is further enhanced by a fireplace

■ Well-designed Kitchen has a desirable island cooktop and accesses the bright Breakfast Nook

■ Large Family Room opens to a rear sundeck and includes a second fireplace

■ Master Suite has a terrific private bath w corner whirlpool tub, double vanity, line closet and a walk-in closet

■ Two additional bedrooms share a full ha bath

■ No materials list is available for this plan

First floor — 1,240 sq. ft.
Second floor — 819 sq. ft.
Width — 52'-6"
Depth — 50'-0"

An EXCLUSIVE DESIGN *B* CRANE DESIGN

Four Dramatic Gables

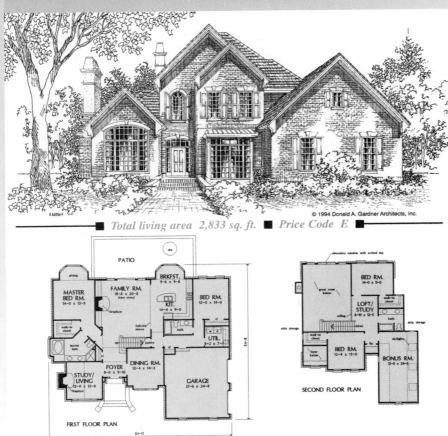

■ *Total living area 2,833 sq. ft.* ■ *Price Code E* ■

© 1994 Donald A. Gardner Architects, Inc.

FIRST FLOOR PLAN

SECOND FLOOR PLAN

No. 99841

■ **This plan features:**

— Three bedrooms

— Two full and one half baths

■ Four dramatic gables lend curb appeal to this impressive executive home

■ Two fireplaces add warmth to this home one in the two-story Family Room, the ot in the Study/Living Room

■ Vaulted and nine foot ceilings create maximum volume

■ First floor Master Suite, with an angled h entrance for privacy, features a sitting ba whirlpool tub, a double vanity and a separate shower

■ Extra room is added on the upper level b skylight bonus room and attic storage

First floor — 2,162 sq. ft.
Second floor — 671 sq. ft.

A Modern Look At Colonial Styling

■ *Total living area 2,024 sq. ft.* ■ ● *Price Code C* ■ ●

No. 93287

This plan features:

Three bedrooms

Two full and one half baths

Brick detailing and keystones highlight elevation

Two-story Foyer opens to formal Living and Dining rooms

Expansive Family Room with a hearth fireplace between built-in shelves and Deck access

U-shaped Kitchen with serving counter, Breakfast alcove, and nearby Garage entry

Elegant Master Bedroom with a decorative ceiling, large walk-in closet and a double vanity bath

Two additional bedrooms share a full bath, laundry and Bonus area

First floor — 987 sq. ft.
Second floor — 965 sq. ft.
Finished staircase — 72 sq. ft.
Bonus — 272 sq. ft.

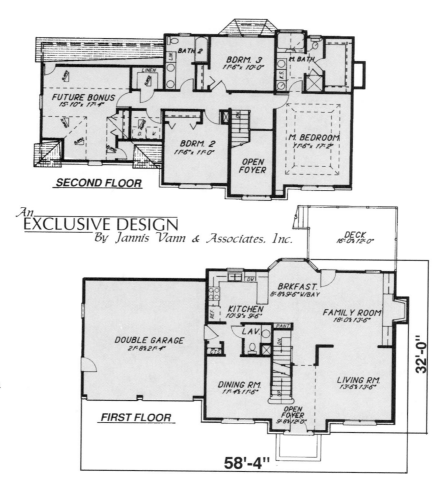

An
EXCLUSIVE DESIGN
By Jannis Vann & Associates, Inc.

Lattice Trim Adds Nostalgic Charm

■ *Total living area 1,359 sq. ft.* ■ *Price Code A* ■

No. 99315

■ This plan features:

— Three bedrooms

— Two full and one half baths

■ Wood and fieldstone exterior

■ A vaulted Living Room with balcony view and floor to ceilin corner window treatment

■ A Master Suite with private bat and dressing area

■ A two car Garage with access to Kitchen

First floor — 668 sq. ft.
Second floor — 691 sq. ft.

MBr
11-8x13

Loft/
Br 3
9x11

Br 2
10x9-8

DN

skylight

open to below

SECOND FLOOR

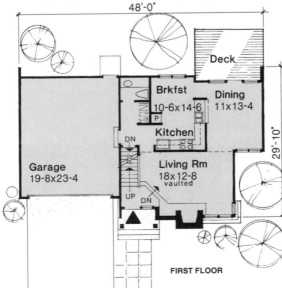

48'-0"

Deck

Brkfst
10-6x14-6

Dining
11x13-4

Kitchen

DN

Garage
19-8x23-4

Living Rm
18x12-8
vaulted

29'-10"

UP   DN

FIRST FLOOR

The Perfect Home

No. 20199

This plan features:

- Four bedrooms
- Three full and one half baths
- A stunning fireplace in the Breakfast/Hearth Room with a built-in TV cabinet and plant shelf
- A spacious Living Room with ten-foot ceiling height
- A decorative ceiling enhancing the elegant Dining Room
- An efficient Kitchen with all the amenities
- A sloped ceiling in the Master Suite and a private full bath with walk-in closet
- Three additional bedrooms, one with a private bath and two with walk-in closets

First floor — 1,760 sq. ft.
Second floor — 785 sq. ft.
Basement — 1,760 sq. ft.
Garage — 797 sq. ft.

An EXCLUSIVE DESIGN *By Karl Kreeger*

■ *Total living area 2,545 sq. ft.* ■ *Price Code D* ■

Stucco, Brick and Elegant Details

No. 99400

This plan features:

- Four bedrooms
- Three full and one half baths
- Majestic Entry opens to Den and Dining Room highlighted by boxed windows and decorative ceilings
- Expansive Great Room sharing a see-thru fireplace with Hearth Room, and French doors to a Covered Veranda
- Lovely Hearth Room enhanced by three skylights above triple arched windows and an entertainment center
- Hub Kitchen with work island/snack bar, pantry, bright Breakfast bay and nearby Laundry/Garage entry
- Sumptuous Master Bedroom suite with corner windows, two closets and vanities, and a garden whirlpool tub
- Second floor bedrooms with walk-in closets and private bathroom access

First floor — 2,084 sq. ft.
Second floor — 848 sq. ft.
Garage — 682 sq. ft.

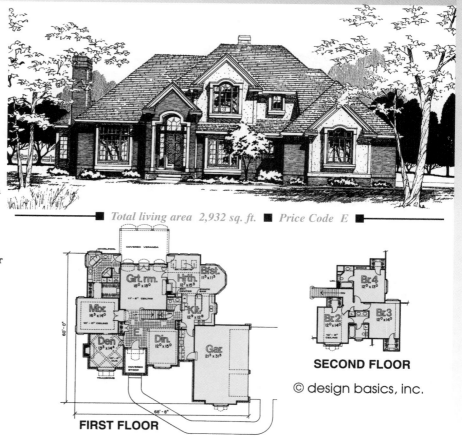

■ *Total living area 2,932 sq. ft.* ■ *Price Code E* ■

© design basics, inc.

Extraordinary Elegance

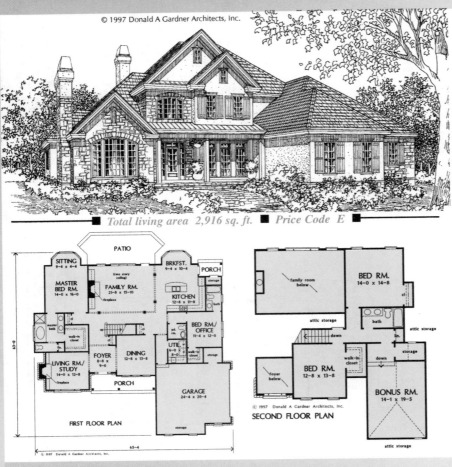

© 1997 Donald A Gardner Architects, Inc.

Total living area 2,916 sq. ft. ■ Price Code E

FIRST FLOOR PLAN

SECOND FLOOR PLAN
© 1997 Donald A Gardner Architects, Inc.

No. 99821

■ This plan features:

— Four bedrooms

— Three full and one half baths

■ Stone and stucco exterior and contemporary interior offer class and convenience

■ Formal Dining and Living rooms at front of home, while casual areas located in back

■ Columns offer definition for open Family Room, Kitchen and Breakfast bay

■ Master Bedroom suite features sitting bay, luxurious bath and walk-in closet

■ Second floor includes two more bedrooms, full bath and Bonus Room

First floor — 2,293 sq. ft.
Second floor — 623 sq. ft.
Bonus room — 359 sq. ft.
Garage & storage — 641 sq. ft.

Curb Appeal

Total living area 3,773 sq. ft. ■ Price Code G

FIRST FLOOR PLAN

SECOND FLOOR PLAN
© 1996 Donald A Gardner Architects, Inc.

No. 99898

■ This plan features:

— Four bedrooms

— Three full and one half baths

■ Inviting front porch, dormers, gables, and windows topped by half rounds give this home curb appeal

■ An open floor plan with a split bedroom design and a spacious bonus room

■ Two dormers add light and volume to the Foyer

■ A cathedral ceiling enlarge the open Great Room

■ Accent columns define the Great Room, Kitchen, and Breakfast Area

■ Private Master Suite, with a tray ceiling and a lavish bath, accesses the rear deck through sliding glass doors

First floor — 2,920 sq. ft.
Second floor — 853 sq. ft.
Garage & storage — 680 sq. ft.
Bonus room — 458 sq. ft.

■ *Total living area 2,301 sq. ft.* ■ *Price Code D* ■

No. 96404

This plan features:

■ Three bedrooms

■ Two full and one half baths

■ Open floor plan plus Bonus Room great for today's family needs

■ Two-story Foyer with palladian, clerestory window and balcony overlooking Great Room

■ Great Room with cozy fireplace provides perfect gathering place

■ Columns visually separate Great Room from Breakfast area and smart, U-shaped kitchen

■ Privately located Master Bedroom accesses Porch and luxurious Master Bath with separate shower and double vanity

■ First floor — 1,632 sq. ft.

■ Second floor — 669 sq. ft.

■ Bonus room — 528 sq. ft.

■ Garage & storage — 707 sq. ft.

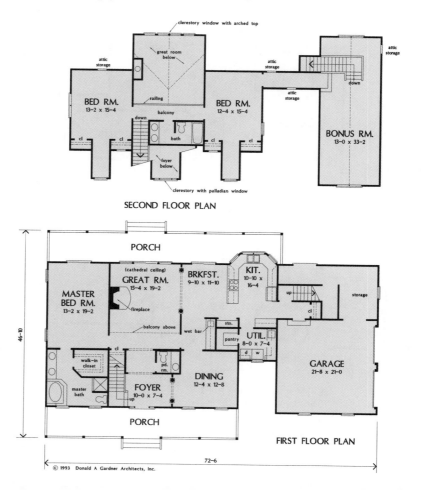

SECOND FLOOR PLAN

FIRST FLOOR PLAN

© 1993 Donald A Gardner Architects, Inc.

Impressive Two Story Entrance

Total living area 2,957 sq. ft. ■ Price Code E ■

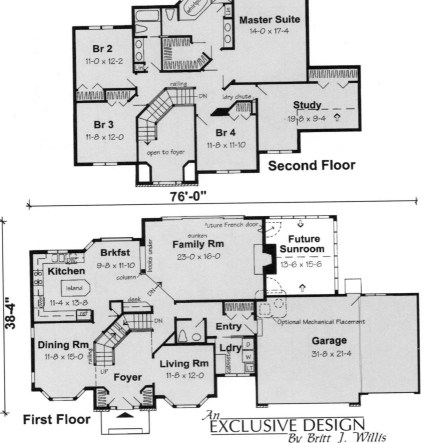

Second Floor

Master Suite
14-0 x 17-4

Br 2
11-0 x 12-2

Br 3
11-8 x 12-0

Br 4
11-8 x 11-10

Study
19-8 x 9-4

whirlpool

railing

DN

ldry chute

open to foyer

76'-0"

First Floor

Kitchen
11-4 x 13-8

island

Brkfst
9-8 x 11-10

column

books under

desk

DN

Family Rm
23-0 x 16-0

sunken

future French door

Future Sunroom
13-6 x 15-6

Optional Mechanical Placement

Dining Rm
11-8 x 15-0

railing

UP

Living Rm
11-8 x 12-0

Foyer

Entry

Ldry

D
W

Garage
31-8 x 21-4

38'-4"

An EXCLUSIVE DESIGN
By Britt J. Willis

No. 24594

■ **This plan features:**

— Four bedrooms

— Two full and one half baths

■ Two-story Foyer highlighted by lovely, angled staircase and decorative window

■ Bay windows enhance Dining a[] Living rooms

■ Kitchen with work island and a[] open Breakfast area

■ Family Room with a fireplace a[] Future Sunroom access

■ Private Master Suite offers a wa[] in closet and pampering bath

■ Three additional bedrooms sha[] a double vanity bath and large Study

First floor — 1,497 sq. ft.
Second floor — 1,460 sq. ft.
Future Sunroom — 210 sq. f[]
Garage — 680 sq. ft.

Elegant Executive Home

No. 96448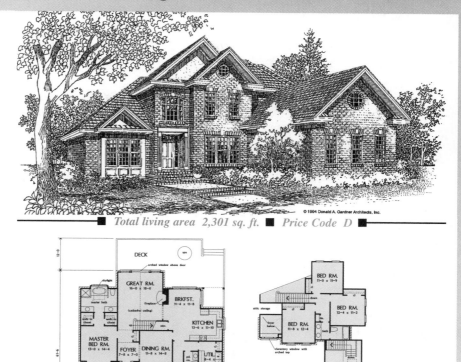

This plan features:

Four bedrooms

Two full and one half baths

Understated elegance with arched clerestory window lighting the two-story Foyer

With a cathedral ceiling topping it, the Great Room has an arched transom window above the slider to Deck and a fireplace

Open and efficient the Kitchen with adjacent Breakfast area accesses the Deck, Dining Room and the Garage

First floor Master Bedroom offers twin closets and vanities, plus a skylight over the garden tub

Second floor boasts three bedrooms, and a full bath

First floor — 1,639 sq. ft.

Second floor — 662 sq. ft.

Bonus room — 336 sq. ft.

Garage & storage — 520 sq. ft.

■ *Total living area 2,301 sq. ft.* ■ *Price Code D* ■

© 1994 Donald A. Gardner Architects, Inc.

FIRST FLOOR PLAN

SECOND FLOOR PLAN

Room for a Large Family

No. 99129

This plan features:

Four bedrooms

Two full and one half baths

Gracious Living Room archway leads into a formal Dining Room

Family Room with fireplace

The L-shaped Kitchen opens into the nook and has a built-in planning desk

The Master Bedroom is located on the second floor and has a private bath

Three more bedrooms and a full bath complete the plan

There is no materials list available for this plan

Main floor — 1,000 sq. ft.

Second floor — 960 sq. ft.

Basement — 1,000 sq. ft.

■ *Total living area 1,960 sq. ft.* ■ *Price Code C* ■

MAIN FLOOR PLAN

SECOND FLOOR PLAN

EXCLUSIVE DESIGN
By Ahmann Design Inc.

273

Bay Windows Add Airyness to Traditional Gem

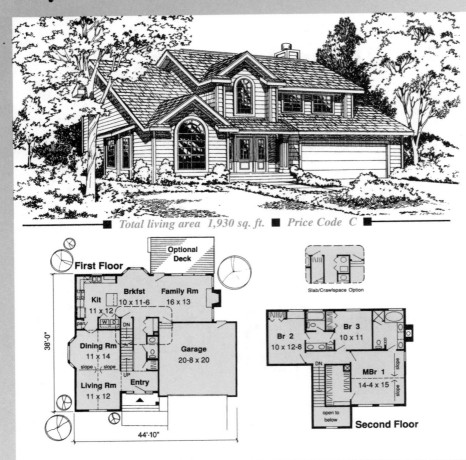

■ Total living area 1,930 sq. ft. ■ Price Code C ■

First Floor

Optional Deck

Kit 11 x 12

Brkfst 10 x 11-6

Family Rm 16 x 13

Dining Rm 11 x 14

Living Rm 11 x 12

Entry

Garage 20-8 x 20

38'-0"

44'-10"

Slab/Crawlspace Option

Br 2 10 x 12-8

Br 3 10 x 11

MBr 1 14-4 x 15

open to below

Second Floor

No. 34851

■ This plan features:

— Three bedrooms

— Two full and one half baths

■ A sloped-ceiling Living/Dining Room combination that is brightened by abundant windows

■ A Family Room with a cozy fireplace and direct access to the deck

■ An efficient, well-appointed island Kitchen with a built-in pantry and laundry facilities that serves both the Breakfast area and the formal Dining Room

■ A Master Suite with a sloped ceiling, and a private Master Bath, and a walk-in closet

■ Two additional bedrooms with direct access to a full bath

First floor — 1,056 sq. ft.
Second floor — 874 sq. ft.
Basement — 1,023 sq. ft.
Garage — 430 sq. ft.

Good Things Come in Small Packages

■ Total living area 1,253 sq. ft. ■ Price Code A ■

No. 20303

■ This plan features:

— Three bedrooms

— Two full baths

■ An air-lock vestibule entry that keeps the chill outside

■ A cozy sitting nook in the Living Room

■ A well-equipped Kitchen with a Breakfast nook

■ A sky-lit hall bath shared by two of the bedrooms

■ A Master Suite with his-n-her closets and private, sky lit full bath

First floor — 885 sq. ft.
Second floor — 368 sq. ft.
Basement — 715 sq. ft.

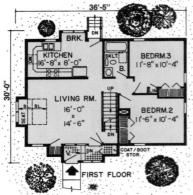

36'-5"

BRK.

KITCHEN 16'-8" x 8'-0"

BEDRM.3 11'-8" x 10'-4"

LIVING RM. 16'-0" x 14'-6"

BEDRM.2 11'-6" x 10'-4"

30'-0"

COAT/BOOT STOR.

FIRST FLOOR

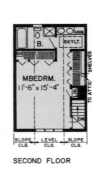

MBEDRM. 11'-6" x 15'-4"

TO ATTIC SHELVES

SLOPE CLG. LEVEL CLG. SLOPE CLG.

SECOND FLOOR

274

Tradition Combined with Contemporary

■ *Total living area 1,289 sq. ft.* ■ *Price Code A* ■

No. 99327 ✖

This plan features:

Three bedrooms

Two full baths

A vaulted ceiling in the Entry

A formal Living Room with a fireplace and a half-round transom

A Dining Room with sliders to the deck and easy access to the Kitchen

A main floor Master Suite with corner windows, a closet and private bath access

Two additional bedrooms that share a full hall bath

Main floor — 858 sq. ft.
Upper floor — 431 sq. ft.
Basement — 858 sq. ft.

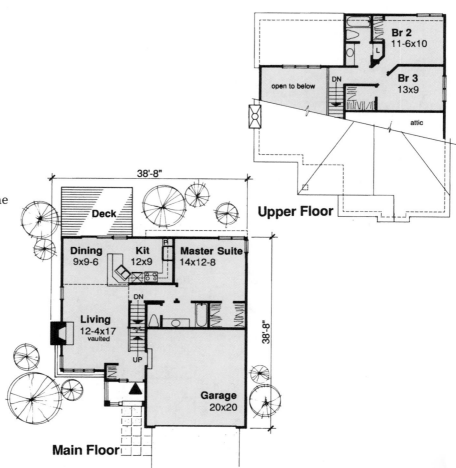

Delightful Home

■ *Total living area 1,853 sq. ft.* ■ *Price Code C* ■

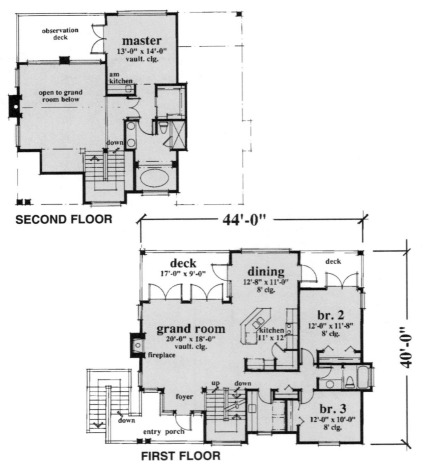

observation deck

master
13'-0" x 14'-0"
vault. clg.

am kitchen

open to grand room below

down

SECOND FLOOR

44'-0"

deck
17'-0" x 9'-0"

dining
12'-8" x 11'-0"
8' clg.

deck

grand room
20'-0" x 18'-0"
vault. clg.

kitchen
11' x 12'

fireplace

br. 2
12'-0" x 11'-8"
8' clg.

up   down

foyer

down

entry porch

br. 3
12'-0" x 10'-0"
8' clg.

40'-0"

FIRST FLOOR

No. 94248

■ This plan features:

— Three bedrooms

— Two full baths

■ Grand Room with a fireplace, vaulted ceiling and double Fren doors to the rear deck

■ Kitchen and Dining Room open continue the overall feel of spaciousness

■ Kitchen has a large walk-in pantry, island with a sink and dishwasher creating a perfect triangular workspace

■ Dining Room with doors to bot decks, has expanses of glass looking out to the rear yard

■ Master Bedroom features a dou door entry, private bath, and a morning kitchen

■ No materials list is available for this plan

First floor — 1,342 sq. ft.
Second floor — 511 sq. ft.

Compact With Style

No. 94030

This plan features:

Three bedrooms

Two full and one half baths

Formal Living Room features a bay window and vaulted ceiling

Efficient Kitchen includes a double sink, built-in pantry and a peninsula counter

Formal Dining Room is perfectly located for entertaining as it adjoins both the Living Room and the Kitchen

Expansive Family Room has a fireplace and access to the sundeck and utility area

Master Suite includes a walk-in closet and private bath

Two additional bedrooms share a full hall bath

No materials list is available for this plan

This plan is available with a basement or crawl space foundation please specify when ordering

First floor — 952 sq. ft.

Second floor — 648 sq. ft.

Width — 40'-0"

Depth — 42'-0"

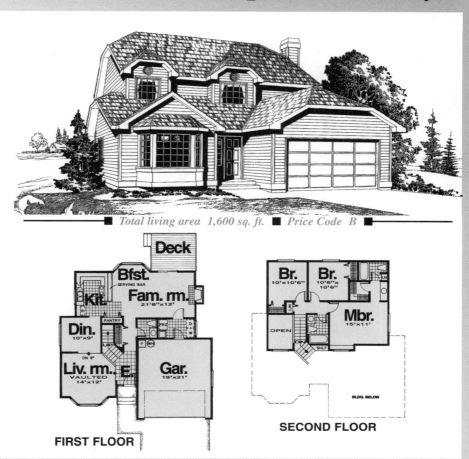

■ Total living area 1,600 sq. ft. ■ Price Code B ■

FIRST FLOOR

SECOND FLOOR

Friendly Front Porch

No. 96500

This plan features:

Three bedrooms

Two full and one half baths

Wrap-around front Porch and double French doors are an inviting sight

Central Foyer with a lovely landing staircase opens to the Dining and Great rooms

The fireplace is framed by a built-in credenza in the Great Room

Kitchen boasts a buffet, pantry and a peninsula counter/snack bar

Master Bedroom offers direct access to the Sun Room, a walk-in closet and a luxurious bath

First floor — 2,361 sq. ft.

Second floor — 650 sq. ft.

Detached carport/workshop — 864 sq. ft.

■ Total living area 3,011 sq. ft. ■ Price Code E ■

277

Country Exterior With Formal Interior

— *Total living area 2,068 sq. ft.* ■ *Price Code C* ■

No. 90451

■ **This plan features:**

— Three bedrooms

— Two full and one half baths

■ Wrap-around Porch leads into central Foy[er] and formal Living and Dining rooms

■ Large Family Room with a cozy fireplace and Deck access

■ Convenient Kitchen opens to Breakfast ar[ea] with a bay window and built-in pantry

■ Corner Master Bedroom with walk-in clos[et] and appealing bath

■ Two additional bedrooms plus a bonus room share a full bath and Laundry

■ An optional basement or crawl space foundation — please specify when orderin[g]

First floor — 1,046 sq. ft.
Second floor — 1,022 sq. ft.
Bonus — 232 sq. ft.

Contemporary Flair

— *Total living area 1,961 sq. ft.* ■ *Price Code C* ■

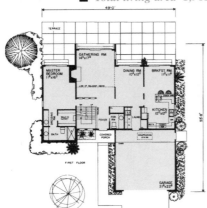

No. 99229

■ **This plan features:**

— Three bedrooms

— Two full and one half baths

■ A huge skylight in the stairwell giving ligh[t] to a typically dark area

■ Two second-floor bedrooms with use of a full hall bath and a balcony lounge area

■ A Master Suite with well-proportioned dressing suite and sliding doors to the pa[tio]

■ A Kitchen area that combines with an ope[n] Breakfast Room, and has a handy pass-through counter and snack bar

■ A large Gathering Room with cozy firepla[ce]

First floor — 1,342 sq. ft.
Second floor — 619 sq. ft.
Garage — 506 sq. ft.

■ *Total living area 2,090 sq. ft.* ■ *Price Code C* ■

No. 91416 ⚒

This plan features:

Three bedrooms

Two full and one half baths

An expansive, two story Great Room and full-length deck behind atrium doors

A Kitchen, with rangetop island, flowing into the Dining Room; which has access to the deck

A vaulted ceiling in the Master Suite, which includes two walk-in closets, a private Master Bath with garden tub and double vanity

An optional basement, slab or crawl space foundation — please specify when ordering

First floor — 1,440 sq. ft.
Second floor — 650 sq. ft.
Basement — 1,440 sq. ft.
Garage — 552 sq. ft.

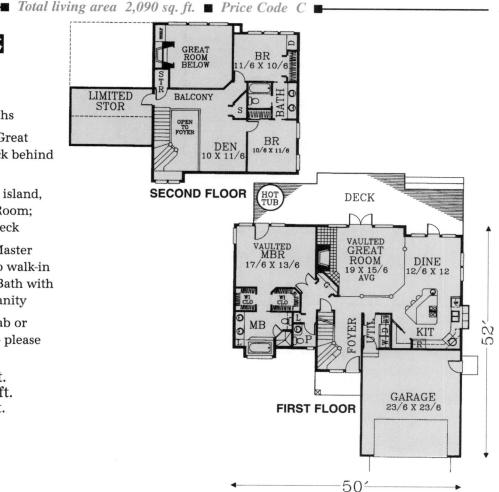

Loads of Natural Light

■ *Total living area 1,562 sq. ft.* ■ *Price Code B* ■

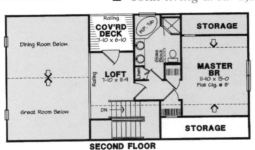

SECOND FLOOR

FIRST FLOOR

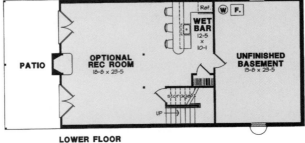

LOWER FLOOR

No. 24705

■ This plan features:

— Three bedrooms

— Two full baths

■ Double French doors with arched transom windows access an elevated Deck

■ Spacious feeling created by open Great Room, Dining area and Kitchen

■ Two first floor bedrooms with ample closets, share a full bath

■ Secluded Master Bedroom with Covered Deck, plush bath, loads of storage and a Loft

■ Lower level offers an optional Recreation Room with Patio, fireplace and wetbar

■ No materials list is available for this plan

First floor — 1,062 sq. ft.
Second floor — 500 sq. ft.
Bonus — 678 sq. ft.
Basement — 384 sq. ft.

Elegantly Styled

No. 98449

This plan features:

Three bedrooms

Two full and one half baths

Architectural details create eye-catching appeal to this home's facade

The two-story Foyer is flanked by the formal Living and Dining rooms

A convenient Kitchen with angled snack bar has easy access to the Dining Room, Breakfast area, back yard and the Laundry/Garage

Open and comfortable, the Family Room is highlighted by a fireplace and windows

The Master Bedroom suite is enhanced by a tray ceiling and a plush bath with a vaulted ceiling

The Second floor offers an optional Bonus Room for future expansion

An optional basement or crawl space foundation — please specify when ordering

First floor — 922 sq. ft.

Second floor — 778 sq. ft.

Bonus Room — 369 sq. ft.

Garage & storage — 530 sq. ft.

■ *Total living area 1,700 sq. ft.* ■ *Price Code B* ■

Farmhouse Favorite

No. 99262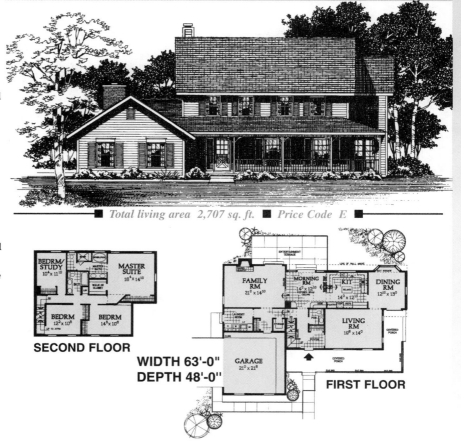

This plan features:

Four bedrooms

Two full and one half baths

Covered Porch adds living space outdoors and shelters entrance into Foyer

Formal Living Room highlighted by full length windows and open to formal Dining Room with bay window and Porch access

Spacious Kitchen with work island, pass-thru to Morning Room and Terrace beyond, and nearby Laundry/Garage entry

Comfortable Family Room with a raised hearth fireplace and access to Entertainment Terrace

Corner Master Bedroom offers two closets and pampering bath

Two or three additional bedrooms with ample closets, share a double vanity bath and attic storage

First floor — 1,595 sq. ft.

Second floor — 1,112 sq. ft.

■ *Total living area 2,707 sq. ft.* ■ *Price Code E* ■

WIDTH 63'-0"

DEPTH 48'-0"

Sense of Spaciousness

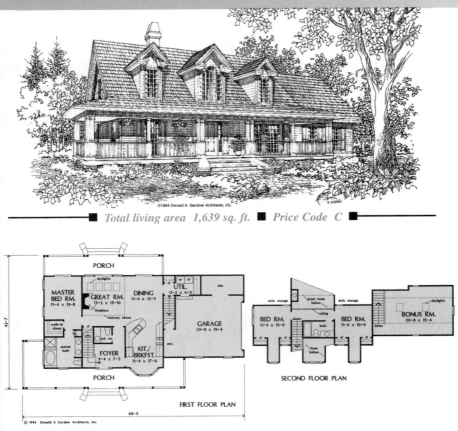

■ *Total living area 1,639 sq. ft.* ■ *Price Code C* ■

FIRST FLOOR PLAN

SECOND FLOOR PLAN

No. 96456

■ This plan features:

— Three bedrooms

— Two full and one half baths

■ Creative use of natural lighting gives a feeling of spaciousness to this country home

■ Traffic flows easily from the bright Foye into the Great Room which has a vaulted ceiling and skylights

■ The open floor plan is efficient for Kitchen/Breakfast area and the Dining Room

■ Master Bedroom suite features a walk-in closet and a private bath with whirlpool tub

■ Two second floor bedrooms with storage access, share a full bath

First floor — 1,180 sq. ft.
Second floor — 459 sq. ft.
Bonus room — 385 sq. ft.
Garage & storage — 533 sq. ft.

Created in Perfect Balance

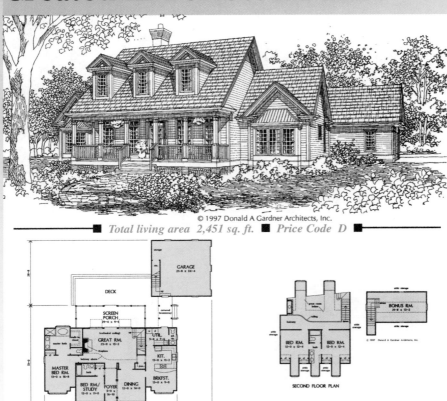

■ *Total living area 2,451 sq. ft.* ■ *Price Code D* ■

FIRST FLOOR PLAN

SECOND FLOOR PLAN

No. 99822

■ This plan features:

— Four bedrooms

— Three full and one half baths

■ Perfectly balanced, inside and out, this country home offers style and convenien in a home equipped for today's busy families

■ Two clerestory dormers cast natural ligh into the Great Room with a fireplace and cathedral ceiling

■ A large screened Porch and a Deck, beyo expand living and entertaining space through French doors

■ Staircase leads to a Loft which overlooks Great Room and accesses two family bedrooms

■ First floor Master Suite offers a charmin box bay window and generous bath with walk-in closet

■ Flexible swing room serves as a Study or Bedroom with an adjacent full bath

First floor — 1,776 sq. ft.
Second floor — 675 sq. ft.
Bonus — 382 sq. ft.

■ *Total living area 2,031 sq. ft.* ■ *Price Code C* ■

No. 90606 ✕

This plan features:

Four bedrooms

Two full and one half baths

A beautiful circular stair ascending from the central foyer and flanked by the formal Living Room and Dining Room

Exposed beams, wood paneling, and a brick fireplace wall in the Family Room

A separate dinette opening to an efficient Kitchen

First floor — 1,099 sq. ft.
Second floor — 932 sq. ft.
Basement — 1,023 sq. ft.
Garage — 476 sq. ft.

SECOND FLOOR

2x6 studs for added insulation

BED RM
12'-8" x 11'-4"

BED RM
11'-4" x 10'-4"

cl.

W.I.C.

BATH

cl.

cl.

lin.

dn.

H.

railing planter

railing
open

MASTER
BED RM
16' x 11'

BED RM
12'-8" x 10'-8"

BATH

FIRST FLOOR

56' - 8"

34' - 2"

PATIO

sl. gl. dr.

cl.

exposed
beams

DINETTE
10' x 8'

cook-top

s.

dw ov

closet

service
entry

d.

w.

STORAGE

FAMILY RM
16' x 11'-4"

KITCHEN
11'-4" x 10'

dn.

MUD RM

heat-circulating
fireplace

LAV.

ref.

dn.

railing
open
abv.

up

DINING RM
14' x 11'

TWO CAR
GARAGE
20' x 20'

LIVING RM
19'-6" x 12'-8"

cl.

FOYER

PORCH

Luxury Personified

■ *Total living area 2,653 sq. ft.* ■ *Price Code E* ■

No. 92623

■ **This plan features:**

— Four bedrooms

— Three full baths

■ A tray ceiling in the formal Livi
Room and Dining Room with
corner columns

■ An island Kitchen with a corner
sink with windows to either sid

■ A sunken Family Room with a
cozy fireplace

■ A luxurious Master Suite with
double walk-in closets, sloped
ceiling and private Master Bath

■ Three additional bedrooms that
share a skylit full bath with
laundry chute located close by

■ A balcony overlooking the foyer
with a plant shelf, arched windo
and skylight

First floor — 1,365 sq. ft.
Second floor — 1,288 sq. ft.
Basement — 1,217 sq. ft.
Garage — 491 sq. ft.

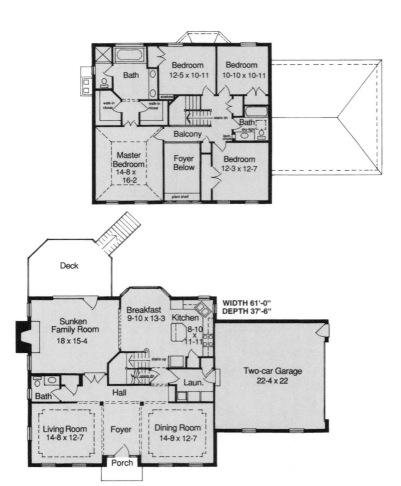

Traditional Splendor

No. 91339

This plan features:

- Six bedrooms
- Four full and one half baths
- This home easily accommodates a large or extended family with style and grace
- Two-story Entry illuminated by palladian window opens to gracious Living Room
- Bright and efficient Kitchen with angled counter/eating bar and walk-in pantry opens to Family Room and Deck
- Luxurious Master Bedroom suite shares two-way fireplace with Den
- Four second floor bedrooms share two full baths
- No materials list is available for this plan
- First floor — 2,498 sq. ft.
- Second floor — 1,190 sq. ft.

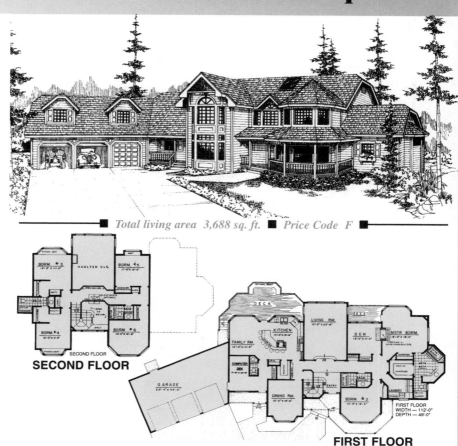

Total living area 3,688 sq. ft. ■ *Price Code F*

SECOND FLOOR

FIRST FLOOR

Spacious Stucco

No. 20368

This plan features:

- Three bedrooms
- Two full and one half baths
- A vaulted foyer flanked by a soaring Living Room with huge palladium windows
- A Family Room with a massive two-way fireplace
- A Master Suite with garden spa, private deck access, and a walk-in closet
- First floor — 1,752 sq. ft.
- Second floor — 620 sq. ft.
- Basement — 1,726 sq. ft.
- Garage — 714 sq. ft.

Total living area 2,372 sq. ft. ■ *Price Code D*

First Floor

Second Floor

Impressive Image of Luxury

Total living area 1,911 sq. ft. ■ **Price Code C**

44' - 10"

51' - 1"

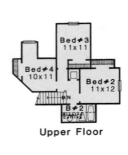

Main Floor

Patio
Din 10x12 8'Ceiling
FmlDin 9x10 8'Ceiling
Patio
Kit
LivRm 16x19
Ent 10'Ceiling
Cathedral Ceiling
Por
MstrBed 15x15
Mstr
Pwd
Utl
Gar 20x22

Bed #3 11x11
Bed #4 10x11
Bed #2 11x12
B #2

Upper Floor

No. 98507

■ **This plan features:**

— Four bedrooms

— Two full and one half baths

■ Full brick gables and a lovely palladian window present an impressive image of luxury

■ The spacious Living Room with a fireplace and a cathedral ceiling is separated from the Dining Room by a plant ledge

■ The angled Kitchen with a cooktop island efficiently serves the Dining areas and the Patio

■ The Master Bedroom suite offers a private Patio, double vanity bath and a walk-in closet

■ There is no materials list available for this plan

■ This plan is available with a basement or slab foundation, please specify when ordering this plan

First floor — 1,354 sq. ft.
Second floor — 557 sq. ft.
Garage — 440 sq. ft.

A Center Family Room

© 1992 Donald A. Gardner Architects, Inc.

Total living area 2,647 sq. ft. ■ **Price Code E**

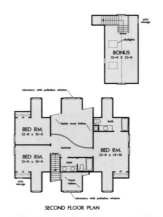

No. 99892

■ **This plan features:**

— Four bedrooms

— Three full and one half baths

■ At the center of the home is a fireplaced family room with a rounded balcony overlooking from above.

■ Master Suite enhanced by a sitting area with a unique window, a walk in closet & spacious bathroom with a dual vanity

■ Dining Room and Breakfast area both off the island Kitchen

■ A huge wrap-around porch extending to deck, complete with built-in seating and spa

■ A covered breezeway joining the garage & the utility/laundry room

First floor — 1,759 sq. ft.
Second floor — 888 sq. ft.
Garage — 532 sq. ft.

A Whisper of Victorian Styling

■ *Total living area 3,198 sq. ft.* ■ *Price Code E* ■

No. 93333

This plan features:

Four bedrooms

Two full and one half baths

Formal Living Room features wrap-around windows and direct access to the front Porch

An elegant, formal Dining Room accented by a stepped ceiling

Efficient Kitchen is equipped with a cooktop island/eating bar and a double sink

A bright, all-purpose Sun Room, with glass on four sides adjoining an expansive Deck

A private Master Suite with a decorative ceiling and a luxurious Bath with a raised, atrium tub, oversized walk-in shower, two vanities, and a pocket door leading into an oversized walk-in closet

Three additional bedrooms sharing a full, hall bath with double vanity

No materials list available

First floor — 1,743 sq. ft.

Second floor — 1,455 sq. ft.

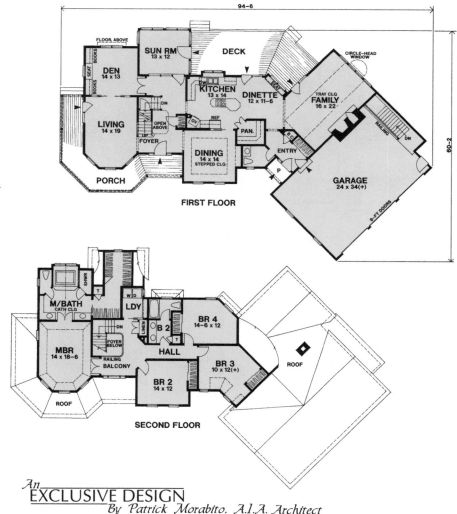

An
EXCLUSIVE DESIGN
By Patrick Morabito, A.I.A. Architect

Contemporary Features Sunken Living Room

■ *Total living area 1,487 sq. ft.* ■ *Price Code A* ■

FIRST FLOOR

SECOND FLOOR

No. 26112

■ This plan features:

— Two bedrooms, with possible third bedroom/den

— One full and one half baths

■ A solar design with southern gla[...] doors, windows, and an air-lock entry

■ R-26 insulation used for floors a[...] sloping ceilings

■ A deck rimming the front of the home

■ A Dining Room separated from the Living Room by a half wall

■ An efficient Kitchen with an eating bar

First floor — 911 sq. ft.
Second floor — 576 sq. ft.
Basement — 911 sq. ft.

Elegant Elevation

No. 92662

This plan features:

- Three bedrooms

- Two full baths

- Brick trim, sidelights, and a transom window give a warm welcome to this home

- High ceilings continue from foyer into Great Room which counts among it's amenities a fireplace and entertainment center

- The Kitchen serves the formal and informal dining areas with ease

- The Master Suite is positioned for privacy on the first floor

- The second floor has loads of possibilities with a Bonus space and a Study

- Two bedrooms each with walk in closest share a full bath

- No materials list is available for this plan

First floor — 1,542 sq. ft.
Second floor — 667 sq. ft.
Bonus — 236 sq. ft.
Basement — 1,367 sq. ft.
Garage — 420 sq. ft

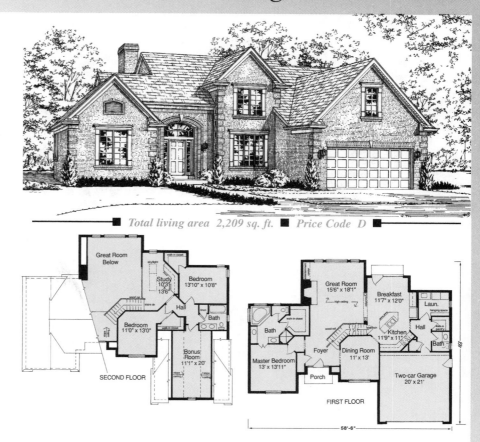

■ *Total living area 2,209 sq. ft.* ■ *Price Code D* ■

"English Manor" House

No. 99402

This plan features:

- Four bedrooms

- Two full, one three quarter and one half baths

- Quarried stone facade enhances Covered stoop and impressive Entry with columns and a curved staircase

- Double doors open to private Den with built-in bookshelves and triple, transom window

- Formal Dining Room accented by a decorative ceiling, and hutch space

- Spectacular bow window and a raised, hearth fireplace highlight Living Room

- Ideal Kitchen with walk-in pantry, built-in desk, angled serving counter/snack bar, bright Breakfast alcove, and spacious Family Room

- Private Master Bedroom suite includes a charming Sitting area, decorative ceiling, two walk-in closets and a luxurious bath

- Three second floor bedrooms with walk-in closets and private bath access

First floor — 2,813 sq. ft.
Second floor — 1,091 sq. ft.
Basement — 2,813 sq. ft.
Garage — 1,028 sq. ft.

■ *Total living area 3,904 sq. ft.* ■ *Price Code F* ■

© design basics, inc.

289

Year Round Retreat

■ Total living area 1,432 sq. ft. ■ Price Code A ■

No. 90613 ⚒

■ **This plan features:**
— Three bedrooms
— Two full baths
■ A Living Room with a dramatic sloping ceiling and a wood burning stove
■ A Kitchen and Living Room opening ont the rear deck
■ A Master Suite with a full bath, linen clo and ample closet space

First floor — 967 sq. ft.
Second floor — 465 sq. ft.
Basement — 811 sq. ft.
Garage — 234 sq. ft.

FIRST FLOOR

SECOND FLOOR

Ultimate Rambling Farmhouse

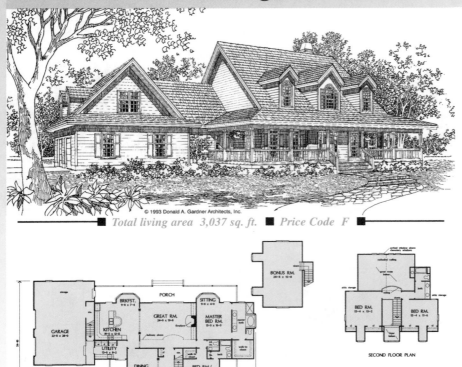

© 1993 Donald A. Gardner Architects, Inc.

■ Total living area 3,037 sq. ft. ■ Price Code F ■

No. 99887 ⚒

■ **This plan features:**
— Four bedrooms
— Three full and one half baths
■ Living space abounds both downstairs a up, with four large Bedrooms, a Bonus room and a generous Kitchen
■ The Great Room, with a balcony overlooking above, includes a large firep and adjoins with a spacious Kitchen
■ Columns define the Dining Room from Foyer in an elegant style
■ First floor Master Suite is the perfect ret with a bayed sitting area and a five-piec master Bath
■ Front Bedroom/Study has private access a full Bath and a walk-in closet creating terrific guest room

First floor — 2,316 sq. ft.
Second floor — 721 sq. ft.
Bonus — 545 sq. ft.
Garage — 974 sq. ft.

Angular Elegance

■ *Total living area 2,707 sq. ft.* ■ *Price Code E* ■

No. 91509 ⚒ Ⓡ

This plan features:

Three bedrooms

Two full and one half baths

A unique Living Room with a vaulted ceiling, and columns separating it from the formal Dining Room

A wide-open arrangement between the Family Room, Nook and island Kitchen

A fireplace in both the Family Room and the Living Room

A skylight and double vanity in the full hall bath

A Master Suite with a walk-in closet, garden spa tub, and bay window

First floor — 1,675 sq. ft.
Second floor — 1,032 sq. ft.
Bonus room — 450 sq. ft.

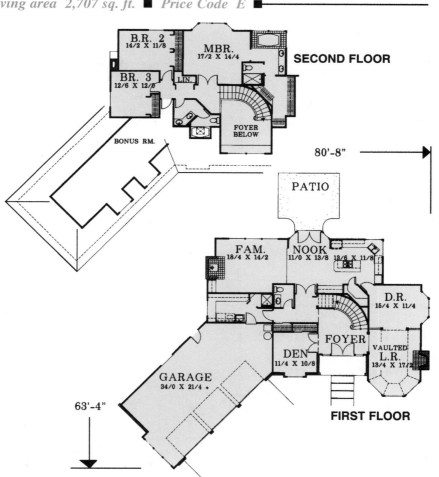

Charming Country Home

■ *Total living area 1,434 sq. ft.* ■ *Price Code A* ■

No. 24711

■ **This plan features:**

— Three bedrooms

— Two full baths

■ Cozy fireplace below a vaulted ceiling and dormer window in Living Room

■ Kitchen with a peninsula counter/snack bar, built-in pant and access to laundry, Screened Area-way and Garage beyond

■ Two first floor bedrooms share full bath and laundry

■ Private second floor Master Suit offers a dormer window, walk-in closet and private bath

■ No materials list is available for this plan

First floor — 1,018 sq. ft.
Second floor — 416 sq. ft.
Garage — 624 sq. ft.

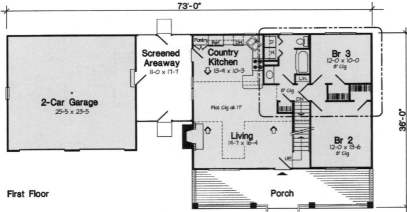

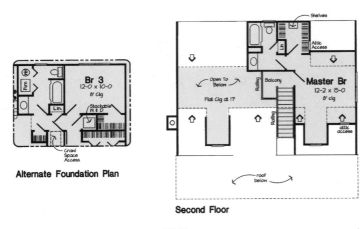

Alternate Foundation Plan

Second Floor

First Floor

Classic Victorian

No. 94721

This plan features:

- Four bedrooms

- Three full and one half baths

- Large open areas that are bright and free flowing

- Great Room accented by a fireplace and large front window

- Sun Room off of the Great Room viewing the porch

- Dining Room in close proximity to the Kitchen

- Efficient Kitchen flows into informal Breakfast Nook

- Private first floor Master Suite highlighted by a plush Master Bath

- Three bedrooms on the second floor, two with walk-in closets and one with a private bath

First floor — 1,868 sq. ft.

Second floor — 964 sq. ft.

Garage — 460 sq. ft.

An
EXCLUSIVE DESIGN
By United Design Associates

■ *Total living area 2,832 sq. ft.* ■ *Price Code E* ■

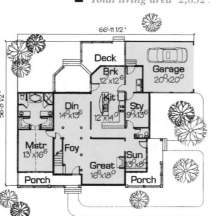

SECOND FLOOR

FIRST FLOOR

Casually Elegant

No. 99890

This plan features:

- Four bedrooms

- Three full and one half baths

- Two-level Foyer, naturally illuminated by the Palladian window above

- Great Room topped by a cathedral ceiling and highlighted by a balcony above and a fireplace

- Columns defining the Great Room from the Kitchen and Breakfast Room

- First floor Master Suite opening to the screened porch through the bay area

- Two additional bedrooms on the second floor, each with a private bath

First floor — 1,766 sq. ft.

Second floor — 670 sq. ft.

Garage & storage — 624 sq. ft.

© 1992 Donald A. Gardner Architects, Inc.

■ *Total living area 2,436 sq. ft.* ■ *Price Code D* ■

Savor the Summer

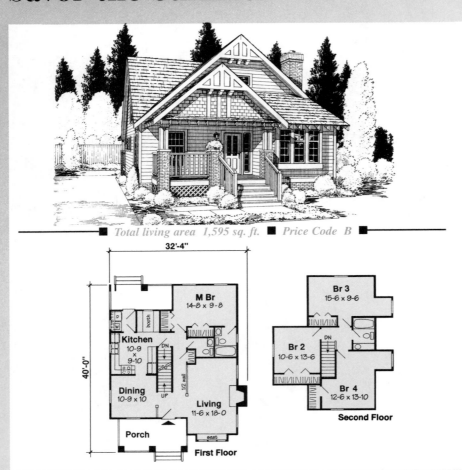

Total living area 1,595 sq. ft. ■ Price Code B

32'-4"

40'-0"

M Br
14-8 x 9-8

Kitchen
10-9 x 9-10

Dining
10-9 x 10

Living
11-6 x 18-0

Porch

seat

First Floor

Br 3
15-6 x 9-6

Br 2
10-6 x 13-6

Br 4
12-6 x 13-10

Second Floor

No. 24242

■ **This plan features:**

— Four bedrooms

— Two full and one half baths

■ A efficient home with a friendly front Porch and a practical back porch

■ A cozy fireplace and a boxed window with a built-in seat in the Living Room

■ A formal Dining Room opening to front entrance and Kitchen

■ A well-equipped Kitchen with an old-fashion booth and ample cabinet and counter space adjoining Laundry area and back porch

■ A convenient, first floor Master Suite with two closet and a private Bath

■ Three additional bedrooms, on second floor, sharing a full hall bath

First floor — 931 sq. ft.
Second floor — 664 sq. ft.

Luxuriant Living

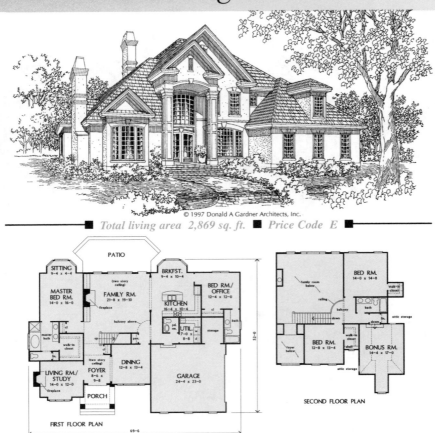

© 1997 Donald A Gardner Architects, Inc.

Total living area 2,869 sq. ft. ■ Price Code E

PATIO

SITTING
9-4 x 4-4

MASTER
BED RM.
14-0 x 16-0

FAMILY RM.
21-8 x 19-10

BRKFST.
9-4 x 10-4

KITCHEN
16-4 x 10-4

BED RM./
OFFICE
12-4 x 12-0

UTIL.
7-0 x 8-8

LIVING RM./
STUDY
14-0 x 12-0

FOYER
8-6 x 9-8

DINING
12-8 x 13-4

GARAGE
24-4 x 23-0

PORCH

FIRST FLOOR PLAN

69-6

© 1997 Donald A Gardner Architects, Inc.

BED RM.
14-0 x 14-8

BED RM.
12-8 x 13-4

BONUS RM.
14-4 x 17-0

attic storage

SECOND FLOOR PLAN

No. 99825

■ **This plan features:**

— Four bedrooms

— Three full and one half baths

■ French doors, windows, and a high gable Entry make a dramatic entrance to this home

■ Formal Living Room features a box bay window and a fireplace

■ Dining Room is illuminated by a bank of windows

■ Large family room has a two-story ceiling fireplace and accessed the rear patio

■ Kitchen and Nook adjoin handy home Office that has a full bath

■ The Master Suite features a private bath a sitting area

■ Upstairs find two bedrooms each with a walk-in closet, a full bath and a Bonus Room

First floor — 2,249 sq. ft.
Second floor — 620 sq. ft.
Bonus — 308 sq. ft.
Garage — 642 sq. ft.

Adapt This Colonial To Your Lifestyle

■ *Total living area 1,587 sq. ft.* ■ *Price Code B* ■

No. 90671 ✖

This plan features:

Four bedrooms

Two full baths

A Living Room with a beam ceiling and a fireplace

An eat-in Kitchen efficiently serving the formal Dining Room

A Master Bedroom with his and her closets

Two upstairs bedrooms sharing a split bath

First floor — 1,056 sq. ft.
Second floor — 531 sq. ft.

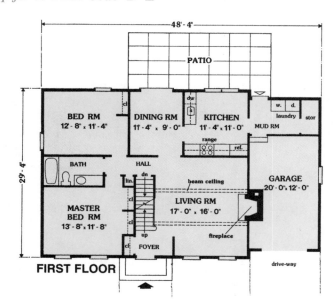

FIRST FLOOR

48'-4"

29'-4"

PATIO

BED RM
12'-8" x 11'-4"

DINING RM
11'-4" x 9'-0"

KITCHEN
11'-4" x 11'-0"

w. d.
laundry   stor

MUD RM

BATH

HALL

range

ref.

GARAGE
20'-0" x 12'-0"

MASTER
BED RM
13'-8" x 11'-8"

beam ceiling

LIVING RM
17'-0" x 16'-0"

fireplace

FOYER

drive-way

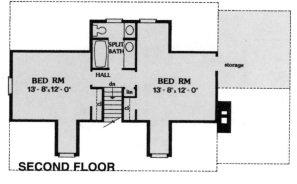

SECOND FLOOR

SPLIT
BATH

HALL

BED RM
13'-8" x 12'-0"

BED RM
13'-8" x 12'-0"

storage

Exciting Arched Accents Give Impact

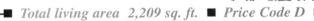

Total living area 2,209 sq. ft. ■ **Price Code D** ■

SECOND FLOOR

Great Room Below

Study 10'3" 13'6"

Bedroom 13'10" x 10'8"

Hall

linen

Bath

Bedroom 11'0" x 13'0"

Bonus Room 11'1" x 20'

skylight

walk-in closet

walk-in closet

wood rail

stairs dn

slope ceiling

slope ceiling

slope ceiling

FIRST FLOOR

Great Room 15'6" x 18'1"

Breakfast 11'7" x 12'0"

Laun.

hanging space

Bath

walk-in pantry

Hall

Kitchen 11'9" x 11'

Master Bedroom 13' x 13'11"

Bath

walk-in closet

Foyer

Dining Room 11' x 13'

Porch

Two-car Garage 20' x 21'

entertainment center

wood rail

stairs dn

high ceiling

58'6"

49'

No. 92643

■ This plan features:

— Three bedrooms

— Two full and one half baths

■ Keystone arch accents entrance

■ Great Room enhanced by an entertainment center, hearth fireplace and a wall of windows overlooking back yard

■ Efficient, angled Kitchen offers work island/snackbar, Breakfast area with access to back yard, a next, Laundry, Bath and Garage

■ Master Bedroom wing features lavish Bath with two vanities, and corner window tub

■ Two bedrooms with walk-in closets share a skylit Study, double vanity bath and a Bonus Room

First floor — 1,542 sq. ft.
Second floor — 667 sq. ft.
Bonus — 236 sq. ft.
Garage — 420 sq. ft.

Not a Typical Farmhouse

No. 96470

This plan features:

- Four bedrooms
- Two full and one half baths
- A large center gable with a palladian window and a gently vaulted portico
- Formal Dining Room and a Living Room/study highlighted by tray ceilings
- Spacious Family Room, adjoining the Living Room and the Breakfast area
- Nine foot ceilings adding volume to the first floor
- Efficient Kitchen with a center work island and a roomy pantry
- Gracious Master Suite topped by a tray ceiling and highlighted by a generous walk-in closet and a skylit bath with a double bowl vanity, linen closet and a garden tub
- Three additional bedrooms sharing a full bath

First floor — 1,299 sq. ft.
Second floor — 1,176 sq. ft.
Garage & storage — 641 sq. ft.
Bonus room — 464 sq. ft.

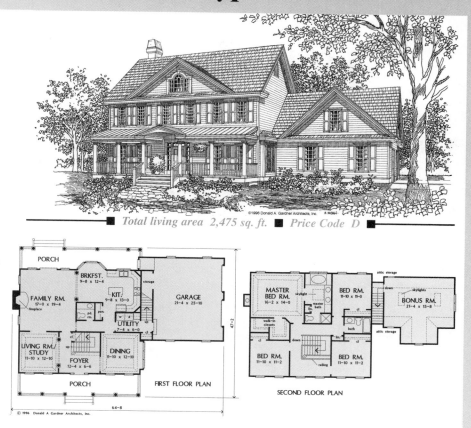

■ *Total living area 2,475 sq. ft.* ■ *Price Code D* ■

Grandeur Within

No. 99443

This plan features:

- Four bedrooms
- Two full, one three quarter, and one half baths
- Cascading staircase dominates the tiled front entry hall
- Den has a bay window and built-in bookcases
- The Living and Dining Rooms have ten foot ceilings and access a Screened Porch
- The upstairs Master Suite has built-ins, a sitting area and a wonderful bath
- Three secondary bedrooms all have walk-in closets and share two baths

First floor — 1,923 sq. ft.
Second floor — 1,852 sq. ft.
Basement — 1,923 sq. ft.
Garage — 726 sq. ft.

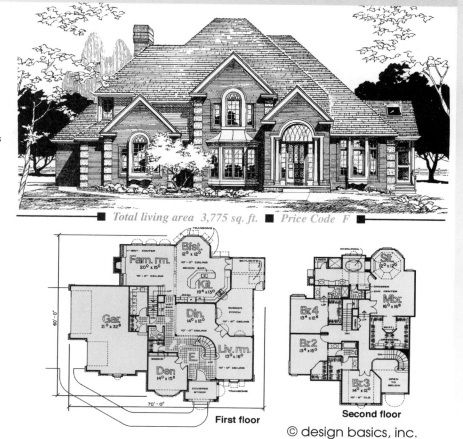

■ *Total living area 3,775 sq. ft.* ■ *Price Code F* ■

© design basics, inc.

Traditional Warmth

No. 34073

This plan features:

— Four bedrooms

— Two full and one half baths

■ Abundant windows and a covered porch

■ A sunken Living Room off the entry

■ An efficient island Kitchen

■ A Great Room with access to both a screened porch and an outdoor deck

■ A graceful staircase leading to three ample bedrooms, each with a walk-in closet

First floor — 1,469 sq. ft.
Second floor — 1,241 sq. ft.

■ *Total living area 2,710 sq. ft.* ■ *Price Code E* ■

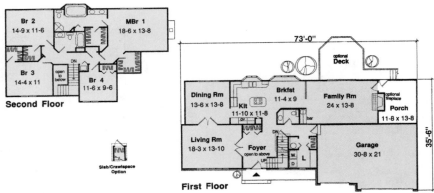

Comfortable Family Living

No. 99881

This plan features:

— Four bedrooms

— Three full and one half baths

■ Traditional plan offers comfortable family living space and well placed formal areas

■ Formal Living and Dining rooms are accentuated by columns

■ The Family Room features a cathedral ceiling, a fireplace, and access to the back porch

■ The private Master Suite has it's own bath with a sunny window

■ Upstairs find three bedrooms, two full baths and a Bonus Room

First floor — 1,847 sq. ft.
Second floor — 964 sq. ft.
Bonus — 413 sq. ft.
Garage — 651 sq. ft.

■ *Total living area 2,811 sq. ft.* ■ *Price Code E* ■

Contemporary Cape

■ *Total living area 1,739 sq. ft.* ■ *Price Code B* ■

No. 93501

This plan features:

Four bedrooms

Two full baths

Covered Entry leads into Living Room with barrel vault ceiling, arched window and cozy fireplace dividing Family/Dining area

Skylight highlights compact Kitchen with open snack bar serving Dining area and Patio/Optional Sunspace beyond

Private Master Bedroom offers a wall of closets, a double vanity bath with skylight and nearby bedroom or multi-purpose room

Two first floor bedrooms with ample closets, share a full bath

First floor — 1,154 sq. ft.
Second floor — 585 sq. ft.

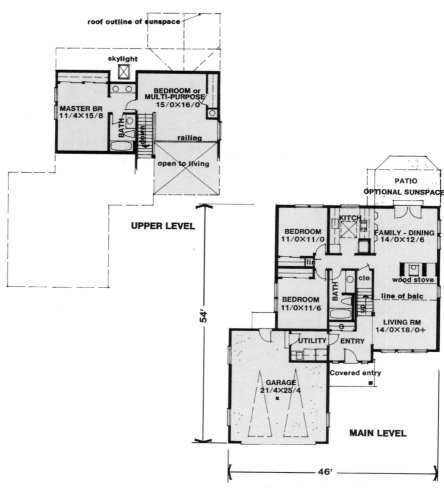

Charming and Convenient

■ Total living area 2,209 sq. ft. ■ • Price Code D ■

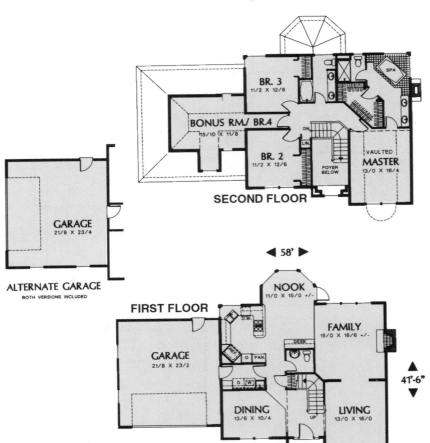

SECOND FLOOR

BR. 3
11/2 X 12/6

BONUS RM./ BR.4
15/10 X 11/8

BR. 2
11/2 X 12/6

VAULTED
MASTER
13/0 X 16/4

FOYER
BELOW

GARAGE
21/6 X 23/4

ALTERNATE GARAGE
BOTH VERSIONS INCLUDED

FIRST FLOOR

◄ 58' ►

NOOK
11/0 X 15/0 +/-

FAMILY
15/0 X 16/6 +/-

GARAGE
21/8 X 23/2

DESK

DINING
13/6 X 10/4

LIVING
13/0 X 16/0

▲
41'-6"
▼

No. 91534

■ **This plan features:**

— Three bedrooms

— Two full and one half baths

■ Central entrance opens to form[a
Dining and Living areas

■ Spacious Family Room offers a
fireplace and back yard view

■ Kitchen with peninsula
counter/snackbar, pantry, built-
desk, glass eating Nook and
nearby laundry/Garage entry

■ Corner Master suite offers an
arched window below vaulted
ceiling, a walk-in closet and spa
tub

■ Two additional bedrooms with
ample closets, share a double
vanity bath and Bonus Room

First floor — 1,214 sq. ft.
Second floor — 995 sq. ft.
Bonus Room 261 sq. ft.

Expansive Entertainment Room

No. 99500

This plan features:

Three bedrooms

Two full and one half baths

Charming porch and quaint dormers enhance curb appeal

Formal Foyer with half bath and staircase to the left and elegant Dining Room with a bay window to right

Great Room, with fireplace, is open to the efficient Kitchen except for extended counter/snack bar

First floor Master Suite has a five-piece bath and a walk-in closet

Entertainment room on second floor keeps playful children happy and the noise upstairs

Two additional bedrooms share a full bath

Please specify a slab or a crawl space foundation when ordering this plan

No materials list is available for this plan

First floor — 1,218 sq. ft.

Second floor — 864 sq. ft.

Garage — 472 sq. ft.

An **EXCLUSIVE DESIGN**
By Georgia Toney Cesley.
Residential Designer

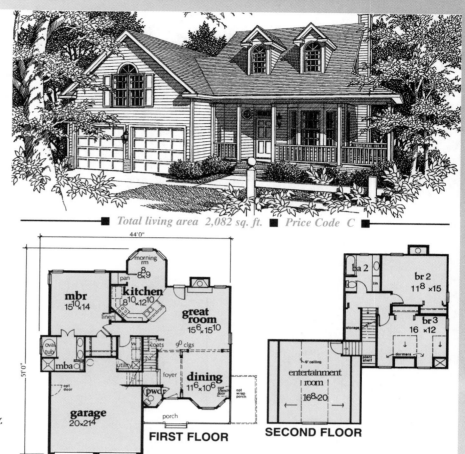

Total living area 2,082 sq. ft. ■ Price Code C

FIRST FLOOR

SECOND FLOOR

Country Porches Front and Back

No. 99894 ✗

This plan features:

Four bedrooms

Three full baths

Elegantly bayed Dining Room directly accesses the cook top island Kitchen

Breakfast Bay flows into the efficient Kitchen

Great Room, directly accesses the back porch, and is highlighted by a cathedral ceiling, fireplace and a balcony above

Master Suite enhanced by a lavish private bath and a walk-in closet

Two additional bedrooms on the second floor share the full double vanity bath in the hall

First floor — 1,871 sq. ft.

Second floor — 731 sq. ft.

Bonus room — 402 sq. ft.

Garage & storage — 600 sq. ft.

© 1993 Donald A. Gardner Architects, Inc.

Total living area 2,602 sq. ft. ■ Price Code E

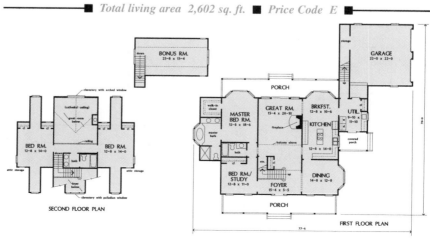

SECOND FLOOR PLAN

FIRST FLOOR PLAN

Narrow Lot Home

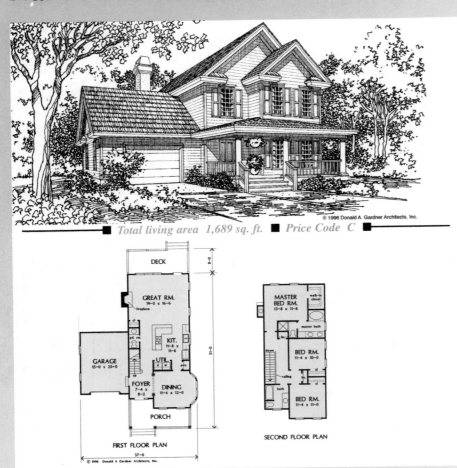

© 1996 Donald A. Gardner Architects, Inc.

Total living area 1,689 sq. ft. ■ Price Code C

DECK

GREAT RM.
19-0 x 16-6
fireplace

KIT.
11-8 x
11-6

UTIL.

GARAGE
15-0 x 20-0

FOYER
7-4 x
8-2

DINING
11-4 x 12-0

PORCH

FIRST FLOOR PLAN

37-0

© 1996 Donald A Gardner Architects, Inc.

MASTER
BED RM.
13-8 x 11-8

walk-in
closet

master bath

down

BED RM.
11-4 x 10-0

railing

bath

BED RM.
11-4 x 11-0

SECOND FLOOR PLAN

No. 99884

■ **This plan features:**

— Three bedrooms

— Two full and one half baths

■ Double gables and a porch with a hip roof giving this narrow lot home a storybook look

■ Deck at the rear expanding living and entertaining space from the Great Room

■ Great Room open to the center island Kitchen with pantry

■ Formal Dining Room accented by column located directly off the Foyer

■ Second floor Master Suite placed for utmost privacy with separate shower, garden tub and double vanity

■ Two additional bedrooms sharing a full bath

First floor — 875 sq. ft.
Second floor — 814 sq. ft.
Garage & storage — 317 sq. ft.

Wonderful Windows

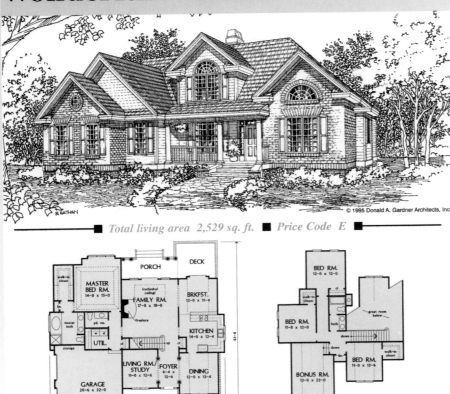

B. NATHAN

© 1995 Donald A. Gardner Architects, Inc.

Total living area 2,529 sq. ft. ■ Price Code E

walk-in
closet

MASTER
BED RM.
14-8 x 15-0

PORCH

DECK

cathedral
ceiling
FAMILY RM.
17-8 x 18-8

fireplace

BRKFST.
12-0 x 11-4

master bath

pd. rm.

UTIL.

storage

KITCHEN
14-0 x 12-4

LIVING RM./
STUDY
11-0 x 12-6

FOYER
6-4 x
7-0

DINING
12-0 x 13-4

GARAGE
20-6 x 22-0

PORCH

storage

FIRST FLOOR PLAN

55-4

© 1995 Donald A Gardner Architects, Inc.

BED RM.
12-0 x 12-0

walk-in
closet

great room
below

BED RM.
11-8 x 12-0

bath

down

down

BED RM.
11-0 x 12-6

walk-in
closet

BONUS RM.
13-0 x 22-0

SECOND FLOOR PLAN

No. 99897

■ **This plan features:**

— Four bedrooms

— Two full and one half baths

■ Covered front porch supported by column and decorative windows make this home special

■ Enter the Foyer and columns greet you i the entrances to the Living and Dining Rooms

■ An efficient U-shaped Kitchen opens into the breakfast nook and rear deck beyond

■ The large Family Room contains a firepla and a cathedral ceiling

■ The hallway to the first floor Master Suit includes a laundry and half bath

■ The Master Suite has lovely windows, a decorative ceiling, and a private bath

■ Upstairs find three bedrooms, a full bath and a bonus room for future expansion

First floor — 1,799 sq. ft.
Second floor — 730 sq. ft.
Bonus — 333 sq. ft.
Garage — 563 sq. ft.

English Country Architecture

■ *Total living area 2,878 sq. ft.* ■ *Price Code E* ■

No. 94400

This plan features:

Four bedrooms

Four full baths

Two-story Foyer

Open, island Kitchen blends with the Breakfast Room

Family Room with a vaulted ceiling has a fireplace and wetbar

Formal Living Room is accented by a fireplace

Each of the four upstairs bedrooms has access to a full bath

Master Bedroom with a private bath and a large walk-in closet

An optional basement or crawl space foundation — please specify when ordering

No materials list available

First floor — 1,563 sq. ft.
Second floor — 1,315 sq. ft.
Basement — 1,547 sq. ft.
Garage — 434 sq. ft.

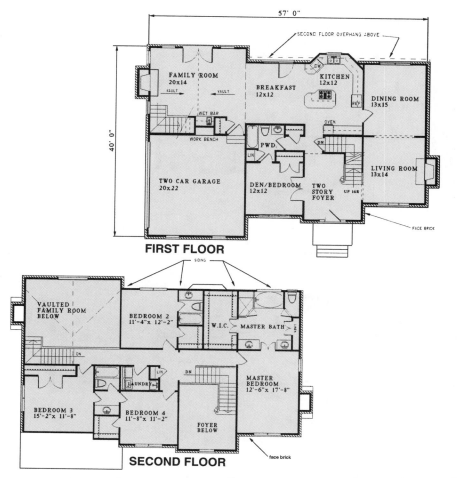

Distinctive Detail and Design

■ *Total living area 1,897 sq. ft.* ■ *Price Code C* ■

walk-in closet

Master Bedroom
12' x 14'11"

Bedroom
10'6" x 11'2"

Great Room Below

Bath

Bath

computer desk

Balcony

Bedroom
11' x 12'

stairs dn

window seat

SECOND FLOOR

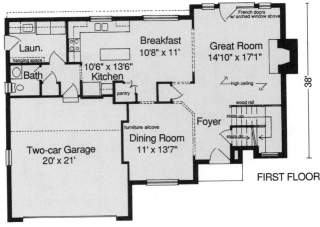

French doors w/ arched window above

Laun.

hanging space

Bath

Breakfast
10'8" x 11'

Great Room
14'10" x 17'1"

10'6" x 13'6"
Kitchen

pantry

high ceiling

Two-car Garage
20' x 21'

furniture alcove

Dining Room
11' x 13'7"

Foyer

wood rail

stairs up

stairs dn

38'

FIRST FLOOR

48'

No. 92644

■ **This plan features:**

— Three bedrooms

— Two full and one half baths

■ Impressive pilaster entry into open Foyer with landing staircas[e]

■ Great Room accented by hearth fireplace and French doors

■ Formal Dining Room enhanced by furniture alcove

■ Efficient, L-shaped Kitchen with work island, walk-in pantry, bright breakfast area

■ Quiet Master Bedroom offers a walk-in closet, and plush bath with two vanities and whirlpool tub

■ Two additional bedrooms share full bath and computer desk

First floor — 1,036 sq. ft.
Second floor — 861 sq. ft.
Garage — 420 sq. ft.

No. 92663

This plan features:

Four bedrooms

Two full and one half baths

A covered front porch coupled with the fieldstone and brick exterior provide warmth and a welcoming effect to this home

A butler's pantry is located between the Kitchen and Dining Room for ease in serving

A tray ceiling tops the formal dining area, adding style and charm

The oversized Kitchen offers an abundance of storage and work area

A corner fireplace warms the Great Room

A sloped ceiling is featured in the Master Bedroom along with the luxurious dressing/bath area

There is no materials list available for this plan

First floor — 1,573 sq. ft.

Second floor — 1,152 sq. ft.

Basement — 1,534 sq. ft.

Garage — 680 sq. ft.

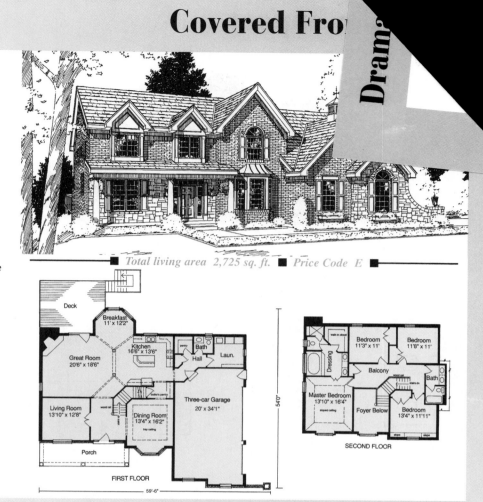

■ *Total living area 2,725 sq. ft.* ■ *Price Code E* ■

Country Charm and Modern Convenience

No. 96459

This plan features:

Three bedrooms

Two full and one half baths

Great Room crowned in a cathedral ceiling and accented by a cozy fireplace with built-ins

Centrally-located Kitchen with nearby pantry serving Breakfast area and Dining Room with ease

Master Suite elegantly appointed by a walk-in closet and a lavish bath

A Sitting Room with bay window off the Master Suite

Two secondary bedrooms sharing a full bath

First floor — 1,778 sq. ft.

Second floor — 592 sq. ft.

Garage & storage — 622 sq. ft.

Bonus Room — 404 sq. ft.

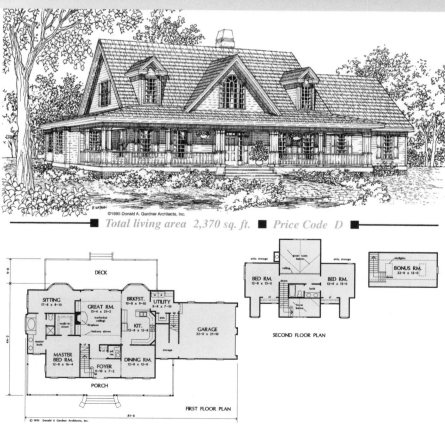

■ *Total living area 2,370 sq. ft.* ■ *Price Code D* ■

atic Impact

■ *Total living area 3,542 sq. ft.* ■ *Price Code F* ■

FIRST FLOOR

SECOND FLOOR

No. 98237

■ **This plan features:**

— Four bedrooms

— Three full and one half baths

■ Double door entry Foyer, that is two-stori high, is accented by natural light from th high arched window above

■ Bay window encompasses the elegant formal Dining Room

■ A cascading staircase graces the Living Room, while a fireplace radiates with warmth

■ Efficient Kitchen flows into an octagonal shaped Breakfast Area

■ A vaulted ceiling crowns the Keeping Roo that is highlighted by a large fireplace

■ Luxurious first floor Master Suite with direct access to the deck is topped by a vaulted ceiling

■ Three additional bedrooms on the second floor, each have access to a full bath

■ This plan is available with a basement, crawl space or a slab foundation, please specify when ordering

■ No material list is available for this plan

First floor — 2,552 sq. ft.
Second floor — 990 sq. ft.
Width — 70'-0"
Depth — 58'-0"

Dazzling Space And Style

© 1997 Donald A Gardner Architects, Inc.

■ *Total living area 3,517 sq. ft.* ■ *Price Code G* ■

FIRST FLOOR PLAN

SECOND FLOOR PLAN

No. 99823

■ **This plan features:**

— Four bedrooms

— Three full and one half baths

■ Exterior includes an arched Entry, hip ro mixed with gables, and brick detailing, while its interior dazzles with space and style

■ Double doors lead into the Living Room/Study with exposed beams, a fireplace, and bay window

■ A second fireplace is located in the two-st Family Room overlooked by a loft with curved balcony

■ Large center island Kitchen is accessed easily by the Breakfast Room, Great Roo and Formal Dining Room and is adjacen a walk-in pantry and Utility Room

■ Master Suite features a tray ceiling, rear porch access and a lavish bath with a wa in closet

First floor — 2,330 sq. ft.
Second floor — 1,187 sq. ft.
Garage — 676 sq. ft.

Two-story Bay Window Adds Appeal

■ *Total living area 1,815 sq. ft.* ■ *Price Code C* ■

No. 91543

This plan features:

Three bedrooms

Two full and one half bath

Portico entrance leads into central Foyer with banister staircase

Combination Living/Dining Room brightened by lovely bay window

Family Room with fireplace and corner windows

Kitchen with peninsula serving/eating counter

French doors lead into Master Suite with vaulted ceiling, a bay window and double vanity bath

Two additional bedrooms share a full bath and laundry closet

Second floor Bonus Room

First floor — 972 sq. ft.
Second floor — 843 sq. ft.
Bonus Room — 180 sq. ft.
Garage — 437 sq. ft.

Farmhouse Flavor

■ *Total living area 1,770 sq. ft.* ■ *Price Code B* ■

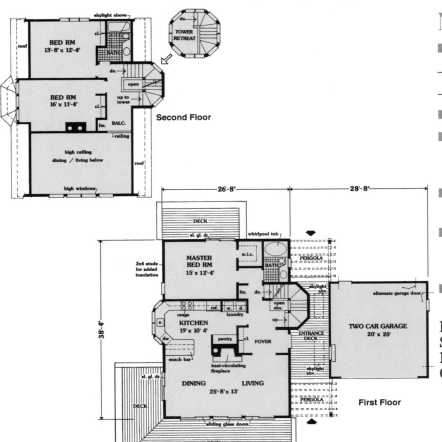

BED RM
13'-8" x 12'-4"

BED RM
16' x 11'-4"

skylight above

TOWER RETREAT

BATH

open

up to tower

BALC.

railing

high ceiling
dining / living below

high windows

Second Floor

roof

roof

DECK

sl. gl. dr.

whirlpool tub

w.i.c.

MASTER BED RM
15' x 12'-4"

BATH

PERGOLA

2x6 studs
for added
insulation

lin.

dn.

skylight abv.

open abv.

up

KITCHEN
19' x 10'-4"

range

ref.

w.

d.

laundry

ENTRANCE DECK

TWO CAR GARAGE
20' x 20'

alternate garage door

pantry

cl.

FOYER

s.

dw

snack bar

heat-circulating fireplace

DINING

LIVING

25'-8" x 13'

skylight abv.

PERGOLA

sl. gl. dr.

DECK

sliding glass doors

DECK

26'-8"

28'-8"

38'-4"

First Floor

No. 90685

■ This plan features:

— Three bedrooms

— Two full baths

■ An octagonal stair tower

■ A Foyer opening to a Living and Dining Room combination, enhanced by a striking glass wa

■ A heat circulating fireplace addi welcome warmth

■ A galley-style Kitchen including large pantry, snack bar, and laundry area

■ A Master Suite with a private de overlooking the backyard

First floor — 1,073 sq. ft.
Second floor — 604 sq. ft.
Retreat tower — 93 sq. ft.
Garage — 428 sq. ft.

No. 98524

This plan features:

Four bedrooms

Three full and one half baths

The entry of this home offers French doors into the Study and columns define the Gallery and formal areas

The expansive Family Room with an inviting fireplace and a cathedral ceiling opens to the Kitchen

The Kitchen features a cooktop island, butlers pantry, Breakfast area and Patio access

The first floor Master Bedroom offers a private Patio, vaulted ceiling, twin vanities and a walk-in closet

Three second floor bedrooms each access a full bath

No materials list is available for this plan

This plan is available with a basement or a slab foundation — please specify when ordering this plan

First floor — 2,036 sq. ft.

Second floor — 866 sq. ft.

Garage — 720 sq. ft.

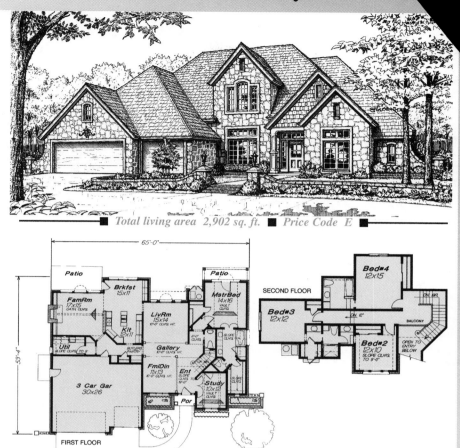

Total living area 2,902 sq. ft. ■ *Price Code E* ■

Rambling Farmhouse

No. 99848 ✖

This plan features:

Four bedrooms

Three full and one half baths

Two-story Foyer flooded with light from the palladium window above

Great Room topped by a vaulted ceiling and highlighted by a fireplace with built-ins and a balcony overlooking the room

Great Room, Breakfast Room, and Master Bedroom accessing the porch for open circulation

Nine foot ceiling throughout the first floor

Island Kitchen with direct access to formal and informal eating areas

First floor Study/bedroom with private full bath

First floor — 2,064 sq. ft.

Second floor — 594 sq. ft.

Garage & storage — 710 sq. ft.

Bonus room — 483 sq. ft.

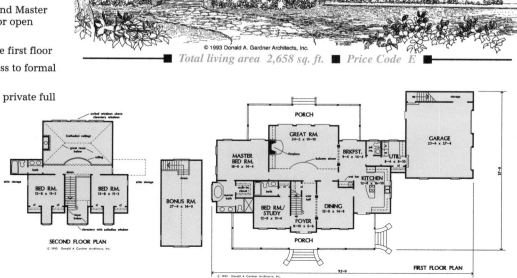

© 1993 Donald A. Gardner Architects, Inc.

Total living area 2,658 sq. ft. ■ *Price Code E* ■

rious Master Suite

■ *Total living area 2,893 sq. ft.* ■ *Price Code E* ■

62'-0"

64'-0"

First Floor

Second Floor

Alternate Foundation Option

No. 24657

■ **This plan features:**

—Four bedrooms

—Three full and one half baths

■ Fireplace in the formal Living Room and one in the Family Room

■ Optional Sun Room expanding living spa

■ Kitchen located between the Breakfast Ar and the formal Dining Room

■ A plush bath with a whirlpool tub, vaulte ceiling over the bath and a tray ceiling ov the bedroom highlighting the Master Sui

■ Two additional bedrooms, each with private access to full bath

■ Bonus room available for future expansio

First floor — 1,523 sq. ft.
Second floor — 1,370 sq. ft.
Bonus — 344 sq. ft.
Basement — 1,722 sq. ft.
Garage — 484 sq. ft.

An
EXCLUSIVE DESIGN
By Plan One Homes, I

Towering Windows

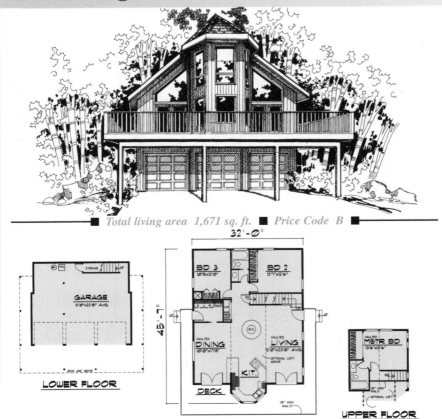

■ *Total living area 1,671 sq. ft.* ■ *Price Code B* ■

32'-0"

45'-7"

LOWER FLOOR

MAIN FLOOR PLAN

UPPER FLOOR

No. 91071

■ **This plan features:**

— Three bedrooms

— Two full baths

■ A wrap-around Deck above a three car garage with plenty of work/storage space

■ Both the Dining and Living areas claim vaulted ceilings above French doors to th Deck

■ A octagon-shaped Kitchen with a view, a cooktop peninsula and an open counter the Dining area

■ A Master Bedroom on the upper level, w an over-sized closet, a private bath and a optional Loft

■ Two additional bedrooms sharing a full bath

■ No materials list is available for this plan

■ This plan is available with a crawl space slab foundation — please specify when ordering

First floor — 1,329 sq. ft.
Second floor — 342 sq. ft.
Garage — 885 sq. ft.
Deck — 461 sq. ft.

Expandable Home

■ *Total living area 1,757 sq. ft.* ■ *Price Code B* ■

No. 34077

This plan features:

Four bedrooms

Three full baths

Front Entry into open Living Room highlighted by double window

Bright Dining area with sliding glass door to optional Patio

Compact, efficient Kitchen with peninsula serving/snackbar, laundry closet and outdoor access

Two first floor bedrooms with ample closet share a full bath

Second floor Master Bedroom and additional bedroom feature dormer windows, private baths and walk-in closets

First floor — 957 sq. ft.
Second floor — 800 sq. ft.

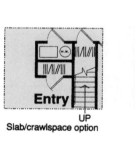

Entry
Slab/crawlspace option
UP

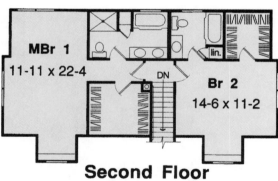

MBr 1
11-11 x 22-4

DN

lin.

Br 2
14-6 x 11-2

Second Floor

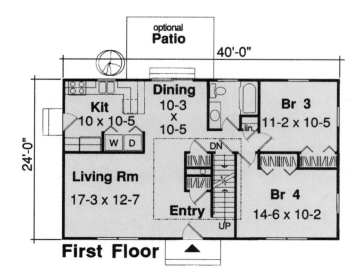

optional **Patio**

40'-0"

24'-0"

Kit
10 x 10-5

W D

Dining
10-3
x
10-5

Living Rm
17-3 x 12-7

DN

Entry
UP

Br 3
11-2 x 10-5

lin.

Br 4
14-6 x 10-2

First Floor

Large Front Window Provides Streaming Light

■ *Total living area 1,707 sq. ft.* ■ *Price Code B* ■

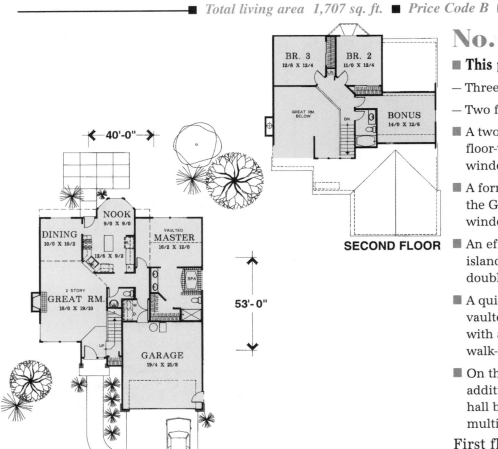

FIRST FLOOR

SECOND FLOOR

No. 91514

■ This plan features:

— Three bedrooms

— Two full and one half baths

■ A two story Great Room with a floor-to-ceiling, corner front window and cozy, hearth firepl

■ A formal Dining Room adjoinin the Great Room which has a bay window and a Nook

■ An efficient Kitchen with a worl island, pantry and a corner, double sink

■ A quiet Master Suite with a vaulted ceiling and a plush Bath with a double vanity, spa tub ar walk-in closet

■ On the second floor, two additional bedrooms share a fu hall bath and a Bonus area for multiple uses

First floor — 1,230 sq. ft.
Second floor — 477 sq. ft.
Bonus area — 195 sq. ft.

Abundance of Windows for Natural Lighting

No. 94902

This plan features:

- Four bedrooms
- Two full and one half baths
- Interesting staircase with landing in volume Entry
- Ten foot ceiling above transom windows and hearth fireplace accent the Great Room
- Island counter/snack bar, pantry and desk featured in Kitchen/Breakfast area
- Kitchen conveniently accesses laundry area and Garage
- Beautiful arched window under volume ceiling in Bedroom two
- Master Bedroom suite features decorative ceiling to walk-in closets and double vanity bath with a whirlpool tub
- Two additional bedrooms with ample closets share a full bath

First floor — 944 sq. ft.
Second floor — 987 sq. ft.
Basement — 944 sq. ft.
Garage — 557 sq. ft.

■ *Total living area 1,931 sq. ft.* ■ *Price Code C* ■

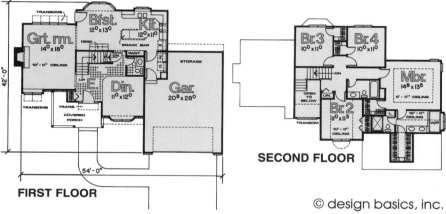

FIRST FLOOR

SECOND FLOOR

© design basics, inc.

Stately Stone and Stucco

No. 98402

This plan features:

- Four bedrooms
- Three full and one half baths
- Two story Foyer with angled staircase, welcomes all with elegance
- Expansive two-story Great Room enhanced by a fireplace, wetbar, and French doors to rear yard
- Convenient Kitchen with a cooktop island, pantry, Breakfast alcove, and nearby Laundry/Garage entry
- Open Keeping Room accented by a wall of windows and back yard access
- Master Suite wing offers a tray ceiling, a plush bath and roomy walk-in closet, and access to a Study/Sitting Room with a fireplace
- Three second floor bedrooms with walk-in closets and private access to a full bath
- An optional basement, crawl space or slab foundation — please specify when ordering

First floor — 2,130 sq. ft.
Second floor — 897 sq. ft.
Garage — 494 sq. ft.

■ *Total living area 3,027 sq. ft.* ■ *Price Code F* ■

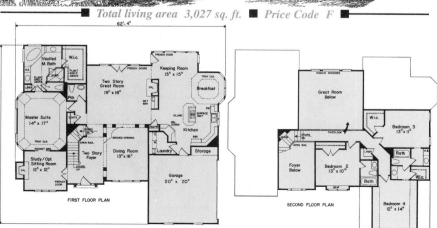

FIRST FLOOR PLAN

SECOND FLOOR PLAN

Country Classic

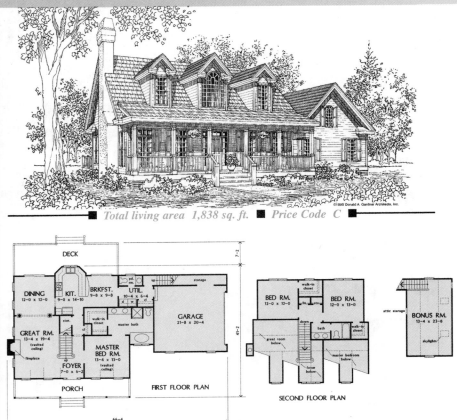

■ Total living area 1,838 sq. ft. ■ Price Code C ■

DECK

DINING 12-0 x 12-0

KIT. 9-0 x 14-10

BRKFST. 9-8 x 9-8

UTIL. 10-4 x 6-4

storage

GARAGE 21-8 20-4

GREAT RM. 13-4 x 19-4 (vaulted ceiling)

fireplace

MASTER BED RM. 13-4 x 13-0 (vaulted ceiling)

FOYER 7-0 6-2

PORCH

FIRST FLOOR PLAN

66-4

© 1995 Donald A Gardner Architects, Inc.

BED RM. 12-0 x 12-0

walk-in closet

BED RM. 12-0 x 13-0

walk-in closet

bath

great room below

foyer below

master bedroom below

SECOND FLOOR PLAN

attic storage

BONUS RM. 13-4 x 23-8

skylights

No. 96461

■ **This plan features:**

— Three bedrooms

— Two full and one half baths

■ Casually elegant exterior with dormers, gables and a charming front porch

■ U-shaped Kitchen easily serves both adjacent eating areas

■ Nine foot ceilings amplify the first floor

■ Master Suite highlighted by a vaulted ceiling and dormer

■ Garden tub with a double window are focus of the master bath

■ Two bedrooms with walk-in closets shari a hall bath, while back stairs lead to a spacious bonus room

First floor — 1,313 sq. ft.
Second floor — 525 sq. ft.
Bonus room — 367 sq. ft.
Garage — 513 sq. ft.

Craftsman Inspired Two-Story

■ Total living area 2,588 sq. ft. ■ Price Code E ■

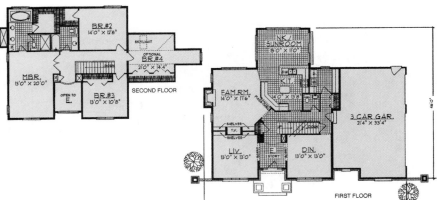

BR.#2 14'0" x 17'8"

SKYLIGHT

OPTIONAL BR.#4 21'0" x 14'4"

MBR. 13'0" x 20'0"

OPEN TO E.

BR.#3 13'0" x 10'8"

SECOND FLOOR

SINK / SUNROOM 8'0" x 11'0"

KIT. 14'0" x 13'8"

FAM.RM. 14'0" x 17'6"

3 CAR GAR. 21'4" x 33'4"

SHELVES
T.V.
SHELVES

LIV. 13'0" x 13'0"

DIN. 13'0" x 13'0"

FIRST FLOOR

60'4"

No. 99144

■ **This plan features:**

— Three bedrooms

— Two full and one half baths

■ Family Room and Living Room have buil in shelves

■ Unique Kitchen design is convenient and functional

■ Upstairs the Master Bedroom has a priva bath and a walk-in closet

■ Two bedrooms, an optional third, and a bath round out the second floor

■ Three-car garage — perfect for a car hobb enthusiast

■ There is no materials list available for th plan

First floor — 1,423 sq. ft.
Second floor — 1,165 sq. ft.
Bonus room — 250 sq. ft.
Basement — 1,423 sq. ft.

An EXCLUSIVE DESIGN *By Ahmann Design*

Total living area 1,552 sq. ft. ■ Price Code B

No. 90844 ⚒

This plan features:

Three bedrooms

Two full and one half baths

A wrap-around Deck providing outdoor living space, ideal for a sloping lot

Two and a half-story glass wall and two separate atrium doors providing natural light for the Living/Dining Room area

An efficient galley Kitchen with easy access to the Dining area

A Master Bedroom suite with a half bath and ample closet space

Another bedroom on the first floor adjoins a full hall bath

A second floor Bedroom/Studio, with a private Deck, adjacent to a full hall bath and a Loft area

First floor — 1,086 sq. ft.
Second floor — 466 sq. ft.
Basement — 1,080 sq. ft.

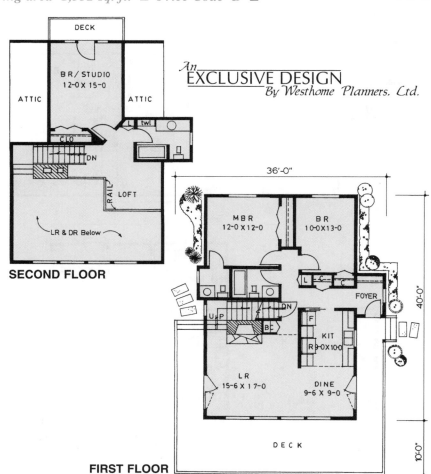

An EXCLUSIVE DESIGN
By Westhome Planners, Ltd.

SECOND FLOOR

FIRST FLOOR

cluded Master Suite

■ *Total living area 1,741 sq. ft.* ■ *Price Code B* ■

No. 24720

■ This plan features:

— Three bedrooms

— Two full and one half baths

■ Arched Porch leads into an open Foyer with a cascading staircase

■ Great Room with a vaulted ceiling, sunburst window and hearth fireplace

■ Columns frame entrance to formal Dining Room with decorative ceiling

■ Kitchen with breakfast bar, Breakfast area with Screened Porch access and nearby

■ Master Bedroom has angled ceiling, private Deck

■ No materials list is available for this plan

First floor — 900 sq. ft.
Second floor — 841 sq. ft.
Garage — 609 sq. ft.

Crawl/Slab Plan
NOTE: Mechanicals to
be placed in Utility
Room with this option.

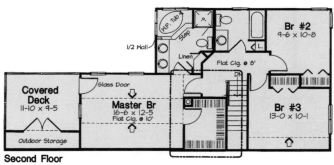

Covered Deck
11-10 x 9-5

Glass Door

Outdoor Storage

Master Br
16-6 x 12-5
Flat Clg. @ 10'

1/2 Wall

Linen

W.P. Tub

Flat Clg. @ 8'

DN

Br #2
9-6 x 10-8

Br #3
13-0 x 10-1

Second Floor

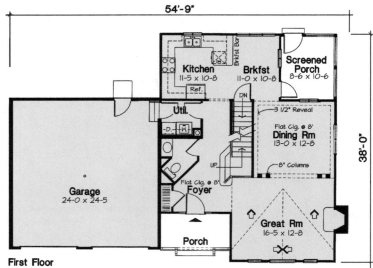

54'-9"

38'-0"

Garage
24-0 x 24-5

Kitchen
11-5 x 10-8

Ref.

Brkfst
11-0 x 10-8

Brkfst Bar

Screened Porch
8-6 x 10-6

Util.

3 1/2" Reveal

Flat Clg. @ 8'
Dining Rm
13-0 x 12-8

DN

UP

8" Columns

Flat Clg. @ 8'
Foyer

Great Rm
16-5 x 12-8

Porch

First Floor

Amenities Galore and Room to Grow

No. 90971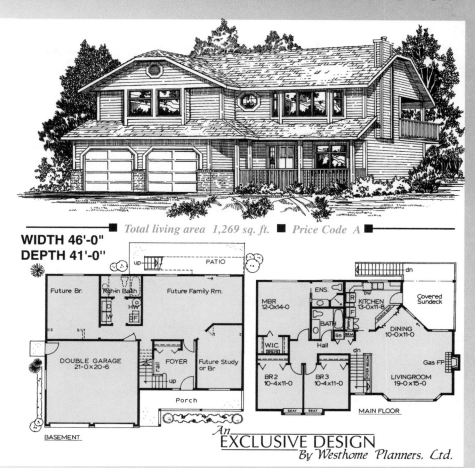

This plan features:

- Three bedrooms (future five)

- Two full baths (future three)

- A front door Porch that shelters your arrival and adds a traditional flavor

- A Foyer stairway that ascends to a truly unique and spacious Living/Dining Room graced by a gas fireplace and views from both front bay window and rear sliding glass doors to the covered Deck

- An L-shaped Kitchen complete with built-in pantry, double sink, and a convenient snack bar for informal meals

- A Covered Sun Deck accessed by both Kitchen and Dining Room extending entertainment possibilities

- A large Master Suite with a walk-in closet and private full Bath

- Two secondary bedrooms with large closets, window seats for sunny relaxations, and access to the hall full bath

- A basement ready to finish into a spacious Family Room, two additional bedrooms, and a bath/utility room

Main floor — 1,269 sq. ft.
Basement — 1,034 sq. ft.
Garage — 462 sq. ft.
Covered porch — 140 sq. ft.

Total living area 1,269 sq. ft. ■ Price Code A

WIDTH 46'-0"
DEPTH 41'-0"

An EXCLUSIVE DESIGN
By Westhome Planners. Ltd.

Grand Living

No. 34047

This plan features:

- Three bedrooms

- Two full and one half baths

- Impressive two story entrance into Foyer with a graceful angled staircase

- Formal Living and Dining rooms, and private study highlighted by triple windows

- Angled and efficient Kitchen with cooktop island/snackbar, built-in pantry and desk, bright Breakfast alcove with Patio access

- Two-story Family Room with an inviting fireplace and sliding glass door to three-season Porch

- French doors open to an elegant Master Bedroom with double windows, walk-in closet and a corner garden tub

- Two additional bedrooms with large closets and triple windows, share a full bath

First floor — 1,511 sq. ft.
Second floor — 1,163 sq. ft.
Basement — 1,511 sq. ft.
Garage — 765 sq. ft.

Total living area 2,674 sq. ft. ■ Price Code E

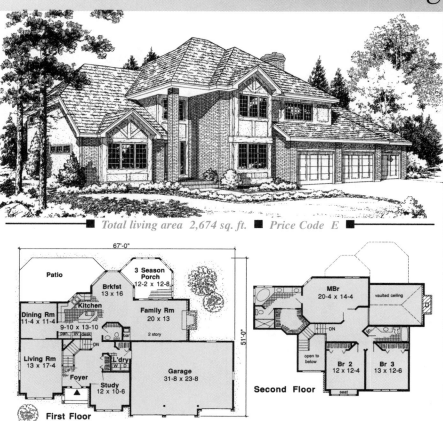

Deck Includes Spa

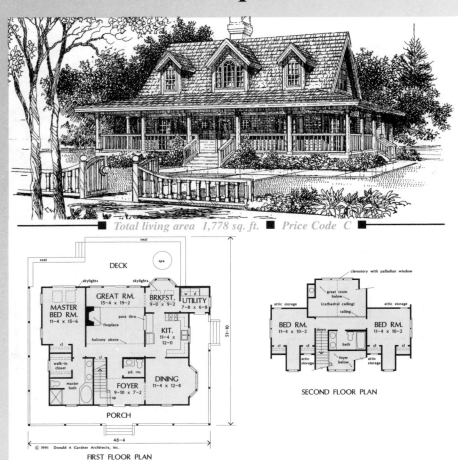

■ Total living area 1,778 sq. ft. ■ Price Code C ■

FIRST FLOOR PLAN

SECOND FLOOR PLAN

© 1991 Donald A Gardner Architects, Inc.

No. 99873

■ **This plan features:**

— Three bedrooms

— Two full and one half baths

■ An exterior porch giving the home a traditional flavor

■ Great Room highlighted by a fireplace a a balcony above as well as a pass throug into the kitchen

■ Kitchen eating area with sky lights and windows overlooking the deck with a sp

■ Two additional bedrooms with a full bat on the second floor

■ Master Suite on the first floor and natur illuminated by two skylights

■ Specify a basement or a crawl space foundation when ordering this plan.

First floor — 1,325 sq. ft.
Second floor — 453 sq. ft.

Picture Perfect

© 1995 Donald A. Gardner Architects, Inc.

B. NATMAN

■ Total living area 2,535 sq. ft. ■ Price Code C ■

FIRST FLOOR PLAN

SECOND FLOOR PLAN

No. 99896

■ **This plan features:**

— Three bedrooms

— Two full and one half baths

■ Picture perfect exterior features to be th envy of your neighbors

■ Great Room is the center of attention wi cathedral ceiling, fireplace and rear deck access

■ Formal and informal dining spaces with easy access to the Kitchen complete with center island

■ Private first floor Master Suite has a decorative ceiling and a sumptuous bath

■ Upstairs a balcony over looks the Great Room and Foyer below

■ Two secondary bedrooms and full bath bonus space round out the upstairs of th home

First floor — 1,894 sq. ft.
Second floor — 641 sq. ft.
Bonus — 375 sq. ft.
Garage — 578 sq. ft.

■ *Total living area 1,303 sq. ft.* ■ *Price Code A* ■

o. 99339

This plan features:

Three bedrooms

Two full baths

A vaulted ceiling in the Living
Room with a half-round transom
window and a fireplace

A Dining area flowing into either
the Kitchen or the Living Room
with sliders to the deck

A main floor Master Suite with
corner windows, walk-in closet,
and private access to a full Bath

Two additional bedrooms on the
second floor, one with a walk-in
closet, having use of a full bath

ain floor — 857 sq. ft.
per floor — 446 sq. ft.

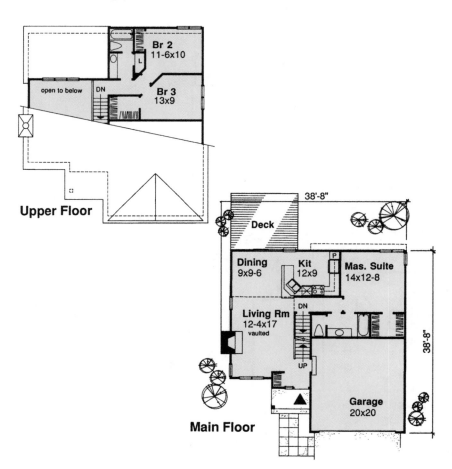

Beckoning Country Porch

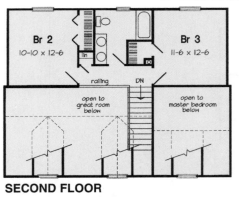

■ *Total living area 1,560 sq. ft.* ■ *Price Code B* ■

Br 2
10-10 x 12-6

Br 3
11-6 x 12-6

railing   DN

open to
great room
below

open to
master bedroom
below

SECOND FLOOR

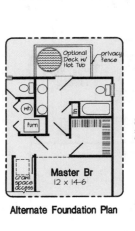

Optional
Deck w/
Hot Tub

privacy
fence

furn

crawl
space
access

Master Br
12 x 14-6

Alternate Foundation Plan

Kitchen
8-1 x 12-7

Ref

island

DW

Dining
9-8 x 12-7
8' clg

D

Optional
Deck w/
Hot Tub

privacy
fence

stor.

8' clg

DN

Master Br
12 x 14-6
vault clg

17' flat clg

Great Room
19-7 x 14-10
vault clg

UP

flat clg
@15'-7"

34'-0"

Porch

FIRST FLOOR

40'-0"

No. 34603

■ **This plan features:**

— Three bedrooms

— Two full and one half baths

■ Country styled exterior with dormer windows

■ Vaulted ceiling and central fireplace in the Great Room

■ L-shaped Kitchen/Dining Room with work island and atrium d to back yard

■ First floor Master Suite with vaulted ceiling, walk-in closet, private bath and optional priva Deck with hot tub

■ Two additional bedrooms on th second floor with easy access t full bath

First floor — 1,061 sq. ft.
Second floor — 499 sq. ft.
Basement — 1,061 sq. ft.

o. 24301

his plan features:

- ur bedrooms
- vo full and one half baths
- Family Room opening to a large deck in ar
- Master Bedroom with a private bath and ple closet space
- large Living Room with a bay window
- modern Kitchen with many amenities

t floor — 987 sq. ft.
ond floor — 970 sq. ft.
ement — 985 sq. ft.

EXCLUSIVE DESIGN
By Marshall Associates

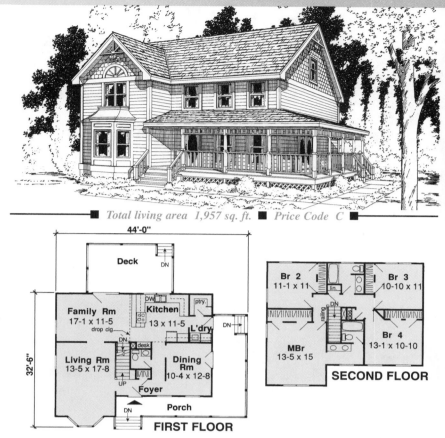

■ *Total living area 1,957 sq. ft.* ■ *Price Code C* ■

FIRST FLOOR

Deck
Family Rm 17-1 x 11-5 drop clg.
Kitchen 13 x 11-5
ptry.
L'dry
Living Rm 13-5 x 17-8
desk
Dining Rm 10-4 x 12-8
Foyer
Porch
44'-0"
32'-6"

SECOND FLOOR

Br 2 11-1 x 11
Br 3 10-10 x 11
MBr 13-5 x 15
Br 4 13-1 x 10-10
railing

Two-Story Entry Adds Grace

o. 93041

his plan features:

- ve bedrooms
- vo full and one half baths
- stucco designed accented by an arched, o-story Entry
- major living areas are located with ews to the rear grounds
- e Kitchen, Breakfast Room and Family om are adjacent and open to one another
- island cooktop and double sinks, along th an abundance of storage space making e Kitchen even more convenient
- e Master Suite with an angled whirlpool , separate shower and his-and-her nities
- ree additional bedrooms located on the ond floor
- materials list is available for this plan

floor — 1,973 sq. ft.
nd floor — 1,060 sq. ft.
age — 531 sq. ft.

■ *Total living area 3,034 sq. ft.* ■ *Price Code E* ■

FIRST FLOOR

WIDTH 64'-4"
DEPTH 53'-4"

MASTER BDRM.
LIVING RM.
DINING RM.
FAMILY ROOM
MASTER BATH
BREAKFAST
HALL
KITCHEN
ENTRY
UTIL.
PDL.
CLO.
PORCH
GARAGE

SECOND FLOOR

OPEN TO LIVING ROOM BELOW
STUDIO/ BEDROOM 5
OPEN TO FAMILY ROOM BELOW
OPEN TO FOYER BELOW
LOFT
BEDROOM 4
BATH 2
HALL
BEDROOM 2
BEDROOM 3

Luxury at it's Finest

■ Total living area 3,992 sq. ft. ■ Price Code F ■

No. 92116

■ **This plan features:**

— Three bedrooms

— Three full and one half baths

■ Brick and stucco make an exciting combination

■ Grand Foyer with curved staircase enjo the Living and Dining rooms

■ Kitchen has a unique geometric shape, a center island

■ Rear staircase accesses the three Bedro and Baths on the second floor

■ Sunken Family room has a fireplace

■ Den is illuminated by a huge front win

First floor — 2,108 sq. ft.
Second floor — 1,884 sq. ft.

Cottage Influence

■ Total living area 2,533 sq. ft. ■ Price Code D ■

FIRST FLOOR   **SECOND FLOOR**

No. 94614

■ **This plan features:**

— Three or four bedrooms

— Three full and one half baths

■ Cozy porch entrance into Foyer with banister staircase and coat closet

■ Expansive Great Room with focal point fireplace and access to Covered Porch a Deck

■ Cooktop island in Kitchen easily serves Breakfast bay and formal Dining Room

■ Large Master Suite with access to Cover Porch, walk-in closet and double vanity

■ Study/Guest Bedroom with private acc a full bath, offers many uses

■ Two second floor bedrooms with dorm private vanities and walk-in closets

■ An optional crawl space or slab founda — please specify when ordering

■ No materials list is available for this pl

First floor — 1,916 sq. ft.
Second floor — 617 sq. ft.
Garage — 516 sq. ft.
Width — 66'-0"
Depth — 66'-0"

Beautiful Balconies

■ *Total living area 3,443 sq. ft.* ■ *Price Code F* ■

No. 91562

This plan features:

- Three bedrooms

- Two full and one half baths

- Vaulted Living Room enhanced by French doors to balcony and sharing a see-thru fireplace with a corner Den

- Elegant ceiling tops decorative window in Dining Room

- Kitchen with a cooktop island/snack bar, corner pantry and eating Nook

- Corner fireplace and a triple window accent the Family Room

- Master Bedroom offers a balcony, decorative ceiling and deluxe bathroom

- No materials list is available for this plan

First floor — 1,989 sq. ft.
Second floor — 1,349 sq. ft.
Lower floor— 105 sq. ft.
Bonus room — 487 sq. ft.

A Touch of Old World Charm

■ *Total living area 2,320 sq. ft.* ■ *Price Code D* ■

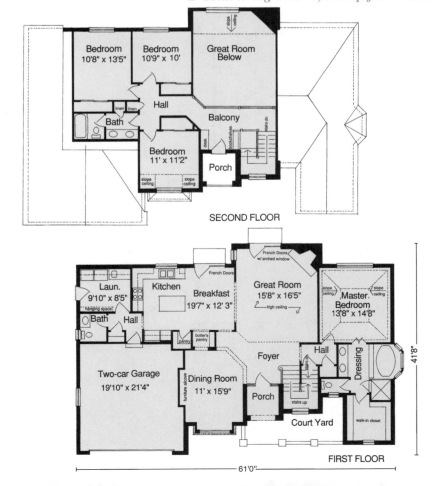

SECOND FLOOR

Bedroom 10'8" x 13'5"
Bedroom 10'9" x 10'
Great Room Below
slope ceiling
Hall
linen linen
Bath
Balcony
desk
bookshelves
stairs dn
Bedroom 11' x 11'2"
Porch
slope ceiling
slope ceiling

FIRST FLOOR

Laun. 9'10" x 8'5"
hanging space
Kitchen
Breakfast 19'7" x 12'3"
French Doors w/ arched window
French Doors
Great Room 15'8" x 16'5"
slope ceiling
high ceiling
Master Bedroom 13'8" x 14'8"
slope ceiling
Bath
Hall
pantry
butler's pantry
Foyer
Hall
stairs dn
Dressing
Two-car Garage 19'10" x 21'4"
furniture alcove
Dining Room 11' x 15'9"
Porch
stairs up
Court Yard
walk-in closet
61'0"
41'8"

No. 92646

■ **This plan features:**

— Four bedrooms

— Two full and one half baths

■ Authentic balustrade railings and front courtyard greet one and a

■ High ceiling in Great Room top corner fireplace and French doo

■ Formal Dining Room enhanced by a decorative window and furniture alcove

■ Country Kitchen with work island, two pantrys, Breakfast a with French door to rear yard, Laundry and Garage entry

■ Master Bedroom wing offers a sloped ceiling, and a plush bath

■ Three additional bedrooms sha second floor, balcony and doub vanity bath

First floor — 1,595 sq. ft.
Second floor — 725 sq. ft.
Garage — 409 sq. ft.

Plan Yields Lots of Living Space

No. 10519

This plan features:

- Three bedrooms
- Two full and one half baths
- Sloped ceilings and an open central stairway
- An efficient, U-shaped Kitchen with easy access to the Dining Room and a laundry facility
- Ample closet space throughout the home
- First floor — 872 sq. ft.
- Second floor — 483 sq. ft.

■ *Total living area 1,355 sq. ft.* ■ *Price Code A* ■

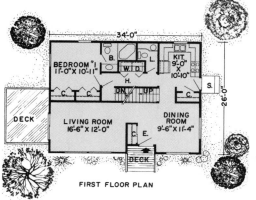

FIRST FLOOR PLAN

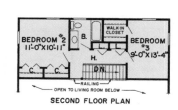

SECOND FLOOR PLAN

Eye-Catching Elevation

No. 94305

This plan features:

- Two bedrooms
- Two three-quarter baths
- An entrance to a Spa Deck with hot tub and a few steps down to an open Living area with a cozy fireplace, a vaulted ceiling and atrium door to the side Deck
- An efficient Kitchen with a peninsula counter/eating bar opens to Living area
- A first floor bedroom next to the full bath and utility area
- A second floor Master Bedroom with an over-sized and private bath
- No materials list is available for this plan
- First floor — 680 sq. ft.
- Second floor — 345 sq. ft.

An
EXCLUSIVE DESIGN
By Marshall Associates

■ *Total living area 1,025 sq. ft.* ■ *Price Code A* ■

LOWER/MID LEVELS   UPPER LEVEL

Details Distinguish This Home Design

■ Total living area 2,539 sq. ft. ■ Price Code E ■

No. 92537

■ This plan features:

— Four bedrooms

— Three full and one half baths

■ Gracious entrance into Open Foyer is highlighted by an arched window and banister staircase

■ Formal Living and Dining rooms conveniently located off Foyer

■ Expansive Den accented by a decorative ceiling over hearth fireplace and access t backyard

■ Hub Kitchen with peninsula counter/snackbar, two pantries, a bright Breakfast area, Utility room, and Garage entry

■ Spacious Master Bedroom suite enhance by a large bath with two walk-in closets vanities

■ Three additional bedrooms, one with a private bath, share second floor

■ An optional crawl space or slab — please specify when ordering

First floor — 1,809 sq. ft.
Second floor — 730 sq. ft.
Garage — 533 sq. ft.

Conventional and Classic Comfort

■ Total living area 1,961 sq. ft. ■ Price Code C ■

No. 93349

■ This plan features:

— Three bedrooms

— Two full and one half baths

■ Cozy Porch accesses two-story Foyer wit decorative window highlighting a landi staircase

■ Formal Dining Room accented by a rece window adjoins Kitchen

■ Spacious Family Room crowned by a vaulted ceiling over a hearth fireplace surrounded by more decorative window

■ Efficient Kitchen with an extended counter/eating bar and bright Dinette a with bay window and access to Deck

■ Convenient Laundry, Powder Room and Garage entry near Kitchen

■ First floor Master Bedroom with walk-i closet and Master Bath with double van

■ No materials list is available for this pla

First floor — 1,454 sq. ft.
Second floor — 507 sq. ft.
Basement — 1,454 sq. ft.
Garage — 624 sq. ft.

An EXCLUSIVE DESIGN
By Patrick Morabito, A.I.A. Architect

Versatile Chalet

■ *Total living area 1,360 sq. ft.* ■ *Price Code A* ■

No. 90847

This plan features:

Two bedrooms

Two full baths

A Sun deck entry into a spacious Living Room/Dining Room with a fieldstone fireplace, a large window and a sliding glass door

A well-appointed Kitchen with extended counter space and easy access to the Dining Room and the Utility area

A first floor bedroom adjoins a full hall bath

A spacious Master Bedroom, with a private Deck, a Suite bath and plenty of storage

Main floor — 864 sq. ft.
Second floor — 496 sq. ft.

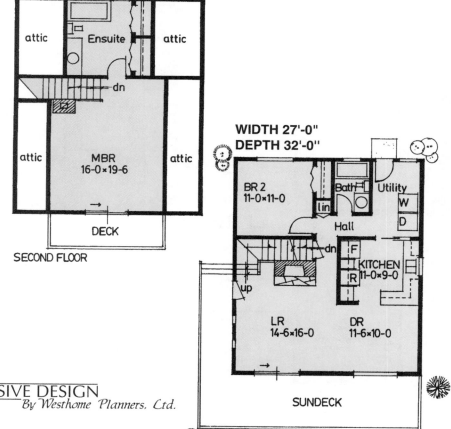

An EXCLUSIVE DESIGN
By Westhome Planners, Ltd.

Traditional Ranch has Many Modern Features

■ *Total living area 2,301 sq. ft.* ■ *Price Code D* ■

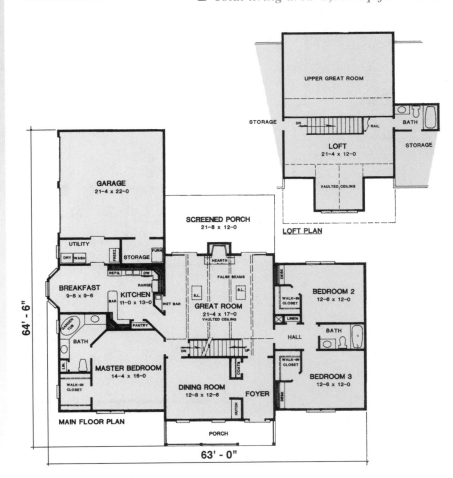

No. 90444

■ **This plan features:**

— Three bedrooms

— Three full baths

■ A vaulted-ceiling Great Room w skylights and a fireplace

■ A double L-shaped Kitchen with an eating bar opening to a baye Breakfast Room

■ A Master Suite with a walk-in closet, corner garden tub, separ vanities and a linen closet

■ Two additional bedrooms each with a walk-in closet and built-desk, sharing a full hall bath

■ A loft that overlooks the Great Room which includes a vaulted ceiling and open rail balcony

■ An optional basement or craw space foundation — please spec when ordering

Main floor — 1,996 sq. ft.
Loft — 305 sq. ft.

Elegant Elevation

No. 92634

This plan features:

Four bedrooms

Two full and one half baths

A wide-apron staircase and plant shelf highlight open Foyer

An arched entrance frames formal Living Room with high ceiling

Decorative bay window enhances formal Dining Room

Expansive Family Room with focal point fireplace and view of rear yard

Hub Kitchen with Breakfast area, Garage entry, Laundry, and peninsula counter/snackbar

Comfortable Master Bedroom with sloped ceiling, large walk-in closet and plush bath

Three additional bedrooms share a double vanity bath with skylight

No materials list is available for this plan

First floor — 1,309 sq. ft.

Second floor — 1,119 sq. ft.

Basement — 1,277 sq. ft.

Garage — 452 sq. ft.

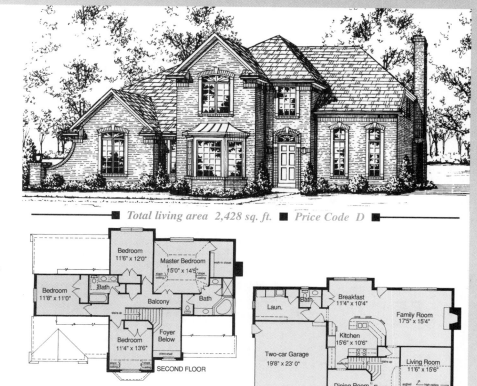

Total living area 2,428 sq. ft. ■ Price Code D

Colonial with Contemporary Flair

No. 94141

This plan features:

Four bedrooms

Two full and one half baths

The Master Bedroom has a walk in closet and an attached Bath with a skylight

Upstairs there are three additional Bedrooms and one full Bath

The Dining Room and Living Room are traditionally placed

The Family Room and Dinette are laid out with plenty of open space

The island Kitchen has a useful snack bar

No materials list available

First floor — 1,108 sq. ft.

Second floor — 942 sq. ft.

Basement — 1,108 sq. ft.

Garage — 455 sq. ft.

Total living area 2,050 sq. ft. ■ Price Code D

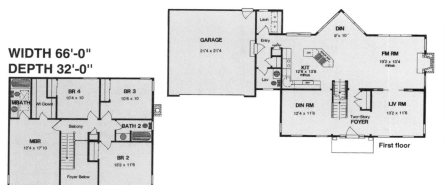

Dignified Family Home

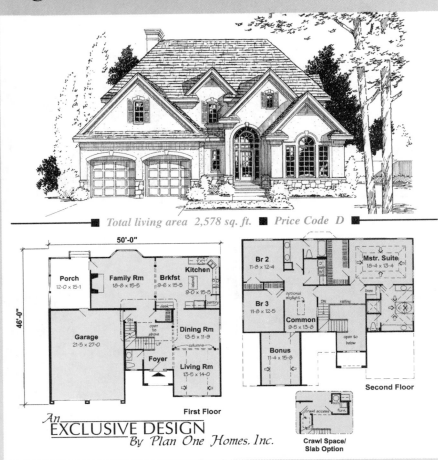

— Total living area 2,578 sq. ft. ■ Price Code D —

An
EXCLUSIVE DESIGN
By Plan One Homes, Inc.

First Floor

Second Floor

Crawl Space/Slab Option

Porch 12-0 x 15-1
Family Rm 18-8 x 15-5
Brkfst 9-6 x 15-5
Kitchen 9-0 x 15-5
Garage 21-5 x 27-0
Dining Rm 13-5 x 11-9
Foyer
Living Rm 13-5 x 14-0

50'-0"
46'-0"

Br 2 11-8 x 12-4
Mstr. Suite 18-4 x 13-4
Br 3 11-8 x 12-5
Common 9-5 x 13-8
Bonus 11-4 x 15-8

No. 24653

■ **This plan features:**

— Three bedrooms

— Two full and one half baths

■ Multi-paned windows and an arched, highly-windowed entrance

■ A formal Living Room that adjoins the formal Dining Room with columns between the two rooms

■ A U-shaped Kitchen with a built-in pantry a built-in planning desk and an island

■ A large Family Room flowing from the Kitchen, equipped with a focal point fireplace and a bright bay window

■ A second floor Master Suite topped by a decorative ceiling and a lavish bath

■ A Common Area, brightened by a skylight

■ A convenient second floor laundry next to the bedrooms

■ Two additional bedrooms that share a full hall bath

■ A bonus room for future needs

■ No materials list is available for this plan

First floor — 1,245 sq. ft.
Second floor — 1,333 sq. ft.
Bonus room — 192 sq. ft.
Garage — 614 sq. ft.

Family Favorite

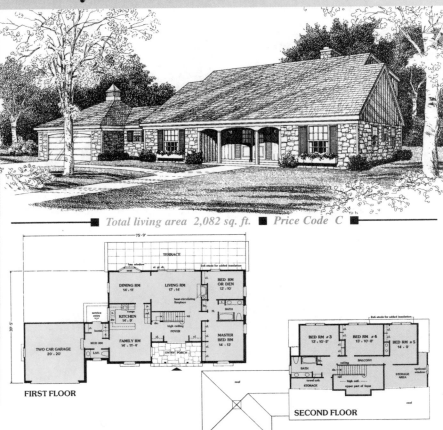

— Total living area 2,082 sq. ft. ■ Price Code C —

FIRST FLOOR

SECOND FLOOR

TERRACE
DINING RM 14 x 11
LIVING RM 17 x 14
BED RM OR DEN 12 x 10
KITCHEN 14 x 9
FOYER
FAMILY RM 14 x 11-4
MASTER BED RM 14 x 12
TWO CAR GARAGE 20 x 20
ENTRY PORCH

75'-9"
39'-5"

BED RM #3 13 x 10'-8"
BED RM #4 13 x 10'-8"
BED RM #5 14 x 9
BALCONY
STORAGE AREA

No. 90690

■ **This plan features:**

— Five bedrooms

— Two full and one half baths

■ An efficient Kitchen with a peninsula counter opening into the Family Room

■ A cozy bay window seat in the formal Dining Room

■ A first floor Master Bedroom with an adjoining private Bath including double vanities

■ A heat-circulating fireplace in the Living Room which has sliding glass doors to the Terrace

■ Three bedrooms located on the second floor that share a full bath

First floor — 1,407 sq. ft.
Second floor — 675 sq. ft.

■ *Total living area 3,220 sq. ft.* ■ *Price Code F* ■

No. 93505 ✂

This plan features:

Four bedrooms

Three full baths

A vaulted ceiling foyer

A Living Room with a vaulted ceiling and elegant fireplace

A formal Dining Room that adjoins the Living Room, with a built-in buffet

An island cooktop in the well-appointed Kitchen with a walk-in pantry and an open layout to the Family Room

A vaulted ceiling in the Family Room with a, corner fireplace

A huge walk-in closet, built-in entertainment center, and a full bath with every amenity in the Master Suite

First floor — 2,125 sq. ft.

Second floor — 1,095 sq. ft.

Basement — 2,125 sq. ft.

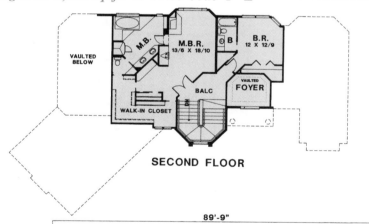

SECOND FLOOR

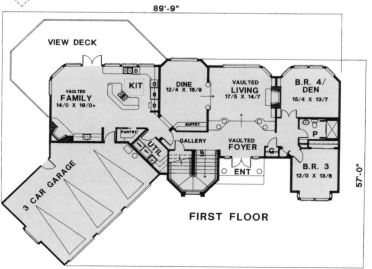

FIRST FLOOR

Colonial Charmer

■ *Total living area 1,920 sq. ft.* ■ *Price Code C* ■

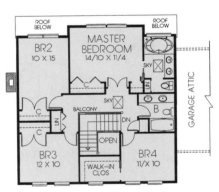

SECOND FLOOR

Second floor labels: ROOF BELOW, BR2 10 X 15, MASTER BEDROOM 14/10 X 11/4, SKY, ROOF BELOW, GARAGE ATTIC, C, SKY, B, BALCONY, LN, DN, C, C, OPEN, BR3 12 X 10, BR4 11/X 10, WALK-IN CLOS

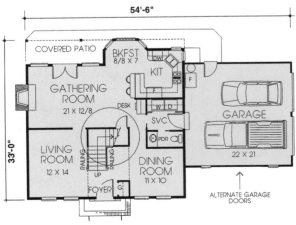

FIRST FLOOR

First floor labels: 54'-6", COVERED PATIO, BKFST 8/8 X 7, DW, KIT, F, GATHERING ROOM 21 X 12/8, DESK, F, GARAGE, W D, SVC, LIVING ROOM 12 X 14, RAILING, RAILING, PDR, DINING ROOM 11 X 10, UP, 22 X 21, 33'-0", FOYER, G, ALTERNATE GARAGE DOORS

OPTIONAL BASEMENT

No. 93523

■ **This plan features:**

— Four bedrooms

— Two full and one half baths

■ An oversized Family Room that opens into the Kitchen/Nook ar creating a feeling of space

■ A large fireplace and access to th patio in the Family Room

■ A peninsula counter and double sinks in the Kitchen

■ A formal Living Room and Dini Room for entertaining

■ A Master Suite with two closets, jacuzzi and double vanity

■ Three additional bedrooms, one with a walk-in closet, that share full hall bath

First floor — 970 sq. ft.
Second floor — 950 sq. ft.
Basement — 970 sq. ft.
Garage — 462 sq. ft.

No. 92543

This plan features:

- Three bedrooms
- Two full and one half baths
- Two-story Foyer with a lovely, landing staircase and balcony
- Spacious Den with an inviting fireplace between windows
- Convenient Kitchen with an open serving counter for Eating bay, and nearby Dining area, Utility and Garage entry
- Elegant Master Bedroom wing with a plush dressing area
- Two second floor bedrooms with large closets and separate vanities, share a full bath
- An optional crawl space or slab foundation — please specify when ordering

First floor — 1,322 sq. ft.
Second floor — 536 sq. ft.
Garage & Storage — 565 sq. ft.

■ *Total living area 1,858 sq. ft.* ■ *Price Code D* ■

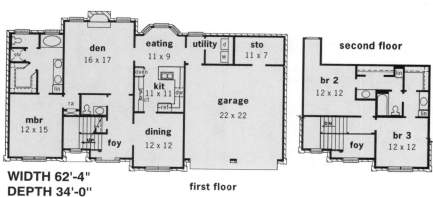

WIDTH 62'-4"
DEPTH 34'-0"

first floor

Welcoming Wrap-Around Porch

No. 94932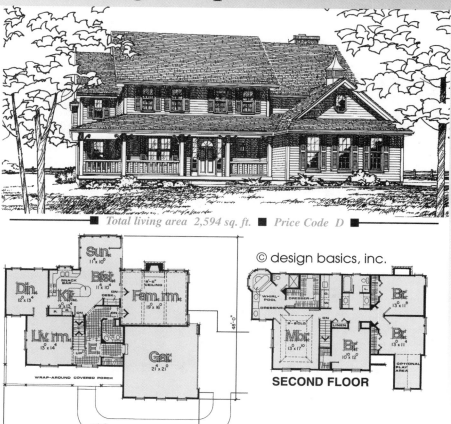

This plan features:

- Four bedrooms
- Two full and one half baths
- Front porch expands living space and accesses easy-care tile Entry
- Formal Living and Dining rooms connected by French doors
- An efficient Kitchen with serving counter/snackbar, pantry, Breakfast area and Sunroom beyond
- Sunken Family Room with beamed ceiling and inviting fireplace
- Corner Master Bedroom with decorative ceiling and French doors into spacious dressing area with a whirlpool window tub and large walk-in closet
- Three additional bedrooms, one with an optional play area, share a double vanity bath

First floor — 1,322 sq. ft.
Second floor — 1,272 sq. ft.
Basement — 1,322 sq. ft.
Garage — 468 sq. ft.

■ *Total living area 2,594 sq. ft.* ■ *Price Code D* ■

© design basics, inc.

FIRST FLOOR

SECOND FLOOR

Comfort and Style

■ *Total living area 1,326 sq. ft.* ■ *Price Code A* ■

FIRST FLOOR
WIDTH= 36'-0"
DEPTH= 34'-0"

SECOND FLOOR

No. 93359

■ **This plan features:**

— Three bedrooms

— One full and one half bath

■ Covered entrance leads into open Foyer with banister staircase and convenient closet

■ Spacious Living Room with a cozy fireplace below a vaulted ceiling

■ Bay window highlights formal Dining Room adjoining Living Room

■ Efficient, L-shaped Kitchen with built-in pantry, a Dinette area with access to back yard, Laundry area and Garage

■ Three second floor bedrooms with ample closets, share a full bath

■ No materials list is available for this plan

First floor — 748 sq. ft.
Second floor — 578 sq. ft.
Basement — 748 sq. ft.
Garage — 360 sq. ft.

An
EXCLUSIVE DESIGN
By Patrick Morabito, A.I.A. Archit

Elegant Country Farmhouse

■ *Total living area 2,570 sq. ft.* ■ *Price Code E* ■

No. 96433

■ **This plan features:**

—Four bedrooms

—Two full and one half baths

■ Spacious Great Room open to the Kitchen/Breakfast area

■ Living Room/Study distinguished by elegant columns

■ Breakfast area and Great Room open to a covered porch and deck beyond

■ Great Room and Living/Study include co fireplaces

■ Second floor Master Suite with sitting ba walk-in closet, whirlpool tub, shower, an dual vanity

First floor — 1,381 sq. ft.
Second floor — 1,189 sq. ft.
Garage & storage — 747 sq. ft.
Bonus — 400 sq. ft.

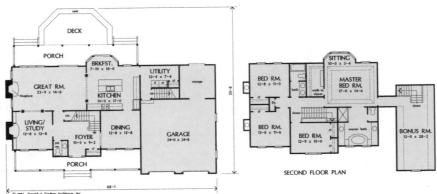

FIRST FLOOR PLAN

SECOND FLOOR PLAN

A-Frame for Year-Round L...

■ *Total living area 1,702 sq. ft.* ■ *Price Code B* ■

No. 90930 ⚒

This plan features:

Three bedrooms

Two full baths

A vaulted ceiling in the Living Room with a massive fireplace

A wrap-around sun deck that gives you a lot of outdoor living space

A luxurious Master Suite complete with a walk-in closet, full bath and private deck

Two additional bedrooms that share a full hall bath

Main floor — 1,238 sq. ft.

...ft — 464 sq. ft.

...sement — 1,175 sq. ft.

...dth — 34'-0"

...pth — 56'-0"

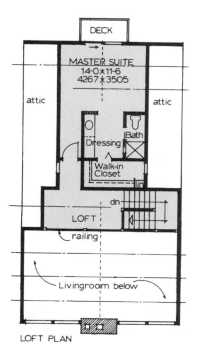

DECK

MASTER SUITE
14-0 x 11-6
4267 x 3505

attic — attic

Dressing | Bath

Walk-in Closet

dn

LOFT

railing

Livingroom below

LOFT PLAN

An **EXCLUSIVE DESIGN**
By Westhome Planners, Ltd.

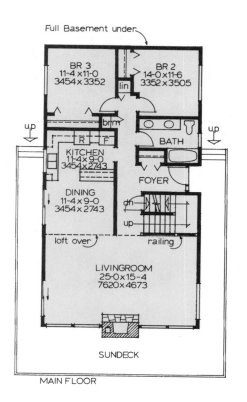

Full Basement under

BR 3
11-4 x 11-0
3454 x 3352

BR 2
14-0 x 11-6
3352 x 3505

up

KITCHEN
11-4 x 9-0
3454 x 2743

BATH

FOYER

DINING
11-4 x 9-0
3454 x 2743

dn

up

loft over

railing

LIVINGROOM
25-0 x 15-4
7620 x 4673

SUNDECK

MAIN FLOOR

■ *Total living area 2,362 sq. ft.* ■ *Price Code D* ■

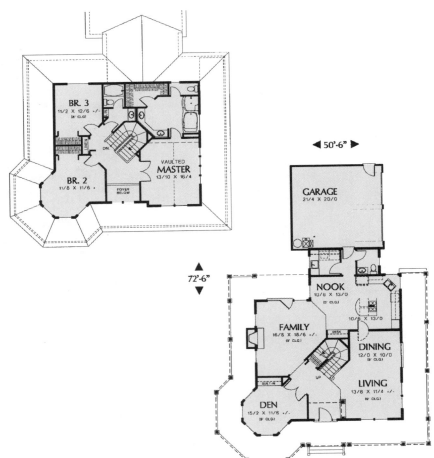

◄ 50'-6" ►

▲
72'-6"
▼

No. 91565

■ **This plan features:**

— Three bedrooms

— Two full and one half baths

■ Extensive porch wraps around and is accessed by active areas home

■ Combined Living and Dining a offers comfortable entertaining

■ Efficient Kitchen with a cookto work island, built-in desk, near laundry and Garage entry

■ Family Room with a cozy fireplace and atrium door to Porch

■ Unique Den with loads of light and built-in shelves

■ Vaulted ceiling, walk-in closet a luxurious bath in Master Sui

■ Two bedrooms, one with a uni shape, share a full bath

First floor — 1,337 sq. ft.
Second floor — 1,025 sq. ft.

Lasting Elegance

No. 92508

This plan features:

- Four bedrooms

- Three full and one half baths

- Rich lines, bays and detailed window treatments add lasting elegance to this home

- Large Foyer leads directly into huge den with hearth fireplace and built-ins

- Both the Living and Dining Rooms have bays which add style and character

- The convenient U-shaped Kitchen is fully complimented and opens into a Nook

- The large first floor Master Suite is second to none and features a private bath

- Upstairs find three bedrooms and two full baths

- No materials list is available for this plan

- This plan is available with a crawl space or a slab foundation, please specify when ordering

First floor — 2,008 sq. ft.
Second floor — 943 sq. ft.
Garage — 556 sq. ft.

Total living area 2,951 sq. ft. ■ Price Code F

WIDTH 50'-7"
DEPTH 66'-2"

FIRST FLOOR PLAN

SECOND FLOOR PLAN

Two-Story Glass Entry

No. 93013

This plan features:

Three bedrooms

Two full and one half baths

A Living Room and Dining Room with openings defined by traditional square columns

A large fireplace to add warmth and interest to the Living Room

An ample Kitchen with cook top island, built-in pantry, angled double sink, and eating bar

A Master Suite with a lavish Master Bath equipped with oval tub, step-in shower, and double vanity

Two additional bedrooms with walk-in closets that share a full hall bath

No materials list is available for this plan

First floor — 1,831 sq. ft.
Second floor — 632 sq. ft.
Garage — 525 sq. ft.
Width 50'-7"
Depth 66'-2"

Total living area 2,463 sq. ft. ■ Price Code D

FIRST FLOOR

SECOND FLOOR

For the Executive

■ *Total living area 2,428 sq. ft.* ■ *Price Code D* ■

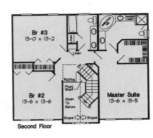

No. 24246

■ **This plan features:**

— Three bedrooms

— Three full baths

■ A sloped, two-story ceiling in the Foyer giving a definite impression of distinguished elegance

■ A double door entrance into the formal Living Room adding anticipation while the corner fireplace adds warmth and atmosphere to the room

■ A built-in china alcove in the formal Dining Room

■ A U-shaped Kitchen directly accessed form the Dining Room

■ A built-in pantry, breakfast bar, double sink and ample counter and storage space in the Kitchen adding to its efficiency

■ A second corner fireplace accenting the Family Room

■ A whirlpool corner tub, two vanities, a separate shower and a walk-in closet in the Master Suite

■ A full bath, easily accessible from the two additional bedrooms

First floor — 1,368 sq. ft.
Second floor — 1,060 sq. ft.
Basement — 1,340 sq. ft.
Garage — 578 sq. ft.

Vacation Cottage

■ *Total living area 796 sq. ft.* ■ *Price Code A* ■

FIRST FLOOR

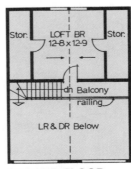
SECOND FLOOR

No. 90821

■ **This plan features:**

— Two bedrooms

— One full bath

■ An economical, neat and simple design

■ Two picture windows in the Living/Dining Room

■ An efficient Kitchen design

■ A large, cozy loft bedroom flanked by big storage rooms

■ An optional basement or crawl space foundation — please specify when ordering

First floor — 616 sq. ft.
Loft — 180 sq. ft.
Width — 22'-0"
Depth — 28'-0"

An
EXCLUSIVE DESIGN
By Westhome Planners, Ltd.

Today's Family Living Made Easy

■ *Total living area 1,609 sq. ft.* ■ *Price Code B* ■

No. 35001

This plan features:

Three bedrooms

Two full and one half baths

A large Living Room that flows into the Dining Room

An efficient U-shaped Kitchen that includes an informal Breakfast area and a laundry center

A private Master Suite with a full Bath and two closets

A Den/Office with ample closet space, enabling it to double as a Guest Room

Two additional bedrooms on the second floor that share a full hall bath

An optional Deck/Patio that will increase your living space in the warmer weather

First floor — 1,081 sq. ft.
Second floor — 528 sq. ft.
Garage — 528 sq. ft.

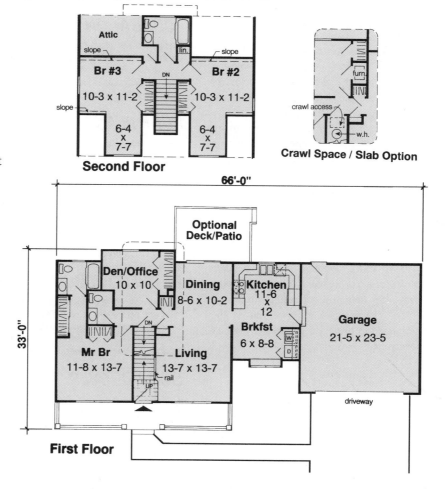

Second Floor

Attic

slope   lin.   slope

Br #3   DN   Br #2
10-3 x 11-2   10-3 x 11-2

slope

6-4 x 7-7   6-4 x 7-7

Crawl Space / Slab Option

furn.

crawl access

w.h.

First Floor

66'-0"

33'-0"

Optional Deck/Patio

Den/Office
10 x 10

Dining
8-6 x 10-2

Kitchen
11-6 x 12

Garage
21-5 x 23-5

DN

Brkfst
6 x 8-8

Mr Br
11-8 x 13-7

Living
13-7 x 13-7

rail

UP

W D

driveway

Everything You Need...
...to Make Your Dream Come True

You pay only a fraction of the original cost for home designs by respected professionals.

You've Picked Your Dream Home!

You can already see it standing on your lot... you can see yourselves in your new home... enjoying family, entertaining guests, celebrating holidays. All that remains ahead are the details. That's where we can help. Whether you plan to build-it-yourself, be your own contractor, or hand your plans over to an outside contractor, your Garlinghouse blueprints provide the perfect beginning for putting yourself in your dream home right away.

We even make it simple for you to make professional design modifications. We can also provide a materials list for greater economy.

My grandfather, L.F. Garlinghouse, started a tradition of quality when he founded this company in 1907. For over 90 years, homeowners and builders have relied on us for accurate, complete, professional blueprints. Our plans help you get results fast... and save money, too! These pages will give you all the information you need to order. So get started now... I know you'll love your new Garlinghouse home!

Sincerely,

EXTERIOR ELEVATIONS

Elevations are scaled drawings of the front, rear, left and right sides of a home. All of the necessary information pertaining to the exterior finish materials, roof pitches and exterior heig dimensions of your home are defined.

CABINET PLANS

These plans, or in some cases elevations, will detail the layout of the kitchen and bathroom cabinets at a larger scale. This gives you an accurate layout for your cabinets or an ideal start point for a modified custom cabinet design.

TYPICAL WALL SECTION

This section is provided to help your builder understand the structural components and mater used to construct the exterior walls of your home. This section will address insulation, roof components, and interior and exterior wall finishes. Your plans will be designed with either 2x 2x6 exterior walls, but most professional contractors can easily adapt the plans to the wall thickness you require.

FIREPLACE DETAILS

If the home you have chosen includes a fireplace, the fireplace detail will show typical method to construct the firebox, hearth and flue chase for masonry units, or a wood frame chase for a zero-clearance unit.

FOUNDATION PLAN

These plans will accurately dimension the footprint of your home including load bearing point and beam placement if applicable. The foundation style will vary from plan to plan. Your local climatic conditions will dictate whether a basement, slab or crawlspace is best suited for you area. In most cases, if your plan comes with one foundation style, a professional contractor ca easily adapt the foundation plan to an alternate style.

ROOF PLAN

The information necessary to construct the roof will be included with your home plans. Some plans will reference roof trusses, while many others contain schematic framing plans. These framing plans will indicate the lumber sizes necessary for the rafters and ridgeboards based the designated roof loads.

TYPICAL CROSS SECTION

A cut-away cross-section through the entire home shows your building contractor the exact correlation of construction components at all levels of the house. It will help to clarify the load bearing points from the roof all the way down to the basement.

DETAILED FLOOR PLANS

The floor plans of your home accurately dimension the positioning of all walls, doors, window stairs and permanent fixtures. They will show you the relationship and dimensions of rooms, closets and traffic patterns. Included is the schematic of the electrical layout. This layout is clearly represented and does not hinder the clarity of other pertinent information shown. All t details will help your builder properly construct your new home.

STAIR DETAILS

If stairs are an element of the design you have chosen, then a cross-section of the stairs will included in your home plans. This gives your builders the essential reference points that they need for headroom clearance, and riser and tread dimensions.

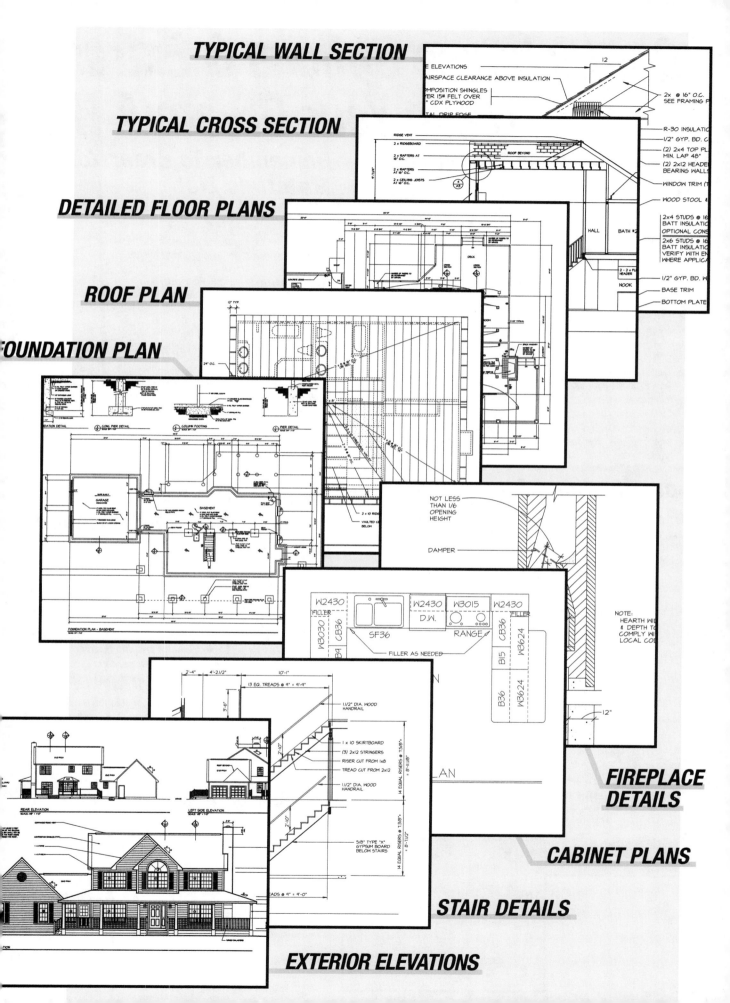

TYPICAL WALL SECTION

TYPICAL CROSS SECTION

DETAILED FLOOR PLANS

ROOF PLAN

FOUNDATION PLAN

FIREPLACE DETAILS

CABINET PLANS

STAIR DETAILS

EXTERIOR ELEVATIONS

Garlinghouse Options & Extras
...Make Your Dream A Home

Reversed Plans Can Make Your Dream Home Just Right!

"That's our dream home...if only the garage were on the other side!"
You could have exactly the home you want by flipping it end-for-end. Check it out by holding your dream home page of this book up to a mirror. Then simply order your plans "reversed." We'll send you one full set of mirror-image plans (with the writing backwards) as a master guide for you and your builder.

The remaining sets of your order will come as shown in this book so the dimensions and specifications are easily read on the job site...but most plans in our collection come stamped "REVERSED" so there is no construction confusion.

As Shown   Reversed

We can only send reversed plans with multiple-set orders. There is a $50 charge for this service.

Some plans in our collection are available in Right Reading Reverse. Right Reading Reverse plans will show your home in reverse, with the writing on the plan being readable. This easy-to-read format will save you valuable time and money. Please contact our Customer Service Department at (860) 343-5977 to check for Right Reading Reverse availability. (There is a $125 charge for this service.)

Specifications & Contract Form

We send this form to you free of charge with your home plan order. The form is designed to be filled in by you or your contractor with the exact materials to use in the construction of your new home. Once signed by you and your contractor it will provide you with peace of mind throughout the construction process.

$19.95 per set
(includes postage)

Remember To Order Your Materials List

It'll help you save money. Available at a modest additional charge, the Materials List gives the quantity, dimensions, and specifications for the major materials needed to build your home. You will get faster, more accurate bids from your contractors and building suppliers — and avoid paying for unused materials and waste. Materials Lists are available for all home plans except as otherwise indicated, but can only be ordered with a set of home plans. Due to differences in regional requirements and homeowner or builder preferences... electrical, plumbing and heating/air conditioning equipment specifications are not designed specifically for each plan. However, non-plan specific detailed typical prints of residential electrical, plumbing and construction guidelines can be provided. Please see below for additional information. If you need a detailed materials cost you might need to purchase a Zip Quote. (Details follow)

Detail Plans Provide Valuable Information About Construction Techniques

Because local codes and requirements vary greatly, we recommend that you obtain drawings and bids from licensed contractors to do your mechanical plans. However, if you want to know more about techniques — and deal more confidently with subcontractors — we offer these remarkably useful detail sheets. These detail sheets will aid in your understanding of these technical subjects. **The detail sheets are not specific to any one home plan and should be used only as a general reference guide.**

RESIDENTIAL CONSTRUCTION DETAILS

Ten sheets that cover the essentials of stick-built residential home construction. Details foundation options — poured concrete basement, concrete block, or monolithic concrete slab. Shows all aspects of floor, wall and roof framing. Provides details for roof dormers, overhangs, chimneys and skylights. Conforms to requirements of Uniform Building code or BOCA code. Includes a quick index and a glossary of terms.

RESIDENTIAL PLUMBING DETAILS

Eight sheets packed with information detailing pipe installation methods, fittings, and sized. Details plumbing hook-ups for toilets, sinks, washers, sump pumps, and septic system construction. Conforms to requirements of National Plumbing code. Color coded with a glossary of terms and quick index.

RESIDENTIAL ELECTRICAL DETAILS

Eight sheets that cover all aspects of residential wiring, from simple switch wiring to service entrance connections. Details distribution panel layout with outlet and switch schematics, circuit breaker and wiring installation methods, and ground fault interrupter specifications. Conforms to requirements of National Electrical Code. Color coded with a glossary of terms.

Modifying Your Favorite Design, Made EASY!

OPTION #1

Modifying Your Garlinghouse Home Plan

Simple modifications to your dream home, including minor non-structural changes and material substitutions, can be made between you and your builder by marking the changes directly on your blueprints. However, if you are considering making significant changes to your chosen design, we recommend that you use the services of The Garlinghouse Co. Design Staff. We will help take your ideas and turn them into a reality just the way you want. Here's our procedure!

When you place your Vellum order, you may also request a free Garlinghouse Modification Kit. In this kit, you will receive a red marking pencil, furniture cut-out sheet, ruler, a self addressed mailing label and a form specifying any additional notes or drawings that will help us understand your design ideas. Mark your desired changes directly on the Vellum drawings. NOTE: Please use only a **red pencil** to mark your desired changes on the Vellum. Then, return the redlined Vellum set in the original box to The Garlinghouse Company 282 Main Street Extension, Middletown, CT 06457. **IMPORTANT:** Please **roll** the Vellums for shipping, **do not fold** the Vellums for shipping.

We also offer modification estimates. We will provide you with an estimate to draft your changes based on your specific modifications before you purchase the vellums, for a $50 fee. After you receive your estimate, if you decide to have The Garlinghouse Company Design Staff do the changes, the $50 estimate fee will be deducted from the cost of your modifications. If, however, you choose to use a different service, the $50 estimate fee is non-refundable.

Within 5 days of receipt of your plans, you will be contacted by a member of The Garlinghouse Co. Design Staff with an estimate for the design services to draw those changes. A 50% deposit is required before we begin making the actual modifications to your plans.

Once the preliminary design changes have been made to the floor plans and elevations, copies will be sent to you to make sure we have made the exact changes you want. We will wait for your approval before continuing with any structural revisions. The Garlinghouse Co. Design Staff will call again to inform you that your modified Vellum plan is complete and will be shipped as soon as the final payment has been made. For additional information call us at 1-860-343-5977. Please refer to the Modification Pricing Guide for estimated modification costs. Please call for Vellum modification availability for plan numbers 85,000 and above.

OPTION #2

Reproducible Vellums for Local Modification Ease

If you decide not to use the Garlinghouse Co. Design Staff for your modifications, we recommend that you follow our same procedure of purchasing our Vellums. You then have the option of using the services of the original designer of the plan, a local professional designer, or architect to make the modifications to your plan. With a Vellum copy of our plans, a design professional can alter the drawings just the way you want, then you can print as many copies of the modified plans as you need to build your house. And, since you have already started with our complete detailed plans, the cost of those expensive professional services will be significantly less than starting from scratch. Refer to the price schedule for Vellum costs. Again, please call for Vellum availability for plan numbers 85,000 and above.

IMPORTANT RETURN POLICY: Upon receipt of your Vellums, if for some reason you decide you do not want the modified plan, then simply return the Kit and the unopened Vellums. Reproducible Vellum copies of our home plans are copyright protected and only sold under the terms of a license agreement that you will receive with your order. Should you not agree to the terms, then the Vellums may be returned, **unopened,** for a full refund minus the shipping and handling charges, plus a 15% restocking fee. For any additional information, please call us at 1-860-343-5977.

MODIFICATION PRICING GUIDE

CATEGORIES	ESTIMATED COST
KITCHEN LAYOUT — PLAN AND ELEVATION	$175.00
BATHROOM LAYOUT — PLAN AND ELEVATION	$175.00
FIREPLACE PLAN AND DETAILS	$200.00
INTERIOR ELEVATION	$125.00
EXTERIOR ELEVATION — MATERIAL CHANGE	$140.00
EXTERIOR ELEVATION — ADD BRICK OR STONE	$400.00
EXTERIOR ELEVATION — STYLE CHANGE	$450.00
NON BEARING WALLS (INTERIOR)	$200.00
BEARING AND/OR EXTERIOR WALLS	$325.00
WALL FRAMING CHANGE — 2X4 TO 2X6 OR 2X6 TO 2X4	$240.00
ADD/REDUCE LIVING SPACE — SQUARE FOOTAGE	QUOTE REQUIRED
NEW MATERIALS LIST	$.20 SQUARE FOOT
CHANGE TRUSSES TO RAFTERS OR CHANGE ROOF PITCH	$300.00
FRAMING PLAN CHANGES	$325.00
GARAGE CHANGES	$325.00
ADD A FOUNDATION OPTION	$300.00
FOUNDATION CHANGES	$250.00
RIGHT READING PLAN REVERSE	$575.00
ARCHITECTS SEAL	$300.00
ENERGY CERTIFICATE	$150.00
LIGHT AND VENTILATION SCHEDULE	$150.00

Questions?

Call our customer service department at 1-860-343-5977

"How to obtain a construction cost calculation based on labor rates and building material costs in <u>your</u> Zip Code area!

ZIP-QUOTE!
HOME COST CALCULATOR

ZIP QUOTE
HOME COST CALCULATOR

WHY?

Do you wish you could quickly find out the building cost for your new home without waiting for a contractor to compile hundreds of bids? Would you like to have a benchmark to compare your contractor(s) bids against? *Well, Now You Can!!,* with **Zip-Quote** Home Cost Calculator. Zip-Quote is only available for zip code areas within the United States.

HOW?

Our new **Zip-Quote** Home Cost Calculator will enable you to obtain the calculated building cost to construct your new home, based on labor rates and building material costs within your zip code area, without the normal delays or hassles usually associated with the bidding process. Zip-Quote can be purchased in two separate formats, an itemized or a bottom line format.

"How does **Zip-Quote** actually work?" When we receive your **Zip-Quote** order, we process your specific home plan building materials list through our Home Cost Calculator which contains up-to-date rates for all residential labor trades and building material costs in your zip code area. "The result?" A calculated cost to build your dream home in your zip code area. This calculation will help you (as a consumer or a builder) evaluate your building budget. This is a valuable tool for anyone considering building a new home.

All database information for our calculations is furnished by Marshall & Swift, L.P. For over 60 years, Marshall & Swift L.P. has been a leading provider of cost data to professionals in all aspects of the construction and remodeling industries.

OPTION 1

The **Itemized Zip-Quote** is a detailed building material list. Each building material list line item will separately state the labor cost, material cost and equipment cost (if applicable) for the use of that building material in the construction process. Each category within the building material list will be subtotaled and the entire Itemized cost calculation totaled at the end. This building materials list will be summarized by the individual building categories and will have additional columns where you can enter data from your contractor's estimates for a cost comparison between the different suppliers and contractors who will actually quote you their products and services.

OPTION 2

The **Bottom Line Zip-Quote** is a one line summarized total cost for the home plan of your choice. This cost calculation is also based on the labor cost, material cost and equipment cost (if applicable) within your local zip code area.

COST

The price of your **Itemized Zip-Quote** is based upon the pricing schedule of the plan you have selected, in addition to the price of the materials list. Please refer to the pricing schedule on our order form. The price of your initial **Bottom Line Zip-Quote** is $29.95. Each additional **Bottom Line Zip-Quote** ordered in conjunction with the initial order is only $14.95. **Bottom Line Zip-Quote** may be purchased separately and does NOT have to be purchased in conjunction with a home plan order.

FYI

An **Itemized Zip-Quote** Home Cost Calculation can ONLY be purchased in conjunction with a Home Plan order. The **Itemized Zip-Quote** can not be purchased separately. The **Bottom Line Zip-Quote** can be purchased seperately and doesn't have to be purchased in conjunction with a home plan order. Please consult with a sales representative for current availability. If you find within 60 days of your order date that you will be unable to build this home, then you may exchange the plans and the materials list towards the price of new set of plans (see order info pages for plan exchange policy). The **Itemized Zip-Quote** and the **Bottom Line Zip-Quote** are NOT returnable. The price of the initial **Bottom Line Zip-Quote** order can be credited towards the purchase of an **Itemized Zip-Quote** order only. Additional **Bottom Line Zip-Quote** orders, within the same order can not be credited. Please call our Customer Service Department for more information.

SOME MORE INFORMATION

The Itemized and Bottom Line Zip-Quotes give you approximate costs for constructing the particular house in your area. These costs are not exact and are only intended to be used as a preliminary estimate to help determine the affordability of a new home and/or a guide to evaluate the general competitiveness of actual price quotes obtained through local suppliers and contractors. However, Zip-Quote cost figures should never be relied upon as the only source of information in either case. The Garlinghouse Company and Marshall & Swift L.P. can not guarantee any level of data accuracy correctness in a Zip-Quote and disclaim all liability for loss with respect to the same, in excess of the original purchase price of the Zip-Quote product. All Zip-Quote calculations are based upon the actual blueprint materials list with options as selected by customer and do not reflect any differences that may be shown on the published house renderings, floor plans, or photographs.

What Garlinghouse Offers

Home Plan Blueprint Package

By purchasing a single or multiple set package of blueprints from Garlinghouse, you not only receive the physical blueprint documents necessary for construction, but you are also granted a license to build one, and only one, home. You can also make simple modifications, including minor non-structural changes and material substitutions, to our design, as long as these changes are made directly on the blueprints purchased from Garlinghouse and no additional copies are made.

Home Plan Vellums

By purchasing vellums for one of our home plans, you receive the same construction drawings found in the blueprints, but printed on vellum paper. Vellums can be erased and are perfect for making design changes. They are also semi-transparent making them easy to duplicate. But most importantly, the purchase of home plan vellums comes with a broader license that allows you to make changes to the design (ie, create a hand drawn or CAD derivative work), to make an unlimited number of copies of the plan, and to build one home from the plan.

License To Build Additional Homes

With the purchase of a blueprint package or vellums you automatically receive a license to build one home and only one home, respectively. If you want to build more homes than you are licensed to build through your purchase of a plan, then additional licenses may be purchased at reasonable costs from Garlinghouse. Inquire for more information.

IMPORTANT INFORMATION TO READ BEFORE YOU PLACE YOUR ORDER

The Standard 8-Set Construction Package

Our experience shows that you'll speed every step of construction and avoid costly building errors by ordering enough sets to go around. Each tradesperson wants a set — the general contractor and all subcontractors; foundation, electrical, plumbing, heating/air conditioning and framers. Don't forget your lending institution, building department and, of course, a set for yourself.

The Minimum 4-Set Construction Package

If you're comfortable with arduous follow-up, this package can save you a few dollars by giving you the option of passing down plan sets as work progresses. You might have enough copies to go around if work goes exactly as scheduled and no plans are lost or damaged by subcontractors. But for only $50 more, the 8-set package eliminates these worries.

The Single Study Set

We offer this set so you can study the blueprints to plan your dream home in detail. As with all of our plans, they are stamped with a copyright warning. Remember, one set is never enough to build your home. In pursuant to copyright laws, it is _illegal_ to reproduce any blueprint.

All plans are drawn to conform to one or more of the industry's major national building standards. However, due to the variety of local building regulations, your plan may need to be modified to comply with local requirements — snow loads, energy loads, seismic zones, etc. Do check them fully and consult your local building officials.

A few states require that all building plans used be drawn by an architect registered in that state. While having your plans reviewed and stamped by such an architect may be prudent, laws requiring non-conforming plans like ours to be completely redrawn forces you to unnecessarily pay very large fees. If your state has such a law, we strongly recommend you contact your state representative to protest.

The rendering, floor plans, and technical information contained within publication are not guaranteed to be totally accurate. Consequently, no information from this publication should be used either as a guide to constructing a home or for estimating the cost of building a home. Complete blueprints must be purchased for such purposes.

GARLINGHOUSE

Order Form

Plan prices guaranteed until 4/1/99 —After this date call for updated pricing

Order Code No. **CHPO**

Ⓔ

____ set(s) of blueprints for plan #_____	$_____	✓ Itemized ZIP Quote for plan(s) # 96403 N/A $
✓ Vellum & Modification kit for plan # 94965	$665 (＊730)	Shipping (see charts on opposite page) 30. $25
____ Additional set(s) @ $30 each for plan #____	$_____	Subtotal $_____
____ Mirror Image Reverse @ $50 each	$_____	Sales Tax *(CT residents add 6% sales tax, KS residents add 6.15% sales tax) (Not required for all states)* $_____
____ Right Reading Reverse @ $125 each	$_____	
✓ Materials list for plan # 94965 N/A	$50	**TOTAL AMOUNT ENCLOSED** $855
____ Detail Plans @ $19.95 each		
☒ Construction ☐ Plumbing ☐ Electrical	$ 19.95	
✓ Bottom line ZIP Quote @ $29.95 for plan # 94965	$29.95	
✓ Additional Bottom Line Zip Quote		
@ $14.95 for plan(s) # 96403		
____	$ 14.95	

Send your check, money order or credit card information to:
(No C.O.D.'s Please)
Please submit all United States & Other Nations orders to:
Garlinghouse Company
P.O. Box 1717
Middletown, CT. 06457

614765 Order
ZIP quote # 614769 - 29.95   614770 - 19.95
"   "   - 14.95

NAME: Twendy / POC - _____

STREET: _____

CITY: _____ **STATE:** _____ **ZIP:** _____

DAYTIME PHONE: _____

TERMS OF SALE FOR HOME PLANS: All home plans sold through this publication are copyright protected. Reproduction of these home plans, either in whole or in part, including any direct copying and/or preparation of derivative works thereof, for any reason without the prior written permission of The L.F. Garlinghouse Co., Inc., is strictly prohibited. The purchase of a set of home plans in no way transfers any copyright or other ownership interest in it to the buyer except for a limited license to use that set of home plans for the construction of one, and only one, dwelling unit. The purchase of additional sets of that home plan at a reduced price from the original set or as a part of a multiple set package does not entitle the buyer with a license to construct more than one dwelling unit.

Payment must be made in U.S. funds. Foreign Mail Orders: Certified bank checks in U.S. funds only

Credit Card Information

Charge To: ☐ Visa   ☐ Mastercard

Card # | | | | | | | | | | | | | | | | | |

Signature _____ Exp. ____ / ____

ORDER TOLL FREE — 1-800-235-5700
Monday-Friday 8:00 a.m. to 8:00 p.m. Eastern Time
or FAX your Credit Card order to 1-860-343-5984
All foreign residents call 1-800-343-5977

Please have ready: 1. Your credit card number   2. The plan number   3. The order code number ⇨ CHPO1

arlinghouse 1998 Blueprint Price Code Schedule

Additional sets with original order $30

PRICE CODE	A	B	C	D	E	F	G	H
8 SETS OF SAME PLAN	$375	$415	$455	$495	$535	$575	$615	$655
4 SETS OF SAME PLAN	$325	$365	$405	$445	$485	$525	$565	$605
1 SINGLE SET OF PLANS	$275	$315	$355	$395	$435	$475	$515	$555
VELLUMS	$485	$530	$575	$620	$665	$710	$755	$800
MATERIALS LIST	$40	$40	$45	$45	$50	$50	$55	$55
ITEMIZED ZIP QUOTE	$75	$80	$85	$85	$90	$90	$95	$95

hipping — (Plans 1-84999)

	1-3 Sets	4-6 Sets	7+ & Vellums
Standard Delivery (UPS 2-Day)	$15.00	$20.00	$25.00
Overnight Delivery	$30.00	$35.00	$40.00

hipping — (Plans 85000-99999)

	1-3 Sets	4-6 Sets	7+ & Vellums
Ground Delivery (7-10 Days)	$9.00	$18.00	$20.00
Express Delivery (3-5 Days)	$15.00	$20.00	$25.00

International Shipping & Handling

	1-3 Sets	4-6 Sets	7+ & Vellums
Regular Delivery Canada (7-10 Days)	$14.00	$17.00	$20.00
Express Delivery Canada (5-6 Days)	$35.00	$40.00	$45.00
Overseas Delivery Airmail (2-3 Weeks)	$45.00	$52.00	$60.00

r Reorder and Exchange Policies:

If you find after your initial purchase that you require additional sets of plans you may purchase them from us at special reorder ces (please call for pricing details) provided that you reorder within 6 months of your original order date. There is a $28 reorder pro- sing fee that is charged on all reorders. For more information on reordering plans please contact our Customer Service Department 860) 343-5977.

We want you to find your dream home from our wide selection of home plans. However, if for some reason you find that the plan you e purchased from us does not meet your needs, then you may exchange that plan for any other plan in our collection. We allow you y days from your original invoice date to make an exchange. At the time of the exchange you will be charged a processing fee of 15% he total amount of your original order plus the difference in price between the plans (if applicable) plus the cost to ship the new plans ou. Call our Customer Service Department at (860) 343-5977 for more information. Please Note: Reproducible vellums can only be hanged if they are unopened.

portant Shipping Information

Please refer to the shipping charts on the order form for service availability for your specific plan number. Our delivery service must e a street address or Rural Route Box number — never a post office box. (PLEASE NOTE: Supplying a P.O. Box number only will ay the shipping of your order.) Use a work address if no one is home during the day.

Orders being shipped to APO or FPO must go via First Class Mail. Please include the proper postage.

For our International Customers, only Certified bank checks and money orders are accepted and must be payable in U.S. currency. speed, we ship international orders Air Parcel Post. Please refer to the chart for the correct shipping cost.

☙ Thank you.

ADDING SPACE WITHOUT ADDING ON

Cramped for space? This book, which replaces our old book of the same title, shows you how to find space you may not know you had and convert it into useful living areas. 40 colorful photographs and 530 full-color drawings.

BOOK #: 277680   192pp.   8½"x10⅞"

BASIC WIRING
(Third Edition, Conforms to latest National Electrical Code)

Included are 350 large, clear, full-color illustrations and no-nonsense step-by-step instructions. Shows how to replace receptacles and switches; repair a lamp; install ceiling and attic fans; and more.

BOOK #: 277048   160pp.   8½"x10⅞"

BATHROOMS: Design, Remodel, Build

Shows how to plan, construct, and finish a bathroom. Remodel floors; rebuild walls and ceilings; and install windows, skylights, and plumbing fixtures. Specific tools and materials are given for each project.

BOOK #: 277053   192pp.   8½"x10⅞"

Designing and Planning: BATHROOMS

From the planning stage to final decorating, this book includes innovative and dramatic ideas for master baths, fitness bathrooms, powder rooms, and more. 200 inspirational color illustrations and photographs.

Book #: 287627   96 pp.   8½"x10⅞"

BUILD A KIDS' PLAY YARD

Here are detailed plans and step-by-step instructions for building the play structures that kids love most: swing set, monkey bars, balance beam, playhouse, teeter-totter, sandboxes, kid-sized picnic table, and a play tower that supports a slide. 200 color photographs and illustrations.

Book #: 277622   144 pp.   8½"x10⅞"

CABINETS & BUILT-INS

26 custom cabinetry projects are included for every room in the house, from kitchen cabinets to a bedroom wall unit, a bunk bed, computer workstation, and more. Also included are chapters on tools, techniques, finishing, and materials.

BOOK #: 277079   160 pp.   8½"x10⅞"

DECKS: Plan, Design, Build

With this book, even the novice builder can build a deck that perfectly fits his yard. The step-by-step instructions lead the reader from laying out footings to adding railings. Includes three deck projects, 500 color drawings, and photographs.

BOOK #: 277180   176pp.   8½"x10⅞"

Furniture Repair & Refinishing

From structural repairs to restoring older finishes or entirely refinishing furniture: a hands-on step-by-step approach to furniture repair and restoration. More than 430 color photographs and 60 full-color drawings.

BOOK #: 277335   192pp.   8½"x10⅞"

HOUSE FRAMING

Written for those with beginning to intermediate building skills, this book is designed to walk you through the framing basics, from assembling simple partitions to cutting compound angles on dormer rafters. More than 400 full-color drawings.

BOOK #: 277053   192pp.   8½"x10⅞"

the Home Planner, Builder & Owner

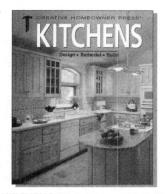

KITCHENS: Design, Remodel, Build

This is the reference book for modern kitchen design, with more than 100 full-color photos to help homeowners plan the layout. Step-by-step instructions illustrate basic plumbing and wiring techniques; how to finish walls and ceilings; and more.

BOOK #: 277065   192pp.   8½"x10⅞"

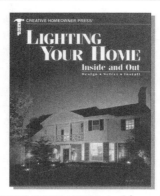

LIGHTING YOUR HOME: Inside and Out

Lighting should be selected with care. This book thoroughly explains lighting design for every room as well as outdoors. It is also a step-by-step manual that shows how to install the fixtures. More than 125 photos and 400 drawings.

BOOK #: 277583   160pp.   8½"x10⅞"

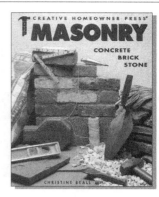

MASONRY: Concrete, Brick, Stone

Concrete, brick, and stone choices are detailed with step-by-step instructions and over 35 color photographs and 460 illustrations. Projects include a brick or stone garden wall, steps and patios, a concrete-block retaining wall, a concrete sidewalk.

BOOK #: 277106   176pp.   8½"x10⅞"

PLANNING A BETTER KITCHEN

From layout to design, no detail of efficient and functional kitchen planning is overlooked. Covers everything from built-in ovens and ranges to sinks and faucets. Over 260 color illustrations and photographs.

Book #: 287495   96 pp.   8½"x10⅞"

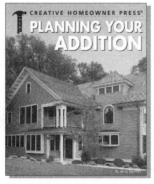

PLANNING YOUR ADDITION

Planning an addition to your home involves a daunting number of choices, from choosing a contractor to selecting bathroom tile. Using 280 color drawings and photographs, architect/author Jerry Germer helps you make the right decision.

BOOK #: 277004   192pp.   8½"x10⅞"

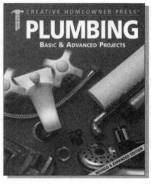

PLUMBING: Basic & Advanced Projects

Take the guesswork out of plumbing repair and installation for old and new systems. Projects include replacing faucets, unclogging drains, installing a tub, replacing a water heater, and much more. 500 illustrations and diagrams.

BOOK #: 277620   176pp.   8½"x10⅞"

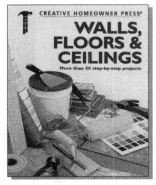

WALLS, FLOORS & CEILINGS

Here's the definitive guide to interiors. It shows you how to replace old surfaces with new professional-looking ones. Projects include installing molding, skylights, insulation, flooring, carpeting, and more. Over 500 color photos and drawings.

BOOK #: 277697   176pp.   8½"x10⅞"

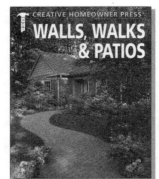

WALLS, WALKS & PATIOS

Learn how to build a patio from concrete, stone, or brick and complement it with one of a dozen walks. Learn about simple mortarless walls, landscape timber walls, and hefty brick and stone walls. A special design section helps turn your dreams into reality. 50 photographs and 320 illustrations.

Book #: 277994   192 pp.   8½"x10⅞"

QUICK GUIDE: FENCES & GATES

Learn how to build and install all kinds of fences and gates for your yard, from hand-built wood privacy and picket fences to newer prefabricated vinyl and chain-link types. Over 200 two-color drawings illustrate step-by-step procedures.

BOOK #: 287732   80pp.   8½"x10⅞"

Place your Order ....

The Smart Approach to BATH DESIGN

Everything you need to know about designing a bathroom like a professional is explained in *this book*. Creative solutions and practical advice about space, the latest in fixtures and fittings, and safety features accompany over 150 photographs.

BOOK #: 287225   176pp.   9"x10"

COLOR IN THE AMERICAN HOME

Find out how to make the most of color in your American home with ideas for analyzing, selecting, and coordinating color schemes. Learn how differently light affects the colors you choose depending on where you live. Over 150 photographs of traditional and contemporary interiors.

BOOK #: 277344   176pp.   9"x10"

CHOOSING A COLOR SCHEME

Plan colorful and imaginative decorating schemes for your home with the style and flair of a professional interior decorator. Learn how color, light, pattern, and texture work together. Over 170 full-color illustrations and photographs of wallcovering, paint, fabric, and floor covering design schemes.

BOOK #: 287531   96pp.   8½"x10⅞"

BOOK ORDER FORM   *Please Print*
SHIP TO:

Name:

Address:

City: State: Zip: Phone Number:

(Should there be a problem with your order)

Quantity	Title	Price	CHP #	Cost	Quantity	Title	Price	CHP #	Cost
	450 Two-Story Home Plans	$9.95	277042			Quick Guide - Decks	$7.95	277344	
	Adding Space without Adding On	14.95	277680			Quick Guide - Fences & Gates	7.95	287732	
	Basic Wiring	14.95	277048			Quick Guide - Floors	7.95	287734	
	Bathrooms: Design, Remodel, Build	14.95	277053			Quick Guide - Garages & Carports	7.95	287785	
	Bird Feeders	9.95	277102			Quick Guide - Gazebos	7.95	287757	
	Build a Kids' Play Yard	14.95	277662			Quick Guide - Insulation & Ventilation	7.95	287367	
	Cabinets & Built-Ins	14.95	277079			Quick Guide - Interior & Exterior Painting	7.95	287784	
	Color in the American Home	16.95	287264			Quick Guide - Masonry Walls	7.95	287741	
	Complete Guide to Wallpapering	12.95	278910			Quick Guide - Patios & Walks	7.95	287778	
	Custom Closets	9.95	277132			Quick Guide - Plumbing	7.95	287863	
	Decks: Plan, Design, Build	14.95	277180			Quick Guide - Ponds & Fountains	7.95	287804	
	Decorative Paint Finishes	9.95	287371			Quick Guide - Roofing	7.95	287807	
	Fences, Gates & Trellises	14.95	277981			Quick Guide - Shelving & Storage	7.95	287763	
	Furniture Repair & Refinishing	19.95	277335			Quick Guide - Siding	7.95	287892	
	Gazebos & Other Outdoor Structures	14.95	277138			Quick Guide - Stairs & Railings	7.95	287755	
	Home Landscaping: Mid-Atlantic Region	19.95	274537			Quick Guide - Storage Sheds	7.95	287815	
	Home Landscaping: Northeast Region	19.95	274618			Quick Guide - Swimming Pools & Spas	7.95	287901	
	Home Landscaping: Southeast Region	19.95	274762			Quick Guide - Trim & Molding	7.95	287745	
	House Framing	19.95	277655			Quick Guide - Walls & Ceilings	7.95	287792	
	Kitchens: Design, Remodel, Build (New Ed.)	14.95	277065			Quick Guide - Windows & Doors	7.95	287812	
	Lighting Your Home Inside & Out	14.95	277583			Quick Guide - Wiring, Second Edition	7.95	287884	
	Masonry: Concrete, Brick, Stone	14.95	277106						
	Plumbing: Basic and Advanced Projects	14.95	277620						
	Planning Your Addition	14.95	277004						
	Smart Approach to Bath Design	16.95	287225						
	Spas & Hot Tubs, Saunas & Home Gyms	10.95	277845						
	Walls, Floors & Ceilings	14.95	277697						
	Walls, Walks & Patios	14.95	277994						
	Wood Finishing & Refinishing	10.95	277121						
	Working with Tile	14.95	277540						
	Quick Guide - Attics	7.95	287711						
	Quick Guide - Basements	7.95	287242						
	Quick Guide - Ceramic Tile	7.95	287730						

Number of Books Ordered _____   Total for Books _____

NJ Residents add 6% tax _____

Prices subject to change without notice.   Subtotal _____

Postage/Handling Charges _____
$2.50 for first book / $1.00 for each additional book

Total _____

Make checks (in U.S. currency only) payable to:
CREATIVE HOMEOWNER PRESS®
P.O. BOX 38, 24 Park Way
Upper Saddle River, New Jersey 07458-9960